BTEC

First in C_____

Neil Moonie • Kath Bulman • Yvonne Nolan

Heinemann Educational Pub...
Halley Court, Jordan Hill, Oxford OX2 8EJ
a division of Reed Educational & Professional Publishing Ltd
Heinemann is a registered trademark of Reed Educational & Professional Publishing Limited

OXFORD MELBOURNE AUCKLAND
JOHANNESBURG BLANTYRE GABORONE
IBADAN PORTSMOUTH NH (USA) CHICAGO

First published 1999

2003 2002 2001 2000 1999
11 10 9 8 7 6 5 4 3 2 1

A catalogue record for this book is available from the British Library on request.

ISBN 0 435 40156 4

Designed by Artistix

Typeset by TechType, Abingdon, Oxon

Printed and bound in Great Britain by The Bath Press, Bath

CONTENTS

PREFACE

This book has been written to provide the knowledge and understanding needed to achieve the outcomes and assessment criteria for any BTEC First in Caring programme.

- The book covers all 15 units in the BTEC First syllabus and will support students on First Certificate or First Diploma programmes covering both the Care and the Early Years pathways.
- The book is designed to provide easy access to knowledge. Each chapter covers the corresponding unit of the BTEC First course, and chapters are organised in the order of the outcomes and assessment criteria for the course. Content is set out using subheadings and bullet points for ease of reference.
- Chapters are designed to support coverage of BTEC grading criteria. Knowledge is illustrated and supported with case studies and diagrams to help relate knowledge to practice. The level and depth of content is written to assist with the development of analytical skills. Sections are designed to relate to work or placement experience.
- While each chapter covers a specific unit, readers may wish to explore chapters that cover units not included on their programme. Additional sources of information may be found in the different chapters of this book.
- Tasks labelled 'Do it' are provided to focus attention on the assessment criteria for each outcome. The 'Do its' provide ideas for evidencing the outcomes of the programme, but they are not intended as an alternative to the detailed and placement-linked assignment guidance that centres will supply.

VALUES AND INTERPERSONAL SKILLS

What is good quality care? What skills should a care worker have? What are your responsibilities as a care worker?

Social care work is 'working with people' – and people are all different from one another. Examine your fingerprints – there are about 6,000 million people in the world today and yet it is very

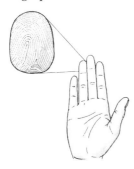

unlikely that you will have exactly the same fingerprints as anyone else. Each person is different from other people physically, and each person also has different life experiences.

The great thing to enjoy about care work is getting to know so many different people, with their different views of life. Although each person is special, there are patterns which mean that some people are similar in some ways to other people – they may share similar life experiences. This chapter will explore some of the social and political factors that influence people's lives, making us different from each other but also creating patterns we can recognise.

Figure 1.1 There are 6,000 million people in the world, but each person's fingerprint is different

Because people have different life experiences, it is very important that people are not treated as if they were all the same. Each person who needs care will have his or her own individual, social and cultural needs. If people are to receive a fair and equal service, their different needs have to be understood. This chapter will explore the risk of discriminatory practice. Discrimination can happen when people are seen as being 'all the same'.

Factors that influence diversity and equality

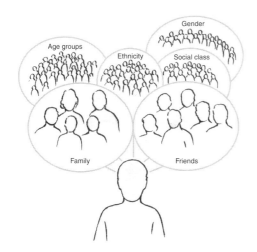

The rich range of differences between people is called 'diversity'. It is important that people working in care should recognise diversity and treat people with equal respect whoever and whatever they are. Many factors make people different from one another. They include:

- social class
- income and lifestyle
- geographical location
- family structure
- ethnicity
- gender
- age

The groups we belong with can have a strong influence on how we think, what we value, how we act and what we do. For example, when people are with their friends they will behave differently than when at work.

Figure 1.2 Most people feel that they belong with groups such as their family and friends – but people also belong with other groups such as their social class, age group and ethnic group

It is important not to make assumptions that other people will have the same views, attitudes or needs as we do. Men often react to things differently from women. Older people don't necessarily see things the same way that younger people do, and so on.

Social class

┌─ **CASE STUDY WILLIAM, MISCHEL AND SEAN: SCHOOLS** ─┐

William is 16, and his father works in the diplomatic service as a senior civil servant. He boards at a private residential school, which charges fees of £8,000 per year. In the holidays he stays with his parents on their five-acre estate in the country. He is studying four A-levels and has advanced skills in sailing. He is not sure about his career, but after completing his degree he may choose to take a post within the civil service. If he chooses this option he would expect to achieve a senior post by the age of 30.

Mischel is 16, and her father is a senior teacher at a comprehensive school. Mischel attends a different school three miles away from the semi-detached home where she lives with her family. Her mother takes Mischel to school each day by car – and will do so until Mischel is old enough to take her driving test. Mischel hopes to stay on at school and take A-levels. She would like to get the qualifications to work as a journalist.

Sean is 16. His father is currently working as a technician at a tyre-fitting company. Sean walks or catches a bus to school each day. Sean lives on a large housing estate in an urban area which is very congested with traffic. He is not sure what he wants to do when he leaves school, but hopes he can get bar work or some sort of hourly paid employment locally.

These three people are the same age – yet they have very different lifestyles. One boards at school, one travels by car to the best school in the area, and one walks to the local school. Their lives will be different in many other ways. The friends they mix with, education, career opportunities and future income will probably be very different. Sociologists would explain these differences in terms of **social class**.

└──┘

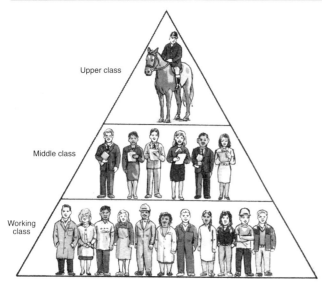

Upper class

Middle class

Working class

Social class is a way of categorising the social status that different occupations have. In other words, some jobs are seen as high status or high class, while other jobs have less status. Your social class is concerned with the way other people think about your job – not just about the money you have.

Social class is a term that has been used to describe different groups of people for a very long time in Britain. Mostly, people are used to the terms 'upper class', 'middle class', and 'working class'. Upper-class people have more power, influence and status than middle-class people, but middle-class people have more power, influence and status than working-class people. Before the 1960s, class differences were open and obvious. People usually wore different clothes which showed the class they belonged to and they usually only mixed socially with members of their own class.

Historically, social class was often seen as being like a pyramid, the upper class at the top and depending on the work of the other classes.

Although it is common to think in terms of three classes, the official system for grading the jobs people do contains five classes. This system was officially designed for the Government Census in 1971 and is known as The Registrar-General's Social Class Index.

Class level	Definition	Examples of occupations in each class
Social Class I (1)	Professional occupations	Company secretary, doctor, judge, lawyer, university teacher, solicitor, scientist
Social Class II (2)	Intermediate occupations	Aircraft pilot, police or fire brigade officer, teacher, manager, farmer
Social Class III N (3N)	Skilled non-manual occupations	Cashier, clerical worker, estate agent, sales representative, secretary, typist
Social Class III M (3M)	Manual occupations	Bus driver, bricklayer, carpenter, electrician, hairdresser, baker, butcher
Social Class IV (4)	Partly skilled occupations	Agricultural worker, bar staff, hospital porter, street trader
Social Class V (5)	Unskilled occupations	Road sweeper, kitchen labourer, refuse collector, window cleaner, office cleaner

Since this classification system was developed, a number of variations have been proposed. Market research agencies use a system first developed for the National Readership Survey, which divides the population into classes called A, B, C1, C2, D and E. These letters group people in a similar way to the Registrar General's classification above. Social Class I is known as A, Social Class II is known as B, Social Class III is known as C1, and so on. When companies want to send out advertisements to people through the post they will often use postcode analysis of social class in an attempt to send product information to the right homes.

The government is planning a new system to measure social class, which is expected to be introduced for the Census in 2001. The new system is expected to focus on issues to do with job security and pensions as well as the skill levels needed to do a job. In general, the type of differences between occupations listed above will still show up in the new system. An outline of the new system is shown below.

Social classifications expected to be used in the 2001 census

1.1 Employers and managers in larger organisations, for example company directors.

1.2 Higher professionals, for example doctors, solicitors, teachers.

2 Lower managerial and professional occupations, for example nurses, journalists.

3 Intermediate occupations, for example clerks, secretaries.

4 Small employers and own account workers, for example taxi drivers, painters and decorators.

5 Lower supervisory, craft and related occupations, for example plumbers, train drivers.

6 Semi-routine occupations, for example shop assistants, hairdressers.

7 Routine occupations, for example cleaners, refuse collectors.

Those who are long-term unemployed form a final, eighth group.

CASE STUDY WILLIAM, MISCHEL AND SEAN: MONEY

William comes from a wealthy family, and mixes with people who are used to taking money for granted. If William wants extra tuition to help him with his studies, the money is there. If he needs a car, it will be bought for him. William can expect to travel widely – expense isn't an issue. If he wants books or sailing lessons, he gets them. William mixes with other people who have very high expectations of life. William listens to people who have direct experience of how government and business work. He is very clear about the possibilities for his future. He works very hard – but he knows what he is working for. He would describe himself as middle class – but his father's occupation and his family's status would be Social Class I.

Mischel lives a lifestyle that could be a bit like William's. Mischel can buy the latest clothing and CDs – she has a Saturday job that gives her a small income. Mischel's parents can pay for little extras, but money is always an issue that has to be talked about. Mischel mixes with people who don't know much about government or business, but they get advice on careers from the local school. Mischel is interested in her future career and her parents put pressure on her to do well in exams – telling her that qualifications are very important. Mischel's parents are middle class.

Sean's parents are working class. Sean goes to a school similar to Mischel's, except that many of the students there don't believe that school is important. Most of Sean's friends say that school is boring and that what matters is getting out and earning money. Once you get some money you can be independent – you can do what you want. Sean hasn't got a job yet, but he is looking forward to getting the latest clothes, CDs, etc. when he can get one. Sean's parents often worry about money and are looking forward to Sean going out to work so that he can contribute to the household budget.

Think it through

What are the differences in lifestyle for these three people? How do you think their views on education would be different. What will happen to each person in the future?

Does social class matter?

Social class can make a difference to how people live their lives – whether they think about social class or not. One reason social class matters is that class can influence the attitudes and values that people have.

People whose work roles place them in Social Classes 1 and 2 often believe that they control their own lives. They expect to choose where to buy their own house or flat, they choose entertainment, what they eat and what they wear. People in classes 1 and 2 or children with parents in classes 1 and 2 may not see themselves as being wealthy, but often they do not worry too much about the cost of items, or about getting into debt.

Some people in Social Classes 4 and 5 often feel that they cannot control their income, their jobs and housing needs. They may sometimes feel worried about money. If you are short of money, you have to be careful what clothes and what food you buy. Money worries can limit where you can go out – where you can go on holiday and what social life you can have. If you have to rent a house or flat, you may feel that you have less choice of where to live than if you can afford to buy your own property.

Sociologists explain that people who belong to the higher social classes often feel they can choose their own lifestyle, whereas people in the lower classes may have less chance to choose how they live and what they do.

Does social class influence happiness?

Happiness is a very personal issue, and happiness comes and goes each day. The psychologist Michael Argyle has studied social class and happiness and come to the conclusion, from a large range of studies, that people in the higher social classes are generally 'somewhat happier' than people in the lower social classes. Why does higher class lead to more happiness for many people?

- **Money** Jobs in a lower social class often don't pay very well. People in classes 4 and 5 may have less to spend and less saved than people in the higher classes.
- **Enjoyable work** The more prestigious jobs, like lawyer or accountant, may often be more enjoyable than routine or boring jobs.
- **Respect** People with high-status jobs may be treated with more respect than people with low-status jobs.
- **Self-esteem** People who feel they have been successful and have developed their abilities may feel good about life.
- **Stress** People who have money worries, or who live in poor quality housing – in areas of crime and so on – often feel that life is difficult and full of stress. Upper-class people may be more free of this stress.
- **Holidays** The higher classes take more holidays and more days out from home than working-class people.
- **Sport and exercise** Generally, Social Classes 1 and 2 enjoy more sport and exercise than classes 4 and 5 and they also have more social activity.
- **Health** On average, people in Social Classes 1 and 2 have less chronic (or long term) illness, less sickness and even live longer than people in Social Classes 4 and 5.
- **Job security** Unskilled people (Social Class 5) are ten times more likely to be out of work than people with a high level of education and training.

Naturally, not every person who is in a job of high social class is happy, and not every person who is in an unskilled job is sad. All sorts of things can go right or wrong for anyone, but the evidence is that people with high-status jobs do seem to have more chances of being happy over their lifetimes.

Income and lifestyle

In modern Europe, it seems that you are what you buy. Whenever you read a newspaper, watch TV, look at the Internet or just walk down the street, you see advertisements. Adverts don't just tell you about things you can buy – they often invite you to join in a way of life.

Adverts offer a lifestyle.

Some sociologists say that it's not so much the work you do that will matter in the new millennium, it's more how you spend your money – what lifestyle you buy into.

Many people now buy four-wheel-drive cars, yet rarely use them in the way they are intended to be used – in the country. Most of the time they may sit in traffic jams. But owning a four-wheel-drive says 'I'm part of the sporting outdoor set'. It's the image or lifestyle that people spend their money on.

When it comes to spending money, people are not equal – some have far more money to spend than others.

DID YOU KNOW?

In 1998 the richest 10 per cent of the population had, on average, five times more to spend than people who had below average income, even after tax.

About a fifth of Britain's population and a quarter of Britain's children were considered to be living in poverty in 1995. There are different ways of measuring what it is to be poor. One measure is to use the amount of money paid to people receiving Income Support – this level can be understood as being the poverty line. Brief details on Income Support can be found in the section on Benefits – see page 8.

Key groups of people who have to live on or below the poverty line include:

- one-parent families
- elderly people
- single-earner, unskilled couples (where only one person works in an unskilled job)
- people who are unemployed
- people who are sick or disabled

In 1998 an estimated 10.3 million people in Britain lived on or below this poverty line; in 1979 only 4.4 million people were estimated to live in poverty. The number of people who can be considered to be poor has increased during the 1990s and may continue to increase as time goes on.

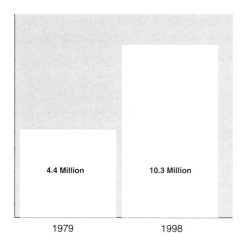

Figure 1.3 'Poverty' has more than doubled since 1979

4.4 Million   10.3 Million

1979   1998

People who are poor may have enough money for food, for some clothes and for heating, but poverty means that there is little money for the interesting purchases that make exciting lifestyles. People who depend on benefits have limited life choices.

The latest clothes, comfortable and reliable cars, the latest electronic equipment, digital TV, and so on may not be possible choices for people on a low income. People with little money have to restrict what they can buy when they visit a supermarket or shopping centre.

Many lifestyles are not possible for people in poverty. Belonging to a sports club is not possible if you can't afford the membership fees, the equipment and so on. Even jogging isn't possible if you feel your neighbourhood isn't safe to go out in.

Children living in poverty may have limited life choices and limited life chances to develop their full social, emotional and intellectual potential.

Think it through

Do people on low incomes generally eat the same healthy food as well-paid people? Have you seen any evidence of poor diet or hunger among families on a low income?

Geographical location

People who feel confident about their future income and finances can choose their lifestyle. They can also choose where they would like to live.

Social Class 1 and 2 tend to live in more expensive housing, areas with good facilities for travel and education. People with lower incomes tend to live in more densely occupied housing areas. People on lower incomes are often forced to rent rather than buy their homes.

Figure 1.4 Housing areas chosen by wealthier people tend to be spacious

Figure 1.5 People on low incomes tend to live in high density housing

Different social class groups often live in different neighbourhoods – this is why marketing companies can use postcodes to work out what advertisements to send to different areas.

Does it matter what kind of location you live in? Many people would say that the important thing is to get on with the people you live with and that money, or the size of your house, doesn't matter. But there can be disadvantages to living in poor-quality or high-density housing. These can include noise, pollution, overcrowding, poor access to shops and other facilities, and stress from petty crime. When people are on a low income, household maintenance can become a problem. Poorly maintained housing can create health hazards.

If you live on a low income in a crowded block of flats or high-density housing, you may get:

- noise from neighbours
- more chance of being woken up in the night
- stress from neighbours' behaviour
- nearby busy roads where traffic fumes create pollution
- a number of children or relatives crowded into bedroom
- more burglary, car crime and personal attacks
- poor car parking and travel facilities.

Do It

Explain what is meant by social class and the relationship to geographical location.

Look at a map of your local area. Work out if the housing differs in different areas on your map. You may need to walk round the streets to note the kind of housing that exists. What lifestyles do people have in the different areas? How do you think lifestyles and stress levels might vary between areas of housing in your area? What conclusions can you draw about social class in different areas?

The Welfare State

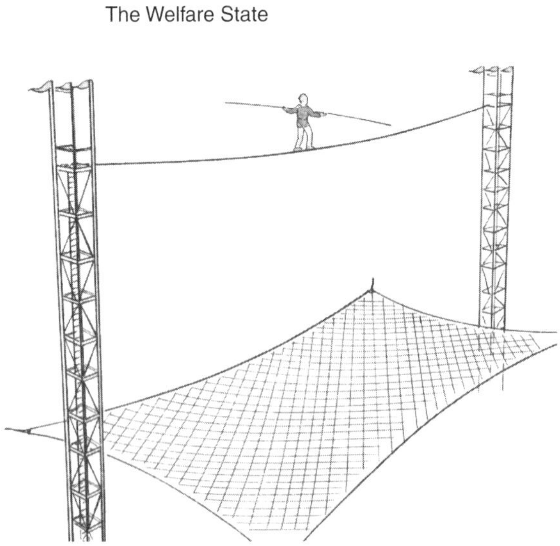

The Welfare State

Figure 1.6 Benefits are intended to provide a safety net for people as they go through life

The government of the country is sometimes called the State. The State provides a range of welfare services to meet people's health and welfare needs. These services include the National Health Service, local authority social services, and Social Security benefits administered through the Benefits Agency. The welfare services provided by the government are sometimes described as being part of a Welfare State.

People may be entitled to a range of financial benefits in order to meet social needs. Benefits are generally intended to help people who have low or even no income, and to provide a basic level of financial security.

Benefits are often re-examined by parliament and details of benefits are likely to change. Benefits that were available in July 1998 are described below.

There are three types of benefit to which a person may be entitled:

1. **Contributory benefits:** People pay towards or 'contribute to' these benefits when National Insurance is deducted from their earnings at work. These benefits may not be available to you if you haven't paid enough National Insurance.

2. **Non-contributory benefits:** These benefits are available to British citizens regardless of whether they have paid National Insurance. You don't have to contribute to get the benefit.

3. **Means-tested benefits:** Means-tested benefits are intended for people with low incomes and not for people who have enough money to meet their welfare needs. 'Means-tested' is the term for benefits that are 'income-tested' – the benefit is only available to people who can show their income is below a certain level.

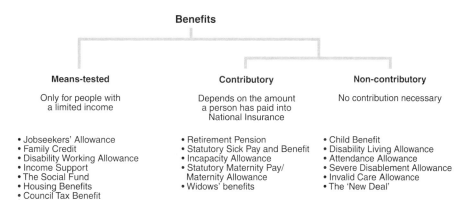

Figure 1.7 The benefits system

Contributory benefits

Retirement Pension: People who have paid full National Insurance contributions are entitled to a full retirement pension. People who have paid only part of their contributions receive a part pension. At the moment men receive their pension at 65 years of age and women at 60. In the future, both men and women will receive their pension at 65. The current retirement pension is worth less than one fifth of average male earnings.

Statutory Sick Pay and Sickness Benefit: If you are employed but are sick, you are paid a sum of money through your employer. Self-employed people can claim a similar benefit.

Incapacity Allowance: This allowance is paid to people who are unable to work because of injury. People who claim this allowance have to be able to show that they fit medical assessment criteria.

Non-contributory benefits

Child Benefit: A benefit is paid to every family with dependent children. An additional benefit is paid to lone parents, called One-Parent Benefit.

Disability Living Allowance: A benefit is paid to people under 65 years of age who need help with personal care because of disability.

Attendance Allowance: This benefit is for people who are over 65 and who are severely disabled.

Severe Disablement Allowance: This is a benefit for people under 65 who do not qualify for contributory benefits, which otherwise might meet their needs.

Invalid Care Allowance: An allowance which can be paid to carers who look after people claiming attendance allowance. Wives may not claim for their husbands, and carers can only claim if they are on a low income.

Means-tested benefits

Job Seekers' Allowance: This benefit is paid to people who are unemployed. Job Seeker's Allowance has a contributory part to it – a person can claim a contribution-based allowance for up to six months if he or she has enough National Insurance contributions. There is a means-tested allowance for people who are not entitled to the contributory allowance, or who are still unemployed after six months of claiming the allowance. People can lose this benefit if they do not keep to an agreement to be available for work and look for work.

Family Credit: This benefit is paid to employed people on low incomes who have dependent children.

Disability Working Allowance: This is a benefit for working people with disabilities and a low income.

Contributory benefits

Statutory Maternity Pay: A payment is made for 18 weeks to employed women who take time off work to give birth.

Maternity Allowance: This is an alternative payment for women who need time off work to give birth, but who can't claim maternity pay – perhaps because they have not been with the same employer for long enough.

Widows' benefits: Widows' Bereavement Payment is a single payment to help with funeral expenses and other costs. Widowed Mothers' Allowance is an allowance to help support dependent children. Widows' Pensions are paid to widows from age 45.

Non-contributory benefits

The New Deal: This system provides skills training and work experience to people under the age of 25. They can lose payments from their Job Seeker's Allowance if they refuse to join or stay with the scheme. The New Deal also offers help to lone parents to help them find work, to people over 25 who have been unemployed for more than two years, and to people with disabilities who may need specialist training to find work.

Means-tested benefits

Income Support: Income Support provides benefits for people on low incomes. Sometimes it is possible to claim an allowance for partners and children, and increased payments can be made for people with special needs.

The Social Fund: People on low incomes – usually those eligible for Income Support – can claim grants or loans for such things as funeral payments or major household items. This fund is limited, and claimants are not always able to get the loans they apply for.

Housing Benefit: This benefit is for people on low incomes, and is paid through the local authority housing department to cover the costs of rent and local government tax.

Council Tax Benefit: People on low incomes can receive help with payment of council tax.

Do it

Identify what is meant by the Welfare State and the financial benefits that are available to meet specific care needs.

Think about a person who has a low income, perhaps a person who is unemployed, retired, disabled, on a low wage or a lone parent. Work out what the person's weekly living costs might be – costs for rent, food, heating, lighting, travel, clothing, council tax, and entertainment. Make an allowance for costs of holidays, and the replacement or repair of household items like fridges, washing machines and so on.

Find out what benefits this person could claim and how much he or she might receive in benefit. How far does benefit income cover this person's needs?

Family structure

People differ from one another in the kinds of families or groups that they live in. In the early 1990s over a quarter of homes were occupied by single people. Over a third of all homes were occupied by couples, either with no children at all or no dependent children. Many people do live as couples with their children, but it would be a mistake to imagine that all people are born into and grow up in small families.

What is a family?

A family is a social group made up of people who are 'related' to each other. This means that other people (society) recognise that this group is related. In British society, 'family' is the word used to describe groups where adults act as parents or guardians to children. Belonging to a family can have many advantages - family relationships can provide a safe, caring setting for children.

Family groups can guide and teach children, and they can provide a source of social and emotional support for adults and older family members as well as children.

Modern sociologists identify four different types of family:

- extended families
- reconstituted families
- nuclear families
- lone-parent families.

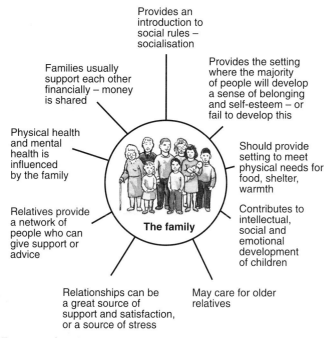

Figure 1.8   What the family does for people

Extended families

An extended family is where parents, children and grandparents all live together or near each other, so that they are often together. Between 1800 and 1900 in England, many families lived in this way. The extended family can have many advantages. Parents can work all day without having to worry about who is looking after the children - the grandparents might do this. If the grandparents needed care, then the parents or even the older children could help. The extended family provides a network of people who can support each other.

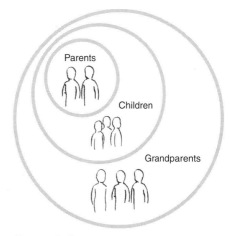

Figure 1.9   The extended family

Nuclear families

A nucleus is the centre of a living cell, and the nuclear family is like the centre of the extended family on its own. By the 1950s, many people in Britain no longer lived with grandparents. The term nuclear family was invented to describe this new, smaller family. The original nuclear family was usually a husband who would go out to work, a wife who would look after the children while they were young, and the children.

Nowadays many couples no longer fit this description. Often both parents will have full-time work and the children are cared for by childminders, nannies, or nursery services. Male and female roles have been changing – men and women are now usually seen as equally responsible for household tasks. However, studies suggest that women still undertake the majority of child care and housework tasks.

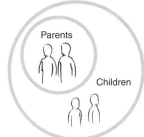

Figure 1.10 The nuclear family

Reconstituted families

Approximately one marriage in every three now ends in divorce, and some people think this figure will increase. Many young people live together before marriage and have children, but there is evidence that a large number of these couples split up too. Over a third of marriages each year are likely to be re-marriages, and about one million children live with a step parent. Roughly a quarter of children might experience their parents divorcing before the age of 16.

The reconstituted family is where the couple are not both the parents of each child in the family. One partner might have been divorced from an earlier marriage, and has now re-married to create a new family. Sometimes children from different relationships may be included in a new, reconstituted family. One partner may have been single but is now married to a partner who has children from a previous relationship.

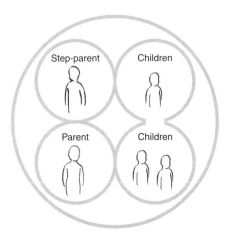

Figure 1.11 The reconstituted family

Lone-parent families

Nearly a quarter of all families with dependent children are now lone-parent families. Of families with dependent children, 21 per cent are lone-parent families led by a lone mother, with just 2 per cent led by a lone father.

Whilst some lone-parent families may be well off, many are disadvantaged. Studies suggest that 70 per cent of lone parents have incomes equivalent to the poorest 10 per cent of couples with dependent children. Many lone parents rely on benefits or receive low wages.

The type of family that a child lives in can change. An extended family can turn into a nuclear family if the grandparents die or move away. Families can become 'reconstituted' if one partner leaves and is replaced by a different person. Few people can guarantee a family style for life. When people leave their partners, divorce or die, a lone-parent family may be created. If the remaining parent finds a new partner, the lone-parent family becomes a reconstituted family. The same child might live in different family structures during childhood and adolescence.

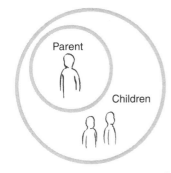

Figure 1.12   The lone-parent family

Example of an extended family

Ross lives with his brother and his mother and father on the top two floors of a very large semi-detached Victorian house near the centre of a city. Ross's mother's parents live on the ground floor of the building. They have their own bathroom and kitchen, although the whole family sometimes eat together at the weekend. Ross's parents were able to buy such a large house only because the grandparents sold their home to make it possible. The grandparents own part of the new house, but they have left their share of the house to Ross's parents in their will.

Example of a nuclear family

Meena lives with her sister, mother and father in a three-bedroom, semi-detached house. Meena's grandmother (her mother's mother) lives in the Caribbean and she has not seen her for two years. Meena's father's parents live about eighty miles away, and she sees these grandparents about five to eight times each year. Meena's family moved to the house they live in three years ago when her father got a better job.

Example of a reconstituted family

Sarosh lives with his mother and stepfather in a modern terraced house in a small town. His mother and stepfather have been married for two years. Sarosh's 'real' father calls every other Saturday to collect him for a visit. Sarosh's mother and father divorced four years ago. His new stepfather has a daughter, Zara, who lives with her mother over two miles away. Sarosh has met Zara and they like each other, but Sarosh thinks his stepfather cares more about Zara than him.

Example of a lone-parent family

Janice is a single mother with an eight-year-old son, living in a fourth-floor flat on a large housing estate. Janice is looking for part-time work, but her son has an attention problem at school and the school often telephones her to ask her to come and collect him or to calm him. Janice depends on Income Support to get by. She doesn't have enough money for holidays or to take her son out for the day. Janice cannot afford leisure activities which cost money. At night Janice usually stays in and watches TV. There is a high drug-related crime rate on the estate and Janice worries that her flat may be broken into.

Changing family patterns

In the past 40 years there has been a gradual change in the way people live. Fewer people now live in extended families than at any time in the past century, fewer people live in nuclear families than in the 1960s and 1970s. There are more reconstituted and lone-parent families with dependent children than 20 years ago.

Why do family patterns change?

There are many issues that influence people's lifestyles, but it is important to understand how money and economic factors influence family patterns. People do not simply 'choose' their pattern of family life like picking clothes from a catalogue.

When people worked on the land as farmers and farm labourers, the extended family was a very effective way to live. There was little reason for children to move away from the village when they grew up – the work went with the house where they lived. The more people that lived together, the more they could help each other and share the work.

When most people stopped working on farms and worked instead in businesses and factories, it was hard for young people to stay in the same area as their parents. If a new factory opened 20 miles away, it was best to move to the area where the new work had developed. Because younger people moved away from their parents to get work, fewer extended families existed and more nuclear families developed.

At the beginning of a new millennium, we live in an information age where each person may do individual work – men and women increasingly share employment opportunities. Running a home can be done much more easily than forty years ago. People may not need to live as a couple in order to cope with the dual pressures of employment and running a home.

Economic pressures no longer encourage or force people to live in traditional types of family to the same extent as in the past.

Advantages and disadvantages of family patterns

EXTENDED FAMILIES

Advantages

Children	*Parents*	*Grandparents*
You have grandparents to look after you as well as parents. You learn from a wider group of people.	Grandparents can look after your children.	You feel you belong and are needed. Both children and grandchildren can help you and talk with you
	Shared income from parents and grandparents. You may be able to afford a bigger house.	

Security and stability – there is usually someone at home all day.

Disadvantages

Children	*Parents*	*Grandparents*
Adults may boss children about. You may have less space.	You may have to look after your parents as well as your children. It may be difficult to move house and relocate for work reasons. Larger houses cost more to run. Small houses become crowded.	You have to get on with your children. You may have less independence.

Family relationships have to work across three generations. Each has to respect the needs of the other.

NUCLEAR FAMILIES

Advantages

Children

Consistent relationship with parents. Perhaps more money to spend on you. Perhaps more space. Security and stability.

Parents

Family can prioritise one parent's career. Family can move house to further a career. You may have two incomes. Security and stability.

Grandparents

Independence from children.

Disadvantages

Children

May tend to receive care from one person only (often the mother).

Parents

The division of work may not satisfy both people. Child care may be needed if both parents work full-time.

Grandparents

May lose contact with children and grandchildren. May become lonely – may have little support in old age.

RECONSTITUTED FAMILIES

Advantages

Children

Similar to nuclear family.

Parents

Similar to nuclear family – may have two incomes and financial security.

Grandparents

Few responsibilities.

Disadvantages

Children

May have difficulty making relationships with a new parent or with new brothers and sisters. May have to live in more than one home.

Parents

Similar to nuclear family.

Grandparents

Possibly feel cut-off from grandchildren or from child to a greater extent than in nuclear family. May have to establish new relationships.

LONE-PARENT FAMILIES

Advantages

Children

Only one parent to relate to.

Parents

Independence, and control of your own life.

Grandparents

Similar to nuclear family.

Possible freedom from stressful or abusive relationships.

Disadvantages

Children

Only one parent to guide and help you.

Parents

Generally more risk of low income and poverty. Responsibilities for home and child care fall on one person. Controlling your own life can be stressful on low income.

Grandparents

Similar to nuclear family.

DO IT

Identify different family structures and the implications for children, parents and grandparents.

Talk to a group of friends or students and find out how many of them live in extended, nuclear, reconstituted or lone-parent families. Using your knowledge of different types of family, imagine two different family groups. Describe what kind of family structure it is and what living in each of the families might be like for children, parents and grandparents.

Ethnicity

For many people their race is of vital importance and it enables them to understand who they are. Race is not easy to define, however. In the past, people believed that different races of people were somehow biologically different, but it is almost impossible to define racial groups in terms of genetic differences or features to do with skin colour or physical appearance. Nevertheless people do classify themselves and are classified by others in terms of the social and cultural groups to which they belong. A person's culture, religion, style of dress, way of speaking, and so on may lead to classification in terms of ethnic group.

A key way in which people distinguish themselves is in terms of being Black or White. Some people talk in terms of a Black, White or Asian group. But there is no single Black culture, and no single White culture.

Every ten years the Government collects information on people in the country. This collection of information is called a Census. The 1991 census gathered information on where people were born, and 4 million people stated that they were born outside Great Britain. The largest single group born outside Great Britain were from Ireland. Other large groups originated from Germany, the USA, Italy, Cyprus, Poland, Australia, Canada and France. In the 1991 census over 3 million people born outside Great Britain identified themselves as non-White.

The Census in the year 2001 is expected to provide more information on ethnicity and to include the category of 'Black British', as many Black people were born in Britain and identify themselves with this term.

Laws have been in force to prevent discrimination on the basis of race since 1965. The Race Relations Act passed in 1976 set up the Commission for Racial Equality, which seeks to investigate cases of discrimination based on racial or ethnic group.

Despite the law and the powers of the Commission, however, there is evidence of inequality between White and Black groups in Britain. Black and Asian people are more likely to be victims of crime than are White people. In general, people from ethnic minority groups were less likely to achieve top professional and management positions as compared to White people. Unemployment rates vary between different Black and White groups, but generally rates of unemployment are higher for Black people than for White people. In 1991, 12 per cent of White men were unemployed compared with 22.6 per cent of non-White men. Among White women, 7.4 per cent were unemployed, compared to 18.4 per cent of non-White women.

Many Black and Asian people feel that services and employers do discriminate against them. A report in September 1998 by the University of Warwick found that four out of five young Black people felt that race relations were getting worse. Employment opportunities and police behaviour are seen by many Black people as key areas where they are subjected to discrimination.

Gender

It was only in 1928 that women were granted equal rights with men to vote in elections. Before that, women were considered to have a lower social status than men. Assumptions were made that women should look after children, do housework, cook and tidy and do light jobs. Men did the more valuable administrative, management and labouring jobs.

Great changes have come about in the nature of work and the nature of family life since 1928. Women are now generally given equal opportunities in education and employment – the Sex Discrimination Act of 1975 made it illegal to discriminate against women in education or employment.

However, current studies claim that women's pay is as much as 17 per cent lower than men's. Women still hold fewer top jobs and seem to profit less from promotion. Women far outnumber men in jobs like nursing and primary school teaching – often, these jobs are not highly paid. Men often get the more highly paid jobs, such as becoming head teachers, even within areas of work dominated by women. When it comes to domestic work, men still generally do less of the child care, washing and cooking, although they may do more gardening and maintenance jobs.

Think it through

Look at the table below. In general, it would appear that men and women still make assumptions about who should do what within the household.

Hours spent on household tasks by parents:[1] by gender, August 1996

United Kingdom	Hours and minutes per week	
	Fathers	Mothers
Cooking/preparing meals	2:50	13:30
Cleaning	2:00	13:15
Washing and ironing clothes	0:55	9:05
Spending time with the children	5:05	8:45
Shopping	2:50	5:50
Washing up	2:00	3:40
Driving children to school	1:45	2:55
Gardening	3:00	2:00
Sewing/mending clothes	0:10	1:20
Other household tasks	2:25	1:40
All household tasks	23:00	62:00

[1] Adults with children aged 18 and under.

Source: Social Trends 1997.

How are tasks shared between men and women in households you know?

Age

Over 20 per cent – one in five – of people are over the age of 60. In 1900, if you were over 60 you would generally have been considered old. In 1900 the average life expectancy of a newborn boy was 55, and the average life expectancy of a newborn girl was 57. Today a boy might expect to live to 73 and a girl to 79. Far fewer people die young, and far more people live to be old. People live longer because of better food, better housing, better public health and better medical care.

DID YOU KNOW?

An Age Concern survey asked people when old age began. 16- to 24-year-olds' average suggestion was 63 years. People aged over 75 suggested age 76, and were more hesitant to give an answer at all!

Most people want a long life, but people don't want to be old! In many Black and Asian societies being an elder is a very positive thing. As an old person you may not have the physical fitness you had when young, but you have developed wisdom instead. In Britain a large number of people seem to think that being old is a very bad thing.

Discrimination

Discrimination means telling things apart – knowing the difference between similar things. It's quite alright to discriminate between, say, a sandwich filling that you don't like and one that you do. Telling things apart is a vital part of life – if we didn't do it we wouldn't be able to live independently.

But discriminating against people has a different meaning; it doesn't mean 'telling them apart.' It is important to realise that people are all different – with different life experiences.

> *Discriminating against people means giving people an unequal service or treatment because of their differences.*

If an employer did not want to appoint a woman to a job, because she might leave to have children, the employer would be illegally discriminating against her. The discrimination would not be simply that the employer realised she was female. The discrimination would be that she was treated differently from a man who might want to start a family. A man in the same situation would be appointed; the woman gets unequal treatment because the employer thinks she might leave the job or take maternity leave to have a baby.

Discrimination can take place against people who belong to any group. Common forms of discrimination are based on race and culture, gender, age, disability and sexuality.

How does discrimination come about?

All those who work in care have to be interested in learning about other people – interested in diversity and difference. Carers cannot divide people into 'types that I like' and 'types that I don't like'. Carers must never exclude people from receiving a good service because they belong to a different race, culture, religion, gender or age group, or because of their sexuality or abilities.

Seeing the world in terms of 'us and them' leads to certain kinds of thinking. Discrimination sometimes comes about because of assumptions that people make in their thinking – people will sometimes stereotype or label others.

Stereotyping

Figure 1.13 Example of stereotyped thinking

Life is very complicated for everyone, and sometimes people try to make it easier by seeing others as being 'all the same'.

Perhaps a younger person meets an 80-year-old who has a problem with his or her memory. Perhaps the person has seen someone like that on TV – it's then easy to think that 'all old people are forgetful'. This would be a stereotype. A stereotype is a fixed way of thinking about a group of people.

People may make assumptions based on stereotyped thinking. For example, a carer working with older people might say 'I'll just go in and wash and dress this next one – I won't ask what she would like me to do because she's old and old people don't remember – so it doesn't matter what I do'. Stereotyped thinking may cause us to discriminate against people.

When people say 'All women are' or 'all Black people are' or 'all gay people are' they will probably go on to describe a stereotype of these groups. Skilled caring starts from being interested in people's individual differences. Stereotyping lumps people together as if they were all the same. Thinking in stereotypes usually stops a person from being a good carer.

Labelling

Another way in which discrimination can be shown is labelling. Labelling is similar to stereotyping, but labels are brief and simple. Instead of having a set of fixed opinions about a group to which a person may belong, the person is summed up in just one word or term.

Think it through

Some years ago there was a school for children with learning difficulties. When it came to meal times, the children had to sit down for their meal. The 'slow' children were allowed to start first because they took longer. Staff would label children 'slows'. The 'slows' knew who they were, and sat down when 'slows' were called for. Some children were not very skilled with holding plates, etc., and these were labelled 'clumsies'. Children would describe themselves as 'slows' or 'clumsies'.

What effect do you think describing herself as a 'slow' or a 'clumsy' would have on a child's development of self-esteem?

Labels can be words like:

- aggressive
- emotional
- disgusting.

These words might be used to describe ethnic groups, or women or old people. Labels can be used to claim that a group of people are all the same. Labels may say that people are all only one thing, such as aggressive, emotional or disgusting. When individuals are labelled, it's almost as if they stop being people – labels take away people's dignity and individuality.

Prejudice

Prejudice comes from the term 'pre-judgement', and means judging other people without the knowledge to judge properly. No new information or understanding can alter such a judgement. If people believe stereotypes about groups, they may go on to make judgements about individuals. For instance, an employer who believes that 'women don't really care about work – they only care about their family', may develop a prejudice that women aren't suited for promotion to senior positions. Employers with such a prejudice might try to promote only men. Once people develop prejudices against groups of people they are likely to discriminate against them when in a position to make decisions.

The consequences of prejudice and discrimination

Carers have to make decisions about how to help others all the time. If carers have prejudices or if they label or stereotype others, they may discriminate against some people in the way that they care. This is serious because:

- discrimination can damage people's self-esteem
- prejudice and discrimination can lead to verbal and physical abuse
- abuse is only one way in which discrimination may show – carers may also avoid or give a poor service to people they don't like.

Sometimes people communicate in a way that doesn't show equal respect and value for others. A number of staff may not want to sit next to someone he or she has a prejudice about. People may use different body language when they have a prejudice towards someone.

Discrimination is not always obvious – very often carers simply make assumptions that everyone does, or should think like they do, and this can come out in conversation. Clients' rights can often be ignored because of assumptions about people. For instance, the following interaction takes place at 7.30 am in a resident's bedroom in a rest home.

Carer:	Morning, Mabel, let's have you up, then – come on.
Resident:	What time is it?
Carer:	It's 7.30 – time you were up and dressed for breakfast.
Resident:	I want to stay in bed.
Carer:	Now come on, don't give me a hard time. I have to get you up, just like everyone else. They'll say I'm not doing my job if you stay here, and I'm not having that. (*Lifts resident to side of the bed*) Right now, what dress shall we have today? The blue one, that would look nice – let's help you into this.
Resident:	What's for breakfast?

Carer:	Bacon and egg, same as always – nice eh, I wish someone would wait on me and get my breakfast.
Resident:	I don't eat bacon!
Carer:	Well, you ought to be grateful – but you don't have to eat it, you know. Here, you're not one of those nutty ones who don't eat meat, are you? I hate all those moaners, never pleased whatever you do for them.
Resident:	Nurr…
Carer:	Right now, I'll wash your face and hands – it will be quicker, and I haven't got all day you know. After that, I'll put you on the loo whil I help Rose downstairs. (*Shouts down the corridor*) I'm just putting this one on the loo, I won't be a minute, Rose.

This is not a pleasant way to wake up! The client has no power – the carer does everything and decides everything. The client's rights are not respected and the following problems arise.

1. **Discrimination:** The client may not like bacon because of her ethnic customs, religious or moral beliefs. People who do not like meat are labelled 'nutty ones' by the carer. The carer is discriminating against people who do not think the way she does. The carer is also forcing opinions on a powerless client.

2. **Communication:** The communication consists of orders from the carer and self-opinionated comments. It fails to value the client and ignores what she thinks or wants. In the end, the client is reduced to groaning 'Nurr…'.

3. **Respect for others:** There is no evidence of respect. The client is accused of being 'nutty'. She is not allowed to stay in bed (although she may have been used to getting up late). The client's routine is not respected. Finally, the client is left on the toilet while the carer helps Rose. This must be a shock. The client is treated like an object rather than a person.

4. **Choice:** The client's rights are not respected, because she has no choice. She has no dignity, and is pulled out of bed against her wishes. The client is not given any opportunity for independence and has to follow the carer's routine. The client has no choice of what to wear or to eat for breakfast. Everyone gets bacon and egg.

5. **Confidentiality:** The client has no right to privacy. The carer shouts down the corridor that 'this one' is being put on the toilet. Going to the toilet is now a public event. If these problems were to go on happening through the day, the client would have a very poor quality of life. Some people might even suggest that she would have little to live for. Non-discriminatory practice should look like this:

Carer:	Good morning, Mabel. How are you feeling this morning?
Resident:	What time is it?
Carer:	It's half-past seven. Do you feel like getting up for breakfast yet?
Resident:	No, I want to say in bed a bit longer.
Carer:	That's all right. Shall I come back in half an hour?
Resident:	Mmmmm …
Carer:	See you later.
	[*Later*] Good morning, Mabel. It's 8 o'clock. Are you ready to get up now?
Resident:	All right.
Carer:	What would you like to wear? There's the blue dress or the white one – or the yellow top and skirt – what do you think?
Resident:	Don't know.

Carer:	Well, would the blue dress be good? It matches the colour of your eyes, you know.
Resident:	(*Laughs*) Come on then. What's for breakfast?
Carer:	Well, there is bacon and egg.
Resident:	I don't eat bacon.
Carer:	Oh, I'm sorry, I forgot you don't eat bacon. There are lots of things you can have – toast, cereal, or fruit, coffee, bread rolls and marmalade. What would you like?
Resident:	Don't know.
Carer:	Well, we'll go through the list when we get downstairs.
Resident:	Toast.
Carer:	OK, I'll make sure you get some toast. Would you like to wash now or later? Would you like me to help you? Do you use a flannel? Let me see if I can find it for you.

In this interaction the carer has time for the client. Her needs are understood and she is not discriminated against. Communication is effective because the client is respected, and she makes her own choices. There is no breaking of confidentiality.

Do IT

Explain what is meant by discriminating practice with reference to ethnicity, gender and age.

Get together with other students and discuss the problems that you think might come about if:

- young children in a nursery were all treated the same
- adults with learning difficulties in a residential home were all treated the same
- old people in a rest home were all treated the same.

What assumptions might be made about ethnicity, gender and age if people are treated 'all the same'?

Think of three ways to prevent discrimination in care settings.

Difficulties in communication

When we talk and listen to others it is important to be aware that difficulties in communication can arise. A range of problems can prevent people from communicating with each other. First, the environment can create problems.

The environment

If people cannot hear what is said because of background noise, or if they cannot see one another properly because of poor lighting, then they may not be able to understand one another. Furniture can act as a block. For example, if desks or tables are arranged badly, people may not be able to see or hear one another easily.

Language

If a person speaks a different language, then an interpreter may be needed. If a person communicates in a sign language, such as British sign language or Makaton, then a signer or interpreter may be needed. Sometimes people talk in their own 'slang' language or in jargon (technical talk that is hard for others to understand).

Interpersonal skills

Communication problems can include not showing respect. Both conversations and relationships break down when people do not attempt to communicate respect. Respect involves trying to understand and listen to other people. There are several reasons why people do not listen to one another.

- **Tiredness**   Listening takes up too much mental energy – we might be tired.
- **Too little time and too much work to do**   Sometimes this might be true, sometimes it might be an excuse.
- **Switching off**   We might assume we have heard it all before and there is nothing we can do to help.
- **Discriminating against people**   Some people might be seen as unimportant, and not worth listening to.
- **Talking so much that we don't listen**   It is tempting to think that we should offer advice to anyone with a worry, and even to feel that we need to have an answer for everything.
- **Listening is frightening**   Clients might talk about pain, suffering and grief. Not listening means that we do not have to think about such things.
- **Being in control**   It is quicker and easier just to get on with practical day-to-day tasks – asking the client's opinion gets in the way.
- **Not valuing diversity**   Sometimes we do not understand the backgrounds and lifestyles of other people. It is easier not have to learn about people different from ourselves.

Effective caring involves being interested in how other people understand themselves and their world. If we are not interested in other people's life experience, we are unlikely to understand them. If we can't understand other people, we will have difficulty communicating with them. A knowledge of diversity can help us to understand and communicate with clients.

Do It

Evaluate own current knowledge of difficulties in communication.

Think of three people you have spoken to at work or on placement in the past month, where there have been difficulties in communication. Without using people's real names, give a mark out of five as to how much the difficulties are to do with practical and environment problems, language problems or difficulties in understanding.

Practical and environment problems	Language problems	Difficulties in understanding
e.g. Seeing, hearing each other	e.g. You speak different languages – need to have sign language	e.g. Different backgrounds, different ages, different abilities, different life experiences

What can you do to improve your understanding of other people's backgrounds?

See Chapter 4 which looks at communication skills in more detail – the task above may link with your work for Chapter 4.

The skills required of a care worker

Rights and responsibilities

People who receive care services are usually vulnerable. Being vulnerable means that you are at risk of being harmed. If clients' needs are not met by carers, clients may be harmed, or deprived of the quality of life they might otherwise have had. All people have the right to be cared for in a way that improves their quality of life. People's needs to belong and for safety and self-esteem are discussed in detail in Chapter 3 (pages 87 to 92).

Children

Young children are developing physically, intellectually, emotionally and socially all the time. In order to develop, children need to feel that they are physically and emotionally safe. Children need contact with loving and caring adults. Children need to be able to make a relationship with adults who care for them. They need to feel that they belong within a group of caring people. Children need to find interesting and mentally stimulating activities to assist with their intellectual development.

If young children receive quality care, they are likely to grow up with a sense of being worth something – a sense of self-worth. If children grow up in a caring setting, they should grow to like who they are, to be confident and to have self-esteem.

When children do not receive good care, they may fail to develop a sense of belonging, they may feel very negative about themselves, and they may lack a sense of being worth anything. Children are vulnerable – their sense of who they are can be strongly influenced by the type of care they receive. The carer is intimately involved with the child – giving the child a sense of belonging, of being loved and important.

Figure 1.14 Encouraging a child's social and emotional development

Think it through

In Figure 1.14, how are the child's care needs being met?

The child's physical development is being helped by the trolley – helping the child to stand up. The child's intellectual development can be helped by the exciting 'things to do' offered by the toy. The child's social and emotional development is encouraged by the carer who is using her relationship and communication skills with the child.

Adults with learning disabilities

Adults need a sense of who they are. This sense of self depends on a feeling that you belong with other people and that you have value and worth. It is important that adults develop a sense of self-esteem – a sense of liking who they are. A sense of who you are develops

Figure 1.15   Ignoring a child's needs

Think it through

What is wrong in Figure 1.15?

The carer's attention is focused on the TV – not on the child. The child is strapped into her chair, even though she is not tired. There is little activity to support physical or intellectual development. There is no sense of love or belonging for the child. If this child is often treated in this way, she may not develop fully.

through making choices. Most adults choose what they want to eat, when they want to eat, what they want to wear, who they want to talk to and so on.

Children are often not trusted to make good decisions about food and clothes. Parents may say things like 'You have to eat your dinner before you can have sweets to eat.' 'You have to wear your coat to school – you will get cold if you don't.'

As people grow up they need to make their own choices and become independent. Adults usually feel angry and hurt if they get treated like children – it is hard to develop self-esteem if you are not allowed to make your own choices.

People with a learning disability will need advice and guidance to do things. There is a danger that carers can 'take over' and not treat them as adults. It can be easy to think 'these people need help and guidance – children also need help and guidance – so these people should be cared for as if they were children.'

Older people

Many, if not most, adults establish a sense of belonging, a sense of self-worth and self-esteem during their adult life. Most adults are used to organising their own lives; they may feel that their life has been important. People may take pride in their family or in their career, or in leisure activities that give a sense of achievement.

In later life there are many changes that can threaten to harm self-worth and self-esteem. When their children grow up and move away, some older people feel they are no longer important as parents. Sometimes when people retire, they lose the self-esteem that their job gave them. If people lose their partner, the loss can make them feel that they are no longer the valuable person they used to be. When people can no longer cope alone – when they need day or residential care – there can be a feeling of a loss of self-worth and self-esteem. Losing a home can be very damaging to a person's sense of who he or she is. A few older people become ill or develop disabilities. All these threats and losses can add up to make elderly people feel vulnerable, lose self-confidence and self-esteem, and feel worried and threatened about the future.

Carers working with older people need to understand the emotions they may have. Skilled care involves getting to know individuals and showing respect for their rights. Skilled relationship and conversation work can help people to a sense of worth and self-esteem, even though they are facing difficult challenges.

If clients are receiving care because they are vulnerable, one of the main purposes of care must be to prevent clients from suffering disadvantage or damage. Care workers have a responsibility to protect clients from physical harm and to ensure that basic physical and safety needs are met. If clients went without food or if they were injured it would be obvious that they were not cared for. But clients' rights go much further than safety and physical care. Caring includes the client's needs for a sense of belonging and their needs for self-esteem and self-worth. The development and maintenance of the client's sense of self lies at the heart of caring. Clients should be in control of their own lives, as much as possible. Clients should be given the power (empowered) to control their own lives as far as it is possible to do this.

Clients' rights

A range of rights are generally seen as applying to all clients who receive care services. Some of these rights have been defined in NVQ standards and some in other works on quality care. As well as these general rights, specific care settings may define the quality of care and clients' rights within their own publications about their service. The way rights are explained can vary between work settings and services for different client groups.

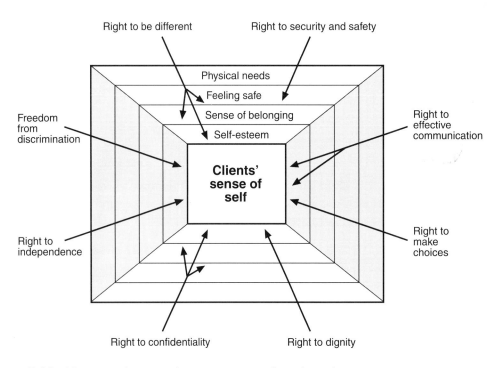

Figure 1.16 Various rights contribute to meeting clients' needs

The right to be different

Care work involves supporting clients as they develop a clear sense of who they are and a feeling of self-worth. People are different from one another because of their age, gender, sexuality, where they live, their race, health, abilities and class, among other things. People have different values and beliefs based on their culture, political beliefs, religion and the social groups they belong to. People also have different personalities – they enjoy different things and develop different ways of understanding life. Two people can live in the same family, go to the same school, have similar life experiences and yet develop quite different attitudes and beliefs about themselves.

Care work involves celebrating the fact that people are different or 'diverse' – understanding and enjoying the fact that people have different beliefs and views. People should never be expected to be all the same, or to fit in with the views of a care worker. Carers need to avoid making assumptions or judgements about what is normal or what is the right way to live.

Freedom from discrimination

Receiving a worse service than others because of your age, gender, race, sexuality or ability would strike at the heart of a client's sense of belonging, self-esteem and self-worth. When services or workers make assumptions about people, discrimination can easily follow. Architects in the 1960s designed buildings with steps and stairs – without lifts or ramps. Part of the reason they did this was that they thought 'everyone walks – like me and the people I know'. Architects didn't hate or want to discriminate against people in wheelchairs – they simply didn't think about it, so disabled people were discriminated against. Making assumptions that everyone eats the same food or everyone celebrates the same religious festivals results in people being excluded and discriminated against. Discrimination damages a sense of belonging and self-esteem.

It is important to find out about individuals and try to check that our own personal behaviour and the service we provide meets the needs of people. Where services do not provide equal quality to different groups of people it is important to challenge discrimination, first by raising the issue with managers. There should be a policy in every care setting to help prevent discrimination.

The right to confidentiality

Care services have to keep detailed information on clients in order to meet their needs. Care workers also have to find out a great deal of personal information about clients in order to ensure they can work effectively and not discriminate against people. It is vital that this information is shared only with people who have a genuine need to know it.

If care workers were to pass information on to friends, neighbours or members of the public, it could have the following effects.

- Clients could feel that they didn't matter, and their sense of belonging and self-esteem could be damaged if they thought personal details could become public.
- Clients could lose trust in a care worker if they thought their personal details were being discussed by others.
- Clients could lose control over their lives if relatives or neighbours knew details of their medical conditions and made assumptions. For instance, if neighbours found out that a

person had cancer, they might assume that he or she would go into hospital and perhaps die. It could be difficult for the client to deal with this.

● Clients' property and personal safety could be at risk if information became known to the wrong people about their savings and where they keep their money or valuables. If it becomes public knowledge that a client keeps a door key under a flowerpot in the front garden, the client could be burgled. If a client is known to be forgetful, he or she could be exploited by criminals on the lookout for a potential victim.

The right to make choices

None of us can have everything we wish for all of the time. Part of being an adult is to make day-to-day choices about our activities, personal appearance, diet, and so on. Where clients have serious disabilities or illnesses, or when they are very young, care workers sometimes limit what they are allowed to do – usually in order to preserve the client's health and safety.

Where clients are deliberately restricted there should be clear reasons for this, and normally those reasons should be recorded in writing so that they can be checked. Where clients have difficulty in expressing their wishes, care workers should try to find ways of helping them to choose and to communicate their choice. Care plans should normally list details of clients' choices, although care workers need to check clients' wishes on a day-to-day basis.

If a client feels that his or her wishes and needs are not being respected, this is likely to damage the person's sense of belonging and self-esteem. Being able to choose makes us who we are.

Dignity

People may need assistance with very personal tasks in a care setting. They may need help with eating food, help to dress and wash, and help to use the toilet. With all these activities it isn't just a matter of getting the task done – the way the task is done matters very much.

Showing respect for clients involves understanding their feelings and wishes. Respect involves ensuring that clients have privacy when undressing, washing or going to the toilet. Respect involves not expressing negative attitudes towards difficulties that clients may have with eating, washing, dressing and toileting.

The right to independence

A sense of self, a sense of belonging and self-esteem are often developed or maintained by involving clients in their own care as much as possible. It is important to do things *with* clients rather than do things *to* clients. Wherever possible, clients should be helped to take control of their own care, and when people cannot do things for themselves they can still be asked to say how they would like care to be given. Feeling independent may increase a client's self-esteem.

The right to effective communication

Respecting diversity, avoiding discrimination, showing respect for dignity and offering choices all depend on understanding the clients you work with. Before we can understand people, it is necessary to communicate with them. Communication is not just a matter of giving and receiving messages – it requires active listening as well as appropriate verbal and non-verbal skills. If clients do not feel that they are understood and listened to, they are unlikely to develop a sense of belonging.

The right to security and safety

If you are afraid or worried, you will not be developing a sense of belonging or self-esteem. If you feel in danger, the first thing you may want is to feel safe again! Clients have a right to feel that they are safe from risks of pain and abuse. Clients have a right to expect that they will not suffer accidents or harm whilst receiving care, and that their property is safe in care settings. These basic rights lay a foundation for the rights discussed above.

Clients' responsibilities

Rights are agreed upon because people are members of a community or group that shares ideas and values about how people should work together. The right to self-esteem is a central principle of a modern democratic society. Rights of individuality, freedom from discrimination, confidentiality, choice, dignity, independence, effective communication and safety all protect individual well-being and encourage self-development and self-esteem.

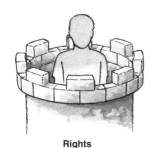

Rights can be seen as protecting vulnerable clients.

Rights

Rights may work best when everyone shares the values on which they are based and when people's rights and responsibilities go together.

Rights and responsibilities

Figure 1.17 Rights and responsibilities go together

Rights usually carry responsibilities with them – they are balanced with responsibilities because membership of a community involves both. Clients can expect respect, but they have a responsibility not to interfere with or damage other clients' rights. Clients have a right to be free from discrimination, but also a responsibility not to discriminate against others. Usually, little is said about clients' responsibilities because they have less power than staff and the managers of services. Clients are generally vulnerable, while care workers usually have a degree of control over their own lives. But because clients are vulnerable, it doesn't mean they have a right to interfere with other people's rights, or for instance threaten people with racist or sexist behaviour. The rights that each client may expect to enjoy must be shared with other clients and staff.

It is a care worker's responsibility to respect client rights, but in turn care workers should expect to enjoy similar rights in their place of work. It is a manager's responsibility to check that clients' rights are respected, but once again managers can expect to be treated with respect, not be discriminated against and to have a safe working environment.

DO IT

Identify the rights and responsibilities of the individual carer, client and professional team when providing care.

One way to identify the rights and responsibilities of carers might be to make a list of clients' rights. Interview a supervisor or manager in care and ask him or her to explain how good care practice makes sure these rights are respected. Write up the details of this interview and include your own ideas on how rights and responsibilities should apply to people in care.

Professional roles and the qualities of a carer

Taking on a professional role is like becoming a character in a play. The role includes everything that an actor is supposed to do and say during a play. An actor has to do and say the things expected if the play is to succeed. Being a professional carer means that what you do and say has to fit the expectations of the people who are relying on you.

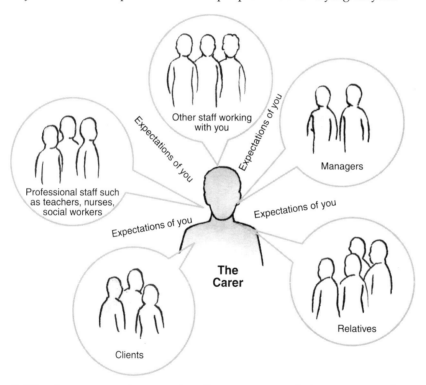

Figure 1.18 As a carer, other people will expect you to behave as a professional

Think it through

If you work as a carer, who will have expectations as to how you should behave? There may be a large range of people, usually including the clients, managers, other staff, relatives and other professionals who work with clients.

Each care role may involve differences in what other people expect from you. Not everyone will expect exactly the same things. There are some general expectations of professional behaviour, however.

- Carers must have respect for the fact that people are different from each other, or 'diverse'. Carers must be careful not to discriminate against people because of differences.

- Carers must maintain confidentiality.

- Carers must show respect for clients and their rights including the right to control their own lives and make choices.

- Carers should develop good communication skills and make appropriate relationships with clients.

- Whilst at work, carers have to meet the needs of employers and clients rather than putting their own wishes first.

- Carers should think carefully about the work they do with clients – care work is not always easy, and it involves lifelong learning.

Time management

Different people expect different things from you as a care worker. Clients will often want you to spend time and give your attention to them. Many clients feel special if you can spare time to listen and talk with them. Managers will expect that, as well as doing this, you will do all the tasks that are needed for all the other clients. Other professionals will want you to understand how busy they are and perhaps hope that you have the time to do things that they can't – like spending time talking to clients. Relatives will expect you to put their child, relative or parent first, perhaps before other clients.

People will all expect different things from you. Carers often have difficulty being able to please everyone!

1. Mrs Benson calls you over. 'Could you take me down the corridor in a wheelchair please?' 'Oh, but the nurse said that walking was good for your circulation,' you reply. 'Never mind all that – I'm 86 years old and it's just too much for me. It's my choice, and I want you to wheel me down!'

    Who do you please, the nurse or Mrs Benson?

2. You are working in a small hostel, and one of the residents comes to you looking sad. She holds your hand, hoping for attention, saying she is 'not well'. This means she is not feeling happy. Just at this moment another carer puts his head round the door and says 'Give us a hand with the shopping, can you?'

    Which do you put off for a moment, the client or your colleague?

Figure 1.19 Care roles involve balancing different people's expectations to get the best results

1. With Mrs Benson you have to balance her health needs – assessed by the nurse – for walking as exercise, against her wish to use the wheelchair. If she always uses the wheelchair she may lose her ability to walk. If she doesn't get her way and have the wheelchair, she will feel her rights have not been respected. She may lose self-esteem if her wishes are ignored. A balanced answer might be to agree her wishes now but offer to help her with walking on other occasions – or to ask her to discuss the issue with a manager and/or the nurse as soon as possible.

2. In this situation you could try to find out whether you can help with the shopping in 'just a minute'. Or you may be able to leave the client and come back. You have to balance the client's needs against the needs of your colleague.

It is important to manage your time so that you can work efficiently with a range of people. It is always possible to explain that you need to leave someone and be polite – perhaps offering to return at a later date.

Self-presentation

Carers need to behave appropriately in order to show respect for clients. Many people spend a great deal of time and money trying to look good – sometimes people want to attract attention, to shock others or to be different. It is important to celebrate differences in people and care workers will want to dress in a way that acknowledges their cultural and lifestyle differences. However, there is an important issue to consider as a member of a care team. Team members are employed to care for others, not to be the centre of attention themselves.

The way carers present themselves to clients and other staff should convey respect for their rights. In turn, others have a responsibility to respect cultural diversity.

Self-presentation includes personal hygiene, which means clean hair, teeth, hands and nails. Many clients or relatives may view body odour or a dirty appearance in a carer as a sign of not caring about others. Carers need to be sensitive to the messages that their appearance sends. They also need to consider health and safety.

- Flat shoes are necessary when lifting or physically supporting people. High-heeled shoes can increase the risk of falling or twisting an ankle.
- Long earrings could be dangerous – children could pull them or they could become caught in clothing.
- Necklaces and ties can get caught in clients' clothing or dangle into food.
- Some rings, especially those with stones, may provide an opportunity for bacteria to collect or might tear protective gloves.
- Long hair can brush over clients' faces and perhaps touch food – it may need to be tied back.
- Personal habits should include careful washing of hands to prevent the spread of infection. Lifestyle habits such as smoking need to be carefully thought through. Many parents may be concerned that their children may grow up to copy what they see adults around them doing. If you smoke in front of children, you may be sending a message that smoking is good. Parents may find this offensive.

As a care worker you need to check policies on self-presentation with senior staff. There can be variations in policies between different settings.

Effective and efficient care

Giving effective care means meeting people's needs (including the needs outlined in their plan of care). Effective care always develops a sense of belonging and self-esteem, and giving effective care always takes time. If you worked with one child or adult all day, you would get to know each other really well, and you might understand their needs in detail and find it easy to encourage the development of self-esteem. But many caring jobs involve working with a large number of people. If you have to care for many people, working efficiently means providing a service for everyone to an equal standard. Carers often have to achieve a balance between the efficiency of their work (giving everyone a service) and their effectiveness at meeting individual social and emotional needs.

Caring usually means balancing effectiveness with the need to give a service to a number of people. Carers always have to respect the dignity and rights of clients, but at some times in the day it is not possible to restrict care to one person only.

Carers have to think about the needs of all the people they work with and plan to have enough time to provide quality service for all the clients. A carer working with children will need to make sure that he or she gives time and attention to all the children. It is possible to find that you give attention to only the interesting or the demanding children.

As well as balancing the pressures of time with the need to give effective care, carers have to be clear about the boundaries of their role.

Boundaries

A boundary is like a fence – it marks where your role ends. You can think of a boundary as the line between your caring role and your ordinary relationships.

A boundary is a line you go up to – but should not cross over.

Boundaries of the care-worker role clarify what you should not be expected to do. Deciding on the boundaries of your role means that you need to decide the limits of what you can do and what you should refuse to do. If you are at work or on a placement, then understanding the boundaries of your care role may be an important task. Setting boundaries may help you to feel safe and comfortable with the pressures that the caring role might place on you.

Whether you work with children, people with learning disabilities, or other adults, there are some general boundary areas. You need to decide:

● how much time it is right for you to give clients
● how far you should become emotionally involved with clients' needs
● how far you should tell your clients about your own life history, lifestyle and feelings
● how much practical support you should provide for certain individuals.

Do it

Describe the qualities required for an effective and efficient carer.

The work you do to evaluate your own caring skills – see page 38 – may include drawing up a list of skills and rating how good you are at these areas. Effective care will depend on these caring skills and behaviours. But how efficient are you as a carer? Use the rating scale again to decide if you spend the right amount of time keeping records, attending meetings, talking to clients, doing activities with clients. Discuss with your supervisor how much time you should spend talking to clients and doing other duties. How effective and efficient does your supervisor think you are at communication skills?

Reviewing your own performance

Caring for vulnerable people is not a simple task. People have complex feelings and thoughts, and each person is unique. Because people can vary so much, and because people's needs are different, care work involves constant learning. How do you learn about people?

- Do you read about theories of needs and behaviour?
- Do you sit in a comfortable chair and think about care work?
- Do you get into discussion groups and talk about care work with others?
- Do you work with clients – talk to them and listen to them?

Figure 1.20   Some ways of learning about clients

All these ways of working could be useful. Many people would say that the best place to start would be to actually do the work – talk and listen to clients. But the very best way of learning about people's needs is to use all the ideas listed above.

Working with people gives you experience, lets you learn naturally by watching other people and copying the way they do things. If you listen to the people you work with, you may get some feedback on how good your practice is. Gradually, you can change what you do – until things seem to work well.

Working with people gives you 'know-how' on care work.

Sitting and thinking is useful because it's only by thinking things over that people realise what is going on. Sometimes difficulties can be sorted out if you think things over, and thinking things through often helps you to feel confident about their ideas. If you picture things you have done, you can work out why certain things happened, and it can help you to see things from other people's point of view. Thinking things through can help us to have new ideas.

Thinking about your work with others can help make sense of things and help you plan for the future.

Discussing care work is a great way of learning – when people work on their own, they are likely to develop assumptions. We can all develop stereotypes, label others and even become prejudiced if we never check our ideas with other people. Other people aren't always cleverer or better than we are; it's just that discussing things often helps us to understand things better. There is an old saying: 'I know what I think when I hear what I say.'

Discussion is useful because it can help to make things clearer – it can help to check assumptions in our thinking.

Reading and going on courses is useful because books and teachers may have new ideas, information or ways of looking at things, all of which can help in understanding the situations or needs that carers work with.

Reading is useful because it can help give new ideas and understanding of care issues.

Do it

Evaluate own current knowledge of diversity and equality.

Get together with a team of other students to design a quiz that will test knowledge of diversity and equality. The quiz could consist of a series of cards with numbered questions on one side. The answers to the questions could be kept on a separate sheet. Another team could design a similar quiz and the teams could play each other. Use the information in this chapter on social class, income and lifestyle, geographical location, the welfare state and benefits, family structure, ethnicity, gender, age, discrimination, stereotyping, labelling and prejudice to help you with this quiz.

After you have played the quiz, rate your own knowledge using a five-point scale to evaluate how well you did on various topics. How could you improve your knowledge?

Emotions and working with people

The great thing about working with people is that they are all so different and each person provides a new learning situation, but having to find out about each child in a nursery, each adult in a day or residential centre, takes energy. It is always easier just to see people as being similar, and not to get too involved.

Not thinking about work, not discussing it, not reviewing your own performance saves emotional energy – but it can lead to a feeling that care work is boring. Once work seems boring, negative feelings about people and tasks take over. Emotions connected with boredom can make us want to give up and withdraw.

One reason for reviewing your own performance is so that you don't begin to see clients as 'all the same' and feel the boredom that can go with this.

Working with people creates a lot of emotions and feelings – some of them nice and some not so nice. Some people we work with will be good to us – they may praise us, and tell us that they like us. Working with interesting, attractive or kind people may make us feel good.

Figure 1.21   We need to review our own performance so as to stop negative emotions from blocking us in our work

But many people who receive care will be worried or even depressed or upset; these people may not always be rewarding to work with. Our first emotional reaction may be to want to avoid them. When we have to work with a difficult child it is only natural to feel 'I don't want to – I'd rather do something else'.

If we are to work in a professional way then we have to be sure that we don't follow the emotional urge to withdraw, but instead find ways of coping. Why does the child not want to do the activity? Is the child bored, frustrated? If we can think through some answers, we may be able to understand why the child is 'difficult'. If we can understand, we can cope with our emotions.

One reason for reviewing your own performance is to prevent negative emotions from blocking professional behaviour.

Thinking a situation through can help us to solve problems. Why does a child throw his or her work on the floor? There could be many different reasons. Talking to other staff or to senior staff may help us to understand. Involving other people will probably help us to understand people we work with. Talking to the child may help us to understand. Observing what happens during the day may help. Thinking about our own behaviour – how good we are at talking or listening – may also help us to understand.

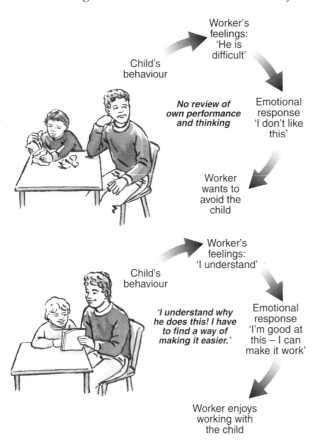

Figure 1.22   Emotions and professional behaviour

One reason for reviewing your own performance is to solve problems we face.

You will have attitudes and beliefs and ways of understanding people based on your own life experience. It is possible that carers can make assumptions about other people – perhaps that they are bad or dangerous. Assumptions can turn into stereotypes and pre-judgements about other people. In the end there is a danger that clients can be judged, labelled and discriminated against because they are different.

One reason for reviewing your own performance is to recognise assumptions in your thinking and to prevent these assumptions turning into discrimination and pre-judgements.

It is very difficult to check our own thoughts alone. A good way to check our assumptions is to discuss practice with colleagues, tutors or workplace supervisors. Skilled supervisors may be able to help us question assumptions in our thinking.

How to review your own performance

It is often difficult to understand how we influence the people we care for. After we have been working with someone it is useful to stop and think about the work we have done. Sometimes discussing our work with supervisors, managers or other staff can be helpful to get new ideas. If we get new ideas they can be tried out in practice to see if they are right. When people have a problem to solve they sometimes go through a process like the one shown in Figure 1.23.

Figure 1.23   A problem-solving process

The important thing is to think about your experiences and learn from them. It is easy to forget our experiences and learn nothing from them if we don't think about them and discuss them. The main ways to review your own performance are to think about your work and discuss your work.

1.   Think about the reactions you get from clients – try to imagine how they see you. What does clients' non-verbal behaviour towards you mean? What do clients say to you? How effective is your care work at meeting clients' needs, including needs to belong and needs for self-esteem?

2.   Review your work by discussing your views of clients' needs and your work with them. You might discuss your practice with your work supervisor, a tutor or with colleagues.

DO IT

Identify the reasons why it is important to review own skills and performance.

Imagine yourself working in a care role two years from now. How would you wish your clients and other staff to think of you? What skills would you want them to say you had? Make a list of skills you would like to develop – how could reviewing your own practice help you to develop these skills? How far would your practice develop if you never thought about or discussed your work?

When and where to review your work

Reviewing work is part of learning and developing care skills. Reviewing could take place at work, but you can think and discuss anywhere. College work should help you to review

DO IT

Evaluate own current caring skills.

Draw up a list of your own responsibilities as a carer. You could use the outline below to help you. You might want to look at the next section of this chapter and Chapter 4 to help explain some areas. Check your completed list with a tutor or supervisor to see if they agree. Then give yourself a mark out of five for how good you are at meeting your responsibilities.

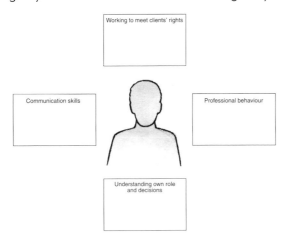

1 = Poor – don't understand – can't do

2 = Needs a lot of improvement

3 = Needs some improvement

4 = Good – but still room for improvement

5 = Expert – excellent at this work

If you rate yourself as a 1, then try to work out why you find this area difficult. How could you learn to understand or develop skills in this area? Ask your tutor or supervisor for help. If you are a 5, then ask yourself how you can share your skills and understanding with others. The act of sharing ideas will help to keep you at a high level of skill.

Figure 1.24   The skills required of a care worker

If you score 2, 3 or 4, then think about how you could develop your practice in order to score higher.

your practice, and the more you review practice, the more you may learn. Many work settings organise formal supervision or training sessions to help staff review their practice. Some work settings may use team meetings to discuss some practice issues. If months go by without any thinking about or any discussion of practice, then the risks of boredom, stress, negative behaviour towards clients, prejudice, discrimination and unmet care needs all increase.

Supervisors, managers, colleagues and tutors should be able to help you review your practice.

Responsibilities of the individual carer

As well as forming professional relationships with clients, it is important to form them with the team of people with whom you work.

Even if you work in the community providing care in clients' own homes, you will probably belong to a 'team'.

Being in a team

Teams are important in care work because it is hard to provide good quality care on your own – support and help from others is needed to provide constant, effective care. Good teams share values and understandings about the purpose of care.

CASE STUDY ONE – PLACEMENT HEAVEN

You arrive for your first day in a small residential centre, and you are greeted by your supervisor. She is very friendly and has time to spare – she gets you a cup of coffee and sits down with you. She tells you about the home and explains who the residents are and how the home tries to respect their rights and meet their needs. She talks about the importance of understanding individual needs and the importance of confidentiality. You are invited to sit in on a team meeting. The meeting includes some administrative issues but also a discussion of some of the residents' needs. Each member of staff looks interested. The staff don't necessarily agree, but they all listen to each other. You can tell from the smiles and eye contact that the staff all care about each other's feelings. They also care about how you feel, and are concerned that you should feel included in their group, even though you don't know much about the home. The manager seems to get on well with the staff, and there is some humour in the group. At the end of the meeting you feel welcome – you feel good about working with these people.

CASE STUDY TWO – PLACEMENT HELL

You arrive for your first day in a small residential centre, and no one knows who you are or why you're there. One staff member says: 'You want to work in care – you must be mad. Anyway, you can come with me, and I'll show you how it's done – I could do with some help, because they leave all the work to me and Iris, you know, the other lot. I came in this morning, and they hadn't even got that end one up – not by 8.30 – I had to do it all. They spend their time jawing away – don't know what work is. Are you on one of those college courses, then? All a lot of nonsense, you know – there's no time here, you've just got to get 'em all up, wash 'em, feed 'em, clean 'em up when it comes out the other end (you know what I mean) and put 'em to bed again. Topping and tailing them, that's what I call it. Yes, it would be lovely to sit round all day talking about it, but who does all the work then!'

In Case Study One there is a team:

- the team shows respect for individuals
- the team values equality
- the team respects self-esteem needs
- the team has good communication skills
- the team believes that to give good quality care you have to benefit from a caring approach by others
- the team believes that clients have rights, staff have rights, and managers have rights.

Because the staff in Case Study One care for each other, they also care effectively for the residents – they share professional values about skilled caring.

In the second Case Study the carer thinks care is about physical needs only, and there is no team:

- the staff don't trust each other
- the staff don't share the same values about rights and responsibilities
- the staff member quoted sees working with people as 'topping and tailing them' – like fish in a canning factory
- the staff don't feel that they belong
- the staff don't feel a sense of self-esteem
- in this situation the staff are unlikely to care about the self-esteem of people working on placement.

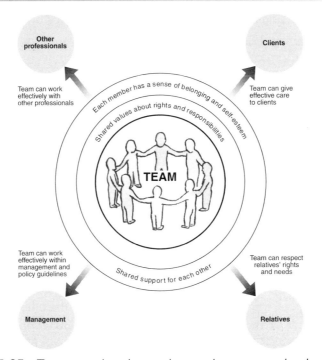

Figure 1.25 Teams need to share values and support each other

Because it is important for team members to work together, it is important for each carer to be committed to professional conduct and values. To become a member of a team you will need to understand the values of that team.

Team values and expectations

Teams in care settings should value:

- the diversity and equality of people
- anti-discriminatory practice (being prepared to challenge discrimination)
- the rights of clients – especially to self-esteem and independence
- confidentiality.

Together with these values, most teams will expect members to:

- present themselves in a way that shows respect for clients, relatives and other staff, and in a way that shows an understanding of safety issues
- maintain health and safety for all
- be reliable, punctual and show commitment to the team, including attending meetings
- maintain the security of clients and property that belongs to both clients and the service
- join in both the practical work and the administrative work that the team has to do
- understand and work within care plan guidance
- understand their own role and be able to prioritise what is important in the job (time management) and show flexibility where necessary
- be able to review their own skills, recognise limitations and ask for help from others when necessary
- be willing to listen and communicate effectively with others, including being able to report and record events.

Being reliable and showing commitment

Most teams of staff have a heavy workload. If you turn up late or not at all, or if you don't let people know where you are, this leaves other people to do work that they were expecting you to do. Even if other people can cover for you, it sends a message: 'I don't care about the team – I don't want to be with you anyway.' It is not always possible to be punctual, and sometimes transport problems prevent people from getting to work or meetings on time. It is always important to apologise and offer a brief explanation for lateness – sending the message: 'I do care about colleagues.' If you are ill, you should always telephone to explain and let people know the situation, so that they can plan ahead. This also lets people know that you care about belonging with them. It is unprofessional not to let colleagues know when they expect you and you can't keep your appointment.

Joining in administrative work

Being a member of a team means sharing the practical and administrative work of the team. If care work is right for you, you will enjoy building relationships with people and probably enjoy a lot of the practical work and activities. But not everyone enjoys the necessary report writing and record keeping.

Reports and records can be very important, however. Records of how children behave, what people with learning difficulties can do, the needs of older people, and so on, help staff to know if care and care plans are meeting objectives. When staff change over on work shifts, it is important that they know what has happened while you were caring for a client. Written records provide evidence that procedures were correctly followed. It is necessary to record details of all accidents and incidents in care that may need to be investigated.

Report-writing and record-keeping are skills. When you explain something in speech, other people can always ask you questions if they are not sure what you mean, and when you speak your non-verbal messages often give the listener a good idea of what you mean. This is not true of written information.

Think it through

If you were working with children you could say: 'Sam had a bad temper this afternoon – he hit me!' The listener could ask questions like: 'Did he hit you hard?' and your non-verbal behaviour would also help to explain how serious the incident was. If you were smiling while you spoke you would send a message saying: 'It's alright – it wasn't a real problem.'

When you have to write reports it is much harder to be sure other people will understand what you mean. Suppose you wrote a report including the comment 'Sam had a bad temper and hit me'. When someone else reads these words later, they will not know exactly what happened – were you hurt, did he become violent and threaten the other children, or did he accidentally touch you when he was feeling angry or frustrated?

The problem with written language is that people have to imagine what words mean when they read them. People often form a mental picture in their heads, based on what they read. Somebody having a bad temper can mean different things. Writing that someone is confused, demented or angry, does not give a clear message, because words like 'confused' can mean different things. A confused person could be a bit forgetful, or seriously physically ill, or very distressed, crying and shouting out. Different people build different pictures in their minds.

When writing reports about people's behaviour, you should:

- say what you saw.
- say what you heard
- be as clear as possible
- not put your own interpretation into your report.

Going back to the example above about Sam, the report writer should write a description like this: 'Sam threw his pencils on the floor and slapped my arm gently. When I asked him why he did this, he just looked at me and then looked away.'

Working within care plan guidance

Under the National Health Service and Community Care Act (1990), clients are entitled to have their needs assessed. Needs include physical, social, financial, transport, mental health, accommodation, education and cultural needs. Needs are assessed by social workers and other professional staff who decide which services need to be purchased for an individual. This first assessment results in a Care Plan, agreeing to buy in certain services. If you are just starting a career in caring, you are unlikely to be directly involved with the purchase of services.

Many clients will have a day-to-day plan for their care, which may be drawn up by providers of care. This day-to-day plan will be based on the original assessment of an individual's needs and may help staff to assess the effectiveness of care. Sometimes the day-to-day care plan is called a 'micro care plan', while the original plan is called a 'Macro plan'.

When you work with adult or older clients there should be a written plan that explains many of the most important needs for which care aims to provide. You may need to discuss each individual's care needs with the team and with supervisors and managers.

Sometimes, individual care needs change and then it is important to discuss new issues with managers. Managers can arrange for a review of a client's care needs where things have changed. You might be providing home care – giving help with shopping and housework – when you notice that your client is become increasingly forgetful and upset. Although the care plan outlines your basic tasks, you will need to report the client's increasing difficulties, and a new assessment of need may be required.

Do it

Describe the importance of care plans, record keeping, team meetings and confidentiality when working as member of a care team.

Make a list of the jobs you are expected to do at work or on placement which include using care plans, making records, attending meetings and keeping things confidential. You could ask your supervisor or a manager to help you with this list if necessary. Discuss with a tutor or supervisor what might happen if you did not have care plans, did not make any records, did not keep things confidential or attend meetings. You can use your discussion to describe why these care tasks are important.

Health and safety

Under the Health and Safety Act of 1974, all employees must take reasonable care for their own safety and that of others. As a team member you will be expected to watch out for risks to your own and clients' safety. This will include looking out for hazards such as wet floors, things you could trip over like boxes on the floor, loose rugs or carpets, trailing leads, overloaded electric points and so on. You must make sure you do not create any hazards and report any problems that you are not sure about. As well as preventing or reporting hazards, you must understand and follow safety procedures while at work or on placement. Unless you have had formal training you should not lift people or heavy objects. You must follow safety procedures when using equipment or cleaning, and also when dealing with body fluids, like blood and urine. Health and safety issues are discussed in Chapter 3.

Maintaining security

Carers have a responsibility to protect themselves and their clients from safety and security risks. You will probably be aware of newspaper stories involving crimes in hospital or social care settings. It is important that you know who visitors to your setting are. You should ask if you can 'be of assistance' to any strangers who enter the building. Many care settings ask visitors to sign in and state who they are visiting or why they are there.

Maintaining security is a role that links with confidentiality. Before giving any information away about a client, you must check who is asking and that they have a need to know. If a telephone caller claims to be a social worker who needs to check on a client, you should ask to call back before giving any information. By calling back you can check that the caller is of the address that he or she claims to be. Your work setting may have a policy about giving information on the telephone – you may be forbidden to give information to mobile phone users.

When contractors enter premises, they will usually carry identification, invoices or order forms proving that they are who they say they are. When relatives arrive it is not usually necessary to ask for identification – instead, you can offer to lead them to the person they are visiting. They should recognise each other or give some sign that all is well.

Think it through

You enter the lounge of a residential home to find a stranger unplugging the video recorder. He says: 'It's OK, I'm just taking it for servicing.' You know nothing about this! Do you:

a. Stand in the way to prevent him from leaving and call for help?

b. Shrug your shoulders and say: 'Nothing to do with me'?

c. Ask him if he would leave the machine for a minute and come to the office to check details of the service contract with the manager?

a. This could be hazardous if the person is stealing the video – he may attack you in order to escape. You should not place yourself at risk in this way.

b. This is wrong – how do you know what he says is true? You should try to protect the home's property, although your own personal safety is more important.

c. This is the best answer. If the stranger is a thief, perhaps he will run off without the video. If he is servicing the machine he might congratulate you on your care – after all, you have been polite and have not jumped to conclusions.

Do it

Explain the reasons why strict security and health and safety rules must be observed.

Think about your placement or workplace. Imagine walking around the building – especially any kitchens, bathrooms or toilets. What safety or security hazards could arise in different areas? Make a map or plan of part of your placement or workplace, and label the hazards that might occur there. What rules are there at your placement or work setting to prevent hazards and maintain security? Make a list of these rules.

Action plans to develop skills

You should try to develop your skills while you are on placement or at work. Think through how you could do this. Developing skills will depend on the following factors.

1. Really wanting to do well – being motivated. If you do not really think something matters then you won't develop the skill.

2. Getting advice and guidance from others. You will need help – developing skills just by thinking is very difficult. Could your supervisor or tutor watch you doing some work, and give you advice, or can the people you work with give advice? Could a manager at your workplace help?

3. Understanding the theory that links with your skills. What reading or discussion work do you need to do in order to understand things better?

4. Having opportunities to practise skills. Do you practise listening and communication skills with other students? How can work or placement help you to fulfil a professional role?

You could write a list of answers to these questions, but designing a form to fill in may be helpful. The form below is one example of an action plan to develop skills.

Do it

Produce a plan to develop own skills further.

Area of skill or practice to be developed	Why is it worth developing this area?	Where can I practise?	Who can give advice?	What theory is it important to know?	Dates to discuss progress
Example:					
Listening skills	To get to know people better	College discussions, talking to clients on placement	Tutor, supervisor	Communication skills, Chapters 1 and 4	
Anti-discrimination practice	To prevent discrimination and work effectively with clients	Discuss issue with supervisor – explore care and check for cultural needs	Tutor, supervisor, 'key workers' on placement	Theory in Chapter 1	

Summary of progress

A plan needs to be checked – this means discussing it with a tutor or supervisor. It is useful to write some notes about progress at or after your meeting to discuss skills development.

LIFESPAN, DEVELOPMENT AND CARE NEEDS

Life stages

Principles of physical growth and development

People do not all grow and develop at exactly the same rate. Many things can influence how an individual develops. Each person is born with a pattern formed by their genes – a 'genetic pattern'. Genes control the sequence of human development, so that many abilities like walking and talking seem to 'unfold from within' a growing child. This unfolding process is often called 'maturation'.

Maturation is not just an unfolding genetic process, however – the environment a person grows up in always influences it. Genetics provide a plan for the building or physical development of a human being, and the environment provides the building materials – and influences what actually happens.

The baby in the womb grows according to a genetic pattern, but this can be influenced by the diet and habits of the mother. For example, alcohol can damage the development of the baby's nervous system. If a mother smokes it can harm her unborn baby, and the mother's diet is important too. After a child is born, he or she will be affected by experiences. A child will not develop language if nobody speaks to him or her. A child will not learn to walk if he or she is prevented from standing. The kind of support and encouragement a child receives will influence the development of skills and abilities.

Diet, illnesses and infections can have a major influence on physical growth. For instance, too little protein in a diet may limit the height to which a child grows. Too much fat in an adult's diet may increase the risk of heart disease. The environment can influence the delicate hormone balance within the body that influences growth. Our genes will influence the type of physical impairments we are likely to develop as we grow old, but a good diet, for example, may help to prevent heart disease, and exercise may help to stop bones from becoming brittle.

Although we all grow up following a similar pattern, we do not all grow exactly the same. There is a pattern to human life stages, but each person will have a different experience of maturation caused by the interaction of his or her genetic plan for development and influences in the environment.

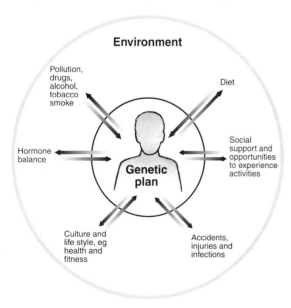

Figure 2.1 Some factors that influence physical growth and development

Do it

Describe the principles of physical growth and development.

Get together with a small group of other students and discuss what you think the ideal environment for a young child would be, in order to help him or her to be healthy and grow to full fitness and height. Use the diagram above to guide your thoughts. Make a list of things that can influence the 'unfolding development' guided by a person's genetic make-up.

Ways of understanding life stages

Human beings grow from a tiny fertilised egg to a baby in nine months. From birth to adulthood takes 18 years. The average life expectancy at birth is now 73 years for boys and 79 years for girls, although some people live well beyond 100 years.

A person's lifespan could be compared to the face of a clock. We grow rapidly in the phases called infancy, childhood and adolescence. We become fully developed adults in the first quarter of the lifespan. Adult life involves very gradual changes, and eventually ageing becomes apparent and a person's life completes its cycle.

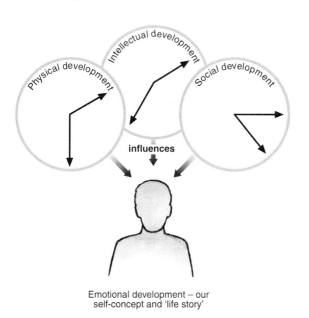

Figure 2.2 Our understanding of who we are is influenced by our social, physical and intellectual development

Society has different expectations of people at different stages of the life cycle. Social development can also be seen as a clock, with different social roles becoming appropriate at different stages. Infants are dependent on their carers. As children grow older so they become more independent, although adolescents are not allowed the responsibility of driving a car until they are 17 and people are not allowed to vote before 18 years of age. Establishing a career, marriage and parenthood are events that are expected in the first half of the life cycle. Retirement might be expected in the third or fourth section of the clock face.

Although we seem to go through an unfolding, physical ageing process, and although society has expectations of us, neither of these clocks makes us who we are. Our physical and social development provides the setting in which our life story is acted out. Our social, physical and intellectual development all influence the development of our self-awareness.

Development of self

Each life story can be seen as being like a journey. When we start our lives we have little sense of who we are, and we react to others 'instinctively'. The first sense of being an individual may not come until we are about two years of age. A child may not develop a general sense of self-worth until eight years of age. Young people often begin to compare themselves with other young people between the ages of 10 and 12, and sometimes after 15 or 16 years of age young adults can explain their sense of who they are, a self-concept. The full development of this sense of self then becomes the goal of adult life. Happy, successful people may have a sense of 'becoming the person they want to be'. This journey of growth and development does not have to end until an individual dies. Some writers feel that the way a person faces his or her own death is in itself a developmental task.

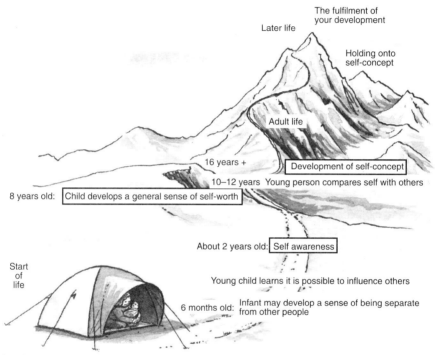

Figure 2.3   Self-awareness, self-worth and self-concept are stages on life's journey

Conception

Human life begins with conception. A fertile woman usually produces one egg cell each month, roughly two weeks after the last menstrual period. The egg cell travels from the ovary, along a tube (known as the fallopian tube) toward the uterus. If sexual intercourse takes place while the egg is in the fallopian tube, then there is a possibility that a new life will be started. Millions of sperm are ejaculated by a man during orgasm. Just one sperm may fertilise the egg. Fertilisation means that the genetic material in the sperm joins with the genetic material in the egg to form a genetic plan for a new human being.

Normally, each sperm and each egg contains 23 chromosomes. Chromosomes contain the genes that control our physical development. Human cells are made from 46 chromosomes, so each egg and sperm contain half the genetic material needed to make the 'plan' for a human being.

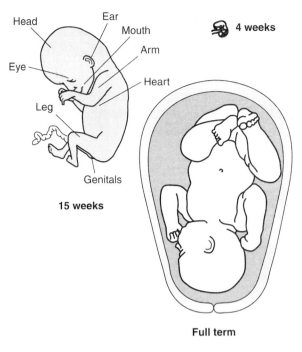

Head
Ear
Mouth
Arm
Eye
Heart
Leg
Genitals

15 weeks

4 weeks

Full term

Figure 2.4 The growth of a baby in the womb

Only about half of all fertilised eggs develop to become babies. Many eggs are lost without the woman knowing that fertilisation ever happened. One to one-and-a-half days after conception, the single egg cell begins to divide. After two or three days there are enough new cells to make the fertilised egg the size of a pin head. This collection of cells travels to the wall of the uterus, where it attaches itself to the wall. The developing collection of cells is now called an embryo. Once the embryo is attached to the uterus wall, a chemical signal stops the woman from having another menstrual period. After eight weeks, the embryo may have grown to between 3 and 4 cm, has a recognisable heartbeat and the beginnings of eyes, ears, mouth, legs and arms. At this stage the growing organism is called a foetus.

During the remaining seven months before birth, all the organs continue to develop. By 20 weeks, the foetus will have reached about half the length of the baby at birth. By 32 weeks, the foetus will be about half its birth weight.

Birth

At about nine months after conception the baby will be born.

Infancy (0–2 years)

Physical development

The newborn baby (or neonate) has to take easily digestible food such as mother's milk in order to grow. A newborn baby does not have a fully developed brain but can usually hear sounds, tell differences in the way things taste, and identify the smell of his or her own mother or carer. Infants are born with various reflexes.

- A newborn baby will turn his or her head toward any touch on the cheek. This reflex is called the rooting reflex, and helps the baby to get the nipple into his or her mouth to feed.
- If you place your finger in the palm of a baby's hand, he or she will grasp your finger tightly. This reflex is called the grasp reflex.
- If a baby is startled – perhaps by a loud noise – he or she will throw hands and arms outwards, arching the back and straightening the legs. This is called the startle reflex.
- If a newborn baby is held upright with the feet touching the ground, he or she will make movements as if trying to walk.

Infants have the physical ability to recognise and interact with people. Babies prefer the sound of human voices to other sounds, and soon learn to recognise their mother's voice. Within a few weeks babies show interest in human faces. It is as if babies come into the world ready to make relationships with their carers.

Babies are helpless when it comes to muscle co-ordination and control. Babies can't hold up their head, roll over, sit up or use their hands to move objects deliberately. The average age for some types of control over the body are shown in the table below:

Ability to lift head slightly	$1-1\frac{1}{2}$ months
Ability to pass an object from one hand to another	6 months
Ability to role over	6 months
Ability to crawl	9–10 months
Ability to stand alone	12 months

See Chapter 10 for more details on development during infancy.

Intellectual development

The first year and a half or two years of life was described as the **sensorimotor** stage of development by a famous psychologist called Piaget (1896–1980). Infants have to learn to co-ordinate their senses and their muscle behaviour (the term 'motor' in the word 'sensorimotor' means control of muscles).

To begin with, a baby will rely on in-built patterns for behaviour such as sucking, crawling and watching. A baby will adapt this behaviour in order to explore a wider range of objects. Babies explore by sucking toys, fingers, clothes and so on. In this way they are slowly able to develop an understanding of objects. According to Piaget, thinking is at first limited to memories of actions. The infant will remember grasping a toy. If given the toy, it may repeat the action. Piaget believed that very young infants would not be able to remember objects they could not see.

Piaget also believed that infants could not understand that objects existed on their own. For instance if an infant's mother left the room, the infant would be afraid that she had gone for ever. Piaget thought that an infant would not be able to understand that the mother still

Piaget's Theory

Stage	Age	Key issue
Sensorimotor stage of development	$1\frac{1}{2}$–2 years	Children don't understand how objects exist
Pre-operational stage (pre-logical stage)	$1\frac{1}{2}$–7 years	Children don't think in a logical way
Concrete operational stage	7–11 years	Children can only understand logic if they can see the issue
Formal operational stage	11 years on	People can understand logical arguments

existed, if he or she could not see, hear, smell or touch the mother. At the end of the sensorimotor period, Piaget thought that infants could at last understand that objects and people continue to exist, even if you can't sense them. Modern research suggests, however, that many eight-month-old infants can understand that people and objects still exist, even when you can't see or hear them. Infants are more able than many people used to think!

Social development

Infants soon learn to recognise their mother's voice and smell, and can probably recognise their mother's face by two months of age. Infants try to attract attention. Many infants will smile and make noises to attract adults. Infants will often respond to the speech and smiles of their carers, and both infants and carers seem to have an inbuilt desire to make an emotional bond that ties them together.

At about 12 months of age infants often develop a fear of strangers, and will protest if they are separated from their parents. After the first year of life infants feel safe with familiar family members if they have formed the necessary social bonds.

Some psychologists believe that this process of bonding is vital for future mental health and well-being. Infants who are rejected or who fail to make relationships during the first few years of life may face great difficulty in coping with relationships in later life. Infants who make safe and secure ties with their carers have a good foundation for future social development.

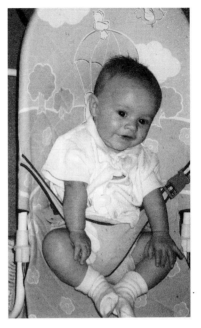

Figure 2.5 Young infants attract their carers to bond with them

Emotional development

Young infants probably do not have a sense of being an individual person. Five- to six-month-old infants do seem to recognise emotions in their carers. As infants grow, they gradually learn that they can influence their carers. Infants may develop the idea that they are a person with a fixed gender at about two years of age. This idea of being a person is called self-awareness. (See Chapter 10 for more details on infancy.)

Childhood (2–12 years)

The word 'childhood' doesn't have a fixed meaning in terms of age. Here, the word is used to cover two to twelve years of age, although exactly where childhood ends and adolescence begins is difficult to say.

Physical development

Children grow steadily at this time but less rapidly than during infancy. By the age of six a child's head will be almost adult size – even though the body still has a lot of growing to do.

Children's practical abilities continue to develop; at two years of age children may be able to run and to climb stairs one step at a time. By four, children may be able to kick and throw a large ball. By six or seven, a child may be able to skip and ride a bicycle.

Puberty often starts for girls between the ages of 11 and 13, although some girls may begin earlier. (See the section on adolescence for more about puberty. See Chapter 10 for more details of development in childhood.)

Intellectual development

By the age of two, children generally start to talk. By the age of six, children can often use language as well as some adults. Language develops very rapidly between two and six years of age.

Between the age of two and seven years, most children learn to count and to explain how much things weigh. Young children don't always fully understand the logic involved in counting and weighing things, however.

Piaget called the period from two to seven years of age the 'pre-operational' period. Pre-operational means 'pre-logical'. Young children make decisions based on what things look like rather than the logic of counting – for example, they will say that there are more sweets in a long line than in a small heap, even though they can count the same number in each.

Older children don't make the mistakes that younger children do. But children aged seven to 12 can often only understand logical problems if they can see what's involved. For example, you could ask a nine-year-old: 'Tanya is taller than Stephen, but Tanya is smaller than Tolu, so who is the smallest out of these three people?' Obviously Stephen is the smallest. A nine-year-old might not be able to work this out without looking at pictures of the people.

Piaget called the period from seven to 12 the 'concrete operational period', because children can only work out logical problems if they can see 'concrete' examples to help them.

Social development

Young children still depend very much on their carers to look after them. They need secure emotional ties with their family. As children develop they become more and more independent, but the family provides safety and a setting in which to learn social roles. Young children use imagination to play-act social roles. Children learn how to behave socially through the process of socialisation in the family (see the section on socialisation in this chapter).

Emotional development

As children develop language skills they can understand and explain who they are in greater detail.

Children develop from being aware of themselves at two years of age to being able to describe their feelings by 12. Children need to develop a sense of being worth something to their friends and family. This sense of self-worth forms a basis for an effective concept of self to develop during adolescence (see the section on self-concept for further details).

Think it through

Try the 'I am' test. Ask children to describe who they are, and six-year-olds will probably just say their name and where they live. They may be able to tell you other factual things like who their brothers and sisters are. Eight- or nine-year-olds may be able to tell you about things they are good at or things they like – they can explain who they are in more depth. By 12, children may be able to compare themselves with others and say things like 'I'm quite good at sport, but not as good as Nisha – she's faster than me.' By 12, children may begin to work out how they fit in with others. Try asking children of different ages and see what kind of answers you can get.

Adolescence (12–18 years)

The word 'adolescence' is used here to cover ages 12 to 18 – 18 is the age when people are first allowed to vote and take on adult responsibilities.

Physical development

Girls generally start puberty before 13, but for boys this comes between 13 and 15. Puberty is a development stage which prepares the body for sexual reproduction. It is setoff by the action of hormones that control sexual development. Both boys and girls may experience a 'growth spurt', where they grow taller at a faster rate than before.

Girls' sexual development during puberty includes the enlargement of breasts, the development of pubic hair, increased fat layers under the skin, and the start of menstrual periods. Boys will experience the enlargement of their testes and penis, the development of pubic and facial hair, and increased muscle strength. Boys' voices also 'break' and become deeper in tone. These major changes mean that adolescents look and behave very differently from children.

Intellectual development

An adolescent may be able to imagine and think about things he or she has never seen or done. By adolescence, people can often imagine their future and how to achieve things. Children are unlikely to plan and think ahead in the same way. Piaget believed that adolescents have the ability to solve problems in an adult way, using formal logic. He called development after about 12 years of age the 'formal operational' (or formal logical) period. Although adolescents may reason in an adult way, many adolescents do not know enough to make good decisions. People continue to improve their decision-making skills during adulthood.

Social development

Adolescents become increasingly independent of their family, and friendship groups can become more important than family for the development of social skills. This phase of development is called secondary socialisation.

Between 13 and 18 years of age, most adolescents will begin to explore relationships with possible sexual partners. Toward late adolescence, people will begin to think about, plan or take on job responsibilities.

The five years between 13 and 18 can involve major changes in social behaviour, as people learn to take on adult roles and adult independence. Some adolescents experience conflict with their parents during this period of change.

Emotional development

Adolescence can involve major emotional stresses as people go through rapid social and physical change. Some adolescents feel a loss of self-esteem as they transfer from school to work. Becoming independent from parents can involve conflict and stress. The search for love and affection from a sexual partner may not be stress free.

The famous psychologist Eric Erikson (1902–1994) believed that a successful adult life depended on people developing a secure sense of self or self-concept. During adolescence people have to work out a self-concept that will guide them through leaving home, perhaps setting up home with a sexual partner, and getting work.

Adulthood (18 onwards)

In Britain the right to vote is granted at 18, and 18 years of age might be taken as the beginning of the social category of adulthood.

Physical development

Young adults are often at their peak of physical performance between 18 and 28 years of age. Most champions of highly active sports are aged between 16 and 30 years. Professional footballers and athletes usually have to retire and move into management roles during their 30s. Older adults generally tend to lose some strength and speed with age, although outside competitive sport these changes can be so gradual as to go unnoticed.

Exercise can help develop physical fitness and athletic skills. An older adult could easily achieve a personal peak of fitness at 40 or 50 years of age if he or she takes up exercise late in life.

There are a number of age-related changes that slowly become apparent as we grow older. Many people develop a need to wear glasses to help with reading during their 40s. Some people cannot hear high-pitched sounds so well during late adulthood. Many adults show a thinning of hair in their 50s, with hair loss being common for men.

Women are most able to conceive children in their late teens and early 20s. The risk of miscarriages and complications rises with age. Usually between 45 and 55 years of age women stop being able to have children when the menopause begins. Older adults in Britain often put on weight. This middle-age spread may be caused because adults still eat the same amount of food that they did when they were younger, but they have become much less active.

The risk of disease and disability rises with age. Older adults are more likely to develop health problems than younger adults.

Intellectual development

Intellectual skills and abilities may increase during adulthood if they are exercised. Older adults may have slightly slower reaction times, but increased knowledge may compensate for this in many intellectual tasks.

Older adults may be more skilled than adolescents and young adults when it comes to making complex decisions. Some adults may develop increased wisdom as they become older.

Social development

Early adulthood is often a time when people continue to develop their network of personal friends. Most young adults establish sexual relationships and partnerships. Marriage and parenthood are important social life events that are often associated with early adulthood. The pressure to obtain paid employment and hold down jobs is also a major social issue for adults.

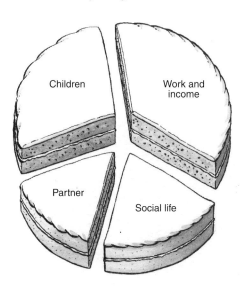

Figure 2.6 Adults have to work out how to divide up their time in order to meet different needs

Many adults experience a degree of stress in trying to cope with the demands of being a parent, a partner and a worker. Nowadays, many individuals work long hours or even take more than one job in order to achieve a high standard of living. If a person has to go to work and maintain a family home, this can create social and emotional problems. Adult life can often involve trying to balance the need to earn money, with the needs of partners and other family members.

Older adults may find that as well as coping with work pressures, they have to provide support for their parents and their children.

Some older adults may feel that they are torn between different demands on their time. When children leave home some pressures may be taken off parents. But some may feel that they have lost part of their social purpose when children no longer need their support.

Many people now retire from paid employment in their 50s, and most people retire by their mid-60s. Retirement is seen as a positive release from pressures by some people, and as an end to usefulness by others.

Emotional development

An individual's sense of self and self-esteem will continue to develop throughout adulthood. During early adulthood, many individuals may struggle to develop the confidence to share life with a partner. Some individuals may prefer to live alone, or may feel that partnership relationships are too demanding. A person's previous family experience may strongly influence his or her expectations of a partner.

Some research suggests that adults often feel more confident and satisfied with their lives in their 30s and 40s than they did in their 20s. It may be that many young adults experience some stress in establishing a satisfying lifestyle.

One theory suggests that older adults may struggle to stay interested and involved with other people after their own family grows up. Some adults may get into 'a rut' and withdraw from active, social involvement as they get older. Successful ageing means remaining emotionally involved with other people.

Old age (65 onwards)

Most people retire by the age of 65 and the period of life after the age of 65 is generally regarded as old age. Most 65-year-olds do not see themselves as 'old', however. Some writers distinguish between the 'young-old' (65 to 80) and the 'old-old' (80-plus). But many 80-year-olds still claim that they are not old!

Physical changes

The period of life after 65 usually involves some reduction in the efficiency of the body:

- the heart, breathing and circulation become weaker
- muscles may become weaker and skin becomes less 'elastic'
- muscles, skin, joints and bones become less flexible and this can mean that people become less mobile, more at risk of fractured bones and more likely to develop wrinkled skin
- blood capillaries in the skin are more likely to burst, meaning that bruising can happen more easily
- most organs in the body, such as the liver and kidneys, work less efficiently
- many people develop problems with arthritis
- there may be a loss of hearing ability
- the risks of impairments and disability rise with increasing age
- reaction times and speed of thinking slow down.

Physical health varies from person to person. Where people have poor health, their ability to remember and think things through can sometimes be affected. Life after 65 involves a general slowing down of physical activity. People can still go jogging, dancing, mountain climbing and so on, but the body becomes less flexible and less able to cope with exertion – limiting the extremes to which people can perform.

Intellectual development

Some people seem to become less able to solve problems and cope with difficult, intellectual challenges in later life. To some extent mental abilities are influenced by physical health. If people develop problems with blood circulation, this can involve the brain and lead to difficulty with mental activities such as problem-solving.

Other people who enjoy good health, and who exercise their minds, often keep their mental abilities and continue to develop their store of knowledge. Some older people seem to develop their ability to make wise decisions and judgements. Even if thinking slows down, the opportunity to develop wisdom may increase with age.

The risk of developing dementia or Alzheimer's disease seems to increase with age; but dementia is not a part of normal ageing. Most old people never develop conditions such as dementia or Alzheimer's disease. There are different types of dementia, but in general dementia can cause a range of disabilities including:

- a loss of ability to control emotion
- difficulty in understanding other people
- difficulties in communicating and expressing thoughts
- loss of memory
- difficulties in recognising people, places and things
- problems with making sense of where they are and what is happening
- problems with daily living activities like getting dressed.

The reasons for dementia are not fully understood, but bad health habits like heavy drinking and smoking may increase the risk of dementia for some people. Other people may inherit a risk factor for dementia with their genetic pattern.

Social development

Older people lead varied and different lives. Many retired people have a greater opportunity for meeting and making new friends than they did while they were working. A network of family and friends can provide vital practical and emotional support. Health problems and impairments can sometimes create difficulties for older people, which might result in social isolation (see case study of Mrs Baddock, page 62).

Emotional development

People continue to develop their sense of self as life progresses. Some theorists suggest that the main challenge of old age is to keep a strong sense of self-esteem, despite the problems that can arise. Older people may not only develop health problems but they can be stereotyped by other people who assume they are less able. Some older people may be at risk of losing their self-confidence and self-esteem because of the way others treat them.

Do It

Identify characteristics of each life stage.

For each life stage from infancy to old age, write down two positive things and two negative things that may happen. For instance, adulthood might involve independence, having your own home and family, but it might also involve little time for yourself or problems with unemployment. Compare your ideas with the ideas of other students in the group and make a general list of positive and negative things that can happen throughout life. What can you do to try to avoid the negative things the group has identified?

Decline and death

Physical processes

There are different theories to explain why we age and die. One theory is that the cells that make up our body have to continually renew themselves, but they can only do this a limited number of times. Eventually, body cells start to go wrong as they try to renew, and other cells die out, causing problems.

Think it through

One way of understanding ageing is to look at what happens when you make photocopies. Imagine you copied a photograph of a face on a photocopier, and then copied your copy rather than the original page. If you keep copying your copies rather than the original, the copies will gradually fade and start to look wrong. You can only copy a limited number of times before you can no longer see the picture clearly.

Some people think that as our cells have to copy themselves, like the photocopier they can manage the task efficiently only a limited number of times. We change as our cells copy and renew themselves. Eventually we lose vital parts of our pattern – and then we die.

Social issues

People think about death and dying in many different ways. Some people fear death and do not like to think about it. Other people have strong religious or personal beliefs which protect them from worry. In general, older people often have less fear of dying than young adults. It may be that some older people feel ready to let go of life at a certain stage of physical decline. Some older people may prepare for their own death by thinking over their lives and the things they have achieved.

Some people who face death want to see family, friends and relatives and need social support to help them cope with dying. Other people may prefer to die alone. Each individual will have his or her own social and emotional needs.

Death as the final stage of growth

Elizabeth Kubler-Ross wrote a book with the title *Death – the Final Stage of Growth*. In this book she explained how people who were dying might go through a process of:

- denying that they were dying
- feeling angry
- trying to bargain or sort things out
- depression
- acceptance of being ready to die.

Being ready to die, not angry, afraid or depressed, might represent the final achievement that a person makes in the journey of emotional development.

The human life cycle – why does it matter?

The genetic material in a sperm and an egg fuse together to create a plan for a new person. This plan is then influenced by the person's environment. If the plan and the environment are good, the person will grow and develop well. We don't just grow physically, we also develop our social and emotional behaviour. Most people develop a sense of self – an idea about who and what they are. Our bodies are not designed to last for ever, and at some age our physical abilities start to decline. The sense of self that we develop never needs to be 'finished' before we die. Our lives influence others, and leave their mark on the history of the world. The world would not be exactly the same if you or I had never existed.

Many of the world's great religions believe that the self we have created (or soul) is 'kept on record', and that God will re-create this self in heaven or in some sort of afterlife.

Quality care depends on workers valuing and caring about other people's sense of who they are. If people do not have a sense of self-worth, they may see little point in living. If we have our basic needs met and a sense of self-esteem, we can go on to enjoy the whole of our lifespan.

DO IT

Relate physical, intellectual, emotional and social aspects of development to two different life stages.

Think of two people at different life stages whom you have talked to and got to know while on placement or at work. Think about each person's stage of physical, intellectual, emotional and social development. Make a list of key issues connected with each stage of development. Use Figure 2.7 to help you.

Figure 2.7 Key issues for four-year-old Yemi

Disability and impairment

The Disability Discrimination Act defines a disability as 'a physical or mental impairment which has a substantial and long-term adverse effect on a person's ability to carry out normal day-to-day activities'.

Physical impairment

A physical impairment results from a part of the body being damaged, lost, or not working as it should. Impairments cause disabilities.

For instance, if you develop cataracts on the lens of the eye, you have a physical impairment which will mean you cannot see clearly. This could lead on to a disability if you can no longer read books or magazines. However, if you had the right computer equipment you could have books and magazine articles scanned and translated into speech that you could hear. The computer could remove the disability of not being able to know what was written down but the impairment would still be there.

Mental impairment

A mental impairment can result from damage to the nervous system or from the experiences that a person has in life. Mental impairments can also come about from a combination of experiences and damage. The cause of some mental impairments is not fully understood.

For instance, a person might have a disability due to slight brain damage at birth. This might involve problems to do reading, writing and spelling. If a person's work doesn't involve reading and writing, people may not know that the person has a disability. If the person uses a computer to help with grammar and spelling, the disability isn't there any more.

DID YOU KNOW?

Over six million people in Britain have a disability, but only 200,000 people use wheelchairs. Wheelchair users are a small proportion of disabled people.

Types of disability

There may be as many types of disability as there are disabled people – no one person's disability is the same as another person's. Equipment and adaptations that are useful for certain people are not useful for other people. It is very important not see disability as some sort of label for people who are different. Disabled people are not 'all the same'.

For instance, people who use wheelchairs may need open, flat spaces where there are no steps. If they have to go up or down levels, ramps are important. People who are partially sighted often like stairs to have a hand rail that they can follow. People who use a wheelchair may need low-level kitchen worktops and sinks, yet people who have arthritis in the back might find it painful and difficult to cope with low-level kitchens. People with disabilities all need different types of support. The most important thing to remember about disability is that people have disabilities – but people *are* not disabilities.

Disabilities can be classified as **sensory**, **physical** or **intellectual** disabilities. All disabilities can interfere with a person's ability to cope with daily living activities. Daily living activities include being able to prepare and eat food, bath or shower, dress, use the toilet, clean, go shopping, read, write, do laundry, use transport, and manage money.

Sensory disabilities

Disabilities of the senses include those of sight and hearing. Many people lose their sense of taste and smell as they get older, but in Western society this impairment rarely results in a disability. People who cannot taste food very well usually have few problems with social life or work – who would know how good your sense of taste was?

People who have impaired vision or hearing usually do have a disability, however. There is no single condition of blindness or deafness. Many people who are 'registered blind' can sense differences between light and dark – they can tell where the window in a room is, because they can sense the light. Others may have tunnel vision, where they can see only a small area, as if they were looking at things at the end of a tunnel. Others may have blurred vision, or be able to see only the outside area of what they look at. So it can be possible for a 'blind' person to see a coin on the floor and pick it up!

People can also have many different types of hearing impairment. As they grow older, many people lose the ability to hear high-pitched sounds. Nearly a fifth of people over the age of 75 wear a hearing aid. Many people can hear the speech of people they are used to hearing, because they know their voices and speech patterns. People can sometimes have difficulty understanding strangers, and those with a different accent. Some people with a hearing impairment can make sense of speech if they can see a person's lips – many people can 'lip-read' a little. So a person with hearing impairment might say 'I can't hear you – I need to put my glasses on'.

People are sometimes born with impairments to hearing or vision. Some people develop impairments due to injuries or accidents and other people develop impairments as they grow older.

Think it through

How can visual or hearing disabilities influence work, meeting people, mobility, shopping and so on?

Disability can be reduced if a person's needs are understood and the right kind of support is provided. People who are born with a serious hearing impairment may never be able to hear spoken language, but many people who are born 'deaf' in Britain may learn British sign language. BSL is a complete language system, and it reduces the disability that having to learn English might create.

TV programmes are now often sub-titled or signed, so that people who have a hearing impairment need not be excluded from enjoying TV. If a deaf person has a signer or interpreter, he or she may be able to engage in the same study, recreational and work activities as hearing people.

People with visual impairment may also be helped by a range of equipment and services that can reduce the restrictions their disability might otherwise create.

Physical disabilities

One of the major causes of physical disability is arthritis. Arthritis can limit people's ability to cope with daily living activities and reduce their mobility. Other causes of physical disability include heart and circulation disorders, which can limit people's ability to undertake any activity requiring physical effort. Some illnesses cause temporary or permanent disability – M.E., for example, is an illness that can leave a person weak and unable to cope with work or daily activities. A range of illnesses and injuries can cause mobility problems, where people lose the use of hands, arms or legs.

The disability of not being able to walk to shops or board a bus can be overcome if a person can use an electric wheelchair or an adapted car and continue with his or her activities. Even if a person cannot use an adapted car, a home carer might be able to assist with shopping and domestic needs. The impairment need not result in a wide range of disability.

Intellectual disability

About 2 per cent of Britain's population has a learning disability. This means that a person may not learn things as quickly or as easily as most people do. People with a serious learning disability may not be able to lead fully independent lives as adults. Some people with a learning disability may not be able to manage money or plan daily activities like cooking or shopping without help.

Various impairments can result in a learning disability. People may be born with genetic abnormalities (Down's syndrome) or with damage to the nervous system due to infection or injury before or during birth. Infection, injury and poor environment (such as poor diet, poor social contact and poor opportunities for learning) can create a learning disability during infancy or childhood.

In the past, people with learning disability were often thought of as being too different to mix with other people. People with serious disabilities lived in long-stay hospitals or other isolated settings away from other people. Over the past 30 years there has been growing concern to protect the rights of people with learning disabilities and to provide opportunities for individuals to live independently in the community. Most services for people with learning disability now try to support individuals to live as independently as possible and make choices. Many people with a learning disability can develop and lead an independent life with the right help and support.

Intellectual disability can include problems other than a learning disability. There are differences in the way people's brains work, and some people have difficulty understanding how sounds link to written words. This can be due to a condition called dyslexia, which involves a difficulty in learning to read and to spell, but is not usually classified as a learning disability. People with dyslexia may be good at learning generally.

Illness and injury can cause impairments that lead to particular disabilities. For example, aphasia is a disability that leads to difficulty with speaking. Agnosia is a disability caused by not being able to make sense of what you see.

CASE STUDY MRS BADDOCK

Mrs Baddock is 84, and lives on her own in a terraced house. Her husband died five years ago and her daughter lives 20 miles away. Mrs Baddock used to do her own housework and shopping, and used to go out to meet friends and to a local club.

Mrs Baddock has a sensory impairment to her vision due to cataracts and long-sightedness, and a physical impairment of the use of her hands and body due to arthritis.

Mrs Baddock has a disability relating to housework and shopping. She has lost her confidence about going out because she cannot read signs and notices clearly. She has some pain when she walks and she cannot carry shopping. Mrs Baddock has difficulty with housework – even making a cup of tea or a sandwich is a serious problem because her two impairments create a lot of small disabilities. When Mrs Baddock tries to make a sandwich, she often drops food on the floor, or spills food on the kitchen work surfaces. Trying to prepare food is painful, stressful and sometimes unsuccessful. Mrs Baddock used to be able to look after her own needs, and she feels depressed that she now has so much difficulty. When Mrs Baddock's care needs are assessed, she says 'I can't cope any more – I can't cook, I don't get out, I can't do anything any more'.

Think it through

Imagine you have poor eyesight, pain in movement, and difficulty using your hands. What disabilities would you develop? You could try this experiment: Find some old glasses, safety glasses or sunglasses, and paste some thin tissue over most of the lens area. Use masking tape to tie your fingers together and restrict the movement of your thumb. Now try making a sandwich! It may be more fun (and safer) to try this experiment with a friend or in a small group.

Mrs Baddock has the disabilities shown in Figure 2.8. New routines and new equipment could prevent the arthritis and poor eyesight from causing Mrs Baddock major problems. Her disability could be reduced if the right assessment and the right help were available. For instance, a wide handle on cutlery could make it easier to use. Changing the kitchen layout might make it easier for her to find things. For jars, labels that can be understood by touch might help. Non-slip mats may help prevent things from falling on the floor. Some ideas to limit disability are shown at the edges of Figure 2.8.

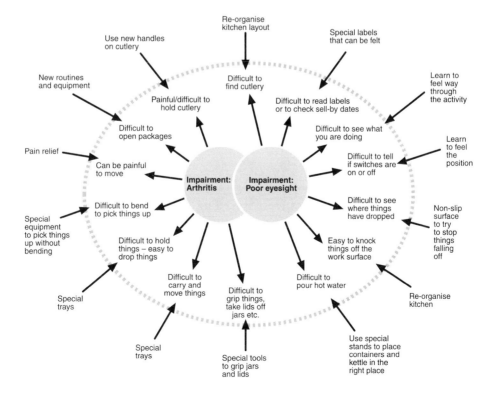

Figure 2.8 Impairments and disabilities

Do it

Define physical, sensory and intellectual disability and impairment.

Write down one physical impairment, one sensory impairment and one intellectual impairment. Explain what the impairments involve. List the types of disability that may follow from each of these impairments. What can be done to reduce the disability that people may face? Now say what the difference between impairment and disability is.

Positive and negative influences on individuals

Life events

Buddhists teach that, apart from birth and death, the only certainty in life is that there will be change. Since you were born you will have experienced many life events that have changed you. As you grow older you will experience many more changes. Everyone has a different life, and some life events seem insignificant to some people; for example, a new job may be something that you just drift into, but for other people their first job may change their lives for ever. Going to school, getting a job, leaving home, marriage, parenthood, retirement, ageing and bereavement are all common events that involve change. Many people will not experience all of these events; and other events such as divorce or changing jobs may be far more important for some people.

Change

Some life events change us for ever. Life events that change us involve some stress, because change can cause:

- a sense of **loss** for the way things used to be
- a feeling of **uncertainty** about what the future will be like
- a need to **spend time** and/or money and/or emotional energy sorting things out
- a need to **learn** new things.

Going to school

Some children are taught at home because of travelling problems or personal needs, but most go to school and many people will remember their first day.

Starting school can involve a sense of loss. This might be the first morning your mother and family have left you to cope with other people on your own. You might cry because you miss them. You also might feel uncertain. Where are the toilets? Who should you speak to? What will happen if you don't eat the food?

Starting school can also be stimulating and positive. Some children feel that it is exciting to meet new people. They might find school interesting and be proud that they are 'grown up' enough to start school activities. Starting school can be a positive experience, involving increasing independence – it all depends on how each child is helped to cope with the change.

Think it through

How positive or negative was your experience of your first day at secondary school? Do you have relatives who started infant school recently? How positive or negative was their first day? Rate experiences on the scale below:

1	**2**	**3**	**4**	**5**
Stressful, frightening	Not good	OK	Good	Great fun, exciting

Think of the reasons why you have rated things this way.

Getting a job

Starting a first job is a different experience for everyone. Many people have part-time jobs, perhaps in a shop, before they start their first full-time job. Part-time work might help you to be prepared for the changes that going out to work involve. Some people only get temporary work and suffer periods of unemployment. Other people have several jobs in order to earn enough money. Some people work for their own family business and don't have to get a job with people they don't know. Many people have to search hard for a full-time job and are anxious to do well when they find one.

Getting and starting a job can involve a feeling of loss – it would be nicer not to have to bother, and to stay at home! Getting and starting a job involves lots of uncertainty: 'Will I like the people there?', 'Will they like me?', 'Can I do the job?'. Getting a job and getting started takes a lot of time and energy. Starting a new job involves a lot of new learning; who is who, where things are, what you have to do, and so on.

For some people, getting and starting a new job is frightening and unpleasant. Some people feel that they are forced to work at things they don't really want to do, or are being paid low wages to do. For these people, starting work is a negative experience. Other people experience getting a job as exciting, and as a chance to develop and improve skills. Some people see going out to work as a sign of freedom and independence, and for these people, starting work is a positive experience.

Leaving home

Moving out of the family home can be a major life event. Sometimes, leaving happens gradually. A person might go away to study or work but return home at weekends or at the end of term. Sometimes people may leave home to marry, and the major life event is getting married. Some people leave home after a dispute with parents – they may 'run away' rather than leave. Some people do not leave their family home during their early life.

Leaving home is a great change for some people, who miss their family and feel a loss of company. Some people will feel uncertain about their future and how to cope with a new house or flat. Those who leave home will need to spend a lot of time and energy sorting their new home out. There is much to learn about paying bills, buying food and doing your own housework. Many people will find that the change is a positive experience, but people who feel that they have been forced to leave, perhaps to find work, or because of arguments, might see the change as a negative life event. For many people, however, 'having your own place' is the final thing you need to be an independent adult.

Leaving home can be a big step to independent life if it is planned carefully. If there are problems with money or with people you share accommodation with, then it can become a negative event.

Marriage

In Britain, marriage is the legal union of one man to one woman. Gay and lesbian couples cannot currently be registered as married. Some other cultures permit a husband to have more than one wife or a wife to have more than one husband, but the legal definition of marriage in Britain restricts marriage to one man and one woman.

Many heterosexual couples live together without marrying – some go on to marry after living together for some years, but about half of all couples who live together do not go on to marry each other. Current trends suggest that perhaps one in five people will never be married during their lives.

Marriage involves a commitment to live with a partner permanently. It ties financial resources and the networks of family relationships together. Marriage is a big change in life, and it can involve moving house and leaving your family. This may cause a sense of loss. Many people feel some anxiety about getting married; are they marrying the right person, will they get on well together, what will living together for ever be like? Learning to cope with married life takes a lot of time, money and energy. Living with a partner involves learning about his or her needs and ways. For some people marriage is the most positive change that can happen in life. Other people regard it as involving a loss of freedom, or even as entering a relationship where one person dominates or exploits another.

Think it through

How positively or negatively do you and your friends see marriage? What rating would you give it on a five-point scale from one (very negative) to five (very positive)

Divorce

At present, one in three marriages is likely to end in divorce. In the 1950s many people stayed married despite being unhappy with their partners – in the past, it was often difficult to get a divorce and there were likely to be serious problems over money and finding somewhere to live following divorce, particularly for women.

Divorce is much more common nowadays, but many people who divorce go on to re-marry. Each year, over a third of marriages are likely to be re-marriages. Nearly a quarter of children in Britain may expect their parents to divorce before they are 16 years old.

Although many people experience divorce as a negative experience, it may often be better than living in a stressful situation. Sometimes people develop a deeper sense of self following divorce. Agencies such as Relate provide counselling services to help people to understand the emotions involved in partnerships. Counselling may help some people to decide whether it is best to divorce or not.

CASE STUDY MARRIAGE

Davinder is 21 years old and is about to complete her studies for a university degree. Davinder is a Sikh, and she has lived in a Sikh community in the UK all her life. Davinder has thought about marriage a lot during the past few years. Many times, she has discussed the possibilities and whom she might marry with her family. Davinder's family are concerned that she should make a good marriage with someone of an equal educational status.

Davinder has met Sohan and thinks he is attractive and intelligent. Davinder's family know Sohan's family and have agreed that they would make a good couple. Sohan has visited Davinder's family and an 'engagement' ceremony has taken place at their local Gurdwara (or temple). Davinder has been given a gold ring by Sohan's mother.

Davinder is now looking forward to her wedding day. She is extremely happy and excited. She will be the centre of attention, and she will go through a ceremony that will mark a major change in her life. Everything about this change is welcome. Davinder will wear red and gold, lucky colours. After the ceremony she will live with her husband, and not with her family. There have been many gifts exchanged between the families. Davinder feels a mixture of joy and anticipation. After the wedding she will be different, she will have her own house, and she will have a husband to care for, although she will not be with her own family. All the changes involved almost make Davinder feel a bit 'giddy'.

Figure 2.9 A Sikh wedding

Davinder will find marriage positive because she wants to be married. She has had a great deal of support from her family and feels that she has some idea of how to cope with her new role. Marriage is a major change that Davinder has looked forward to for a long time, and she is sure that Sohan will be a good husband.

Parenthood

Becoming a parent involves a major change in life. Many parents experience their relationship with their child as an intense and new emotional experience. There may be strong feelings of love and a powerful desire to protect the child. But becoming a parent also involves losses – parents can lose sleep because the baby wakes them up, and they may find that they can't go out very easily – so that they lose touch with friends and social life. Parents can lose money because they have either to pay for child care or give up full-time work to care for their child. Parents can lose career opportunities if they stay out of full-time work to bring up a family. These losses can sometimes place a relationship or marriage under stress – sometimes a parent can even become jealous of the love and attention that a child receives from the other parent.

Becoming a parent can involve some anxiety about the new role of being a parent. 'Will the baby be healthy? 'Is the baby safe?', 'Am I being a good mother/father?'. New parents usually seek advice from family, friends, doctors and health visitors. Parenthood involves a lot of pressure on time, money and energy. A new infant will need nappies, clothes and toys, food, cot, high chair, car seat and so on. An infant needs a lot of attention. Carers will need time and emotional energy to care for the child. Parents often need advice on caring skills – there is new learning involved in being a good parent and always a lot to learn about the child as a new relationship develops.

Retirement

The nature of work is changing rapidly. Many people will work as self-employed or temporary workers in the future, and retirement may become very flexible with some people effectively retiring in their 40s and others continuing to take on work in their late 60s and 70s. Retirement can represent a major change for people who have worked in a demanding, full-time job and then completely stop working. A sudden break from full-time work might cause a feeling of loss. Work roles influence self-concept, so a person's self-concept and self-esteem can change following retirement. People may lose their routine and perhaps their work friends when they retire, and some people may not be prepared for the leisure time they have and be unsure what to do with their time each day. Some people say that retirement makes them feel useless - they are no longer of use to anyone. People who have to live on the state pension alone may experience a loss of income. Some older people live below the poverty line.

On the positive side, people with private pensions and savings often have the time and money to travel, study or take up hobbies and thoroughly enjoy themselves. Some people see retirement as a time of self-fulfilment, when they harvest the rewards of a lifetime's work. Retirement can lead to greater freedom and the opportunity to spend more time with family, relatives and friends.

Think it through

Retirement provides a mixture of positive and negative possibilities. If you were to talk to people who have been through retirement, what would they say were the main problems and the main advantages? How positively or negatively would they rate retirement?

Death of a loved one (bereavement)

People can lose their partners at any stage of life, but as couples grow older the chances that one person will die increase. Bereavement means losing someone you loved, and it causes a major change in people's lives. There is a very strong sense of loss – you might lose the main person you talked to, the main person who helped you, your sexual partner, a person who you shared life with and a person who made you feel good. Living without a partner can involve great uncertainty. Your partner may have helped with household bills or with shopping or housework – now you have to do it all yourself. Bereavement can mean you have to learn to live a new life as a single person again. Learning to cope on your own can take a lot of time and energy.

People who try to cope with a major loss often experience the following feelings:

- not being able to believe that the person is dead
- sadness and depression
- anger or guilt
- stress because they have to learn to cope with a different lifestyle.

Few people describe bereavement as a positive life event, but the final outcome need not only be sadness and grief. Over time, people can take a positive outlook on life again.

Ageing

Most people hope to grow old and many people enjoy a high quality of life in old age. Many cultures honour older people as 'elders', people who have wisdom and who deserve respect. Whether ageing is mainly positive or negative is greatly influenced by a person's level of self-esteem, and the resources and support that person has. If you feel proud of your life, that you have lived a worthwhile life, this will help to make ageing a positive experience. If you enjoy your lifestyle, and you have enough money to meet your needs, this will help to make ageing positive. If you have friends, family and a partner to support you, this will also help to make ageing a positive experience.

Ageing can involve bereavement, but high self-esteem, friends and enough money can all help people to cope with loss. Low self-esteem, poverty and social isolation (no friends or family) can make it harder to cope.

Ageing can involve the development of illnesses and physical or sensory disabilities, for some people. Again, high self-esteem, friends and enough money can all help a person to cope. A lack of self-esteem, money or support can increase the problems caused by a disability.

Some older people live below the poverty line and some lose contact with friends and family. These problems are social problems – they are not caused just because people have lived a long time.

Think it through

Look at the case study of Mrs Baddock on page 62. What are the positive and negative issues involved in ageing here?

Do it

Identify three life events and describe their positive and negative effects on individuals.

Interview three different people who have recently been through a major life event like starting work, leaving home, getting married and so on. Try to work out what was positive and negative in each person's experience. Without using real names, discuss your interview results with other students and work out if issues like loss and uncertainty are involved. Have people come through their experiences in a positive way?

Kinship groups and family

There are many different types of families and relationships within families, but most children are born into some sort of social group. Many children will have brothers and sisters, parents or step-parents, aunts and uncles. Children grow up surrounded by other people and are influenced by the people in their family or **kinship group**.

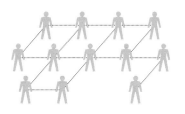

Figure 2.10 A kinship group is like a web or network of contacts

A kinship group means all the people you know who are related to you. This includes the family you might live with and other people and families that are related to you. A kinship group can be like a web or network of contacts – people who can offer advice and help.

Kinship and family groups are very important because they are usually the people who first influence our lives. Infants and young children copy what they see. As we grow up, we may copy what the adults and other children in our kinship network do. We learn from the reactions of parents, brothers, sisters and other relatives towards us.

Socialisation

Kinship and family groups usually provide the first experience of socialisation for children. Socialisation means to become social – children learn to fit in with and be part of a social group. When children grow up within a family group, they will usually learn a wide range of ideas about how to behave. For instance, at mealtimes, some families will have strict rules that everyone must sit down at the table and it is considered 'rude' if one person starts to eat before the others. Other families may not even have set mealtimes – people may just prepare food for themselves when they feel like it.

In the evenings, some families might sit round the TV as a social group, while other families might all sit in different rooms doing different activities. Some families are very concerned that people take their outdoor shoes off before coming into the house, and others have no rules about shoes.

Think it through

Are, or were, any of the following 'norms' important in your family?

- To say 'thank you' or 'thank you for having me' to the head of a household you visited?
- To give thanks in prayer before a meal?
- To eat hot food with your fingers?
- To go to bed at a fixed time – unless there is a special event or festival?
- Never to interrupt when an older member of the family is speaking?
- That children have set tasks to help adults with the housework?
- That male members of the household are responsible for decorating and repairing the house?
- That female members of the household are responsible for all the washing and ironing?

You could compare your list with others in your group.

Families and similar social groups develop attitudes about what is 'normal' or right to do. Sociologists call these beliefs 'norms'. Each family will have 'norms' that cover how people should behave.

By the age of two, children usually understand that they are male or female. During the socialisation process, children learn how to act in masculine or feminine ways. Boys may copy the behaviour of other male members of the family, and girls may copy the behaviour of other female members. Sociologists call this learning a gender (male or female) role. Learning a role means learning to act as a male or female person.

During childhood, children learn ideas about what is right or wrong. They learn the customs of their culture and family, they learn to play gender and adult roles, and they learn what is expected of them and what they should expect from others. Socialisation teaches children ways of thinking, and these ways of thinking may stay with a person for life.

Primary socialisation

Not everything that a child learns during first (or primary) socialisation within the family group is learned by copying adults. Children also spend time watching TV, listening to radio

Think it through

Look at the picture of a breakfast scene in Figure 2.11. Think carefully – how many influences on the children can you spot?

Figure 2.11 Breakfast time in a family home – how many things to do with socialisation can you spot?

Did you notice the media influence in this home? The radio sends messages about love and relationships in the songs that are playing. The TV sends messages about news and opinions. The newspaper invites the reader to share its views on current events. Even the cereal packet has an advert encouraging the family to get money and spend it!

Did you notice the gender roles in this home? Who is preparing the children's breakfast, and who is being waited on? What differences are there in the way the two children are playing – what toys have they chosen?

Does playing with dolls or playing with toy cars influence children's expectations in life? Note the length of hair for males and females and their clothes.

Thinking about this scene, what do you think the children might be learning? Will the daughter tend to copy the mother's behaviour as she grows up – will she see her role as 'looking after people'? Will the son copy the father's role and expect to be waited on at mealtimes. What expectations might people develop just from being with each other? How far does the media influence people's expectations of their lives? Do you think violence on TV could influence these people in any way?

and playing computer games. Children will be influenced by the things they see and hear over the media as well as their experiences within the home.

Secondary socialisation

As children grow older they go to school and learn to read and use computers. The range of influences on them grows larger. Even though children make friends and learn new ideas at school, however, the main group experience for most children will still be with their family and kinship group. Children's need for love and affection and the need to belong to a group will usually be met by the family. If a child is rejected or neglected by the family, he or she will be at risk of developing a low sense of self-worth and poor self-esteem.

During adolescence the importance of the family group begins to change. Between 11 and 15 years of age adolescents become very involved with their own group of friends. Most adolescents have a group of friends who influence what they think and believe, usually people of the same age. This is the second influential group to which people belong, and it creates a second type of socialisation, that sociologists call **secondary socialisation**.

After the age of 12 or 13, a person's sense of self-worth is likely to depend more on the reactions of others of the same age than on what parents say. During adolescence it is important to be accepted and to belong with friends. Adolescents tend to copy the way other adolescents behave.

Think it through

Try to remember when you were 14 or 15 years old. Can you recall what you and others in your class at school thought about the following topics? What sort of beliefs and values did your parents have at that time? Which beliefs are closest to your beliefs now?

1. It is important to get a good job.
2. It is bad and dangerous to use drugs.
3. It is important to go out and have a good time.
4. Wearing the right clothes to look good is a priority.
5. Saving money is a priority.

Socialisation does not finish with secondary socialisation. People continue to change and learn to fit in with new groups when they go out to work and when they start new families.

| **Primary socialisation** | = First socialisation within a family or care group. |
| **Secondary socialisation** | = Later socialisation with friends and peer groups. |

The value of kinship groups

Kinship groups are often important during the whole of a person's lifetime. Kinship groups not only provide the setting for first (or primary) socialisation, but they can also provide a buffer against stress. A buffer is a shock-absorbing barrier that gives protection from an impact. Buffers are used to protect trains at railway stations. Partners, family and friends can act as 'shock absorbers' to protect us from the knocks that we take in life. When we change jobs, move home, get married, become ill or unemployed, partners or relatives might help us to cope with the stress of change.

Talking to family members can help you to feel that you matter to them. Family and relatives might help you with practical jobs if you are ill or too busy to do them. They might help you with shopping, arrange for doctors to visit, sort out bills. Relatives may be able to give you advice or know people who can advise you. A number of studies in both Britain and the USA have found that people with good partnerships, marriages, family and friends are generally happier and healthier than people who do not have these relationships.

Kinship networks can help us with difficult life events, but they can also cause stress. We hope that we would get support, help and advice from our family, so it is only fair that they expect us to help them. Being part of a kinship network means that we have to spend time supporting other people, and often giving practical help. We may have to visit older relatives and listen to them to help them keep a sense of self-worth. Kinship networks involve giving as well as receiving. At some stages in life, such as childhood, we may mainly receive help; at other times during adult life we may have to give more help than we get back.

Kinship relationships can also be stressful when people fail to cope with each other. A third of marriages end in divorce, and a quarter of all children might experience the divorce of their parents before they are 16. Kinship relationships can be very good for us – but very difficult when they break down.

Do it

Explain the effect of kinship groups on individuals at different life stages.

Think about a child being born today. What help and guidance could family and kin provide during that child's life? When the child grows up, what help could he or she expect from a partner or relative? In old age, what help can a relative provide? What can go wrong between relatives and partners?

Get together with a small group of other students and make a list of the benefits and problems that can come from family and kinship groups. You may be able to share your ideas with a wider class group at the end of the exercise. A table like the one below may help you. Produce a final list of all the ideas you have collected.

Effects of kinship groups on:	Benefits	Problems
Infants		
Children		
Adolescents		
Adults		
Older people		

Self-concept

Self-concept is a term used to describe the way a person sees himself or herself. It includes the way we would describe who we are and how much we value ourselves.

Infants develop a sense of their own body before they can use language. We can probably remember our first sense of self as actions or picture memories. As children's understanding of language increases, they are able to describe themselves using words. If you ask an eight-year-old to describe herself, she might say, 'I am a girl, I have dark hair and I like swimming, um, and I like my mum, and I live at 58 Uplands Road'.

This eight-year-old can think only in terms of 'concrete' or factual descriptions of things, and also how much she likes them. Adolescents might be able to describe themselves using more general or abstract words. An adolescent might respond, 'Well, I'd say I was friendly. I get on well with people, I'm a bit attractive – even if I say so myself. I'm broke this week, I work hard, I am kind and I hate people who are cruel to animals. I'm honest … well, most of the time.'

This adolescent is using language to evaluate his sense of who he is. Adolescents may be able to think using abstract words, but young children are not able to do this. An important factor that influences a person's self-concept is his or her level of intellectual development.

Think it through

If you mix with children, you could ask them to explain who they are and what they enjoy. Compare their answers to the type of answers adults would give you.

Self in childhood

A two-year-old may not have an awareness of his or her self-concept. A deeper sense of self probably starts to develop as the child begins to mix with other children and develop socially. George Mead, a theorist famous in the 1930s, believed that children first began to understand an idea of self during their play and social activity with other people. Very young children are excellent imitators – they will copy the actions of older children and adults. Some children will even pretend to be a cat or other animal they have seen. By acting things out, children learn to understand and remember their world. Acting things out soon moves on to acting out the roles that children see other people playing.

Children can only play-act in this way because they can imagine how adults act. They use their imagination to create characters – the child pretending to be the teacher will copy things he or she has seen on television, things the other children have acted out, and adult behaviours experienced. Children's ability to imitate and imagine means that they can begin to use concepts to explain how people behave. Because children can create an imaginary world of other people, they can also begin to imagine themselves. A five-year-old can begin to create an idea of 'me' using his or her imagination.

Children watch the way older children and adults act. They come to understand the roles that adults play, and will copy the way they see their parents behave. They copy shop assistants, bus drivers and various work roles. Children use their imagination to understand how people act.

Children learn about gender roles early on. These roles may become part of their self-concept during adolescence and later life. Of course, not every child lives in the same cultural situation. Britain is a multicultural society, and this means that there are many different beliefs and values about issues such as gender. Some children may grow up to believe that boys should be more important and powerful than girls. Other children will grow up having developed different beliefs. Some children may see girls as clever, resourceful and in control of social situations.

Socialisation will enable many children to develop self-confidence. They will feel that they belong within their family or care group, that they are liked, loved and important. They may develop a sense of being competent and skilled at school, work and sport.

A child's relationships within the groups of people he or she mixes with will create this self-confidence, but socialisation may not go so smoothly for all children. Children also experience rejection, failure and a sense of not being good at school work, sport, etc. Some children may feel that they do not belong to a group. Failure to identify with other people, or failure to belong, may influence the sense of self and self-confidence that a child is developing.

Self-concept in adolescence

At some time during adolescence many people develop a level of physical, intellectual, social and emotional maturity that leads to their sense of self becoming a developed self-concept.

Think it through

At school, did you ever have to wait in line to be picked for a sports team? The team leaders would start by picking the people who were good at the sport, or people who were popular. Everyone would murmur 'Oh good, we've got so and so'. The last people to be picked were those who were poor at sport. The murmurs would change to 'Oh no, we've got that one – do we have to have so and so?' These last people do not belong – they are not wanted in the team. Imagine how this feeling of rejection might influence the sense of self that a person is developing.

Figure 2.12　The last children to be picked may feel rejected

Physical influences

Sexual maturity causes adolescents to become aware of their own sexual needs and desires. A psychologist called Erikson believed that the development of sexuality marked the end of childhood and childhood relationships with parents. Erikson believed that sexual needs causes adolescents to seek independence from their carers. Adolescents need to develop a new sense of themselves, because people need a self-concept before they can have loving, sexual relationships.

Intellectual influences

Many adolescents may be able to think about themselves using abstract concepts. This new power of thought can enable a person to design his or her own self-concept! For instance, an eight-year-old might look in the mirror and think, 'That's me'. That might be all she thinks! A 16-year-old is likely to look in the mirror and evaluate himself. 'So that's me – I'd like to be more like my friend. Yes – shorter hair, earring, leather jacket – more muscles. How do I do it? OK, I buy the earring on Wednesday, have my hair cut next Tuesday, go to the gym every Monday night – I'll need to save money for the jacket.' Many adolescents can plan how they want to look. They take control of their lives, using powers of imagination.

Social influences

Appearance may identify you as a member of a particular group. Your hairstyle, dress and behaviour can send messages about your gender, age group, wealth, social status, beliefs, and culture. It is often important to present an image of ourselves when we first meet people and seek to make relationships with them. Hairstyle and dress can be ways of expressing self-concept – ways of showing whom we identify with and what we want to be.

Friendship groups will influence our style of dress and appearance during adolescence. It is important to be accepted by friends, but also to declare independence from adults who may have controlled our lives up to this point. Adolescents will often adopt clothing styles that are very different from what their parents would wear!

Do it

Describe the positive and negative influences on the development of self.

Think about your early childhood. You will probably not be able to remember much of your life before you were seven years of age, but try to think about things that have happened to you since then. How happy are your memories? What things have made you unhappy? Fill in the graph below with your own 'time line'.

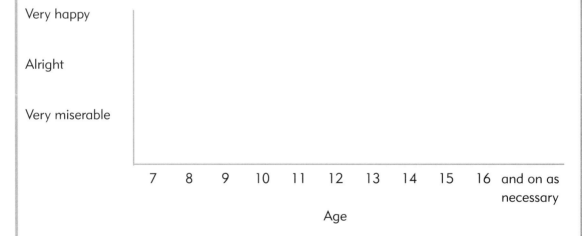

Put dots in for every year and half year, based on your memory for how generally happy you were.

Join up these dots to make a graph of happiness. Share your graph with another student and discuss the kinds of positive and negative influences that have made you happy or sad.

Care needs

People can have four main types of needs.

Physical care needs involve help with tasks like getting meals, help with mobility, help with washing and going to the toilet.

Safety and security needs mean that people have a need to know what to expect, and they need to feel safe from abuse and pain, and from major changes that may alter their lives.

A need to belong involves the feeling of being included – people need to feel that they have a relationship with those who care for them. Young children have a need to build a loving attachment with their carers. Adults need to feel that they fit in with a care setting and that their culture and life experience are respected.

A need for self-esteem is important – most adults have a need to be given respect, a need for dignity, and a need to be treated as a person who is worth something. People receiving care may have a fear of being 'talked down to', or of being seen as a problem rather than as a person.

Caring for people is about meeting all the needs people have. A carer might see his or her task as moving an old person down the corridor so that he can have lunch. Moving the person to the dining room will meet his physical needs. But if this small task is all that is done, the person's other needs may be ignored. Skilled caring is not just doing things to people. A skilled carer would not just take a person to the dining room – he or she would smile, talk to the person, show respect and check that the person was ready to go. A skilled carer would always think about the client's safety and security needs.

Figure 2.13 Four circles of need

If you are sitting in a wheelchair and it suddenly moves off without warning, you cannot feel safe. You can't guess what might happen next in a place where people just do things to you – you might get frightened if you were cared for like this. If you are sitting in a wheelchair and your carer says, 'Right, I'm taking you for lunch now', at least you know what is happening, but you couldn't feel that your feelings mattered or that you were equal to the carer. The carer makes the decision.

The way your carer talks to you is very important. As well as offering you a choice, you will need to feel that your carer values you, and that you are respected by other people. If you don't get respect then you will find it hard to value yourself – your self-esteem needs will not be met.

CASE STUDY MRS MARKOVITZ

Mrs Markovitz is 84 and lives alone in an old terraced house. Her husband died five years ago, and since then she has been supported by her daughter and son-in-law who make regular visits to her. Mrs Markovitz has home help three times a week to collect shopping and help her with housework. Recently, Mrs Markovitz has been increasingly forgetful and has left her front door open at night. Her daughter and son-in-law want to go abroad for a month or so and have arranged with Mrs Markovitz that she should go into a residential care home for a short period.

What kind of care needs will Mrs Markovitz have?

Physical needs	Mrs Markovitz will need a warm, comfortable room. She will need regular meals and clean toilet and washing facilities.
Safety and security needs	Mrs Markovitz will need to be sure that her personal possessions will not be lost or stolen. She will need to feel confident that staff will not abuse her, that she will not fall over or suffer pain if staff use hoists to lift her.
Sense of belonging	Mrs Markovitz is used to her own personal diet. She is hoping that she will not be offered food she doesn't like or that doesn't fit in with her culture. Mrs Markovitz will not know anyone in the home, and she hasn't even left her house for five years. She will need to build a relationship with care staff before she will feel that it is OK to be in the home.
Sense of self-esteem	Mrs Markovitz is very proud of her daughter and of her own life. Now that she has gone into care, Mrs Markovitz feels that her life is over – 'I'm no use to anyone now, I'm just a burden'. Mrs Markovitz might recover her feeling of self-worth if her relationships with carers and other residents makes her feel worthwhile again.

Nearly all care settings would cater for Mrs Markovitz's physical needs. Care homes are inspected to ensure they provide reasonable standards of care, and all care settings will try to provide a safe setting. How Mrs Markovitz gets on in terms of her social and emotional needs will depend on the skills of the care staff.

Maslow's hierarchy of needs

Abraham Maslow (1908–1970) was a psychologist who became famous for his theory of human needs. Young children have an inbuilt need to learn to walk, to learn to talk and to make social relationships, but Maslow believed that humans have a natural need to learn, grow and develop for the whole of their lives – not just during childhood.

Although humans have a tendency to want to learn and to grow and develop emotionally, not everyone does this. Some people get stuck – they stop developing emotionally. Maslow explained why some people grow and others get stuck, in terms of a theory of human needs.

Maslow believed that there were different levels of human need. If your needs are not met at one level, it becomes difficult to develop yourself beyond that level. The levels are shown in

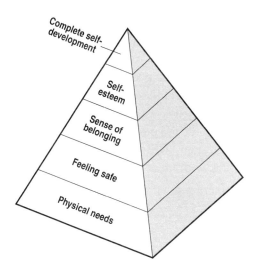

Figure 2.14   Maslow's hierarchy of needs

the diagram in Figure 2.14, which is called Maslow's hierarchy of needs. A hierarchy is a system with different levels; some needs are higher up in the hierarchy.

At the bottom are physical needs. Physical needs include the need for food, water, air, freedom from pain, sleep and sex.

Physical needs

If a person is constantly hungry and can never find enough to eat, that person will not care so much about general safety, and will not be concerned about relationships or what other people think of him or her. If you think you might die of hunger no other needs matter, so all your thoughts will focus on getting food. When people feel that their physical needs are met, they can concern themselves with the next level in the hierarchy – safety needs.

Safety needs

If we have enough food and are free from pain and so on, we will think about our safety needs. People generally need a stable, predictable setting in which to live and work, but many people feel anxious about losing their health, jobs, money, or relationships. Other people are anxious simply because they cannot predict the future – they don't know what might happen to them. Anxious people will try to make their lives more predictable, stable and safe. They will not worry about love and affection until they feel safe.

Belongingness and love

The third level of human need is the need for affection, the need to be with other people, and the need to be accepted. People need to be loved and to love others, but loneliness may only become a worry when you are safe and your basic needs are met.

Self-esteem

Self-esteem means thinking well of yourself, having self-confidence and believing that you have the respect and recognition of others. A high level of self-esteem will mean that you feel good about your performance at work and your relationships with others. Self-esteem is built up from the way other people speak to you and the degree of respect you receive.

When people feel safe, when they have their basic physical needs met, and when they feel they belong with others, they will be concerned about what other people think of them. Life has to be fairly good before people worry too much about being praised or criticised. People who are hungry may steal to get food, because they wouldn't worry what people thought. If your more basic needs are met, however, you will care about the degree of respect you are shown by others.

Self-actualisation

Maslow believed that some people spend most of their lives struggling to feel safe and to find love and affection, but a reasonable number of people do develop good levels of self-esteem in their lives. The goal of living should not be just to get respect from others, however – Maslow thought people should try to develop their abilities and talents to the fullest extent possible. His name for this complete development was 'self-actualisation'. 'Self-actualisation' means achieving everything that you have the potential to achieve. Self-actualisation brings a high level of happiness and contentment to life. Maslow thought that most people never reach this stage, as they become stuck with more basic social and emotional needs.

DO IT

Describe Maslow's hierarchy of care needs and relate it to three different life stages.

Draw your own diagram of care needs, like the diagram in Figure 2.15. Copy the diagram three times. Think of three different people you have met at work or on placement (or who you can imagine) at three different stages. Give examples of their physical care needs, safety needs (from things that could cause anxiety or fear), needs to belong (social needs), and needs for self-esteem (respect and dignity). Write the examples of these different needs on your diagrams.

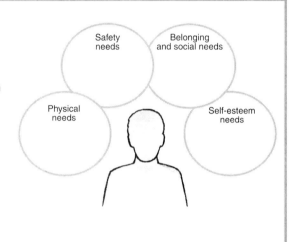

Figure 2.15   A diagram of care needs

Upbringing and health

Most people want to live a long and healthy life – but not everybody does so. Why do some people live to their 90s, or to be over 100, and yet others die young? Why do some people have many health problems and others very little illness?

A general explanation for health differences is that we are influenced by:

1. Our genetic make-up
2. Our behaviour, our diet, our lifestyle, our activities.
3. Our attitudes and beliefs about health.
4. Our socialisation or upbringing.
5. The wider environment we live in.

Genetics

People are born with different genetic patterns, and these patterns can make a person likely to develop certain illnesses or more resistant to particular diseases. Usually an individual might be at risk of one illness, such as cancer, but at less risk of another illness – perhaps heart disease.

Your genetic make-up reacts with the things you do. Steve Jones, a professor of genetics, thinks that as many as one person in every ten has resistance to lung cancer caused by smoking. Some other people may be at great risk from cancer if they ever smoke. At present, we don't know who is at high risk and who is at low risk, so the best advice to everyone is not to smoke.

The same is probably true when it comes to the risks involved in drinking alcohol, not taking exercise or having a high-fat diet. Some people can get away with some unhealthy behaviours, but many people can't. Your genes can influence how much damage a particularly risky behaviour might do to you.

Behaviour

There are a range of risks to health that can be prevented. Health advisors are careful to warn people of the dangers of unsafe sex and of taking non-prescribed drugs.

DID YOU KNOW?

The two main diseases that kill people are heart disease and cancer. In the mid 1990s, 46 per cent of all deaths were caused by heart or circulatory disease. Currently, one in three people are expected to develop a cancer during their lifetime and roughly one in four people in Britain die of cancer.

Is there anything people can do to prevent cancer or heart disease? The main recommendations are as follows.

- Do not smoke
- Eat a healthy diet – low in fat, high in fibre, fruit and vegetables.
- Take regular exercise.
- If you drink alcohol, carefully limit the amount you drink.

If people followed this advice, the amount of cancer and heart disease in the population would be reduced. People can choose to reduce the degree of risk in their lives.

Attitudes and beliefs about health

Advice on how to stay healthy is freely available, but not everyone believes it or takes it seriously.

When people believe there is nothing they can do, or that health is all a matter of luck, they will not try to follow advice on staying healthy. Other people will ignore health advice because they think that having fun or making money is more important. If you only worry about germs, you might not worry about smoking, diet, exercise or sensible drinking. Only people who take their health seriously and who believe that they can influence their own health are likely to make healthy choices and follow health advice.

Think it through

How far do you agree with the following attitudes? Score 1 for totally agree, 2 for partly agree, and 3 for disagree.

a. How healthy you are is all a matter of luck – how you live doesn't matter.

b. How healthy you are is all up to you – if you live your life the right way, you will stay healthy.

c. There is no point in thinking about health. Other things are more important – like enjoying yourself.

d. Disease is caused by germs, genetics and pollution – you need to do what you can to protect yourself.

e. Whatever is going to happen to you will happen anyway – you can't change it.

f. You can't guarantee your health, but you can reduce the health risks you face in life.

Researchers have found that different people agree with each of these statements. People have different attitudes toward their health.

Socialisation

Why do people have different attitudes and beliefs about health? Primary socialisation within a family group and secondary socialisation within an adolescent's age group can influence what people think. Children copy the views and behaviour of their parents. If a child is socialised into a group that does not make healthy choices, he or she may copy negative attitudes and behaviour. If children are brought up to see a high-fat diet, smoking and excessive drinking as normal, they may continue with this behaviour later in life. They may say, 'It must be OK – everybody does it'.

Figure 2.16 Children may learn to copy the lifestyle they see

Later on, young people are influenced by their own age group. Sometimes people ignore their health – take up smoking, take drugs, or drink too much – in order to fit in with what other people do. People often want to look good, and some think that taking drugs or smoking makes them special, or that it brings them more attention and respect. Once you take up an enjoyable but dangerous habit, it can be hard to change the habit later. Other people mix with friends who think that healthy behaviour is important – that smoking or drug-taking is stupid. These people will copy this attitude and perhaps avoid smoking for the rest of their lives.

Sometimes people make choices for complicated reasons. In one study, girls who took up smoking explained that they knew it was unhealthy, but they thought it helped them to stay slim. Being slim was more valuable than health.

The environment

Why do some families and some social groups value health, whereas some don't? Economic and environmental differences may influence people's health directly, but they may also influence group attitudes.

During the 1970s and 1980s many studies showed a link between social class and health. Children born to working-class parents were more likely to be stillborn, more likely to die in childhood and more likely to die during adulthood than children born to middle-class parents. Working-class people had more illness during adulthood, and took more time off work. There appeared to be a health divide, with middle-class people having much better health.

More recent research suggests that poverty causes ill health. Money may not make people healthy, but a lack of it seems to be linked with disease and illness. Reasons why poverty may contribute to poor health include the following.

- Low-income families may live in stressful housing conditions, including overcrowding, noisy neighbours, and property that is poorly maintained or poorly heated and ventilated.
- Low-income families may live in more polluted neighbourhoods.
- Low-income families may find it more difficult to purchase and prepare healthy foods compared with wealthier people.
- Having a low income may create stress and worry about debts, bills and coping with life.
- People who are stressed may have poorer social relationships with family and friends.
- Over-eating, smoking and drinking alcohol may offer simple and relaxing pastimes to stressed people.
- People on a low income and who are stressed may have low self-esteem and may not feel that their future health matters – getting money may seem more important.
- People living in a stressful neighbourhood with little money may feel that health advice about diet, exercise, smoking and drinking only adds to their stress – so they may choose not to believe it.

Do It

Investigate and explain the effects of upbringing on health.

Design a questionnaire to explore other people's beliefs and practices on diet, exercise, smoking and use of alcohol. You might ask people what they do – what type of food they eat, how often they exercise and so on. You could also ask them whether they thought diet, exercise, and so on influence health.

Collect your questionnaires and work out what range of attitudes and behaviour you have found. What kind of influences might have caused the attitudes and lifestyles you found?

Care needs at different life stages

Infancy

Newborn babies are helpless, and completely dependent on parents or carers to provide for their needs. Infants' physical needs have to be met by others – they have to be fed, washed, clothed and kept warm by parents or carers.

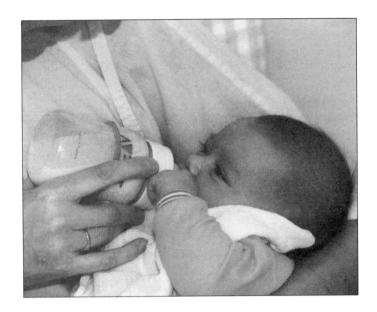

Infants learn to recognise their mother by voice and smell during the first week of life. Infants can usually recognise familiar faces by six months and may cry if separated from carers after this age. Infants need to make a safe and stable relationship with carers during the first year of life, and there is a need to make an emotional bond with carers. Infants will smile and make sounds to attract attention from carers. Relationships are important right from the beginning of life, but infants do not have self-esteem needs because they have not yet developed an understanding of 'self'. The first three levels of Maslow's pyramid are those that are important in infancy.

Childhood

As children grow they learn an ever-increasing range of skills, like running, climbing, skipping, riding a bicycle, and reading. As they gain new skills, children enjoy doing things for themselves and being more independent. Children are still dependent on adult carers to provide a stable, loving home for them, and although children will explore and experiment, carers often need to guide and supervise what they do. Adult carers will need to provide for children's physical needs and create a physically and emotionally safe environment for them. During primary socialisation, children should feel they belong to a family or group; they will have a need to feel loved and wanted.

Children will need to feel approved of and included in care activities. They may often be able to be independent in meeting physical care needs but adults will need to advise on things like diet.

Adolescence

Young people develop an increasing level of skill and understanding as they grow towards adulthood. The need to belong to a family or care group may still be important, but adolescents will be increasingly concerned to fit in with groups of their own age. Around 13 to 15 years of age, young people often copy each other's style of clothing and appearance. Young people learn to become gradually more independent of their parents or carers. Adolescents may be able to make independent choices about physical needs, choose their own friendship groups and lifestyle. When carers work with adolescents they need to encourage and show respect for their developing sense of self.

Adults

People often need practical help and assistance, and they may receive care because they cannot live completely independent lives. Cares may need to provide a range of physical and practical care such as assisting with mobility, cooking, making arrangements for visitors, offering guidance on daily living activities, and so on. Clients will also need to feel safe, to feel included, and to feel respected. Carers will need good communication skills in order to meet all four levels of need.

Older adults

Older people should have the same rights to autonomy, choice and independence that all adults have. Some older people can suffer a range of losses, including a loss of health, of income, of friends and partners. Some older people feel threatened by the changes that can happen. Some older people are stereotyped or labelled as being useless, or a burden. Needs for respect and to be treated as a person with social as well as physical needs may be critically important. Carers will need to pay attention to all four areas of need.

The final stages of life

When people are dying they will often have complex physical needs for comfort, pain relief, keeping the mouth moist, and so on. All the levels of Maslow's pyramid will also be relevant.

People will often be anxious, and will need emotional support. They will often want to see friends and relatives – the need to belong is important. People sometimes need to make sense of their lives and some need a life review or counselling to enable them to cope with the end of life. Self-esteem – the need to feel that life has had value – may be a major factor in enabling people to cope emotionally with the end of life. People who have fulfilled their potential may be able to face the end of life with a sense of inner peace. Self-actualisation links with spiritual needs.

The conversation and communication skills that carers develop may be of great importance for meeting the social, self-esteem, and anxiety needs that people may have in the final stages of their lives.

Different care needs

Some writers have used the word autonomy to sum up clients' rights in care. Autonomy means having freedom and independence to choose what you do – within limits. Most adults are free to choose how they live, but choice is always limited – you can only choose things you can afford and that don't cause serious problems for other people. There are always boundaries to what we can or should choose.

Therefore money may limit some choices and clients must respect other client's and carers' rights, but carers should encourage independence and choice wherever possible. Carers should be careful not to hurry clients by making choices for them and taking independence away.

Do It

Describe how life stage and motivation affect an individual's ability to look after his or her own care needs at two different life stages.

Think of two clients you have met on placement or at work, who are at two different life stages. One person might be an infant or child, and another person an adult or older person. Make a list of physical needs, safety needs, social needs, and self-esteem needs for each person – you may have done this for a previous task. Now make a list of differences in care needs between the two people. Discuss with a small group of colleagues how far these differences are due to life stage. Are older people more able to be independent than young people? How far are differences in care needs due to individual differences in physical, sensory or learning disability? How far are differences due to a person's level of motivation to look after his or her needs?

Rearrange your list under columns headed Life stage, Disability, and Motivation.

CARE PRACTICE FOUNDATIONS

During your placement or work experience you will find that you need to use many of the skills you will learn about in this chapter, regardless of the client group you work with – some basic requirements are the same. On the other hand, each client group will also have its own particular needs and it is important that you learn to recognise the requirements of different groups.

You will need to know how to work safely in a care environment for your own protection, for the safety of work colleagues and especially for the people for whom you are providing care. It is also important that you understand the different types of services that are available to meet the different needs of the many people who require care. This chapter will introduce you to the way in which caring and health services are provided.

Skills required to be an effective care worker

In previous chapters you have learned about the physical, intellectual, emotional and social needs that people have. It is easy to remember this as P.I.E.S., but never forget that you must think about the whole pie, and not just one slice! To be a good care worker you must make sure that you are meeting all of the needs a person has. It is not enough simply to meet their physical requirements – providing them with food and warmth, making sure they are clean and cared for is not enough if you neglect their emotional or social needs.

It is often easy to concentrate on one area of caring and forget about some of the other important aspects. This could mean that while you provided meals and clean clothing for people in your care, you neglected to talk to them, to ensure that they had plenty of interests, that they were able to meet with their friends and people who were important to them, and that they were able to take part in physical activity.

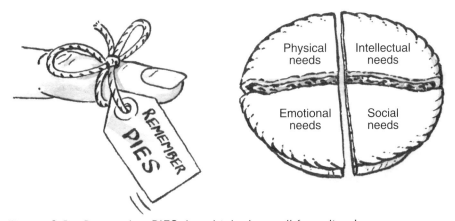

Figure 3.1   Remember PIES, but think about all four slices!

Individuals

To work well in care you need not only to recognise that people have needs in many areas, but to value each person you deal with as an individual. Everyone you meet is interesting, and all human beings have their own fascinating set of experiences, life history and personality. You must never make the mistake of making assumptions about what people want or what they need.

Client groups

Your work in care may well be defined by the group of clients you work with – for instance you may be working with 'the elderly' or 'children' or 'younger people'. Alternatively you could find yourself working with 'people with disabilities', 'people with learning difficulties' or 'people with mental health problems'. These are examples of how people can be put into categories or groups according to age or a particular problem or difficulty they may have.

It can seem natural if you are working in a particular setting to assume that all of the people for whom you provide care will need the same type of care and the same response from you. But look at these three examples:

CASE STUDY THREE CLIENTS

Mr S is 70 years old and has just come out of hospital following a stroke. He can get around slowly, but because he has very little use in his right limbs, he will have problems in cooking or cleaning for himself. As Mr S lives alone, and has no nearby relatives to help, it has been decided that he should come into residential care for a few weeks until he is able to do a little more for himself and feels more confident about returning home.

Joel is 3 years old and attends a day nursery each day. His mother has a full-time job, and his father is a shift worker, so it is often his father who brings and collects Joel. Joel is a lively little boy, who has met all his milestones and is progressing well. He is inquisitive and often asks questions. Joel can tend to be boisterous, and can sometimes hurt other children if he becomes over-excited. It is important that he is given plenty of stimulation as he gets into mischief when he is bored.

F is 17 years old and has multiple disabilities. She has severe physical disabilities and learning difficulties as a result of brain damage at birth. F is in a wheelchair and cannot do anything for herself. She has been in residential care since she was a year old, and has regular visits from her parents, who are not able to manage her at home although they do go away on holidays arranged by the residential home. F is doubly incontinent, is unable to walk or use her arms, and her movements are jerky and uncontrolled. She needs to be dressed, fed and bathed and all personal care must be provided. Although she has no speech she does laugh at things and has a beautiful smile. F is very affectionate and likes to be hugged.

Think it through

Look at the people in your class or tutor group and think about the different ways that you can categorise them. You could start with all the people with brown hair, and all the people with fair hair. Or you could have all the people taller than 5 feet 2 inches and all the people who are 5 feet 2 inches or shorter, and so on.

Choose three different ways of putting people into groups – it does not matter which three you choose. After you have split up your class or group, look at the people who have fallen into each group. You will realise that even though they may all have one factor in common (they are all tall, or short, or they are all wearing navy blue) they are still all very different people. This is clear because you know them. Remember, when you are working in care, that all people are different, despite having some factors and some aspects of their lives in common.

Treating all people as individuals

Not only do you need to recognise that each person is an individual, but you need to treat people with respect and dignity. Treating people with respect is about more than just being polite to them – it is also about respecting their rights to privacy and confidentiality, and their right to have their views taken into account. There are many ways in which this respect for the people you are working with can show itself in the day-to-day tasks you carry out, and the care you give.

Good practice: showing respect for people

✓ Always ask people's permission before you perform any service for them or carry out any activity that affects them in any way. For example, ask, 'Mrs Smith – is it OK with you if I take you to the bathroom now so that you can have your bath?'
✓ Always offer people a choice wherever possible. For example, ask, 'Mr Jones, would you like to have your tea in your room or in the dining room at the table?'
✓ Avoid discussing anything that goes on in your place of work outside.
✓ Avoid discussing individual clients with each other.
✓ Ensure that clients always have privacy for personal matters like using the toilet, dressing and undressing, sleeping.
✓ Provide privacy for people when they are upset.

Communicating well with people

Another important principle of good practice in care is to make sure that you communicate well with all clients and their families. As Chapter 4 explains, there is much more to being a good communicator than simply talking. You will need to make sure that you are also a good listener and use all the listening and communication skills you have learned.

Good communication is the key to providing a good level of service for any client group, regardless of age, disability or need. The communication skills needed, for example, to deal

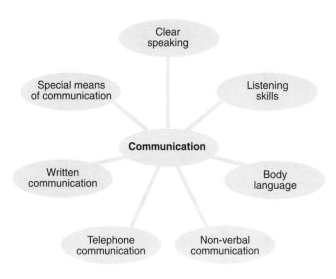

Figure 3.2 Aspects of communication

with children and elderly people may be quite different, but the principles remain the same.

The diagram in Figure 3.2 will show you some of the aspects of communication you need to consider.

Some aspects of good communication may be more important with one client group than with another. For example, the need for non-verbal communication may be greater where people have difficulties in hearing, or where there are language differences. On the other hand if you were dealing with a client who has visual difficulties, your verbal communication and touch may be the most important of your range of skills.

Communicating well with the people you are caring for is a vital part of effective work. There is little value in providing a good level of physical care unless you also practise good communication so that people do not feel isolated, uncertain and unhappy. Research has shown that human beings need to communicate in order to be happy and to feel confident in their environment. Where people are deprived of communication with others they become disturbed, withdrawn and depressed.

Do It

Explain the principles of good practice necessary to be an effective care worker.

The principles of good practice should form the basis of all the work you do. Prepare a journal or diary of just three days of your work experience. In the diary, you should identify where you have used the principles of good practice. Describe the circumstances of each occasion where you demonstrated good practice in your work. Do not name the clients – just use initials.

You could show which principles you are using by notes in the margin, using different colours or using a different typeface if you are word processing the journal.

Care needs and support

You have learned about the life stages everyone goes through, and the needs that people have at different times of their lives. When you were a baby you needed people to carry you and keep you warm, to feed you and keep you clean. As you grew older, your need for physical assistance became less, but your needs in other areas such as making friends and finding interesting activities were more important. For many people, as they grow older physical needs become important again as ill health and infirmity makes it difficult for them to fulfil all of their needs for themselves.

Client group	Needs
Baby	**Regular feeding,** either breast or bottle, prepared hygienically and regularly **Warmth,** both clothing and the surrounding environment **Cleanliness,** bathing, washing and nappy changing **Emotional needs,** stimulation by talking, playing, touching and looking – affection, cuddles, love and care **Mobility,** equipment to carry babies and in which to sleep
Toddler/pre-school child	**Regular, nutritious meals** giving a balanced diet with not too much sugar and fat and plenty of protein, prepared safely and hygienically **Warmth,** good clothing for outdoors and an even temperature indoors **Personal hygiene,** teaching children to use the toilet independently and care for their hair and teeth **Mobility,** space to play, equipment to encourage physical development **Social contacts,** meeting other children and learning to play with others **Intellectual stimulation,** activities to help develop the ability to think and learn **Love and affection,** so that toddlers know they are loved and feel secure
Child	**Regular, nutritious meals** still need to be prepared for them but children become less dependent as they move towards adulthood **Warmth** is still important, but children become better able to regulate their own body temperature **Personal hygiene,** encouragement to follow personal cleanliness routines **Social contacts** with others and support in making friends **Physical activity,** exercise and movement to encourage physical development **Intellectual stimulation,** learning and developing understanding **Love and affection** is essential so that children feel loved, safe and secure
Older person	**Food and warmth** are still vital, meals may be smaller as appetite decreases, need for warmth may increase. May need help with preparing and eating food, for example someone with a stroke may need special cutlery or food that does not need to be chewed **Personal hygiene** – if a person becomes ill or infirm, he or she may need assistance to use the toilet or bathe **Social contacts** are still important to maintain a social life, but this can often decrease as friends die or relatives move away. Assistance may be needed to meet new people **Intellectual stimulation,** since older people should not lose their interests, even if physical abilities decline. Interests may need to be adapted if physical and/or mental abilities change. For example, someone who was previously a footballer might start watching football on TV

	Love and affection – since the close emotional relationship with a partner may be lost, it is even more important that other contacts with friends and family are maintained
People with disabilities	**Food** may be a special diet, or food may need to be prepared in a particular way, with assistance to prepare or eat food
	Warmth may be an increased need if movement is limited
	Personal hygiene may require assistance. There may be special requirements if appliances are worn, for example incontinence pads
	Social contacts are important, both with other people with disabilities and able-bodied people. May need help with practical arrangements like transport and access
	Intellectual stimulation and interests are the same as for able-bodied people at the same life stage. May have to overcome the assumption that physical disabilities mean that people are less intelligent
	Love and affection and emotional needs are the same as for anyone at the same life stage. People with disabilities give and receive love and affection in the same way as everyone else
People suffering from illness	**Food** needs will depend on the illness, but there may be a special diet or special preparations. Otherwise good nutritious meals are important to assist recovery
	Warmth can be a greater need during illness as people are less mobile
	Personal care may, depending on the illness, require help
	Intellectual needs depend on the illness – some people may be too ill to be able to sustain much interest, but stimulation is always important, and everyone should be talked to, even unconscious people. For people who are getting better, or have been ill for a long time, intellectual activity can be very important
	Social and emotional needs – most people especially need to know that they are cared about when they are ill
People with emotional needs	**Physical needs** are likely to be similar to others at the same life stage, but people who have specific mental health problems may need specialist **emotional** support to meet their needs

Why do people need care ?

Think about the different reasons why people may need different sorts of help from you.

- **Life stage** – for example, a baby needs care for all needs.
- **Particular problems** – a person who has a disability or an emotional problem may need support only in one area of life
- **Particular events** – perhaps a fall, illness or injury
- An **emotional reason** – for instance, somebody who has suffered the death of a loved one may not be able to cope for a while.

As well as having different needs and therefore requiring different kinds of help from their carers at various stages of their lives, different client groups will also require different skills from their carers. For example, people who have learning difficulties will require additional support and help in areas where they may be vulnerable, possibly where safety is concerned. People who have physical disabilities may require some very practical help with moving and personal hygiene, whereas they may be completely self sufficient when it comes to judging and assessing any risks to themselves.

There are almost as many different reasons why people need help as there are people needing help! It is important in the work that you are doing that you can recognise the kind of help people need and the different skills that you need to develop in order to offer them the most appropriate type of support.

Do it

Identify the care needs and support of three specific client groups.

In groups in your class, look at case studies or real examples of three different kinds of caring situations for different clients, for example a child, an elderly person and a teenager with special needs. Brainstorm in your group the different help that will be required in each situation and look at the reasons why the different types of help are needed. For each client, create a chart with two lists: one showing the type of help needed, and the other the reasons why that particular help is required.

Practical caring skills

After considering the type of help that people may need you should think carefully about the skills you would need in order to offer that help. Make sure you understand the practical help that you can offer people in order to maintain their personal hygiene, and help with the preparation and serving of food as well as with eating and drinking.

Some clients also need help to move around, either assistance with walking or using aids to do so, or moving around in bed or in a wheelchair. Where clients are suffering pain or discomfort you need to know the most effective ways of helping them to be more comfortable and to rest. Like all other caring skills, the practical skills vary depending upon the client group. You may need to offer help with preparing a meal for a person recovering from an illness or an injury, but you will always have to prepare food yourself for babies, toddlers and young children. If you are working with people who are fit and healthy but have learning difficulties, you may simply need to provide some element of supervision while they prepare their meals and feed themselves. They would require no help at all when it comes to mobility.

These are a few examples of the different kinds of skills that you may need in different situations. You may like to look at Chapter 5 for detailed information on helping clients to eat and drink, maintain personal hygiene and improve mobility. You will learn about the skills in detail in Chapter 5, but the most important are shown in Figure 3.3.

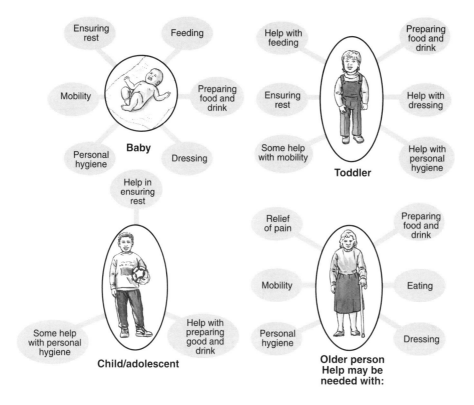

Figure 3.3 The help needed by different client groups

Good practice: practical caring skills

✓ **Helping people to eat and drink** includes storing and preparing food hygienically, knowing how to provide a balanced diet, how to present food and drink attractively, knowing how to use special utensils to assist people with particular problems, knowing how to assist both adults and children to eat.

✓ **Assisting with personal hygiene** includes bathing and changing babies, toilet training toddlers, routines for grooming and cleaning teeth, help with washing, bathing and showering, hair washing and grooming, nail care, eye care, choosing and caring for clothes, assistance with using the toilet.

✓ **Helping with mobility** includes providing supervision and safe areas for babies and toddlers to move and play, using equipment and toys to encourage movement, assisting with walking, ensuring the correct use of mobility equipment, providing support and encouragement to take exercise.

✓ **Providing intellectual stimulation** includes using a range of activities to develop interest, planning and carrying out group and individual activities, encouraging people to keep up interests, obtaining information and advice when requested.

✓ **Maintaining or developing social contacts** includes, encouraging games and activities that develop interaction with others, helping people to keep in contact with others by writing or telephone calls, helping to encourage visitors.

Do It

Describe a range of practical skills to support clients in their activities for three specific client groups

You could do this as either a class activity or on your own. Think of a specific caring skill; it could be helping someone to eat, or perhaps helping someone to dress. Then think about the situations in which that may be needed and three specific groups who may require that help. Using your work experience placement as a guide, create a chart which lists each practical skill, and then identifies the clients for whom you may have to provide this service. If you do this on your own you should list at least five different skills. If you are doing it as a class exercise the groups could take one or two skills each.

Health and safety principles in care settings

Health and safety is very important in all care settings, because the clients you deal with are very vulnerable and you need to be sure that they are protected from risks. It is also essential that you, as a worker in the care setting, are not putting yourself at risk. The whole area of care is covered by comprehensive laws that lay down what can and cannot be done in a care setting.

The main Act of Parliament that affects all care settings is the Health and Safety at Work Act (HASAWA). This law is like an umbrella under which are many other regulations designed to cover particular areas of risk.

The Act broadly identifies which areas are the responsibility of the employer and which are the responsibility of the employee. The employer and employee are jointly responsible for

Figure 3.4 The Health and Safety at Work Act is like an umbrella

safeguarding the health and safety of anyone who uses the premises – this includes both clients and visitors. The employer is responsible for providing a safe place to work, but the employee also has to show reasonable care for his or her own safety.

The Health and Safety at Work Act requires all workplaces where there are five workers or more to have a written health and safety policy.

Employers' duties	Employees' duties
• to plan for safety and security • to provide information about safety and security • to update systems and procedures	• to use the systems and procedures correctly • to report any problems with systems or procedures

Some examples of the HASAWA in practice are shown in the following case studies.

Health and Safety Policy

1. Statement of intention to provide a safe workplace.

2. The name of the person responsible for implementing the policy.

3. The names of any individuals who have particular responsibilities.

4. A list of particular hazards identified for that workplace and the procedures that have to be followed.

5. Procedures for recording accidents at work.

6. Details for the evacuation of the premises.

Figure 3.5 The information required in a health and safety policy

CASE STUDY TREETOPS AND THE BEECHES

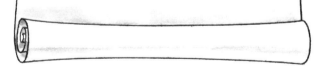

Treetops Day Nursery is registered to take 30 children from birth to five years of age. The nursery is privately owned and managed, and it is mainly used by children whose parents work in the nearby hospital and local college. Under the Health and Safety at Work Act, some of the steps which the owner of the nursery is obliged to take are:

- make sure that the entrance and approach to the nursery are safe for parents and children
- ensure that the inside of the premises is safe with no dangerous wiring (e.g. exposed wires or wrongly fused plugs), plumbing (e.g. scalding hot water where children could reach, or with no warning sign)
- check that all dangerous substances are properly stored and labelled, and are out of reach of the children
- ensure play equipment is regularly checked and repair it or replace it if it is worn or faulty
- make sure that the building is secure and that children are not able to wander off from inside or outside
- develop a system for checking visitors and making sure that no unauthorised people have access to the children.

The Beeches is a large residential home for 40 elderly residents. It is owned and run by the Social Services department. Some of the things the Social Services department must do in order to comply with the Health and Safety at Work Act are:

- ensure the access to and grounds of the home are safe for staff, residents and visitors.
- check that there are no dangers inside the home such as wet floors, trailing flexes, frayed carpets, etc.
- ensure that all dangerous substances are safely stored and properly labelled
- carry out a risk assessment for all residents who require assistance to move
- ensure that equipment such as hoists, slides and slings are supplied for use where necessary
- make sure that all equipment is regularly checked and replaced if faulty or worn
- arrange for staff to receive training in how to move and handle people
- ensure that there is system in place for checking visitors to the premises.

Food handling

If you are involved in handling and preparing food in your workplace, this too is governed by health and safety regulations, and you must be careful that you observe all the regulations to ensure a safe place for people to eat and drink. The regulations cover such areas as storage and refrigeration of food.

The regulations cover both the individual handling the food and the area in which food is prepared. There are regulations about the cooking of food and which foods can be served raw. All care settings are required to follow hygiene rules and also to ensure that they observe the use-by dates on food they offer to clients. Somebody in your workplace will be responsible for ordering food and for regularly checking that food is being stored safely and is within the recommended time limits for safe use.

Do it

Explain the health and safety regulations that apply to clients and workers in the care sectors.

Everyone in your class or group should obtain a copy of the Health and Safety Policy for their workplace. Compare the policies from different workplaces and look at the features that are different.

1.   In your groups, discuss why the policies may be different. For example, if you are working in an early years setting, the Health and Safety Policy may identify different hazards than those identified for a hospital setting or a nursing home.

2.   Look at the things in the policies which are similar. Try to identify the basic principles of health and safety which are the same regardless of the particular considerations of an individual workplace.

Make sure that you consider policies from at least three different types of care settings – one could be from your college.

Prepare a report on what is the same and what is different for the workplaces you have chosen.

Risk assessment

One of the requirements of employers under the Health and Safety at Work regulations is that they must carry out an assessment of risk involved with any work activity. This covers all activities in the workplace, not just those directly concerned with providing care to clients. Activities such as cleaning and working in kitchens, are included, as are risks from visitors to the workplace or from clients' behaviour.

Reducing risks

After employers have carried out an assessment of risk, they have to ensure that they reduce the risk as far as possible by taking whatever steps may be necessary. This could mean:

- providing hoists and slings to lift and move people
- installing a security system
- employing extra staff to ensure that employees are not exposed to risks from violent clients
- providing additional training or further guidelines as how to deal with particular risks.

The responsibility of the employee is to use any equipment provided and to make use of any additional training or to follow any guidelines or advice supplied by the employer.

Manual handling regulations

The manual handling regulations require employers to avoid all manual handling where there is any risk of injury, so far as it is reasonably practical.

Handling and moving clients should always be undertaken using appropriate equipment. Manual lifting is never safe – there is no such thing as a safe lift, and it should never be undertaken in a care setting. The only places where lifting can safely be carried out is on maternity units where babies are being moved around.

As part of a care plan, any moving required for a client (even a child) should be assessed to find out what equipment is needed. The assessment has to be carried out by the employer and should take into account factors such as:

- the extent to which the person to be lifted can help himself or herself
- weight
- risk of injury
- likelihood of pain and discomfort
- height and distance of lift or move
- special circumstances such as skin problems.

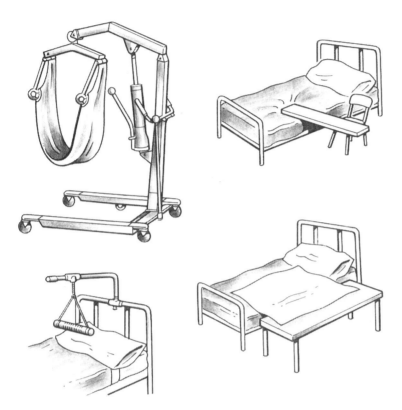

Figure 3.6 Equipment for moving and handling

A risk assessment should also be done before moving large or heavy equipment.

Many serious injuries have been caused to workers in care settings in the past by lifting and moving people without using equipment. You may find that some workers in care settings still believe that it is quicker and easier to carry out a lift or move manually than to use a hoist, a sling or other appropriate equipment. *This is not true.*

Not only care workers can be severely injured by attempting to move and lift people manually – clients can also be injured by a lift carried out without proper equipment. It is never worth the risk – always use the proper equipment.

Do IT

Explain the importance of the main points of the current moving and handling regulations.

Make notes about the way the manual handling regulations affect the way you would work in:

- a hospital geriatric ward
- a hostel for young people with physical disabilities
- a day nursery.

Control of Substances Hazardous to Health (COSHH)

The COSHH regulations cover all the substances you may use in your workplace. This includes everything from cleaning fluids to dangerous drugs. The regulations apply to any caustic or corrosive substances in your workplace and also gases or substances that could potentially release dangerous fumes.

Figure 3.7 These symbols, which warn you of hazardous substances, are always yellow

An employer must meet basic requirements for hazardous substances in a workplace. There must be a COSHH file listing all of the hazardous substances in any workplace, and it has to:

- identify what they are
- say where each is kept
- say what the labels are
- describe the effects of the substances
- state the maximum amount of time it is safe to be exposed to them
- describe how to deal with an emergency.

What to do with a COSHH file

Once you have read the information in the COSHH file in your workplace, you must make sure you follow the advice for working with any particular hazardous substances. The advice could be to wear gloves or protective goggles, or may involve limiting the time you are exposed to the substance. The file will also tell you how the substances must be stored and you must make sure you follow those instructions.

- It is always essential that the correct containers are used and that they are properly labelled.
- You must never use the container of one substance for storing another, and you must *never* change the labels.

Do It

Describe the main points of the COSHH regulations.

Check through the COSHH file in your own workplace. Make a list of the hazardous substances identified there. Compare notes with the rest of your class and see what different substances have been identified in your workplaces. Make a chart for the whole class and look at the range of substances in the different placements.

Prepare an information sheet about COSHH regulations, which could be given to a new employee on the first day in your work placement.

Handling bodily fluids safely

One of the things that you will have to learn to deal with if you are going to work in care is handling the fluids produced by all human beings. These are:

- blood
- saliva
- urine
- mucus.
- vomit
- sweat
- faeces

Regardless of the age range or client group you work with, you will deal with some or all of these fluids at some point. There are important reasons why they must be handled safely and in particular ways. The broad principles which apply are shown below.

Good practice: handling body fluids

✓ Always wear gloves and a plastic apron when you are coming in to contact with any type of body fluid. This will minimise the risk of cross infection if there is any harmful agent present in the bodily fluid. Cross infection occurs where harmful and infectious bacteria are spread from one person to another.

✓ Make sure that body fluids are disposed of safely so that they cannot present a risk to others in the care setting.

Your workplace

All care settings have their own procedures for dealing with disposal of body waste such as urine, faeces and vomit. Normally this will mean disposing of it in a toilet or a sluice – which is designed to dispose of waste hygienically and looks a bit like a sink but flushes like a toilet. However, sometimes waste may need to be retained for measuring or further testing.

There will also be arrangements for disposing of blood, mucus or any other fluids, and these should be listed in the safety procedures in your workplace.

Spills and splashes

If body fluids have been spilt, the area must be thoroughly cleaned and disinfected to minimise the risk of infection. Make sure you wear gloves and an apron while cleaning up any spill.

Soiled linen or clothing should be handled with care. Wear an apron and gloves, and do not place linen or clothes on the floor but put them directly into the container for soiled linen.

> ## *Do it*
>
> **Recognise the importance of safe handling of bodily fluids.**
>
> Consider how many types of body fluids you may come into contact with in your work placement. Note down each one, then check the procedure for dealing with it in your workplace. Prepare a table showing the different methods of disposal.

Health and social care services

Health and social care services cover a vast area of need, ranging from acute medical care to care in the home, from providing advice and support, to providing care and education. The range is enormous and the services are provided in several different ways.

Public provision

The first and largest area of provision is made by the government. This is called **public provision** and is known as the **public** or the **state sector**. This includes the National Health Service, Local Authority Social Services departments, and Local Education Authorities.

It is called the public sector because the funding for the services provided in this sector comes from the government, and is raised from the taxes and National Insurance contributions of the public.

Voluntary sector

The voluntary sector is comprised of charities and similar organisations who either directly provide services for a particular client group, or offer advice and support, and direct clients towards services that are appropriate for them. The sector includes organisations like the Salvation Army, Barnardo's, Scope, Citizen's Advice Bureaux and the NSPCC.

It is called the voluntary sector because it is funded through voluntary contributions made by the general public. A great many charitable bodies also receive grants, either from central or local government or sometimes from other charitable organisations known as the foundations, who provide money for worthy causes. Many organisations in the voluntary sector rely very heavily on fund raising, often arranged by local volunteers.

Private sector

The private sector includes those organisations that provide services in health and care for a profit – these are businesses and are run as such. The profit may go to an individual business owner, or alternatively it may be put back into the services provided, as in many private hospitals owned by organisations such as BUPA. This sector is referred to as the **private sector** because it is funded by people making private payments for the services they receive. If people want to receive medical treatment on a private basis they may pay to do so, either directly to a hospital or through taking out an insurance policy. Many people pay privately for child care and for nursery provision. It is also quite common to find people paying for the care of older people in nursing homes or residential homes in the private sector.

Structure of the public sector

The public sector is by far the largest service provider for health and social care. If you think about the number of hospitals, health centres and Social Services departments there are, you will see that this huge service requires a massive amount of public funding to maintain standards and services. The National Health Service is constantly in the news, as public funding levels are always a matter for political debate and discussion. The present structure of the health service is about to change, and it will soon look like the diagram in Figure 3.8.

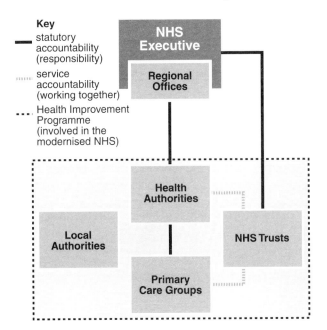

Key
— statutory accountability (responsibility)
⋯⋯ service accountability (working together)
- - - Health Improvement Programme (involved in the modernised NHS)

Figure 3.8   The new NHS

The health service is ultimately the responsibility of the Secretary of State for Health, but the Secretary of State has a great many responsibilities so the particular body within the Department of Health responsible for the health service is the National Health Service Executive.

Health services are provided in two different ways – through local health centres, where GPs, community nurses, midwives, health visitors, chiropodists and other health professionals are based, and through National Health Service Trusts, which provide hospital services, emergency medical services, out-patient care and a wide range of allied services such as physiotherapy, occupational therapy, pathology and dieticians.

In the recent past the health service has been the responsibility of the NHS Executive but it has operated like a 'marketplace' where some people, such as GPs, were 'purchasers', and others – the hospital trusts – were 'providers'. The system worked by GPs purchasing the health care for their patients from a provider.

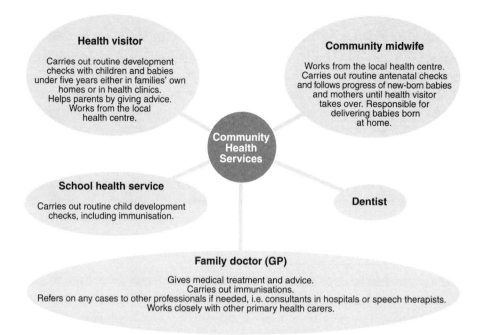

Figure 3.9 Community health services

The modernised National Health Service will operate in a different way. The Executive will work with National Health Trusts, GPs and Health Authorities, but the relationship between them will be quite different. Health Authorities will have the responsibility to look at overall plans for health in their area and to examine the needs there may be among their local population. For example, because of the health risk associated with a particular industry in one area, there may be a greater need for one type of health care. An area may have a particularly large number of older people, and so on. The commissioning of health and care services, however, will come from 'primary care groups', where GPs and community nurses and midwives in an area will work together in a group to look at the level of service needed from their local NHS hospital trust.

Local Social Services providers will also be a part of the process, where decisions are made at a local level about the level of services needed. The system will be different in Northern Ireland, and may be different in Wales after the start of the new Welsh Assembly.

Social Services

Social Services departments are part of local government. This means that they are run by the local council from the local town hall, county hall or council buildings. They usually have a range of local area offices and also a wide range of establishments such as nurseries, children's homes, elderly persons' homes, and resource centres. Social Services departments have a responsibility to provide services for children, people with disabilities, people with mental health problems, people with learning difficulties and older people. The services they provide may be residential, or they may be provided in clients' own homes. Social Services also have a responsibility under the Care in the Community Act to use both private and public sector facilities in order to provide the most appropriate care for any individual for whom they are responsible.

Social Services departments are just one of the many departments in most local councils. They are funded through the local authority annual budget, which in turn receives money from central government and from taxes raised locally. This is called the Council Tax, and everybody who lives in a particular local authority's area must pay Council Tax for the provision of services.

The Social Services department will have its allocation of funding alongside other council departments like education, leisure, and environmental health. Each Social Services department is headed by a Director of Social Services, who works with a committee of local councillors who must decide how the budget is to be spent and which services will be provided. Some services must be provided by law. These are called statutory services and includes such things as provisions to protect children from abuse, provision of accommodation for elderly people, provision of aids and adaptations for people with disabilities, and provision of a service for those who have mental health problems.

Look at the following examples of how clients might use the health and social services.

CASE STUDY MRS J

Mrs J is 83 years old and lives with her daughter and son-in-law. Although she is mentally alert, she is physically frail and her eyesight is poor. Her daughter and son-in-law both go out to work and Mrs J has had a few falls. She also began to feel lonely and isolated in the house all day as she became unable to get out to the shops or the park. Her family contacted Social Services to discuss the help that could be offered. Following an assessment by a social worker, Mrs J now attends a day centre three days each week. She is collected and returned home by the transport service. On the remaining day, she has a visit from a local community group who 'pop in' to make sure she is well.

Which of the services used by Mrs J are provided by:

a. the public sector?
b. the private sector?
c. the voluntary sector?

CASE STUDY ELLEN

Ellen is 10 years old, and she has Down's Syndrome which means that she has some learning difficulties. She is a loving and cheerful little girl who laughs a lot and has a mischievous sense of humour. Ellen attends a local special school, and she is picked up by the school transport service each day. She loves school and has lots of friends. She is looking forward to the next school holiday because her social worker has arranged for her to go away on a week's holiday organised by a local community group.

One evening each week, Ellen goes to a club in the local community centre where she has the chance to play games and sports. Most of her friends from school go too. Ellen has a heart condition and has to attend for regular check-ups at the hospital, and she is also regularly seen by the school nurse and her own doctor. Her eyesight is poor and she wears glasses, but she did not like the frames she was offered this time because they were not trendy enough! So her mother bought her some fashionable ones.

Which of the services used by Ellen are likely to be provided by:

a. the public sector?　　**b.** the private sector?　　**c.** the voluntary sector?

Services provided by the voluntary sector

The services provided by the voluntary sector in many ways mirror those provided by Social Services. They range from residential accommodation to day care and child care facilities, and also include advice, guidance and support services. Usually, however, the service is provided to reflect a particular client group, which is the interest of that particular voluntary organisation. For example, the NSPCC provides services for children, whereas Scope provides services for people with cerebral palsy, and Age Concern provides day care and advice services for older people. You will find this kind of specific service provision throughout the voluntary sector. All services provided by the voluntary sector must meet with the same requirements as those provided by the public sector. They are bound by health and safety regulations, and must provide services to the same standards.

Services provided by the private sector

In the same way as the voluntary sector, the private sector will provide services in all of those areas covered by social service provision. It also provides health care services. No element of public funding is involved in private health and care provision and all of the funding comes from direct payment for the services provided. This payment is either from individuals, insurance companies, or Social Services departments paying for services for particular clients.

DO IT

Describe the range of health and social care services for individuals at two different life stages.

You have been contacted by a friend who is moving to your area. She is moving with her elderly mother, who has difficulty in getting around because of arthritis, and her daughter who is 18 months old. Your friend works full time in a well-paid job. She wants to know what services will be available when she moves. Prepare a list of the services you think she may need for her daughter and her mother.

Range of settings

It is important that you know about the different types of service offered by health and care service providers. You may need to advise clients which services would be of value to them according to the particular needs they may have.

Health service

Hospitals provide both for acute care in emergencies and also for any health care needs where medical treatment is necessary. They also provide out-patient services where people can go to follow up treatment and where clients can receive services such as physiotherapy, occupational therapy and chiropody.

Health Centres are situated in local communities and provide general practitioners, community nurses, community midwives, and health visitors.

Early years services

Services for young children can be provided by the local authority or the voluntary or private sectors, and they include day nurseries (where full-time day care is provided for children from babies to school age), playgroups, nursery education, childminders (who care for children at home) and nannies (who look after children in the child's home).

Services a child may need include:

- full-time care while parents are working
- part-time care while parents are working
- the chance to meet other children
- the opportunity to start learning
- special services to meet special needs.

Playgroups are usually provided by the voluntary sector where children (usually between the age of two and school age) can attend for a short period, normally two to three hours each day. As the name suggests, the major activity is the chance for children to play with others in a safe, supervised setting.

Childminders are normally part of the private sector, but regulated by the local authority. Childminders may care for one or more children in their own home, but there is usually a maximum of three or four. Their homes have to be approved and inspected by the local Social Services department. The charges are usually paid by the child's parents.

Nannies work in a child's home and can provide full- or part-time care. They are almost always employed by the private sector. Most parents insist on qualifications for the nanny they employ, but there are no legal requirements for them to be qualified. Nannies are not subject to any inspections or regulations.

Schools and special schools

These are provided by the local education authority, but can also be part of the private or voluntary sector. They provide education, sometimes with boarding accommodation. Most schools have nursery classes where children can begin to attend school as they reach their fourth birthday. All schools are inspected by OFSTED (the schools inspectors) and have to reach certain standards. If children have special needs, they may attend a particular type of school with special facilities, for example special physiotherapy and hydrotherapy equipment in a school for people with physical disabilities, or lessons using braille or voice-recognition technology for visually impaired people.

Adult services

Day Centres offer contact, support and stimulation to a range of client groups. This can be people with mental health problems, people with disabilities, those with learning difficulties or older people. They can be provided by the public or voluntary sectors. Clients attend each day, or on set days each week. Day centres are often important for people who are cared for at home by a relative.

Residential accommodation, like day centres, can be provided for a wide range of client groups and can also be provided by any of the three sectors. The majority of residential accommodation is for older people, and can be used either to provide a permanent home for people who are unable to care for themselves or as a 'respite' break for people being looked after at home.

Community provision

The term 'community provision' covers support in people's own homes, such as a home help and home care service, and can also be linked to provision of day-care services and supported accommodation services in the community for those who have learning difficulties or who have suffered mental health problems. Services in the community can be provided by any of the three sectors, and can often make it possible for a person to remain at home by providing extra support.

Community provision also covers services such as chiropody and nursing care, laundry services and mobile libraries.

Informal carers

'Informal carers' is the term used to describe people who care for relatives or friends at home. There are many thousands of informal carers carrying out the very difficult job of caring for another person. In the vast majority of circumstances, the carers are relatives who are enabling someone to remain in the community rather than go into residential care or hospital. Carers at home will usually provide all the help their relatives need, from preparing meals to bathing and toileting. They also offer company and support, and will look after the safety and security of the person they are caring for.

The fact that someone has an informal carer can also mean that there is less need for other support services such as home help, district nurses or night sitters. Informal carers save a huge demand on services.

Do It

Identify health and social care services for clients with disability or specific emotional needs.

You have been asked to talk to the mother of Josie, who is blind. Josie will be four years old in a few weeks' time. Her mother wants to know what services are available for Josie, and who she needs to contact to arrange them. Plan what you are going to say to her and prepare an information sheet to leave with her.

VALUES AND COMMUNICATIONS IN CARE SETTINGS

Diversity and rights

We live in a world full of new ways of communicating. Using the Internet, you can easily communicate with individuals all over the world, and you can have conversations with people hundreds of miles away using a mobile phone. New communications technology means that businesses and trade are connected across the world.

A hundred years ago the world was not like this. In 1900, you might meet only people you grew up with. But to be successful in the new world of communication, you will need to value the diversity of people all over the world. Valuing diversity is not just a central principle of care work. You have to be willing and able to understand differences in other people in order to fit in with the new interconnected world of communications. Not valuing diversity may exclude you from the future!

Diversity in individuals

You are special and no one is exactly the same as you. But you will be more like some people and less like others. Many of the differences between people are created by **cultural influences**. Culture means the values and beliefs that different social groups have. We try to make ourselves individual; but we are also influenced by the groups we belong to. Some ways in which people are different from each other (or diverse) are listed below:

- **Age** People may think of others as being children, teenagers, young adults, middle aged or old. Discrimination can creep into our thinking if we see some age groups as being 'the best' or if we make assumptions about the abilities of different age groups.
- **Gender** People are classified as male or female. In the past, men often had more rights and were seen as more important than women. Assumptions about gender can still create discrimination.
- **Race** People may understand themselves as being Black or White, as European, African or Asian. Many people have specific national identities such as Polish, Nigerian, English or Welsh. Assumptions about racial characteristics lead to discrimination.
- **Class** People differ in their upbringing, the kind of work they do and the money they earn. People also differ in the lifestyles they lead and the views and values that go with levels of income and spending habits. Discrimination against others can be based on their class or lifestyle.
- **Caste** The word 'caste' is used where there are rigid social divisions between groups. Caste is like social class, but much more fixed. In some cultures people are born into a caste that they cannot change, whereas you can change social class if you change your type of work. It is important not to see some people as worth more than others in a care setting.
- **Religion** People grow up in different traditions of religion. For some people, spiritual beliefs are at the centre of their understanding of life. For others, religion influences the cultural traditions that they celebrate; for example, many Europeans celebrate Christmas even though they might not see themselves as practising Christians. Discrimination can take place when people assume that their customs or beliefs should apply to everyone else.

- **Sexuality** Many people see their sexual orientation as very important to understanding who they are. Gay and lesbian relationships are often discriminated against. Heterosexual people sometimes judge other relationships as 'wrong' or abnormal.
- **Ability** People may make assumptions about what is 'normal'. People with physical disabilities or learning disabilities may be labelled or stereotyped (see Chapter 1).
- **Health** People who develop illnesses or mental health problems may feel that they are valued less by other people and discriminated against.
- **Relationships** People choose many different lifestyles and emotional commitments, such as: marriage, having children, living in a large family, living a single lifestyle but having sexual partners, being single and not being sexually active. People live within different family and friendship groups. Discrimination can happen if people think that one lifestyle is 'right' or best.

- **Politics** People can develop different views as to how a government should act, how welfare provision should be organised, and so on. Disagreement and debate are necessary; but it is important not to discriminate against people because of their views.

- **Presentation and dress** People express their individuality, lifestyle and social role through the clothes, hairstyle, make-up and jewellery they wear. Whilst it may be important to conform to social expectations at work, it is also important not to stereotype individuals.

Understanding diversity

Familiarity

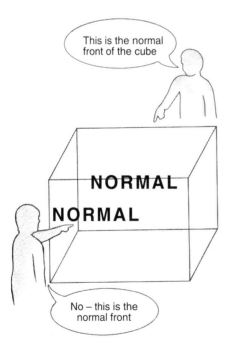

Our own socialisation, culture and life experience may lead us to make assumptions as to what is right or normal. When we meet people who are different, it can be easy to see them as 'not right' or 'not normal'. Different people see the world in different ways. Our way of thinking may seem unusual to others. Look at the illustration in Figure 4.1. Which is the 'normal' front of the cube?

If a person was used to seeing the cube from only one direction, he or she might be sure that view was right. Our culture may lead us to think that some habits are better than others, but often there are many ways of looking at things. For instance, different cultures and different individuals have varying views about what is right to eat or drink.

Figure 4.1 Which is the 'normal' front of the cube?

Diversity in food

Food is quite a personal area of our lives. What we eat or drink is also strongly influenced by our culture and learning. Below is a range of views on different foods.

For	Against
Snake	
A good source of protein enjoyed in many countries.	Not considered acceptable to some Europeans.
Frog	
Eaten by some Europeans.	Once considered offensive by some English people.
Cat, dog or horse	
Regarded as no different from lamb or beef in many cultures.	Seen as pets and 'honorary family members' in some sections of British society.
Insects	
A useful source of protein and a delicacy in some cultures.	May be seen as 'inedible' or disgusting by some people in Britain.
Animals' brains and eyes	
A delicacy in many cultures.	Usually thrown away in Britain.
Alcohol	
Widely consumed in Europe.	Forbidden to many Muslims and forbidden by some Christian and other religious groups.
High fat or sugar products	
Widely consumed in Europe.	Avoided by health-conscious people.
Pork	
Seen as similar to lamb or beef by many Europeans.	Regarded as unacceptable by many Jewish and Muslim people.
Meat	
Seen as good food by many people.	Regarded as unacceptable by vegetarians and many Hindu and Buddhist people.
Genetically modified food	
Argued to be an effective way to produce cheap, high quality food.	Some people think this food is dangerous or wrong because the natural environment may be damaged by genetically altered crops.
Fish	
Widely accepted.	Not acceptable to most vegetarians, vegans and to some religions.
Milk, eggs, cheese	
Widely accepted.	Not acceptable to vegans.

Each person will have a similar range of views on the subjects of clothing, relationships, and social behaviour. The views we are familiar with may not necessarily be held by others. We have a right to our culture and lifestyle, but others have a right to be different from us.

Observing diversity

In order to learn about other people's culture and beliefs, it is necessary to listen and watch what other people say and do. Learning about diversity can be interesting and exciting, but some people feel that finding out about different lifestyles can be stressful. We may feel that our own culture and beliefs are being challenged when we realise the different possibilities that exist. Our emotions may block our abilities to learn.

Skilled carers have to get to know the people they work with in order to avoid making false assumptions. In getting to know an individual, carers will also need to understand the ways that class, race, age, gender and other social categories influence the person. A person's culture may include all the social groups they belong to.

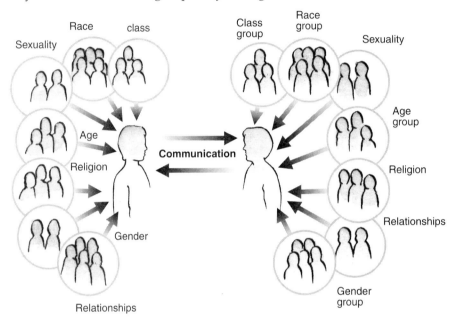

Figure 4.2   The groups a person belongs to will influence his or her beliefs and behaviour

Knowledge of diverse characteristics

There are many different ethnic groups in the world, many different religions, many different cultural values, variations in gender role, and so on. Individuals may belong to the same ethnic group yet belong to different religions or class groups. Knowing someone's religion will not necessarily tell you all of that person's beliefs, or general culture.

You can pick up background knowledge on different ethnic and religious customs, but it is impossible to study all the differences that might exist for individual clients. The best way to learn about diversity is to listen and communicate with people who lead different lives from ourselves.

Valuing diversity

Valuing diversity will enrich your own life. If you are open to understanding other people's life experience and differences you may be able to become more flexible and creative, because you can imagine how other people see things. You may develop a wider range of social skills because you have met different people, and learning about other cultures may provide you with new experiences – such as new foods to try and new places to visit. Understanding other people's lives may also help you to adapt your own lifestyle when you have to cope with change. For instance, if you talk to people who get married or who have children, you may be more prepared if you choose these roles.

Employers are likely to want to employ people who value diversity because:

- Effective non-discriminatory care depends on staff valuing diversity.
- People who value diversity are likely to be flexible and creative.
- People who value diversity may make good relationships with one another and with clients.
- Diverse teams often work together effectively. If everyone has the same skills and interests, then team members may compete. If people have different interests there is more chance that the team will cover all the work and enjoy working together.

Do it

Examine how an understanding of diversity in individuals and culture leads to enrichment and equality.

Get together with some other students and make a list of ways in which you are similar to or different from each other. You could consider all the areas of diversity mentioned in this section, as well as other lifestyle differences. When you have made your list, work out what you could learn from each other. For instance, do some people enjoy different food or go to different clubs or places of worship? Describe some new things you can learn from each other.

Forms of discrimination

In care work, discrimination means treating some groups of people less well than others. People are often discriminated against because of their class, race, gender, religion, sexuality or age.

Discrimination may take the following forms.

- **Physical abuse** means hitting, pushing, kicking or otherwise assaulting a person. People may commit assault because they hate certain groups, or simply because they feel frustrated or annoyed by those who are different.
- **Verbal abuse** means insults, 'put downs' or damaging language. Like physical abuse, it may happen because individuals feel they are more powerful if they can hurt other people.
- **Neglect** occurs when people are discriminated against by being ignored or not offered the help that others might receive.
- **Exclusion** is a more subtle form of discrimination, and may be hard to prove. Exclusion means stopping people from getting services or jobs because they belong to a certain class, race or other group. Disabled people may still be excluded from certain services because access is difficult – some buildings still do not have full disabled access. Some jobs may not be advertised in all local areas, therefore excluding certain communities.
- **Avoidance** is where people try to avoid sitting next to people or working with people who are different from them. Those who decide to discriminate against others may try to avoid contact – perhaps so that they don't need to learn or re-think any of their prejudices.

Figure 4.3 Discrimination through neglect can easily happen

- **Devaluing** involves seeing some types of people as less valuable than others. Some people are helped to build self-esteem because they receive praise and their ideas are valued, but people who are 'different' may be criticised and find their ideas ignored. People who are subjected to constant discrimination and prejudice may develop a low sense of self-esteem.

Direct and indirect discrimination

Direct discrimination is open and obvious. In the 1950s and 1960s, properties for rent in London would sometimes have signs reading 'no blacks, no dogs, no Irish'. Such offensive and obvious discrimination is 'direct' – the advertisements were openly proclaiming racial discrimination.

Indirect discrimination may do equal harm, but it is less clear. An employer once produced an advert stating that applicants for a job must live in certain local areas. At first this sounded all right, but it became obvious that the areas had been carefully chosen to avoid the Black and Asian communities. The advert was indirectly discriminating by identifying areas where only white people lived.

Fifty years ago, you had to be tall to join the police. If the police still had this requirement today, it would indirectly discriminate against women, because on average, men are taller than women.

The effects of discrimination

Discrimination that results in abuse can have permanent and extremely damaging effects on people. All forms of discrimination will cause harm. Some of the possible effects of discrimination and abuse are:

- injury and death
- mental illness triggered by stress
- living in fear of others
- losing a sense of who you are
- withdrawal from social activities

- a low sense of self-worth
- loss of confidence
- depression and anxiety
- feeling stressed or unable to cope with work.

Do It

Describe the forms and effects of discrimination.

Make a list of the major forms of discrimination, and work out what risks are associated with each. You might like to present your task as a table, with forms of discrimination in the left-hand column and the effects of discrimination in the right-hand column.

Legislation, policies and procedures

The main Acts of Parliament that deal with rights and discrimination are:

- Equal Pay Act 1970
- Race Relations Act 1976

- Sex Discrimination Act 1975
- Disability Discrimination Act 1995.

Equal Pay Act 1970

This Act made it unlawful for employers to discriminate between men and women in terms of their pay and conditions of work. Before this law was passed, it was possible for an employer to pay men more than women – even though the women were doing the same job!

Equal pay legislation was updated in 1975 and 1983 to make it possible to claim equal pay for work that was considered to be of equal value.

Sex Discrimination Act 1975

This Act made it unlawful to discriminate between men and women in respect of employment, goods and facilities. The Act also made it illegal to discriminate on the grounds of marital status. It identified two forms of discrimination: direct and indirect discrimination.

The Act tries to ensure equal opportunities for both men and women to get jobs and promotion. In order to make sure that people's rights are protected, the government set up the **Equal Opportunities Commission** to monitor, advise and provide information on men and women's rights under the law. Individuals can ask the Equal Opportunities Commission for help and advice if they believe they have been discriminated against because of their gender.

Race Relations Act 1976

This Act makes it unlawful to discriminate on racial grounds in employment, housing or services. Racial grounds include colour, race, nationality, and ethnic or national origins. The Act makes it an offence to incite or encourage racial hatred. As with the law against sex discrimination, both direct and indirect discrimination are made unlawful.

The **Commission for Racial Equality** was set up in 1976 to make sure that the law against racial discrimination works. The Commission can investigate cases of discrimination and give advice to people who wish to take legal action because of discrimination.

Disability Discrimination Act 1995

This Act is designed to prevent discrimination against people with disabilities, in matters of employment, access to education and transport, housing and obtaining goods and services. Employers and landlords must not treat a disabled person less favourably than a non-disabled person. New transport facilities must meet the needs of disabled people and institutions such as colleges, shops and other services must ensure that disabled people can use their services.

However, as yet there is no body like the Equal Opportunities Commission or the Commission for Racial Equality to help disabled people to take up their rights.

Other laws relevant to care

The Children Act 1989 outlined 'parental responsibility' and established children's right to be protected from 'significant harm'. The NHS and Community Care Act 1990 established that all people who are in need of community care have the right to have their needs assessed and to have services if their needs meet certain criteria.

Policies

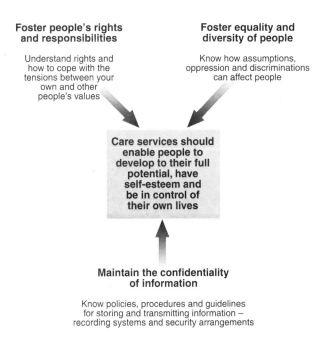

Foster people's rights and responsibilities

Understand rights and how to cope with the tensions between your own and other people's values

Foster equality and diversity of people

Know how assumptions, oppression and discriminations can affect people

Care services should enable people to develop to their full potential, have self-esteem and be in control of their own lives

Maintain the confidentiality of information

Know policies, procedures and guidelines for storing and transmitting information – recording systems and security arrangements

Figure 4.4 The NVQ values

The Care Sector Consortium defined the values that should guide care practice for National Vocational Qualifications (NVQs) in 1997. These values are defined in a unit called 'Foster people's equality, diversity and rights'. There are three main principles, which are intended to enable people to develop or keep high levels of self-esteem and to develop their full potential. These principles are set out in Figure 4.4.

The values set out in the NVQ standards clearly define caring as a service that must meet people's emotional and social needs – not just their physical needs. The policy for good practice is defined in NVQ standards, as set out in the box on page 117:

Principles of good practice

The national occupational standards in the areas of health and social care are built on the following agreed principles of good practice:

- balancing people's rights with their responsibilities to others and to wider society, and challenging those who affect the rights of others
- promoting the values of equality and diversity, acknowledging the personal beliefs and preferences of others and promoting anti-discriminatory practice
- maintaining the confidentiality of information, provided that this does not place others at risk
- recognising the effect of the wider social, political and economic context on health and social well-being and on people's development
- enabling people to develop to their full potential, to be as autonomous and self-managing as possible, and to have a voice and be heard
- recognising and promoting health and social well-being as a positive concept
- balancing the needs of people who use services with the resources available and exercising financial probity (honesty and trustworthiness)
- developing and maintaining effective relationships with people and maintaining the integrity of these relationships through setting appropriate role boundaries
- developing oneself and one's own practice to improve the quality of services offered
- working within statutory and organisational frameworks.

NVQ in Care Standards (Joint awarding bodies 1997)

The role of the care worker

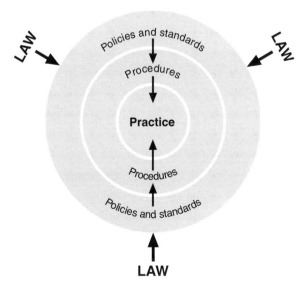

Figure 4.5 Law, policies and procedures influence practice

By itself, the law cannot make sure that discrimination doesn't happen, or that people's rights are always respected. It can be difficult to prove that discrimination has happened and it can be costly in time, energy and money to fight legal battles. Policies and standards of good practice can provide an effective way of making sure that rights are taken seriously. Care services are inspected to make sure that the quality of the service they offer is acceptable. Each service will have policies on equal opportunities and confidentiality to guide staff behaviour.

Laws provide the background to policy making, and policies and standards guide managers when they design procedures. Staff will be given set procedures to follow to ensure that clients' rights are respected.

DO IT

Describe which laws, policies and procedures affect care work settings in respect to individuals' rights, responsibilities and personal beliefs.

While you are at work or on placement, ask if you can have a copy of your agency's policies and procedures which are relevant to rights and responsibilities. These will include those relating to equal opportunity, confidentiality and perhaps training. There may also be written procedures for record-keeping and dealing with enquiries. Design your own diagram listing the relevant law and the policies and procedures that guide your practice with respect to rights, responsibilities and clients' personal beliefs.

Sources of information on rights and responsibilities

One way in which care workers can help people is by providing information. Services, rights and benefits change from time to time and from one location to another. People usually need help to find out which services they may be entitled to or can pay for. The sources of information shown in Figure 4.6 may help carers with detailed information on current support services, rights and benefits.

Figure 4.6   Sources of information that may help carers

The balance of rights and responsibilities

Clients have a right to choose a lifestyle and beliefs, but a person's lifestyle and beliefs must not reduce the quality of other people's lives. Rights are balanced with responsibilities – people have a right to act as they wish, but not a right to cause problems for others. For example, people have a right to smoke, even though smoking causes serious illnesses, including heart disease and cancer. But they don't have a right to make others breathe their smoke and risk their own health.

People in care have a right to:	People in care have a responsibility to:
have control and independence in their own lives	help others to be independent and not try to control other people
be valued and respected	value and respect others
maintain their own beliefs and lifestyle	respect the different beliefs and lifestyles of others
make choices and take risks	not interfere with others, or put others or themselves at risk.
not be discriminated against	not discriminate against others
confidentiality in personal matters.	respect confidentiality for others.

Situations involving rights and responsibility

Consider the following situation. Graham is a 38-year-old man with learning disabilities. He gets great pleasure from eating, and particularly enjoys sweet things such as honey and jam. Graham is overweight and the staff think that he should go on a diet for health reasons. Graham cannot understand their ideas and becomes angry if he can't follow his usual eating pattern.

What are Graham's rights and responsibilities? In general, Graham has the right to choose to eat a lot of sweet things. He also has a right to be overweight! People may choose their own diet and lifestyle. But Graham has a responsibility not to behave in a way that might injure himself or shorten his life. Graham doesn't understand the issues of diet and health, so it is difficult for the staff or for Graham to decide what should be done.

In situations like this, an **advocate** should be appointed to help decide on the balance of rights and responsibilities. An advocate is someone who tries to understand the needs and wishes of a client, and then argues for them. In Graham's situation the advocate might argue that Graham should continue to enjoy his favourite food, but that the care staff should keep an eye on his weight in case this becomes more of a risk to him later.

The balance between rights and responsibility is often hard to decide. Sometimes it is important to involve an advocate for the client, and there is often a need for negotiation and problem-solving work. Care workers should not have to make decisions on their own – they should at least be able to get advice from managers before having to negotiate about rights and responsibilities.

Confidentiality

Confidentiality is an important right for all clients. It is important because:

- clients may not trust a carer if the carer does not keep information confidential
- clients may not feel valued or able to keep their self-esteem if their private details are shared with others
- clients' safety may be put at risk if details of their property or their habits are widely known.
- a professional service that maintains respect for individuals must keep private information confidential
- there are legal requirements to keep personal records confidential.

Trust is important. If you know that your carer won't pass things on, you may feel able to tell him or her what you really think and feel.

Self-esteem is involved, because if your carer promises to keep things confidential, it shows that he or she respects and values you; it shows that you matter.

Safety is an issue, because you may have to leave your home empty at times. If other people know where you keep your money and when you are out, someone may be tempted to break in. Carers need to keep personal details confidential to protect clients' property and personal safety.

Medical practitioners and lawyers have always strictly observed confidentiality as part of their professional role. If clients are to receive a professional service, care workers must copy this example.

Legal requirements

The Data Protection Act 1984 and the Access to Personal Files Act 1987 establish legal obligations to keep recorded information confidential. All agencies will have policies and procedures on recorded information.

Boundaries to confidentiality

Clients have a right to confidentiality, but also a responsibility in relation to the rights of others. Confidentiality often has to be kept within boundaries, or even broken when the rights of others must be balanced with the client's rights. Keeping confidentiality within boundaries means that a carer may tell his or her manager something learned in confidence. The information is not made public, so it is still partly confidential. Information may need to be passed to managers when:

- there is a significant risk of harm to a client
- a client might be abused
- there is a significant risk of harm to others
- there is a risk to the carer's health or well-being.

Some examples of these situations are given below.

- An old person in the community refuses to put her heating on in winter; she may be at risk of harm from the cold.

● A person explains that his son takes his money – he might be suffering financial abuse.
● A person lives in a very dirty house infested with mice and rats. This may be creating a public health risk.
● A person is very aggressive, placing the carer at risk.

CASE STUDY ETHEL

Ethel is 88 years old and receives home care. One day she says to you: 'Keep this confidential, but I don't take my tablets – I'm saving them so that I can take them all at once and finish my life if my pain gets worse.' Ethel manages to say this before you can tell her that some things can't be kept confidential.

Do you have to keep this information confidential? Ethel has a right to confidentiality, but she has a responsibility not to involve other people in any harm she may do to herself – she doesn't have a right to involve you. The information about the tablets should be shared with managers and her GP, who can discuss the matter with Ethel.

Ethel's neighbour stops you as you are leaving one day. The neighbour asks: 'How is Ethel, is she taking her tablets?'

Can you tell the neighbour of your worries? Before giving any information to anyone, carers have to ask the question: 'Does this person have a need to know?' A need to know is different from wanting to know. Ethel's neighbour might just be nosy, and it would be wrong to break confidentiality without an important reason. If the GP knows Ethel doesn't take her tablets, this information may save her life. But the neighbour does not need to be told.

DO IT

Identify how a care worker can best promote individuals' rights and deal with differences and tensions between rights and responsibilities.

Design a poster showing a list of clients' rights and responsibilities. The poster should explain how a care worker might develop his or her own practice to promote individuals' rights.

Design a second poster displaying an idea for getting guidance on balancing rights and responsibilities. The posters could be presented to other students, and a summary of ideas could be listed to meet the assessment criteria.

Effective communication

Forms of communication

Working effectively as a carer involves learning about the individual people you work with. Learning about other people includes listening to what they say and watching the messages that people send with their body language. The skills of listening, taking part in conversation and understanding other people's body language help us to understand each other and to build relationships. It is not always easy to get to know people.

Body language

Within a few seconds of meeting your clients you will usually be able to tell what they are feeling. You will know whether they are tired, happy, angry, sad or frightened - even before they say anything. We can usually guess how people feel by looking at their body language.

Another term for body language is **non-verbal communication**. 'Non-verbal' means without words, so this refers to the messages we send without putting them into words. We send messages using our eyes, the tone of our voice, our facial expression, gestures with our hands and arms, the angle of our head, the way we sit or stand – known as body posture – and the tension in our muscles.

When a person is sad, he or she may signal this emotion with eyes that look down – there may be tension in the face, and the mouth will be closed. The muscles in the person's shoulders are likely to be relaxed, but the face and neck may show muscle tension. A happy person will have wide-open eyes that make contact with you – he or she will smile. When people are excited they move their arms and hands to signal their excitement.

Most people can recognise such emotions in the non-verbal behaviour of others. The skill that care workers need is to go one stage further, and understand the messages that they send with their own bodies when working with other people.

Verbal communication

When we talk to people we have to start the conversation off. Usually we start with a greeting or asking how someone is. Conversations have a beginning, a middle and an end, and this means that we have to create the right kind of atmosphere for a conversation at the beginning. We might need to help someone relax, so we might need to show that we are friendly and relaxed. When we end a conversation we usually say something like 'See you soon'. Ending a conversation has to involve the right feelings.

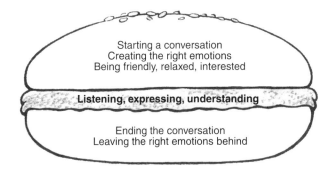

Starting a conversation
Creating the right emotions
Being friendly, relaxed, interested

Listening, expressing, understanding

Ending the conversation
Leaving the right emotions behind

Figure 4.7   The conversation sandwich – beginnings and endings are important

The communication cycle

Communication is not just about giving information to people. While we are having a conversation we go through a process or 'cycle' of:

● hearing what another person says
● watching the other person's non-verbal messages

- having feelings
- beginning to understand the other person
- sending a message back to the other person.

The communication process might look something like the diagram in Figure 4.8.

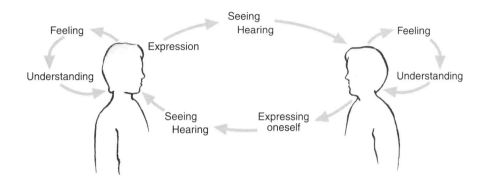

Figure 4.8   The communication cycle involves more than just talking

Listening skills

We can understand other people's emotions by watching their non-verbal communication; but we can't usually understand what is on someone's mind without being good at listening.

Listening is not just hearing the sounds that people make when they talk. Listening skills involve hearing another person's words, thinking about what they mean, then deciding what to reply to the other person. Some people call this process **active listening**. As well as thinking carefully and remembering what a client says, good listeners will make sure that their non-verbal behaviour shows interest.

Skilled listening involves:

- looking interested and ready to listen
- hearing what is said
- remembering what is said
- checking understanding with the other person.

Think it through

Take a piece of paper, divide it into four areas and write out four headings: 'Where I live', 'An important thing that happened in the past', 'Something I am looking forward to', and 'Where I work or study'. Any other titles will do, as long as you can talk in detail about the areas. Think through what you can tell another person about yourself under each heading, then get together with a colleague who has also planned what to say.

Explain your thoughts on the four areas to each other. This should take at least ten minutes. Then see what you can remember about the other person, and how detailed and accurate your memory is! How good are you at understanding and remembering?

Confirming information and reflection

It is usually easier to understand people who are similar to ourselves. We can learn about different people by checking our understanding of what we have heard.

Checking understanding involves hearing what the other person says and asking questions. Another way is to put what a person has just said into your own words and say it to them to check that you did understand. Sometimes this idea of checking our understanding is called 'reflection', because we reflect the other person's ideas.

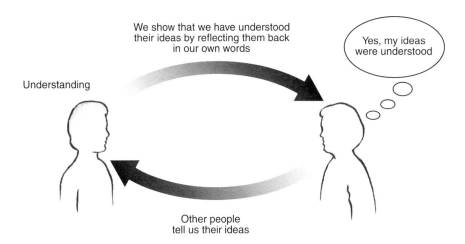

Figure 4.9 'Reflecting' back to the other person proves you have listened

DO IT

Describe the different forms that communication may take.

Make a list of non-verbal ways of sending messages, and another list of the processes involved in verbal communication. Then get together with a small group of colleagues and try a listening and conversation task like the one suggested on page 123. Several members of the group should observe the conversation and record examples of verbal and non-verbal behaviour. Change over so that everyone has a chance to observe and list examples of different forms of communication.

Cultural differences

Skilled carers use a range of conversational techniques when working with others. These include being sensitive to cultural differences and social contexts.

Culture means the history, customs and ways that people learn as they grow up. The expressions that people use and the meanings of non-verbal signs can vary from one culture to another. People from different regions of Britain use different expressions. Non-verbal signs vary from culture to culture. White middle class people often expect others to 'look them in the eye' while talking. If a person looks down or away, it is a sign that he or she may be dishonest, or perhaps sad. In other cultures, for example among some Black communities, looking down or away when talking is a sign of respect – a way to show you are using your listening skills!

Care workers have to be careful not to assume that statements and signs always have the same meaning. Culture, race, class and geographical location can alter what things mean.

Keeping a conversation going (interaction)

It can be hard to get to know people unless you keep a conversation going. Starting a conversation is often easy – we ask someone how he or she is today, we introduce ourselves or we ask a question. If we remember the client, we can mention things that have been talked about before, such as 'How did you get on at the dentist yesterday?'

Once a conversation has started, the trick is to keep it going long enough. Skills that help with this are turn taking, using non-verbal communication to show interest, being good at asking questions and using silence at the right times.

Turn-taking in conversations means taking turns to listen and talk. If you are trying to get to know a client you will probably do less talking and more listening. People normally show when they want you to talk by slowing down the rate at which they speak their last few words, changing the tone of the voice slightly and looking away from you. The person will then stop speaking and look directly at you. If you are sensitive to these messages you will be ready to ask a question or say something that keeps the conversation going.

Showing interest involves giving the other person your full attention. Appropriate body language includes:

- eye contact – looking at the other person's eyes
- smiling – looking friendly rather than 'cold' in expression
- hand movements and gestures that show interest
- slight nods of the head to mean 'I see', or 'I understand', or 'I agree'.

It is important to ask the kind of questions that encourage people to talk. Questions that don't do so are called closed questions, and are not very useful when trying to get to know people. Questions like 'How old are you?' are closed, because there is only one simple answer the person can give: 'I'm eight', 'I'm 84', and so on. Closed questions don't lead on to discussion. 'Do you like butter?' is a closed question – the person can only say yes or no.

Open questions encourage people to think and discuss their thoughts. A question like 'How do you feel about the food here?' asks the other person to think about the food and then discuss it.

The more we know about someone the more we can be sensitive about the type of questions we ask. Some people don't mind questions about their feelings or opinions, but dislike questions that ask for personal information. Getting to know people often takes time and usually involves a number of short conversations, rather than one long conversation.

Sometimes a pause in conversation can make people feel embarrassed, but silence can mean 'let's think' or 'I need time to think'. Silent pauses can show respect and interest, and don't always stop the conversation. Some carers use pauses in a conversation to show that they are listening and thinking about what the client has said.

The skills used in individual communication are also needed for communication in formal and informal group situations. (See Chapter 6, page 180, for more information on formal and informal situations.)

Do It

Describe the stages in communication and methods used to communicate clearly and effectively.

Watch two people having a conversation about a topic that they are both interested in. If possible, videotape this conversation so that you can study it more than once.

Describe the stages you can see in the course of the conversation – do they fit the idea of the 'communication sandwich'? Can you find an example of the 'communication cycle' in what you have watched?

Give examples of verbal and non-verbal communication that showed people were listening. Describe good examples of :

- eye contact
- facial expression
- hand movements and gestures
- head movements

- questions
- silences
- reflecting back.

Constraints on effective communication

There are three main ways that communication becomes blocked:

1. A person can't see, hear or receive the message.
2. A person can't make sense of the message.
3. A person misunderstands the message.

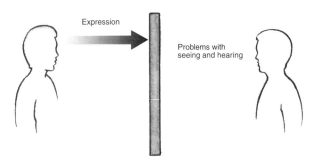

Examples of the first kind of block, where people don't receive the communication, include visual disabilities, hearing disabilities, and environmental problems such as poor lighting, noisy environments, and speaking from too far away.

Figure 4.10   Environmental problems like noise and poor light can create communication barriers

Examples where people may not be able to make sense of the message include:

- the use of different languages, including signed languages
- the use of different terms in language, such as **jargon** (technical language), **slang** (different people using different terms), or **dialect** (different people making different sounds)
- physical and intellectual disabilities, such as being ill, or suffering memory loss, or learning disability.

Reasons for misunderstanding a message include:

- cultural influences – different cultures interpret non-verbal and verbal messages, and humour, in different ways

- assumptions about people – about race, gender, disability and other groupings
- emotional differences – very angry or very happy people may misinterpret communication from others
- social context – statements and behaviour that are understood by friends and family may not be understood by strangers.

Because people are so different from one another, the communication cycle can easily be blocked if professional listening skills are not used.

The effects of communication difficulties

Constantly being unable to communicate with others can make it very difficult to meet any of personal needs.

Human needs	Communication difficulties
Developing your potential	It is difficult to develop well without communication with others.
Self-esteem	It is difficult to value your life if people don't communicate with you.
Belonging	It is difficult to feel that you belong if you can't communicate with others.
Safety	You may feel threatened if people do not understand you.
Physical	If you do not communicate hunger, thirst or pain – people may not respond even to your physical needs.

Labelling and stereotyping

People who have difficulty hearing or seeing are sometimes assumed to be awkward or mentally limited. Older people are sometimes seen as demented or confused if they do not answer questions appropriately.

People can also be labelled or stereotyped when they use different language systems. Some people will shout at those who don't speak the same language, as if increasing the volume would help. People who sign to communicate are sometimes thought to be odd or to have learning difficulties, because they don't respond to written or spoken English.

Cultural differences can also lead to labelling and stereotyping. One person may be using gestures and eye contact to show respect, but another person may misinterpret the messages as aggression or disrespect.

Do It

Identify constraints on effective communication and the effect this has on the individual.

Think about the care setting where you work or are on placement. Make a list of all the constraints that affect people in this setting. You may list these constraints under the following headings.

- Necessary communication (seeing and hearing).
- Making sense of communication (appropriate language).
- Correctly interpreting communication (assumptions and emotions).

What effects do you think each constraint could have on a client? Make another list of the effects that bad communication could have.

Ways of overcoming difficulties

Visual disability

- Use language to describe things.
- Assist people to touch things (e.g. touch your face to recognise you).
- Explain details that sighted people might take for granted.
- Check what people can see (many registered blind people can see shapes, or tell light from dark).
- Check glasses, other aids and equipment.

Hearing disability

- Don't shout, keep to normal clear speech and make sure your face is visible for people who can lip-read.
- Show pictures, or write messages.
- Learn to sign (for people who use signed languages).
- Ask for help from or employ a communicator or interpreter for signed languages.
- Check hearing aids and equipment.

Environmental constraints

- Check and improve lighting.
- Reduce noise.
- Move to a quieter or better lit room.
- Move to smaller groups to see and hear more easily.

Language differences

- Communicate using pictures, diagrams and non-verbal signs
- Use translators or interpreters.
- Be careful not to make assumptions or stereotype.

Jargon, slang and dialects

- Re-word your messages – find different ways of saying things.
- Speak in short, clear sentences.

Physical and intellectual disabilities

- Use pictures and signs as well as clear, simple speech.
- Be calm and patient.
- Set up group meetings where people can share interests, experiences or reminiscences.
- Check that people do not become isolated.

Misunderstandings

- Watch out for different cultural interpretations.
- Avoid making assumptions about or discriminating against people who are different.
- Use reflective listening techniques to check that your understanding is correct.
- Stay calm and try to calm people who are angry or excited.
- Be sensitive to different social settings and the form of communication that would be most appropriate.

DO IT

Explore the ways that communication may be modified to meet the individual's level of understanding, personal beliefs and preferences, culture and background.

Think of a client you have worked with. Without using his or her real name or details, describe the type of language the person uses, his or her personal beliefs, lifestyle and preferences, culture and background. Explain how you might change the way you speak or communicate with this person as compared with speaking to your own friends.

DO IT

Review the types of support available for overcoming communication difficulties.

Think about the care setting you work in or are placed in. Make a list of the communication difficulties that affect people in this setting (you may have already made a list like this). Think of ways in which support can be provided to help overcome communication difficulties, and design a poster explaining these forms of support. Your poster could be designed to appeal to care workers rather than the public. You could present your poster to other students, after you have shared ideas with others. and make a full summary of types of support.

Communicating formally in care settings

Working as a carer involves being part of a large network of people. Each person you work with will have a network of friends, relatives and other professional people who communicate with him or her. You will be working with other people including professionals and managers who also work with your client.

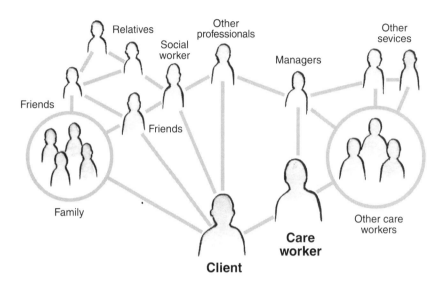

Figure 4.11 Care workers and clients are part of a network of communication

It is an important task to make sure that information gets to the people who need it, and that personal information does not go to those who have no right to know it. Carers may also need to establish how important information is, in order to prioritise it.

The law on information

The **Data Protection Act 1984** was passed to protect people's rights over the way information about them can be stored. The Act originally covered only information stored on computer, but the **Access to Personal Files Act 1987** extended the law to cover manual (paper-based) records kept by local authorities. The **Access to Health Records Act 1990** extended the law to manual records kept by health providers. Private and voluntary services that obtain information on clients from local authority or health services are usually required to keep manual records confidential.

The Data Protection Act requires that anyone who holds computer records must be registered and that:

- all personal information must be fairly and legally obtained
- there must be a specified reason for recording information
- information must be kept confidentially and used only in relation to the reason it was collected

- records should contain only necessary information
- personal information should be accurate and up-to-date
- information should not be held for longer than necessary
- people have a right to know what is recorded about them, and to have records corrected or removed if necessary.
- records must be kept securely.

Whether care workers are working with computerised records or not, they should always follow the principles below:

Good practice: information

✓ Keep information confidential, and only pass information to people who have a right and a need to know it.

✓ Record information accurately.

✓ Keep records safely so that they can't be altered or lost, or seen by people who do not have a need to use them.

Access to records

Not all care staff may have access to all the information about clients. For instance, regulations under the Registered Homes Act 1984 require that residential homes keep a case record for each resident. Some homes maintain personal files on residents to which all permanent staff have access, although some sections may be restricted to senior staff.

The information available to all permanent staff may include personal details such as the person's doctor, next of kin, age and religion. Details about personal finance, action to be taken after a resident's death, and legal arrangements, may be restricted to managers because other staff don't need this information in order to care for residents.

Personal files must be kept for at least three years after a client leaves care. Each home or service will have its own policies on recording information and on who has a need to know it.

Confidentiality and the need to know

Good care practice involves asking clients if we can let other people know things they tell us. It would be wrong to pass on even the date of a client's birthday without asking him or her first. Some clients might not want others to know about a birthday – Jehovah's Witnesses believe that it is wrong to celebrate birthdays! Whatever we know about a client should be kept private unless the client allows us to share the information.

The exception to this rule is that information can be passed on when others have a right and a need to know it. Some examples of people who have a need to know about your work with clients are:

- your manager – he or she may need to help you make decisions that affect the client
- your colleagues – these people may be working with the same client
- other professionals – they may also be working with your client and need to be kept up-to-date.

Giving information

When information is passed to other professionals it should be passed on with the understanding that they keep it confidential. It is important to check that other people are who they say they are. If you answer the telephone and someone says he is a social worker or other professional you should explain that you must phone him back before giving any information. Phoning back enables you to be sure that you are talking to someone at a particular number, or within a particular organisation. If you meet a person you don't know, you should ask for proof of identity before passing on any information.

Relatives will often say that they have a right to know about clients. Sometimes it is possible to ask relatives to discuss issues directly with the client rather than giving information yourself, for example:

Relative: Has the doctor said anything more about my mother's illness?

Care worker: I expect your mother would like to talk to you directly – shall I show you to her room?

It is important to explain that you cannot share confidential information without the client's consent. It will be important to discuss procedures for handling requests for information with your supervisor or manager at work or on placement.

Do it

Describe the relevant legislation and policies which relate to the care worker's responsibility with regard to client information.

Interview your manager at work or on placement, and ask about policies with respect to the confidentiality of records, the accurate recording of information, and the safety and security of records. Your workplace may have forms to help to make sure accurate information is collected, passwords for computer access, or locked filing cabinets to make sure records are secure. Make a list of all the things you can do to help keep records safe, accurate and secure. State which legislation covers the need for confidential, accurate and secure records.

Accuracy of information

Because social care work involves communicating with complex networks of people, it is vital that information is carefully checked and recorded.

When you take phone calls or other messages it is vital that key details are written down, because your memory for what was said will soon disappear. Compare the following two notes in Figure 4.12.

The first note is hard to read and contains little information. The second note follows a set of headings, which helps the worker to record accurate information.

The dangers of inaccurate information include:

- delays in meeting people's needs
- not being able to follow up enquiries

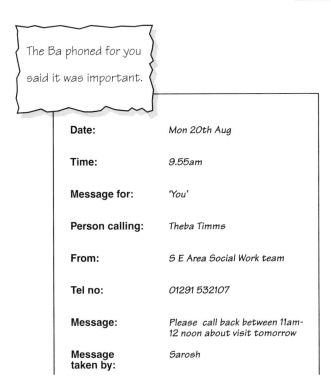

The Ba phoned for you said it was important.

Date:	Mon 20th Aug
Time:	9.55am
Message for:	'You'
Person calling:	Theba Timms
From:	S E Area Social Work team
Tel no:	01291 532107
Message:	Please call back between 11am–12 noon about visit tomorrow
Message taken by:	Sarosh

Figure 4.12 Two telephone messages

- watching what clients do
- listening to what they say
- asking clients questions
- asking relatives or friends for information
- asking other professional workers for information.

Recording information

When recording personal information it is important to be as factual and accurate as possible. Say just what you see and what you hear.

It is important to describe only the facts or the events that happened, without giving your own interpretation or saying how you feel about the person. Some examples to illustrate this principle are given in Chapter 1.

- making mistakes with arrangements for people's care
- missing meetings or important arrangements
- not being able to organise services for clients properly
- other professional workers not having the right information.

When writing information down, it is a good idea to check the spelling of names and repeat phone numbers and key information back to the person in order to check that they are correct.

Care workers sometimes need to search for information in order to help meet a person's care needs. Information can be gained by:

Do IT

Demonstrate effective skills in receiving and transmitting information.

Watch a short video presentation of a conversation between two people (this could be from an acted drama, or from a real-life documentary). Write down what you heard and saw as if you were writing a report about a client. Describe the programme without giving your interpretation or evaluation of the characters; and without recording the conversation word by word.

Storing and retrieving records

Personal records and information may be kept electronically on a computer disk, or manually in handwritten or printed files. Whichever way records are kept, there should be a range of security measures to make sure the information stays confidential and is not lost or inappropriately altered.

Manual records

- Keep records in a locked room or a locked cupboard to which only authorised staff have access.
- Do not take records out of a particular room or area, to avoid the risk of their being lost or left where others might see them.
- File records using a system such as an alphabetical one so that they can be found easily.
- Find out about the policy as to who should update or change details.
- It may be good practice to record the initials of the person who made the records and the date of any changes.

Electronic records

- Keep a back-up copy in case the original is lost or damaged.
- Use a password security check to ensure that only appropriate staff have access.
- Find out about the policy on the printing of details so that hard copies don't get lost, or seen by others.
- Find out about the policy on who is authorised to update or change records. The recording system must prevent information being altered or lost by accident.
- Print out faxed documents in an appropriate confidential area and keep them in a manual system to prevent inappropriate people having access to confidential material.

DO IT

Demonstrate how to store and retrieve records both manually and electronically.

If you have access to manual and electronic systems at work, you could demonstrate and record the procedures you use in the presence of a supervisor. Your supervisor can then confirm your are competent at performing the procedures.

If you are not permitted to access records, you could still ask about and record the steps that a person with access to records would take, together with the safeguards in place. You could then simulate the use of an alphabetical filing system, and view spreadsheets or other database records on a computer.

Protection of individuals from abuse

The word 'abuse' covers a wide range of behaviour. Abuse can include criminal acts of violence, or acts of neglect. Abuse can be caused by the way organisations work, as well as by individuals. Carers need to understand their own and other's behaviour in order to minimise abuse in care settings and care relationships.

Forms of abuse

- **Physical abuse** includes hitting, pushing, pulling, restraining or causing pain or distress by physical actions.
- **Sexual abuse** means sexually exploiting or humiliating others.
- **Emotional abuse** includes bullying, blaming, threatening and damaging others' feelings of self-esteem (this is sometimes called psychological abuse).
- **Financial abuse** involves taking other's property or money, theft and the exploitation of other people's resources.
- **Neglect** means not giving food or physical care, or not giving attention.

Causes of abuse

People abuse children, adults, older people or relatives for complicated reasons. Some different causes of abusive behaviour are listed below.

- **Stress:** When people become tired or exhausted they are more likely to lose their temper – perhaps resulting in emotional abuse, physical abuse or neglect.
- **Past learning:** Some people have experienced abuse in their past and have come to regard physical or emotional abuse as a way of relating to others.
- **Power:** Some people desire to, or believe they have a right to, control and exploit others. A desire for power may motivate sexual abuse as well as bullying and financial abuse. Some people believe that their needs and wishes should come before the rights of others.
- **Social and organisational systems:** Clients who are young, or otherwise unable to protect themselves, are vulnerable. Where staff think they ought to control these vulnerable people, there is a risk of abuse. If staff also become stressed because of lack of time or too much work, they may start to abuse their clients.

Abuse in care settings is often due to stress and a lack of supervision or other systems to prevent abuse. It would be wrong to think that all abuse is caused by individuals who intend to harm other people – when people are under pressure it is easy to neglect the needs of others.

Signs of abuse

It is important not to jump to conclusions, but the following list of possible signs of abuse might alert you to the risk that someone had been physically or emotionally abused. You should always discuss issues with a supervisor or manager before concluding that a person has been abused.

Physical signs

- Bruising or other injuries that are not explained.
- Bruises that look as if they have been caused by objects, such as belts, buckles, shoes or hands.
- Multiple small bruises - which may have been caused by poking.
- Black eyes.
- Bruising to the ears.
- Burns that could have come from a cigarette.

- Burns or scalds in unusual areas of the body.
- Marks to wrists, arms or legs, which could mean the person has been restrained.
- Ulcers or bed sores in older people.
- Unusual sexual behaviour.

Emotional signs

- A client becoming quiet and withdrawn.
- A client having problems with sleeping.
- Children with a sudden change in sexual behaviour or obsession with sexual language.
- Children who are unwilling to change their clothes or participate in sports.
- A child appearing tense or frightened with a particular adult.
- A child finding excuses not to go home.
- Depression or fear of making decisions or choices.
- Disappearance of benefit, pension or bank account books.
- Difficulty getting to see the client (relatives always find a reason why he or she is not available).
- New financial agreements, or arrangements that the client doesn't understand.
- Relatives speaking in a negative way about the client.

Figure 4.13   How would it feel to be in her shoes?

The effects of abuse

Abuse can cause long-term damage to a person, and can limit a person's ability to develop his or her potential. The effects of abuse can vary from person to person, but some likely effects are listed below:

- fear and anger
- loss of self-confidence
- self-destructiveness
- copying the abusive behaviour
- mental illness.

- withdrawal and depression
- loss of self-esteem
- attention seeking
- increased dependency

> ### *DO IT*
>
> **Describe the forms and effects of abuse.**
>
> Make a table of the forms of abuse that could affect the client group you work with. List the possible effects each form of abuse might have on clients.

The law and abuse

Criminal law covers many serious offences such as assault, sexual offences, theft and crimes against property. The police have powers to investigate and take action where many forms of abuse are suspected.

The Children Act 1989 requires that local authority Social Service departments provide protection from abuse for children in their area. In an emergency, a social worker can apply to a magistrate for an Emergency Protection Order to care for a child. The police can also take action to protect a child. Protection Orders are granted if there is reasonable evidence to show that a child may suffer 'significant harm'. Later, court hearings decide what should happen in the longer term. Very often, social workers work with families to prevent abuse and to protect children.

The Mental Health Act 1983 enables Social Service departments to assume responsibility for people who are not able to be responsible for their own affairs. This is called guardianship. However, for adults there is no specific legal duty to protect people from abuse.

Most Social Service departments will have procedures and guidelines to enable them to investigate suspected abuse of vulnerable adults. Where an adult may be at risk, a case conference may be called so that a plan of action can be worked out.

Residential homes and nursing homes are registered with social or health services. All homes are subject to inspection, and inspection units can investigate allegations of abuse, with the power to close unsatisfactory homes. Most homes will have detailed complaints procedures that may be used to challenge incidents of abuse.

What to do if you witness abuse

If you see or hear any abuse you must report what you have seen or heard to your supervisor or manager, who will help you follow the correct procedures. Your manager will make a decision about how to follow up your information. If you think your manager is involved in the abuse, you should report the information to someone more senior.

Sometimes a range of professionals may need to be involved. If there are injuries, a medical examination may be necessary. Decisions about investigating abuse should be taken by senior staff. They will decide what risks can be taken, what should be kept confidential and whether legal action is appropriate.

Very often your information and observations about possible abuse will be shared within the team of people who work with a client. A case conference may be necessary to decide on the best course of action. You must record exactly what happened. Your memory for details will change with time, so it is important that you make a record soon after the event. Your work setting may have a form or a series of headings to help you. Your reports should state just what you saw or heard and any actions you took, not give opinions or try to judge who was right or wrong.

If you find it difficult to write a report, you could describe what happened to another person who might write the report and ask you to check it and sign it. If no report is made, it can be difficult for managers or social workers to take further action.

Do it

Identify legislation, guidelines and procedures which relate to minimising levels and effects of abuse.

Ask your supervisor or manager at work for details of complaints procedures, report forms or procedures and guidelines that could be used to report any concerns about abuse. Make a list of the steps staff should take if they were worried that a client might be abused.

Methods of preventing and dealing with abuse

Abuse can happen in any setting or situation, but some common situations where abuse can occur are listed below.

Abuse of children may happen where:

- parents put their own needs first – before the needs of their children
- parents or carers want to dominate others
- parents have had difficult childhoods or been abused themselves
- families are living in stressful circumstances
- families have a history of violence.

Abuse of adults may happen where:

- carers feel stressed because they have had to change their lifestyle
- the client shows difficult or challenging behaviour such as aggression, or has serious communication problems
- carers have no support
- carers are dependent on drugs or alcohol
- carers have no privacy.

Abuse in care settings may happen where:

- staff are poorly trained or untrained
- there is little supervision or management support
- staff feel isolated
- staff are stressed – perhaps by their workload
- staff feel that clients should be controlled
- relationship and communication skills are poor.

To prevent abuse, it is important that carers receive support and guidance for working with difficult or stressful situations. Some abuse in the community happens because parents or carers do not have enough support or help. One way of preventing abuse to adults is to provide respite care. This is short-term care for a client, to enable his or her carers to have a break.

Staff working in care can take steps to prevent abuse by:

- attending regular supervision and team discussions
- understanding clients' needs and care plans
- learning how to cope with stressful situations, including challenging behaviour
- understanding the risks that can lead to abuse
- believing others when abuse is reported
- challenging bad practice and reporting abuse.

It is important to work as a team member in order to understand client needs, and to cope with the stress that challenging behaviour can cause. Both younger and adult clients can make offensive remarks or physically attack care staff. It is critically important that care staff never decide to 'get their own back' – clients of care services are vulnerable. Most have low or insecure levels of self-esteem. If carers return physical or verbal abuse, they are committing an act of abuse themselves. If you work in a care role you have a responsibility never to lose your temper or return abuse when you are with clients.

To avoid reacting to stress and abusing clients, it is important to learn to:

- prevent others from becoming stressed and aggressive
- stay calm in tense situations
- help others to be calm
- use assertiveness skills, rather than becoming aggressive
- know when you should seek assistance.

Staff training and supervision may help with the development of these skills.

If clients tell you about abuse that has happened to them, it is very important to take what they say seriously and to believe them. It may often be unpleasant to listen to stories of abuse, but it is important not to give in to these feelings and damage the person further by not taking him or her seriously.

If you see or hear other staff failing to respect the rights of clients, it is important to challenge and, if appropriate, report what you have seen. It is vital that you know the procedures you should follow in your work setting.

DO IT

Describe the methods of preventing and dealing with abuse.

Make a list of the skills you need or might develop to help you prevent and cope with abuse within your work setting. Make a second list of the support your work setting needs to supply in order to help prevent and deal with abuse.

Referral to professionals

CASE STUDY MRS MCKENDRICK AND JAMIE

Mrs McKendrick lives alone but has regular home care. One day she says, 'Don't tell anyone, but it makes me so upset – my son is always helping himself to my pension money. But I don't want anything to happen to him – he's my son.'

Jamie is nine years old. He often has bruising to his face, and recently you have noticed bruising on the back of his legs. Jamie has become quiet lately and when asked about his marks he will only say that he has been in a fight.

In both these situations there is a serious possibility that the clients are being abused. In both situations it would be vital to report what you had seen or heard. Both situations may be complex; but both Mrs McKendrick and Jamie need any abuse to stop. If you report what you know, it is likely that Social Services will become further involved.

Professional assessment of the situation may result in new services being made available to both clients' carers. Perhaps Mrs McKendrick's pension can be managed differently. Jamie's family may need a range of support services, together with careful monitoring of his situation. Your own role is to report and seek help – you should not try to sort out these types of situations by yourself.

Preventing and dealing with abuse can often require professional skills, knowledge and experience. Always refer situations to your manager or other senior staff as soon as possible.

A wide range of services may become involved in preventing and dealing with abuse. Social Services can provide social worker support to assess, advise and plan appropriate care packages. Care packages may involve residential, day care and community care services. Some services may be provided by the voluntary or private sectors. The NSPCC (National Society for the Prevention of Cruelty to Children) may enquire into potential abuse of children. The police will enforce the law. Clients are sometimes unable to explain what is happening to them because of disability or dementia. In this situation, an advocate may be appointed to argue for the rights of the person.

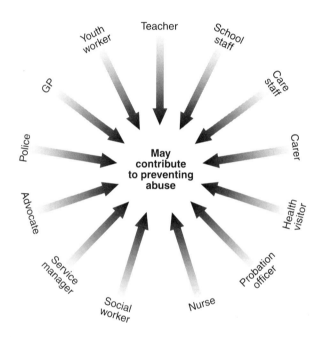

Figure 4.14   People who may be involved in working with abuse

Do It

Explain when and how clients undergoing abuse should be referred to professionals.

If you suspected that a child or adult was being abused by parents, family or relatives, you would report this immediately, but who would you report it to? Ask your manager or supervisor exactly how you should report any suspicions and ask what steps the manager or supervisor might take to gain professional support. Make notes based on your conversation.

PHYSICAL CARE

The hygiene requirements of clients

The skin is the largest organ of the body. It provides a complete covering and protection for the body, and needs to be kept clean. The skin consists essentially of two layers, the outer layer called the epidermis and the inner layer, the dermis.

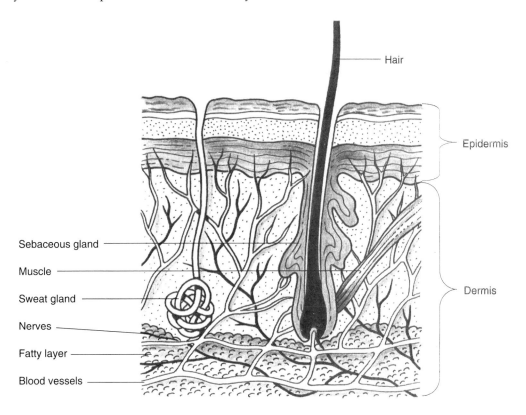

Figure 5.1 A cross-section through the skin

The epidermis is constantly being renewed – it sheds cells and new cells are grown to replace them. You will have noticed how skin cells are shed when you undress or change bed sheets. The skin also contains glands that produce sweat and others (the sebaceous glands) that produce sebum, which is an oily substance that maintains water-proofing of the skin.

Skin becomes dirty because of exposure to the environment, but it also collects dried sweat, dead skin cells and oily sebum. All of these factors combine to provide a breeding ground for an assortment of bacteria. These bacteria can cause offensive odours and lead to infections, so skin needs to be regularly washed so that the bacteria are removed from the skin.

Personal cleanliness is also important because it improves the way people feel about themselves – they tend to feel better after having a bath or shower, so it is good for morale.

Client needs and factors to be considered when planning assistance with hygiene.

Client	Considerations
Older, not disorientated, quite active	Little support needed, may need a check from time to time. Discuss with client the level of assistance required.
Older, disorientated	Needs assistance, extra time necessary to carry out processes, needs supervision.
Client with a physical disability	Unless recently disabled, is likely to have own system of personal hygiene. Discuss the help required, and be guided by the client.
Client with learning disability	May need assistance with particular tasks, depending on level of difficulty. Discuss with client, if possible, the level of help required.

CASE STUDY PHIL

Phil is 25 years old and has spina bifida. He is a wheelchair user, but has achieved a high degree of independence and is as mobile as it is possible to be - he plays sports and has a full-time job. Phil lives in a small group of supported flats. However, his standard of personal hygiene leaves something to be desired. Even after playing basketball or five-a-side football, he does not see the need to bathe or shower. The care staff have begun to get complaints from Phil's workplace and from his team mates. Other tenants in the flats have also demanded that something be done.

1. How do you think this should be handled?
2. Does Phil have the right to decide his own level of hygiene?
3. Is it a different situation if he shares living space with others?
4. Is this the responsibility of the staff?

How to ensure cleanliness

If you are providing care for clients in their own homes, you will need to check:

- that they are able to reach their own bathing facilities – if the bathroom is upstairs it may be necessary to refer your client for special access arrangements such as a stair lift, or a downstairs shower room
- that you have found out about all the equipment that is available to assist clients, and discussed it with them (see Figure 5.2).

Where you are dealing with a client in a residential or supported living setting, it is likely that bathrooms and bathing facilities will have been built to ensure the necessary ease of access.

Client beliefs and preferences

You may find that people have religious beliefs related to maintaining cleanliness, and you must find out about these and make sure that people have the opportunity to carry out cleaning rituals and bathing in whatever way they wish.

- Muslims and Hindus will need to be provided with running water in which to wash, if at all possible. Muslims need to be able to wash their hands, face and feet in running water.
- Hindus will prefer a shower to a bath, and will use a bidet rather than paper to clean themselves after using the toilet.
- Sikhs and Rastafarians believe that hair should not be cut.
- Both Hindus and Muslims will only accept treatment or assistance from a carer of the same gender.

Bathing and showering

Don't forget that sometimes a bathing or showering aid can provide the same sort of help that a care worker could provide, but will enable the client to maintain his or her privacy and dignity. This may be considered preferable to having a carer present. Always make sure

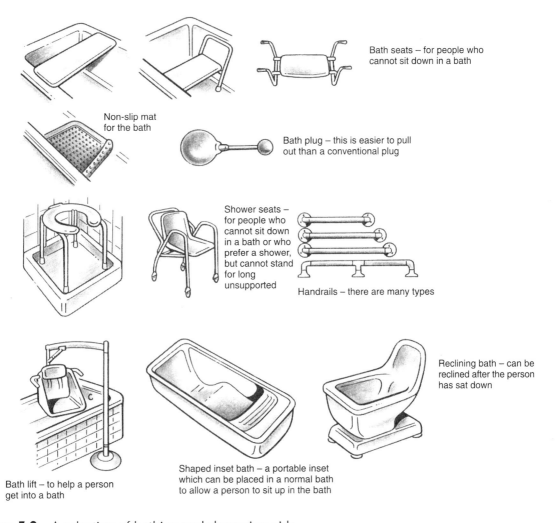

Bath seats – for people who cannot sit down in a bath

Non-slip mat for the bath

Bath plug – this is easier to pull out than a conventional plug

Shower seats – for people who cannot sit down in a bath or who prefer a shower, but cannot stand for long unsupported

Handrails – there are many types

Reclining bath – can be reclined after the person has sat down

Bath lift – to help a person get into a bath

Shaped inset bath – a portable inset which can be placed in a normal bath to allow a person to sit up in the bath

Figure 5.2   A selection of bathing and showering aids

DID YOU KNOW?

It is the responsibility of your employer to carry out risk assessments for all clients who require assistance with personal hygiene. Your employer must ensure that the necessary equipment is available to enable you to assist the client safely. However, it is your responsibility to use it.

that you offer a bath aid as an alternative, if it is available. Some of the aids used are shown in Figure 5.2.

a. Someone who needs a moderate amount of help

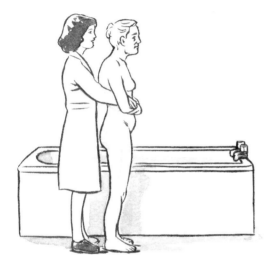

1 Stand behind the client and ask her to clasp her wrists. Put your hands under her armpits and hold her forearms in front of her waist.

2 The client should step into the bath with both feet. Keep your back straight and allow your leg muscles to take the weight. Bend your knees and assist her to lower herself into the bath.

b. Someone who needs only a little help

1 Both you and the client should stand sideways on to the bath. Put your hands under her arms. Help her lift her first leg into the bath.

2 To straighten up, she should lean on your shoulders, step into the bath and grasp the side of the bath. With your hands under her armpits, assist her to lower herself gradually into the bath.

Figure 5.3 Helping a client into a bath

Figure 5.4 Helping an individual into a shower

If you do need to provide manual assistance for someone getting into or out of the bath, you should follow the steps shown in Figure 5.3, being very careful to maintain a straight back throughout the whole process and allowing your legs and thighs to take all of the weight. *You should only follow the technique below if you are assisting a client who is capable of weight bearing, and simply needs some additional support.* Where a client requires a full lift, you must use a hoist or other mechanical aid.

Showering can be a valuable way of people keeping clean. It allows them to stand or sit, unlike a bath, which can avoid the problems some people have climbing in and out of a bath. It is also compatible with the religious views of some people, and the personal preferences of others who like to clean themselves in running water rather than static water. Some clients are able to shower with the assistance of a shower seat or a plastic chair placed in the shower. Others are happy to shower provided that there are grab handles and a non-slip surface.

Washing

If you work with clients who are bedridden, either temporarily because of an illness or permanently, then there may be occasions when bathing or showering is not needed or wanted but a wash would be welcome, and would help to make someone feel a little better.

In all situations, you will need to assess what level of help a client is likely to need, and this should be discussed with the care team and detailed in the client's care plan. The most important views to take into account are those of the client.

Shaving

Shaving is important for most men, because they find it uncomfortable and irritating to have stubble on their faces. If a client is not able to shave himself, you will have to arrange to carry this out. Ask him what kind of help he needs – it may be that he can carry out the shaving himself if you are able to put the soap on his face. Where you need to carry out the whole procedure

A safety razor

An electric razor

Figure 5.5 Find out whether the client shaves with a safety razor or an electric razor

of shaving, you should remember that it is not a straightforward procedure and is not the same for every individual. You will need to establish whether the client shaves with a safety razor or an electric razor.

Mouth care

Mouth care, or oral hygiene, is extremely important for all clients because bacteria will multiply in a mouth that is not kept clean and this will lead to infections.

As long as people maintain a sufficient intake of fluids, the saliva in the mouth normally carries out a great deal of cleaning. However, various illnesses and conditions, as well as the natural ageing process, can change the way the mouth works. Saliva production can be reduced and people may suffer from dry and crusted mouths, and infections such as thrush (a fungal infection), a sore tongue or ulcerated gums or cheeks can develop. A reduction of saliva production will also increase the incidence of bad breath (halitosis).

Oral hygiene involves:

- cleaning teeth or dentures
- cleaning between teeth to ensure the removal of all food particles
- cleaning of gums and soft parts of the mouth
- checking for problems.

DO IT

Explain the consequences of poor personal hygiene.

Complete the following sentences:

Failure to bath or shower will result in............. This is caused by ....

Not cleaning teeth will result in.............. This is caused by.......................................

Add some other sentences of your own to describe the consequences of bad practice in hygiene matters.

Eye care

When people are fit and well their eyes are kept moist and clean naturally by the fluid that fills the eyes and drains into the nose. However, when people are ill their eyes can often become dry, irritated and sore, and you may need to bathe the eyes to soothe them and treat any infection.

Hair washing

Washing the hair of someone who is confined to bed can be extremely difficult. If a client is able to have a bath or a shower, washing the hair is not a problem, but for those who are restricted to bed you need to be able to wash hair.

Figure 5.6 Inflatable hair wash tray

The most effective way is with an inflatable hair wash tray, which allows you to wash the hair and drain the water away without the client having to move from the bed. This is very important for people who are suffering from back injuries or paralysis.

How to deal with problems

The problem you are most likely to come across in the area of personal cleanliness is the client who refuses to wash and bathe, or to be bathed or washed, as often as is necessary in order to maintain hygiene. This situation can often cause problems when clients are living in a residential or hospital setting and there are other people who object to the odour that can come from someone who fails to wash regularly. This is a situation where tact and gentle persuasion are likely to be most effective. An explanation of the reasons for keeping clean should be given, followed by some fairly firm but friendly advice. It may be better to suggest that the client begins slowly – rather than a full bath, he or she should be offered the option of a wash and gradually encouraged over time to accept a bath or shower.

Do it

Explain the hygiene requirements for clients with a range of needs, including clients' preferences.

Prepare a table or chart, showing the hygiene requirements of at least four different clients. Make sure that you look at a range of clients, and choose people who are at different life stages, or who have different care needs.

Ensuring that clients have choice in grooming

It is important that a client's choice should be an informed one, and that you explain to clients if there are changed factors in their lives that need to be taken into account. For example, someone who has become incontinent may need to rethink the kind of fabric that is suitable for clothes and may need to consider buying clothes in fabrics that can be easily laundered. Someone who has developed a sensitive skin condition may have to rethink the use of particular make-up or perfume.

Ultimately, the way people look both in terms of their appearance and their clothing is a matter of individual taste, preferences and beliefs, and it is a personal expression of identity. You can offer only assistance, not direction, and you should encourage clients to make as many of their own decisions as they can.

Helping people get dressed

There are many aids that can assist people in dressing themselves. Several of them are shown in Figure 5.7. They can make the difference between a client having to ask for help and being totally independent. Managing zips and pulling on shoes, stockings and tights can be difficult with limited movement or weak hands. A well-designed dressing aid can make it perfectly possible for a person to dress himself or herself without relying on help from a carer.

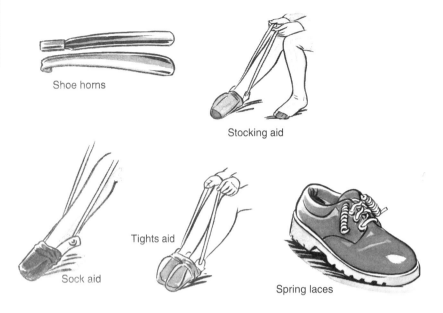

Shoe horns

Stocking aid

Sock aid

Tights aid

Spring laces

Figure 5.7 Dressing aids

Grooming

Grooming is important – if clients are not able to carry out grooming for themselves you need to offer help. The main areas of grooming where you may need to assist are likely to be:

● hair care ● make-up ● manicure.

Hair care

The way that hair is styled and groomed is a matter of individual choice and most people have strong feelings about how they like their hair to be done. If you work in a residential,

day-care or hospital setting, hairdressers may be available to clients on a regular basis. If you are visiting and supporting clients in their own homes, you may be able to arrange for a hairdresser to visit periodically in order to cut and perm or colour hair.

Specially designed combs and brushes can allow clients to continue grooming their own hair – many will prefer this to having to ask for help.

Figure 5.8 Aids for hair grooming

Make-up

You will need to discuss the type of make-up a client uses and establish what sort of help is needed to apply it. Always check with a client which perfume or cologne is preferred.

If you have to apply make-up you should ensure that each client has her own make-up and that it is not shared – this reduces the risk of cross-infection.

Manicure

The day-to-day care of the nails will be partly undertaken during bathing, when you should use a nail brush to keep the nails clean. You will need to ensure that fingernails are regularly cut or filed to a rounder shape, following the shape of the finger.

Toenails can be difficult to cut, particularly in older people where they can become very hard and almost impossible to cut with normal nail clippers. Where it is possible to cut toenails they should be cut in a straight line and never rounded, because this can encourage in-growing toenails.

If there are difficulties in cutting nails, a visit from a chiropodist should be arranged as these professionals have the proper equipment to deal with clients.

Other considerations

Make sure that you always take into account people's personal beliefs and preferences in the question of clothing, hairdressing and personal grooming. They are just as important as in the area of personal cleanliness. For example, Sikhs and Rastafarians believe that hair should never be cut or shaved, and many Orthodox Jewish women wear wigs. Always ensure that you ask the client or seek advice from members of the family or others if it is not possible to ask the client directly.

DO IT

Describe the equipment required for personal hygiene and grooming and how to involve the client in choice.

Draw diagrams of four different pieces of equipment you would use for maintaining personal hygiene for a client. Explain how each one would be used.

Think about the choices that can be made about personal appearance: hairstyle, fragrance, colours, style and so on. Prepare a plan for two different clients at different life stages, showing that they can have the same kind of choices.

Accessing toilet facilities

One of the key areas in maintaining independence is to give clients choice, and this applies no less to toilet facilities than to other matters. It is of course a difficult area to discuss, and you may find it far from easy to talk to clients about their use of toilet facilities and about their body waste. They may be embarrassed by the discussion, but it will be made worse if you show that you are also embarrassed. Try to think about toileting and body waste as a necessary physical process to be undergone in the same way as any other aspect of care. If it is possible for a worker of the same gender to talk with a specific client at his or her request, then that should be offered.

Getting to the toilet

The question of accessing the toilet facilities will need to be looked at in terms of:

- a client's mobility
- the frequency with which the client usually needs to use the toilet.
- the urgency with which the client usually needs to use the toilet.

For example, somebody who has poor mobility may still be able to reach the toilet independently. But a client who suffers with urgency (a feeling of urgent need to empty the bladder) may become incontinent as a result of poor mobility simply because he or she is not able to reach toilet facilities in time. Similarly, frequency (a condition where someone needs to empty the bladder often) can also present problems for a person with mobility problems – it is one thing to undertake a painful, slow walk to the toilet every two to three hours, but it is quite another to do it every half-hour.

Adjusting clothing

The other area that can present difficulties for people with limited mobility is adjusting their clothing once they reach a toilet facility. To undo trouser flies, or adjust buttons, or reach to remove underclothes, may be extremely difficult for people who have limited use of their arms or who are unsteady and need support themselves with both hands.

Accessing the toilet

You may find that you need to offer assistance to a client who needs help to get on and off the toilet. Clients may have difficulty in sitting down or in rising from a seat without help. If a person needs help to get in and out of a chair, it is possible he or she will need similar help with a toilet – but may find it much more difficult to ask, or to accept help.

How to provide help

It is important to bear the following points in mind when arranging help for clients to use toilet facilities.

- Have discussions in private.
- Agree the level of help needed.
- Agree how the client will indicate when he or she needs help.
- Ensure privacy for a client using the toilet – do not interrupt, or allow anyone else to do so.
- Offer help quietly and unobtrusively.

Helping clients to clean themselves is another area of assistance that requires discussion with the client. If you are providing assistance in terms of accessing the toilet, you may be able to observe what a client is able to achieve in terms of cleaning himself or herself appropriately. You will need to:

- establish the level and type of help a client needs
- wear an apron and gloves
- wash or wipe the genital and anal areas gently
- if washing, use clear water, and not use soap
- if using wipes or paper, make sure the area is clean and free from faeces
- wipe from front to back – never from back to front
- after cleaning, dispose of the cleaning materials in a sluice or toilet
- wash your hands.

Make sure that you always assist clients to wash their hands after using the toilet, regardless of the facility they have used.

Do It

Describe how clients can be assisted to access and use toilet facilities.

Note three factors you would take into account when planning how to help someone to access toilet facilities.

Checking for abnormal body waste

The waste expelled from a person's body is a good indicator of any problems that may be developing within the functioning or health of the body. It can often be an early indicator of illnesses or potentially serious conditions, so it is vitally important that you establish a client's normal body waste so that you can identify any changes occurring that would give rise to concerns.

Abnormalities can indicate many potential illnesses or changes, and they can range from the common and easily treatable to serious. It is important that you always report any changes in a client's normal pattern of waste. For example, a change from large, soft stools to small and hard stools indicates that a client is constipated. This may be dealt with by a simple change in diet, or it could be an early indicator of a more serious condition. Stools changing in colour from brown to pale and yellowish may indicate problems with the liver or pancreas. This should be reported immediately as it requires urgent medical attention.

Changes in urine must also be reported – for example, a dark colour may indicate that there is inadequate fluid intake. Cloudy urine or an offensive odour could be indicators of infection. Blood in the urine is always a cause for concern, as is pain on opening the bowels or passing urine. All of these conditions should be recorded in the client's notes.

Do It

Describe the reasons for the monitoring and collection of body waste.

Describe three ways in which body waste can be an indicator of health and well-being.

Prepare and provide food and drink

Hygiene requirements

If you are preparing areas or equipment for people to eat or drink, it is important that you follow basic hygiene procedures. It is also vital that you know how to store and prepare food safely so that people's health is not endangered.

Personal hygiene

If you have long hair, it must be tied back or covered. You should ensure that your nails are short and clean, and that you are not wearing any jewellery in which food could become trapped, such as rings with stones. Wash your hands thoroughly at each stage of food preparation and between handling raw food and cooked food, or raw meat and any food which will not be cooked. You must of course wash your hands after going to the toilet, and avoid touching your nose with your hands during food handling or preparation.

If you have a cut or sore on your hands, you must wear a special blue adhesive plaster dressing. This is because no food is blue, so if the plaster should come off during food preparation it will be easy to locate.

Hygienic food preparation

Food is contaminated by bacteria, which can be spread by infecting food directly if it is not heated or chilled properly, or by cross contamination, which is caused by bacteria spreading from one item of food to another.

The main bacteria that cause contamination of food are salmonella, campylobacter and E-coli. Any of these bacteria can cause food poisoning, which can be very serious in people who are elderly or ill, or in young children.

Raw meat is a source of bacteria, and you should be sure to use separate utensils and chopping boards or surfaces for raw and cooked food. For example, do not chop the raw chicken breasts and then chop the lettuce for the accompanying salad on the same chopping board or with the same knife. This is a recipe for giving everybody who eats your salad a nasty dose of salmonella. You should keep separate chopping boards for meat and vegetables, and ensure that you use different knives. Remember to change knives and wash your hands in between preparing different types of food.

It is possible to kill most bacteria by cooking food, but be very careful with foods that are not cooked, such as salads or mayonnaise, that you use clean utensils to prepare them.

A core temperature of 75°C will kill most bacteria, so hot food should be heated or re-heated to at least this temperature.

Do It

Describe how to handle and prepare food in a safe and responsible manner.

Write a guide that could be given to a new member of staff, outlining the main safety steps to be taken when handling food.

Food storage

By law, food should be stored at 8°C or lower. However, good practice dictates that food should be stored between 5°C and 8°C, and food deteriorates quite quickly at higher temperatures. Food that has been left in a fridge with the door open or where the power has been switched off should be discarded.

Do It

Identify the consequences of poor hygiene techniques in food preparation.

Write an extra page for the guide you have prepared explaining what could happen if the guidelines on food handling and preparation are not followed.

Dietary requirements

All human beings require certain essential nutrients in order to survive. They are classified into five major groups: proteins, carbohydrates, fats, vitamins and minerals. Humans also need to drink about two litres of liquid each day. The liquid can be water, fruit juice, tea, coffee or any kind of non-alcoholic drink.

Nutrient	Where found	Purpose
Proteins	Found in meat, fish, eggs, milk, cheese, nuts, cereals, tofu and beans.	Proteins promote growth and they are also essential for the replacement and renewal of body cells. They are essential for everyone and must be eaten each day as the body is not able to store protein.
Carbohydrates	Found in sugar, potatoes and some root vegetables such as yams, sweet potato, bread, flour, rice, cereals, and pasta.	Carbohydrates, also known as starches, are used by the body to provide energy and heat. They are essential to provide an energy source, but if they are eaten to excess they will be stored as fat.
Fats	Found in butter, margarine, cooking oil, dripping, meat fat, cream, soured cream, milk, cheese, egg yolks.	Fats are a very concentrated source of heat and energy, but if they are eaten to excess they will be stored by the body in the adipose layer just beneath the skin.

Vitamins and minerals

Vitamins are essential to maintaining good health and keeping the body in good condition. Some vitamins are in certain foods in very small quantities, but they are nonetheless essential. Minerals similarly may be found only in quite small quantities, but like vitamins they are essential and have very specific purposes in the body.

It is important that a healthy diet balances the amounts of different nutrients taken each day. Clearly, the necessary amounts will vary depending on the individual. Some elderly people will require less food, for example, than an active teenager. Lifestyle and the amount of exercise taken must be considered when deciding on the overall amounts of food that people will consume. It is important to get the balance right, however, regardless of quantity.

Nutrient	Where found	Purpose
Vitamin A	Found in liver and fish oils, milk, butter, eggs and cheese, and can be made by the body from carotene which is found in carrots, tomatoes and green vegetables.	Protects from infection and contributes to growth. Lack of vitamin A can cause eye problems.
Vitamin B (there are several)	Found in cereals, liver, yeast and nuts.	This is a large group of complex vitamins, all of which are essential for maintaining good skin. Lack of vitamin B may be responsible for some diseases of the nervous system.
Vitamin C	Found in citrus fruits, strawberries, potatoes and some green vegetables.	Vitamin C cannot be stored so it must be taken each day. Lack of vitamin C can cause scurvy, a disease that causes bleeding in the gums and is extremely serious. People who have a lack of vitamin C are also more likely to be affected by viral infections and coughs and colds.
Vitamin D	Found in eggs and fish oils, and made by the body when the skin is exposed to sunlight.	Vitamin D enables calcium to be absorbed to strengthen and develop bones and teeth. A severe shortage of vitamin D will lead to rickets, a deforming disease seen in children whose bones do not develop adequately.
Vitamin E	Found in wheatgerm, cereals, egg yolk, liver and milk.	This helps to prevent cell damage and degeneration.
Minerals	A wide range of minerals are essential for health and are found in eggs, cocoa, liver, baked beans, cheese and milk.	Iron is important for the formation of red blood cells, and a lack of iron can lead to anaemia. Calcium is used for developing firm bones. Sodium is important for maintaining the fluid balance of the body, but an excess of sodium can be a contributory cause of oedema (fluid retention).

Energy requirements

The amount of energy provided by different types of food is measured in calories, which are 'burned' by the body to provide the energy for carrying out activities. The amount of energy needed depends on a person's level of activity; for example, watching television or sitting at a computer does not require much energy, so not many calories are used. Doing housework or running up flights of stairs takes much more energy.

Salads, fruit and vegetables provide fewer calories than fatty foods like chocolate or cream cakes. For people to remain healthy, not only must they eat a diet that is balanced in terms of nutrients (carbohydrates, proteins, fats, etc.) but they must also consume the right amount of calories. If they have too many calories people will gain weight, with too few they may become seriously underweight.

The average adult woman needs 1,940 calories a day to remain healthy and to provide the necessary energy for normal activities. An adult man requires 2,550 calories on average – this is because men generally have a greater weight and body size. Even though children have a smaller body size than adults, they still need approximately the same calories as an adult because they are growing rapidly, which takes a great deal of energy, and they are usually very active. It is especially important that the correct balance of nutrients is maintained for children as this will ensure proper growth and development.

Pregnant women require additional calories in the last three months of pregnancy – but only about 200 extra per day. There is no truth in the old saying about 'eating for two' – in fact, it is not good for women to gain too much weight during pregnancy. However, if a woman is breastfeeding a baby, then she really is 'eating for two' and will need quite a significant number of extra calories, because milk production uses up a great deal of energy. She should increase her calorie intake by approximately 500–600 calories per day.

People who are disabled and not mobile, and older people who are unable to get about as much as they used to, may need to reduce their calorie intake to avoid gaining weight. Calorie intake should not be drastically reduced, however, and even for a very inactive person should not drop below 1400 calories for women and 1700 for men daily.

A balanced diet

Carbohydrates should make up more than 50 per cent of the calories consumed each day – that is, fruits, vegetables, cereals, bread and pasta. The remaining 50 per cent should include about 20 per cent from protein, which comes from lean meat, poultry, fish, nuts and beans.

People who have a dietary problem	Special dietary needs
Diabetes	Regular meals/snacks, controlled amounts of sugar
Allergies – commonly nuts, dairy products, or food additives	Strict avoidance of problem foods, ensuring that information is recorded and people are aware of the allergy
Coeliac disease	Gluten-free diet, i.e. no flour or cereals

People who choose a particular diet	Special dietary needs
Vegetarians	No meat, poultry, game or possibly fish
Vegans	No meat, poultry, game, fish, eggs or dairy products
Cultural preferences	For religious or other reasons, need to eat or not eat certain foods (e.g. pork) or to observe rules at certain times

Total fat intake should be no higher than 30 per cent of daily calories. Eating a variety of foods is the most likely way to ensure a balanced diet and a good intake of vitamins and minerals.

The table opposite shows the special dietary needs of certain groups of people. Information in these needs should be carefully checked, and made available to all carers.

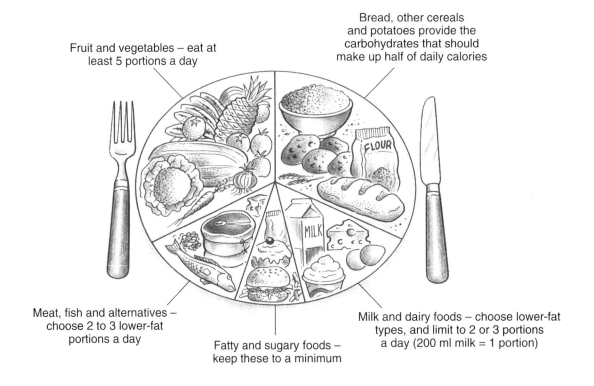

Fruit and vegetables – eat at least 5 portions a day

Bread, other cereals and potatoes provide the carbohydrates that should make up half of daily calories

Meat, fish and alternatives – choose 2 to 3 lower-fat portions a day

Fatty and sugary foods – keep these to a minimum

Milk and dairy foods – choose lower-fat types, and limit to 2 or 3 portions a day (200 ml milk = 1 portion)

Figure 5.9   A balanced diet

Do it

Describe common dietary needs and preferences for three different clients and the effects of diets.

Prepare a chart or report showing the basic dietary needs of human beings. Add separate, more detailed charts for three people at different life stages.

How food is served

The way in which food is served can often reflect the quality of the care setting and can show a great deal about the way in which the clients who use the facility are considered. The significant factors are:

- presentation of food
- the variety of food offered
- choice of seating plan – whether at large tables, in small groups or individually
- whether clients can have a tray on their knees in front of the television
- whether times of the serving of meals are flexible.

All these factors are indications of how much choice and individuality is available for clients in a particular setting. Obviously, for clients who are in their own homes these issues are not so relevant, although those who are dependent on others to prepare and serve their meals may still have some of the same concerns.

Helping clients to eat and drink

The most important thing to establish first is whether the client requires your assistance. You should never impose help on a client – it is far better to encourage independence, if necessary through the use of specially adapted utensils rather than to offer to feed the client yourself. Some clients would be perfectly capable of feeding themselves if they were given a minimal amount of assistance, perhaps in the form of specially designed eating and drinking aids such as the ones shown in Figure 5.10 below.

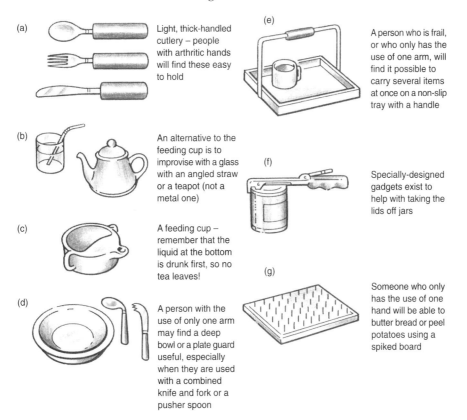

(a) Light, thick-handled cutlery – people with arthritic hands will find these easy to hold

(e) A person who is frail, or who only has the use of one arm, will find it possible to carry several items at once on a non-slip tray with a handle

(b) An alternative to the feeding cup is to improvise with a glass with an angled straw or a teapot (not a metal one)

(f) Specially-designed gadgets exist to help with taking the lids off jars

(c) A feeding cup – remember that the liquid at the bottom is drunk first, so no tea leaves!

(g) Someone who only has the use of one hand will be able to butter bread or peel potatoes using a spiked board

(d) A person with the use of only one arm may find a deep bowl or a plate guard useful, especially when they are used with a combined knife and fork or a pusher spoon

Figure 5.10   Aids for eating and drinking

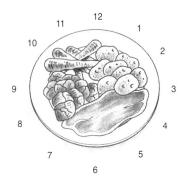

Figure 5.11 Compare the meal to a clockface – potatoes are at 2 o'clock

There are special ways of helping clients who have particular needs. For example, visually impaired clients are often able to feed themselves if you can help to prepare the plate of food in advance. If you arrange the food in separate portions around the plate and then say, using a clock as a comparison, that potatoes are at 2 o'clock, meat at 6 o'clock, sprouts at 8 o'clock and so on, this is often enough to allow the person to enjoy the meal independently (see Figure 5.11).

When feeding people who cannot feed themselves, remember to go through the following steps.

- Help the client to use the toilet or commode if necessary and to wash his or her hands.
- Wash your hands.
- Check that you have everything you will need: the meal, salt and pepper, feeding utensils, etc.
- If the client is completely unable to feed himself or herself because of lack of use of the arms, you should position the client comfortably either propped up in bed or sitting in a chair. The upright position is necessary to assist digestion.
- Ensure that the client is comfortable before you begin the meal.
- Establish whether the client likes to eat food piping hot or to give it the opportunity to cool down.
- Offer the chance to see the meal before you begin to feed, and ask which food the client would like to start with – for example, the potatoes first or meat first.
- Sit down beside the client, slightly to one side and in front.
- Regardless of whether you feed with a fork or spoon, make sure that you leave enough time for each mouthful to be properly chewed and swallowed.
- Bear in mind that if a client is ill it may take a considerable amount of time to finish the meal. Do not rush the client and hover with the next spoonful before the last one is finished.
- Keep up an interesting conversation throughout the meal, even if your client is unable to respond to you – but beware of the dentist's trick of asking a question that requires an answer just after you have put a spoonful of food into the client's mouth!
- Help the client to wash if he or she wishes at the end of the meal, or wipe the mouth and rinse the hands. Remember that some clients may have religious requirements for particular types of washing and cleaning after food.
- Make sure that the client takes regular drinks before and/or after the meal.

DO IT

Explain how clients can be helped to eat and drink food that they have chosen.

Demonstrate, with a partner:

a how to feed someone

b how to present a meal in an attractive way.

People who have been ill, or who have specific disabilities, can experience problems in eating and drinking. This is not restricted to those who have physical difficulty in using eating utensils or sitting at a table – other problems may arise. For example:

- people may find difficulty in swallowing and chewing following a stroke
- some disabilities can cause swallowing problems or digestive difficulties
- people who are ill may lose their appetite and find it difficult to eat
- people who have an illness that affects their sense of smell or taste will find eating difficult or even unpleasant.

Always ensure that you check for these problems with the client and by consulting the care plan. It may be necessary to record and monitor food and drink intake for some clients who are experiencing difficulties.

Do it

Record, report and monitor food and drink intake for two clients.

Keep a record, for two different clients in your workplace, of exactly what they eat and drink for two days. Make sure you include the amounts as well as a description of the meals.

Moving and handling clients safely

Some clients have problems affecting their mobility, and these may involve physical or psychological factors. The table below shows some possible causes of difficulty.

Physical factors	Psychological factors
broken bones, damaged ligaments	fear of painful movement
stroke	loss of confidence – fear of falling
neurological diseases – e.g. motor neurone disease, multiple sclerosis	loss of interest and motivation

Mobility appliances

Mobility appliances assist a client to become or continue to be mobile, either by providing support or, like a wheelchair, by providing the means to mobility.

Mobility appliances such as walking sticks, crutches, quadrupeds, and walking frames provide support where people have become unsteady or where joints or muscles are weak or painful. They also provide additional security where someone has had a fall or is recovering from illness – often the loss of confidence after an incident such as a fall is as damaging to mobility as any injury sustained.

Mobility aids can make a significant difference to a client's quality of life. Rather than be dependent upon assistance for everything, the client with a mobility aid can often maintain his or her independence and freedom to choose.

DO IT

Identify physical and psychological factors which may limit client mobility.

Make a list of the reasons why people may have problems in moving around. Next to each reason, say if it is a physical or psychological reason.

Walking sticks, quadrupeds and tripods

The amount of support a client needs will determine whether a walking stick, a tripod or a quadruped is appropriate. A walking stick would be used for someone who is generally unsteady, needs to regain confidence, or who is recovering from an injury.

A quadruped would only be used for a client who has considerable difficulty in walking on one particular leg, either because of hip or knee degeneration or a stroke. It is not an appropriate aid for somebody who is generally unsteady.

Walking frames

The decision to provide a client with a walking frame would be taken when the client had reached the stage of needing considerable support from one or two care workers, and when he or she is no longer steady on a walking stick or quadruped.

Frames on wheels

The frame on wheels is similar to a walking frame, except that it has wheels on the front legs. This is very useful for clients who are too disabled to be able to cope with learning the walking pattern necessary for an ordinary walking frame, and is also useful for people with particular arm or shoulder problems who would be unable to lift the frame.

Wheelchairs

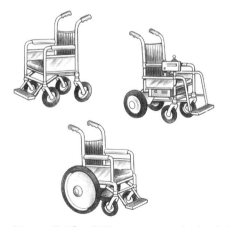

Figure 5.12 Different types of wheelchair

Where an assessment has concluded that a client requires a wheelchair, the client is entitled to be correctly measured and assessed by a physiotherapist. Wheelchairs come in a range of sizes and styles, ranging from chairs that have to be pushed, to chairs that allow clients to propel them and electric wheelchairs. Many younger people with disabilities have decided views about the types of wheelchairs they will use, the amount of equipment and features they should have, the colours they are and the speed at which they travel around in them.

Do It

Describe the common mobility appliances used by clients.

Draw diagrams of, or describe, four different mobility appliances. Describe the circumstances in which each one is used.

Assisting clients to move

As you may remember from Chapter 3, employers have a responsibility under health and safety legislation to examine and assess all risks in your working environment. All risks must be noted and assessed, and steps must be taken to minimise them as far as possible. Employers are required to provide adequate equipment for such tasks as moving and handling individuals who require assistance.

Each time you move or lift any individual, you are responsible for making an assessment of the risks involved in carrying out that particular manoeuvre. You also need to consider the environment. You should take into account all of the following factors:

- Is the floor surface safe, or are there wet slippery patches?
- Are you wearing appropriate clothing – low-heeled shoes, tunic or dress with enough room to stretch and reach?
- Is the immediate area clear of items that may cause a trip or fall, or items that could cause injury following a fall?
- Is all the equipment to carry out the lift available, and is the place to which the individual is to be moved ready?
- Does the individual have privacy and can dignity be maintained during the move?

Many people who have a long-standing disability will be experienced and skilled in dealing with it. They are the best people to ask for advice as they know the most effective ways to lift in a way that will avoid pain and discomfort as far as possible.

Once you have carried out all of the necessary assessments, you should explain carefully to the client what you intend to do and what the client's own role is in contributing to the effectiveness and safety of the move.

Good practice: moving and handling clients

✓   assess risks to the client and to yourself before starting any lift or move

✓   ask clients about the best way of moving or assisting them

✓   explain the procedure to clients at each stage, even where it may not be obvious that you are understood

✓   explain how the equipment operates

✓   check that you have the agreement of the person you are moving

✓   stop immediately if the client does not wish you to continue – you may not move anyone without consent.

A wide range of equipment is available and technological advances are being made continuously in the field of medical equipment. Regardless of the individual products and improvements that may be made to them, lifting and handling equipment broadly falls into the following categories:

- hoists, slings and other equipment to move the full weight of an individual.
- Equipment designed to assist in a move and to take some of the weight of the individual, such as transfer boards.
- Equipment designed to assist individuals to help themselves, such as to pull themselves up. This category includes grab handles, raised toilet seats, and lifting chairs.

There are very few situations in which manual lifting should be carried out. Unless it is an emergency, or a life-threatening situation, there should be no need to move anyone without the correct equipment. Manual handling should be carried out only in situations that do not involve lifting all or most of a client's weight.

Shoulder lifts (like the Australian lift) are no longer considered safe, and there is no safe weight limit for lifting. The only workplaces where lifting should now take place is in units caring for babies and small children. Even there it is important to ensure that risk assessments are carried out to avoid the likelihood of injury.

If you need to move someone manually in order to change a client's position or provide assistance, you should follow the principles of effective manual moving and handling which are:

- it should be well planned and assessed in advance, and technique rather than strength is important
- it should be comfortable and safe for the client, thus creating confidence that being moved is not something to be anxious about and the client can co-operate with the procedure
- it should be safe for the worker carrying out the procedure – a worker injured during a badly planned or executed transfer is likely in turn to injure the client, and similarly a client injured during a move is likely to cause injury to those assisting the move.

Do it

Describe the requirements to prepare, move and handle clients safely with minimum pain and discomfort.

Write a report on three different clients you have moved, assisted with moving, or observed being moved. Include details of how the client was prepared, the equipment used and the amount of assistance given.

Reasons for moving clients

One of the main reasons for moving clients is to prevent the development of pressure sores. Pressure sores are the result of an interruption to the blood supply, which can cause the tissue in that particular area to break down. The interruption to the blood supply is caused by various types of pressure, exerted in different ways, but the effect is the same – the tissue in the effected area begins to degenerate into a sore. Every one of us would get pressure

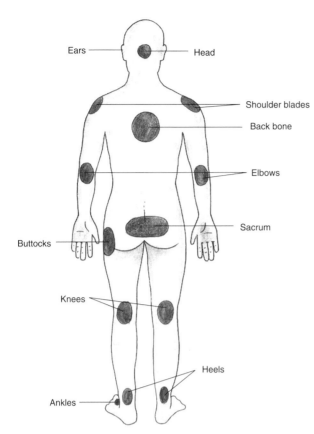

Figure 5.13 labels: Ears, Head, Shoulder blades, Back bone, Elbows, Sacrum, Buttocks, Knees, Heels, Ankles

sores if we were not able to move regularly each night while we were asleep. For individuals who are unable to change their own position regularly, whether that is lying down or sitting in a wheelchair, the pressure can result in a sore. Some areas of the body are particularly vulnerable:

- the back of the head
- the shoulders
- the sacrum (the bottom of the back)
- the buttocks
- the backs of the legs and the calves
- the heels.

The diagram in Figure 5.13 shows the most common sites for pressure sores.

Figure 5.13 Common sites of pressure sores

Preventing pressure sores

It is always better to work on preventing pressure sores than to have to treat them once they have developed. The best way to ensure that pressure sores do not develop is to keep people as active as possible, so that they are less likely to remain in one position. It is also important for individuals who are confined to bed or a chair that they have a special mattress or cushion (such as a Roho cushion), designed to distribute weight more evenly so that the downward pressure is evenly spread.

It is important to ensure, also, that individuals eat a good balanced diet with a significant protein content, as protein is required for cell renewal and can help reduce the risk of tissue breakdown and development of pressure sores.

It is vital to ensure that clients who are incontinent are never left sitting in wet clothes or incontinence pads – the effect of wet, urine-soaked clothing on skin is to make it vulnerable to sores in the pressure areas.

Sheepskin, or artificial sheepskin, is a useful tool in preventing the development of pressure sores, and tends to be used particularly for heels in the form of sheepskin booties. It has the effect of relieving pressure and spreading weight more evenly.

To help prevent pressure sores, remember to:

- move people regularly
- turn an unconscious or paralysed person every two hours

- use aids such as a Roho cushion, special mattress, or fleece pads
- check that the client's diet contains adequate protein.

See the next section of this chapter for information on the signs and indications that a client is in pain, and the ways to meet clients' need for rest.

DO IT

Describe the reasons for moving clients regularly and the risks involved to client and carer.

Explain how pressure sores develop and how they can be avoided. Add a safety checklist related to the risks of moving clients.

Enable clients to achieve physical comfort

Observing and reporting on client's condition

Emotions play a considerable part in the experience of pain. If someone is afraid or tense or has no knowledge of what is happening, he or she is likely to experience more pain than someone who is relaxed, and knows exactly what the cause of pain is. Sometimes the fear of pain can not only make pain worse but can cause additional pain by anticipation. This is commonly seen in a person who has an illness or injury in which movement is extremely painful, and he or she reacts in anticipation of being moved.

There is also compelling evidence that people who have had limbs removed can continue to feel pain in the limb. The evidence shows that pain is more common in a limb that had been painful prior to removal, and would suggest that pain pathways can continue to function after the cause has been removed.

How to help people to express their pain

Because of people's beliefs, values and culture they may not find it easy to say that they are in pain. This can result from a feeling that they do not want to make a fuss, be a nuisance or bother anyone.

It is important that you create as many opportunities as possible for people to express their pain and that you contribute towards creating an atmosphere where people know it is acceptable to say that they are in pain and they want something done about it. You can help by:

- noticing when somebody seems tense or drawn
- noticing facial expressions, if someone is wincing or looking distressed
- observing if somebody is fidgeting or trying to move around to get more comfortable
- noticing when somebody seems quiet or distracted
- checking if someone is flushed or sweating or seems to be breathing rapidly.

All of these are signals which should prompt you to ask a person if he or she is in pain and if any help or relief is needed. Even in the absence of any obvious signals, it is important to check regularly and ask if any of the people that you care for are in pain or discomfort or need any assistance.

You will need to be particularly aware of possible pain when you are providing care for people who are not able to communicate directly with you, including:

- people who do not use English as a first language
- people with speech or hearing difficulties
- people with severe learning difficulties or multiple disabilities
- people who have an illness such as dementia.

You will need to be especially vigilant if you provide care for anyone who comes into these categories.

Care plans

For every client who is being cared for, there will be a written plan called a 'care plan'. The care plan outlines the client's present and future needs and describes how these needs will be met. The following is an example of a care plan for Mrs J, who is 85 years old and mentally alert. Following a fall in which she broke her pelvis, she is confined to bed.

Care plan for Mrs J

Mobility
Mrs J needs to be moved every four hours to prevent her developing pressure sores.

She has a one-hour physiotherapy session every day to improve circulation and muscle strength.

She is confined to bed, so needs assistance with toileting.

Food and drink
Normal diet, but small portions as she is overweight.

Frequent drinks.

Pain control
Pain relief morning and evening as prescribed by Dr N.

Extra pain relief can be given if requested by Mrs J. Refer to main carer, Mr F.

The care plan is very important as it shows exactly how a client is being cared for and what can be done if he or she is in pain or discomfort. In the case of Mrs J, the care plan says that she can be given extra pain relief if she needs it, so you can reassure her that she does not have to suffer.

Do it

Explain the need for a care plan and reporting.

You are caring for someone who is normally cheerful. One day he looks very hot and uncomfortable and complains of pain in his head and neck. How would you report this, and why would it be important to do so? What would you write in the care plan?

Consulting clients

It is important that you talk to your clients about the best way to make them comfortable. After all, they probably have more experience with their illness or disability than you have. Make sure that you ask the client first before carrying out any procedure or activity. Consider the following conversation.

Carer: Oh dear, Edith, is your arthritis bad today? You look a bit uncomfortable. Would it help to put your leg on this stool, or are you more comfortable in the upright chair?

Edith: My foot on the stool is usually best – the upright chair always gives me a sore neck after a while.

Carer: OK then, here's the stool. Is that better? Can I get you a cushion, or is there anything else that usually helps?

Edith: No thanks, cushions make me uncomfortable. They always seem to end up in a hard lump. A hot water bottle is usually good, and if you could bring me one of my tablets, that would help.

Carer: No problem. Would you like a cup of tea to take the tablet?

Edith: That would be lovely.

DO IT

Explain the need for the client to be consulted about treatments.

Write down another conversation like the one above, using a different type of client in different circumstances. You should try to use a conversation you have had, or have heard someone having, while on your work experience placement.

After you have written down the conversation, answer the following questions about it and about the conversation shown above.

1. How many new facts did the carer learn about the client's comfort?
2. What may have happened if the carer had not asked the client about what to do?
3. How do you think the client would have felt if the carer had not asked about what was wanted?
4. How do you think the client felt after being asked?
5. Which part of the care value base is the carer using in this situation?

Resting and sleeping

Rest, not necessarily sleep, is important for individuals who are in a care setting. The rest can be relaxation, a period of quiet, the opportunity to read or meditate, or simply a quiet time alone.

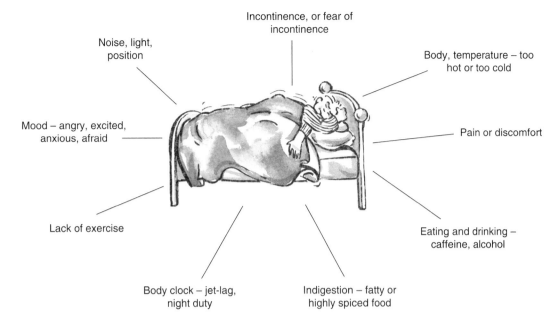

Incontinence, or fear of incontinence

Noise, light, position

Body, temperature – too hot or too cold

Mood – angry, excited, anxious, afraid

Pain or discomfort

Lack of exercise

Eating and drinking – caffeine, alcohol

Body clock – jet-lag, night duty

Indigestion – fatty or highly spiced food

Figure 5.14 Barriers to rest and sleep

Barriers to sleep

A range of factors can make it difficult for people to sleep. These broadly fall into three categories: physical, emotional or environmental.

Physical factors include:

- pain or discomfort
- disturbed body clock
- illness
- too many stimulants, e.g. caffeine or alcohol.
- lack of exercise
- feeling hot or cold
- overeating

Emotional factors include:

- anxiety
- fear of incontinence
- fear of a strange place.
- distress
- fear of disturbing dreams

Environmental factors include:

- noise
- uncomfortable bed or bedding
- temperature
- light.

How to assist rest and sleep

You have an important role in helping people to sleep and to rest. You will need to know how best to support people to sleep well at night and to rest at times during the day.

You can help people to sleep at night:

- by reassuring them and making sure there is nothing they are anxious about
- by encouraging them to carry out some relaxation exercises, which will help both mentally and physically to prepare for sleep

- by offering a warm drink, preferably a milky drink without any caffeine or stimulants
- by offering a hot water bottle
- by ensuring that the individual is comfortable
- by checking whether clients need their position adjusting or their pillows or bed to be made more comfortable
- by offering to take them to the toilet or to provide them with a bed pan – often a full bladder or bowel will prevent people from going to sleep.

The environment in which the individual is sleeping is just as important as the care of the individuals themselves.

- Ensure that noise is kept to a minimum and that squeaking trolleys, noisy shoes, loud laughter or talking amongst the staff are avoided.
- The lights should be dimmed and rooms should be warm but ventilated.

There is much that can be done during the day to help ensure sleep at night. If an individual has physical exercise coupled with mental stimulation, he or she is far more likely to achieve satisfactory rest than somebody who has been left with nothing to do either physically or mentally, and has had little activity of body or brain during the day.

Rest at other times of the day is also important. When planning care, thought should be given to times in the day when individuals are able to have a rest period.

Rest periods should be, as far as possible, uninterrupted by treatments, procedures, observations or activities. Often this period may fit in best immediately after lunch – an early afternoon nap is welcome for many. Rest may not involve sleeping – reading, relaxing or just being quiet and undisturbed may be equally useful.

Everyone who is receiving care should have a plan of that care drawn up by the care team. It is important that plans for rest and sleep are included in the care plan. Establish each individual's normal pattern of sleep and rest by talking to the client and by observation. Any indications of change in an individual's normal sleeping or resting pattern should be recorded and concerns must be passed on immediately to your supervisor or manager.

Do It

Describe the factors which affect the client's ability to rest.

Prepare a table with two columns. In one column write down the factors that may cause problems for a client trying to rest. In the other column, describe how the problems could be overcome.

Minimising pain and discomfort

Carers should respond to pain at the level the client feels it, and not make assumptions about its severity.

You should bear in mind the following points of good practice.

Good practice: moving and handling clients

✓   be alert for signs of pain, even though people may not complain

✓   respond quickly to requests for pain relief

✓   reassure people who are frightened and ensure they are given information by someone who is qualified to do so

✓   ask clients what methods of pain relief work best for them

✓   deal tactfully with the situation where expressions of pain are distressing other people.

Effective responses to pain can be split into three groups: drugs, physical methods and self-help methods.

Drugs

Drugs that are effective in the relief of pain are:

- analgesics (aspirin, paracetamol, etc.)
- anti-inflammatory (ibuprofen)
- opiates (morphine, heroin)
- anaesthetic spinal block (epidural)

Drugs supplied on medical prescription for the relief of pain are likely to be analgesics, but in cases of severe or prolonged pain they may be opiates.

Physical methods

Physical methods are often effective at bringing pain-relief. They include:

- massage (superficial or pressure)
- ice application (with massage)
- transcutaneous electrical nerve stimulation (TENS)
- vibration
- superficial heat or cold
- repositioning of the client's body.

Self-help methods

The client can be encouraged to try various self-help methods for the relief of pain, or may have preferred methods of his or her own, including:

- moving or walking about if possible
- taking a warm bath
- taking recommended exercise
- having a conversation.
- imagining himself or herself in a pleasant and comfortable location
- finding a task to distract from the pain

Dealing with clients in pain

Responding to and dealing with pain effectively can make use of the simplest methods. It may be sufficient to alter the client's position or to provide a hot water bottle or ice pack. Sometimes a distraction, like getting the client involved in an activity or holding a conversation can help.

Self-management is always the most effective method of dealing with pain and discomfort, because it gives the individual the maximum amount of control. Feeling out of control and not having enough information is a contributory factor to experiencing pain in a greater degree.

The so-called 'alternative therapies' are increasingly accepted into mainstream Western medicine, and have an invaluable role to play in the reduction of pain and the improvement of general well-being. These can include the practices shown in the following table.

Alternative therapy	How it works
Aromatherapy	Natural oils are used for massage. Their aroma has a beneficial effect.
Homeopathic medicine	The illness or disease is treated with minute quantities of naturally occurring substances, which would cause similar illness if taken in larger amounts.
Reflexology	Specialised foot massage stimulates particular areas of the feet, which are said to be linked to parts of the body.
Acupuncture	This must be administered by an expert, and uses ancient Chinese medical knowledge about specific points in the body which respond to being stimulated by very fine needles. Acupuncture is now increasingly recognised by Western medical practitioners and is available from the National Health Service in many places.
Yoga and meditation	Yoga and meditation work essentially on the emotional component of pain. Meditation works by dealing with the mental response to pain, whereas yoga combines mind and body in an exercise and relaxation programme.

Do it

Describe ways to help the client achieve physical comfort.

Write a case study about a client who has a painful condition. Explain the different ways in which you could offer assistance to make him or her more comfortable.

CLIENT SUPPORT

The effects of change and ways of providing support

Chapter 2 explored life stages and some of the changes that are likely to happen to people as they grow and develop. Life involves constant change, and change can create stress. A list based on research in 1997 by some American psychiatrists shows the 15 most stressful life events as in the following table.

1997		
1. Death of partner	9.	Pregnancy
2. Divorce	10.	Major business readjustment
3. Death of close family member	11.	Loan repayment demand
4. Marital separation	12.	Gain new family member
5. Fired from work	13.	Marital reconciliation
6. Major illness or injury	14.	Change in health of family
7. Jail term	15.	Change in financial state
8. Death of close friend		

Researchers claim that life stress appears to have increased in recent times and that, in general, unmarried people experience higher life stress than people who have a partner to support them.

The table above shows how stressful general life events can be. Most people do not go into residential care, but if they did, this change would probably come high up on the list of stressful life events.

Why does change cause stress?

Change can cause:

- uncertainty
- a need to learn new things
- a need to change our view of ourselves, or our self-concept
- a sense of loss
- pressure on time, money and emotional energy

Uncertainty

When you start at a new school or job, you don't know how the other students or staff will behave; will they like you, and will you get on all right? Moving house or moving to live with someone can create a lot of worry – all sorts of things could go wrong. Not knowing how things will work out can cause a feeling of stress for many people.

A sense of loss

Serious changes such as redundancy, sudden disability or bereavement can involve multiple losses. Bereaved people may have lost:

- the person they talked to most and who gave them advice
- the person who shared life's tasks with them
- the person who provided most emotional support

- their sexual partner
- the person who made social life fun
- the focus of life at home
- the person who protected them
- a person who helped bring in money.

A person who loses both legs in a road accident may feel that he or she has lost the ability to get out easily, and may fear being labelled and stereotyped as a wheelchair user, or feel like a burden and unattractive. A person may believe that he or she is of no use and that his or her partner might leave. If such a person ends up alone, he or she might also have all the problems listed above for the bereaved person!

A need to learn new things

Moving house, starting a new job, becoming disabled or moving into a care home all involve a great deal of new learning. Moving home may involve organising the move, getting to know new neighbours and learning how to use new household equipment. A new job involves learning new routines, learning about new roles, new tasks and new people. Disability involves learning new ways to be independent and learning to cope with other people's assumptions about you. Going into care might involve learning a whole new lifestyle.

Learning a lot of new things can be tiring and even stressful if you have to learn in a hurry.

Pressure on time, money and emotional energy

It takes time to learn a new job or to make new relationships. Time is often limited. Moving home or getting married may cost a lot of money, and these events may also be emotionally draining.

Changes such as redundancy, serious illness, and bereavement may also involve extra expenditure, additional work and more emotional involvement in order to sort everything out. In these situations you are spending your time and money to sort out things that you never wanted to happen.

A need to change self-concept

The way we see ourselves is partly a result of the way our friends, relatives and other important people see us. When we change friends, relationships, jobs or school, the people we mix with will change. New people might see us differently. Our ideas of our skills and our importance might have to change.

You may have been very good at a previous job, and seen yourself as efficient. When you change jobs, your new colleagues might work in different ways, and they might not see you as efficient. Your concept of yourself might drop in value.

Redundancy, serious illness and bereavement may also damage your self-concept. You may have seen yourself as efficient, physically fit, a partner in a loving relationship, only to find it has all been taken away. You can no longer be the person you used to be. You have to change your whole way of understanding yourself. Having to rebuild your idea of yourself can be a painful process.

What is stress?

Physical and mental pressure can damage health. When a person feels under pressure, he or she often becomes tired. This exhaustion can cause people to worry about aches and pains, and to have migraines, headaches, back pains, sleep disturbances and emotional tension. When stress continues for a long time, it can affect a person's health. Heart disease and strokes have been associated with stress in older adults. Other physical illnesses associated with stress include diabetes, stomach problems and skin problems including eczema and rashes. People who are stressed may be more likely to catch colds, flu, or other infections.

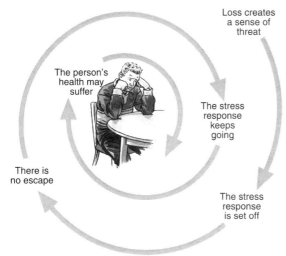

Loss creates a sense of threat

The person's health may suffer

The stress response keeps going

There is no escape

The stress response is set off

Figure 6.1 The stress response can continue until health begins to suffer

People suffer all these physical reactions because of the way our **stress-response** mechanism works. We have all experienced a biological reaction called the stress response, which helps us to jump, run or fight if we feel threatened. If you were crossing the road and suddenly realised there was a speeding car coming towards you, you would feel scared. Because you were in danger your stress response would help you to escape – your senses (eyesight, hearing, etc.) would become clearer, your muscles would become efficient to enable you to jump or run. If you feel threatened, you can run or jump more quickly than normal.

After escaping from the speeding car, you will feel 'wobbly' for a few minutes. You might breathe quickly and feel your heart pounding, but soon you will feel safe and your stress response will switch off.

Major changes in life can cause a feeling of being threatened, and because we feel threatened our stress response is switched on. We want to escape, fight or run away, but there is nowhere to run and no way to escape. The threat is not physical, so we cannot escape it in this way. Our stress response might keep going until we feel exhausted and ill.

Change can make people feel as if they are being attacked. People who feel attacked and threatened are at risk of developing physical and mental illnesses. We might describe such people as being vulnerable.

Think it through

Imagine how you would feel if the following happened to you. You can either read this story and think about it, or listen carefully while someone reads it to you.

Imagine that you have lived to reach old age. Perhaps you have lived to the age of 85. Imagine that you are living alone in the same house or flat that you have lived in for over 30 years.

It is a damp, cold morning and you are sitting in your normal chair in the living room of your own home. You can see a large window – try to imagine it. What colour are the curtains? Are there any blinds at the window? Can you hear bird song, or traffic noise? What sound would come into the room?

Look around, look at your furniture, and notice the colour of the carpet. Perhaps you have a pet dog or cat – imagine whether you would have a pet.

Now imagine your own hands. As you look at your hands you think these do not look right, the skin is wrinkled and hangs too loosely, the veins stand out. These hands don't look the way that you remembered them. Your knees, legs and arms look too thin – not the way you remember them. You think about how painful it can be to move, and how difficult it can be to make meals and drinks. No one has visited you for over a week, you are lonely.

Imagine it is now the afternoon, and you have had a visit from a relative and a government official you have never met before. They both explained that you owe a lot of money for your health care! You do not understand this. They said that you will have to move – because of your debts. Tomorrow at 10 o'clock an ambulance will come to collect you and take you to a little room in a hostel. You have seen this little room with its thin, narrow bed. The room has one locker and a small wash basin.

This is the last day you can be with your pet dog or cat. Tomorrow someone will take him to an animal refuge, as pets are not allowed in the hostel. This is the last day you can look at old photos, books or videos – tomorrow they will be thrown away. You can take only two suitcases with you to the hostel.

How do you feel? How will you act when they come for you? What are you living for at this time?

Imagining yourself in this story may help you to understand the idea of vulnerability and a threat to self-concept. Just imagining this situation might make you feel sad or angry – you might have wanted to withdraw, or to fight the authorities who say you are in debt.

The person in this story was going to a hostel and would be warm, well fed and have a place to sleep there. But meeting a person's physical needs is not enough. The person in this story has lost control – others have all the power. Some people would want to give up on life as a result of this situation.

Supporting clients through periods of stress

Caring means working with people, not working 'on' them. Carers need to be able to understand clients and imagine what they might be feeling. Clients should be able to make choices and feel in control of their lives. Supporting clients may involve the following skills:

- listening and talking with a client in order to understand his or her needs
- listening and talking with other staff, and friends and relatives of a client, in order to understand his or her needs
- helping friends and relatives to keep in touch with a client
- keeping and reading care plan records to do with a client's needs
- good communication skills that show respect for the client and his or her rights, and help to meet the client's emotional needs.
- helping a client to make choices and to be as independent as he or she wants to be
- helping a client to relax using activities and interests (see below).

A carer might help a client cope with change by following the steps below:

1. Give useful information and advice if asked. Information and advice can help reduce feelings of uncertainty. Advice on welfare benefits might help with money worries.
2. Be available to listen. When people are feeling a sense of loss it can help to be able to talk. Advice cannot help people to cope with loss, but talking seems to help many people. Carers can help others just by listening.
3. Provide help with learning new routines or using new equipment. Coping with new learning is easier if you have a friendly guide to help you.
4. Provide physical and practical care. When people are tired and stressed it can be comforting if someone else does housework or cooking, or gives other kinds of help.
5. Show respect and value for the client. People going through change may experience a loss of self-esteem, a carer can show that the client matters. Listening carefully to a client can demonstrate a feeling of concern and respect for a person.

Further information on listening and communication skills can be found in Chapter 4. Further detail on clients' rights can be found in Chapter 1.

DO IT

Identify ways of supporting clients through periods of stress and distress caused by change.

Think of a person you have met or worked with who was going through a major period of change. Briefly describe the situation and map the person's needs as you remember them. You could use the questions in Figure 6.2 to help you. Now think of ways a carer could try to meet each of these needs.

Figure 6.2 A client's needs

When people become ill or disabled or move into care, a range of physical and emotional risks can arise for the individual. These risks can be described as losses and the feeling of being unsafe.

Losses

Illnesses, disabilities and moving into care can mean that a person might experience loss in relation to any of the following factors:

- Body image – a person may feel he or she looks 'different'.
- Mobility – a person may not be able to walk or get up from a chair.
- Vision or hearing – sensory loss may isolate a person.
- Health– illness may restrict what a person can do.
- Friends – it is easy to lose contact with friends if you can't get out and about.
- Status – a loss of self-esteem may result from the way a person is treated by others.
- Income – illness, disability or moving into care may reduce the amount of money a person has to spend on other things.
- Self-worth – the above problems may cause a person to feel that he or she is not worth so much.

Feeling unsafe

Some people feel that illness, disability or moving into care involves an attack on their self-esteem. Other people might attack you by:

- stereotyping or labelling you; perhaps with labels like 'senile', 'wheelchair', or 'daft'
- discriminating against you – you may have needs that can't be met if everyone is treated the same.

People may also feel attacked by their own body if they suffer pain or impairment. They may live in fear of further losses, including losing independence and control over their lives.

DO IT

Describe the effects of change on the physical and emotional needs of clients.

An 85-year-old man is living alone – his partner died a year ago. He has poor eyesight and arthritis. These disabilities mean that it is difficult to go out to shop or to meet people. He is lonely because most of his friends cannot get to see him easily.

Make a list of some physical and emotional needs he will have now that he is trying to cope on his own. Discuss how good physical and emotional care might help meet physical needs and overcome worries.

Carers should work out ways in which they can make sure that they respect the rights of vulnerable people. A full discussion of client rights can be found in Chapter 1.

DO IT

Explain how to ensure that clients' rights, beliefs and preferences are respected during periods of change.

Think of a client you work with now or have worked with in the past. Describe an example of:

1. a conversation where you have listened and learned things about the client
2. offering the client choices that might help him or her to stay in control – perhaps choices of what to eat or drink, or choices to do with physical care

3. giving physical care which has left the client feeling comfortable and valued
4. things that you have done to make the client feel important – remembering a favourite food, telling him or her a little about yourself, or remembering birthdays.

If you can find examples of these behaviours, you can probably explain how you go about treating every person as an individual according to his or her needs.

Roles and responsibilities of carers

The National Vocational Qualifications (NVQ) in Care defines the values that carers must have in their work with others. The NVQ defines three basic values:

- foster the equality and diversity of people
- foster people's rights and responsibilities
- maintain the confidentiality of information.

From these values it follows that carers have certain responsibilities to clients and to their own organisations, as shown in the following table.

Responsibilities towards clients	Responsibilities towards the organisation
Not to stereotype, label or discriminate against people who are different.	To understand the relevant law and policies related to Equal Opportunities and confidentiality.
To show respect to clients.	To follow policy or guidelines on staff behaviour in order to show respect and value for clients.
To develop an understanding of clients' beliefs and preferences.	To manage time to make it possible to get to know the clients.
To offer choices to clients.	To clarify the choices available and the resources needed to offer choice.
To respect clients' rights and support clients to uphold their rights.	To discuss care needs with other team members and managers in order to support clients.
To develop a caring relationship.	To undertake self-development and training to improve communication and supportive skills.
To maintain confidentiality.	To operate record-keeping systems effectively and check if people have a right to know information.
To help clients develop or keep their self-esteem.	To be responsible and reliable to other team members.
To contribute to the full development and independence of others.	To understand and discuss the problems that can arise when trying to respect rights and maintain confidentiality.

DO IT

Identify the roles and responsibilities of a professional care worker in relation to clients and organisations.

Design a poster explaining the main responsibilities of a care worker. The poster could be designed to appeal to other care workers, rather than the general public. You could present your ideas for poster design to other students.

Sources of support for carers

Informal carers

Meeting the needs of vulnerable people cannot be achieved by one person alone. As well as a relationship with individual care workers, vulnerable people may have relationships with friends and family. Carers must work effectively within the organisation and within the client's network of relationships. This network could include family, neighbours, friends, even pets.

Supporting vulnerable people can be tiring work. Sometimes a partner or relative will be the only carer for a vulnerable adult. People who develop mobility problems may rely on a partner to do all the housework and shopping, and people who develop dementia may rely on a partner or relative to provide round-the-clock help. People with dementia may forget where they are; they may constantly ask the same questions, or become lost if they leave their house. The stress put onto a carer can be very great.

Lone carers will often need assistance in supporting their vulnerable relatives. Organisations that may help include both statutory and voluntary services. Services such as home care can take some pressure off carers by working directly with a client or by doing household tasks that the carer has been unable to do because of spending time with a client.

Respite care involves caring for a client for a limited period of time. This allows relatives to take a holiday or other break from caring work. Some residential homes for older people offer this 'respite' or 'short-stay' service.

When people care for their own relatives, they run the risk of becoming not only stressed, but isolated. Lone carers may lack advice or help with problems that they face. **Self-help groups** can provide a source of advice and support. Voluntary groups like the Alzheimer's Society may provide advice and guidance to carers in the community.

Professional carers

Professional care workers also need a source of advice and support to guide their work. Professions such as nursing require that their staff undertake professional training to update their skills at regular intervals. Professional counsellors receive regular supervision to ensure that their counselling practice is satisfactory and ethical. Care workers need supervision sessions on a regular basis to check that their practice respects clients' rights. This is vital because people who feel cared for and supported themselves may tend to treat others in a caring and supportive way, whereas those who feel devalued or stressed may tend to devalue and stress others.

Care workers may also provide more effective care if they can take part in regular training and discussion groups (see Chapter 1).

Do it

Identify sources of support for the care worker.

Either

a. ask your supervisor or manager at placement or work about training opportunities and supervision opportunities for full-time staff – how regular are supervision sessions and how does supervision work?

or

b. research sources of support for relatives who act as carers in the community. What self-help group and what services are available to meet the need of carers? Ask your tutor or supervisor about services provided to carers in relation to The Carers Act.

You could use pattern notes (writing down ideas in lines which branch off from a circle) to report your findings whichever task you take on.

The importance of relationships

Relationships are very important to the health and well-being of most people. Studies show that people who have good relationships with others are usually happier and are often healthier than people who do not enjoy good social relationships. Why are relationships important to people? One answer is that we have an inbuilt need to be with others and that doing so can meet many of our physical, intellectual, social and emotional needs.

Think it through

If you had to draw a simple sketch of yourself in 20 years' time, or write a description of your life, would you include in the picture friends, partners or family? It is likely that you would because many people find it hard to imagine a happy and full life without friends and family around them.

How relationships help

Relationships with other people can help us in many ways, including offering us practical help, enabling us to feel safe, and maintaining our self-esteem.

Practical help that relationships can bring include the following:

- Friends and relatives might help us with shopping, with maintaining a home or car, and other practical activities.
- Close friends or relatives might support us by lending money, sharing or lending things we need.
- People we know may give us useful advice.

Feeling safe is easier if we have supportive relationships.

- Friends and family create groups to which we belong. Many people feel relaxed and safe when they are with their friends or 'at home'.

● Relationships can protect us from feeling stressed about money or other problems in our lives.

Happiness and self-esteem often come from relationships.

● If we get on well with friends and relatives, we may feel that we are valued – relationships can give us a feeling of self-worth.
● Friends and family can provide us with a 'social life'. Without relationships, people often feel lonely and bored.
● Talking and listening to people and planning things with others can create a sense of purpose in life.
● Relationships can meet people's social, love and sexual needs.
● People can be interesting – relationships may help to keep us mentally active.

Different types of relationships

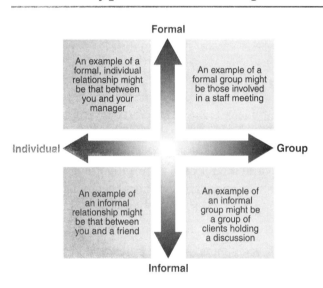

Formal

An example of a formal, individual relationship might be that between you and your manager

An example of a formal group might be those involved in a staff meeting

Individual ← → **Group**

An example of an informal relationship might be that between you and a friend

An example of an informal group might be a group of clients holding a discussion

Informal

Figure 6.3 Types of relationships

We make relationships with individual people, but we may also feel that we belong with groups, such as groups of friends, groups of colleagues at work and family groups. Sometimes our relationships might be part of a formal role that we play – we may get on well with our supervisor or manager at work, but the relationship might be quite formal. Relationships can be very informal, or formal, or somewhere in between. Relationships can be with individuals, with small groups or with large groups.

Types of relationships could be described in a chart like the one in Figure 6.3.

Social and family relationships

Social and family relationships normally involve people who:

● are well known to us and whom we meet regularly
● will be with us throughout life
● we feel are trustworthy and feel tied to emotionally
● support each other, and may share similar views.
● help us develop and keep a sense of who we are.

Because we are involved with family and friends, we share their happiness and celebrate things with them. We also share their pain and grief, and we may become upset if things go wrong for them.

Being closely involved with people causes a great deal of happiness; but it can also create stress and tension. Arguments and anger can easily break out between people who are emotionally involved with each other. When relationships break down, this can cause a great deal of unhappiness and stress.

Professional relationships

When we work with people in social care, we take on a professional role. We have to use personal skills in order to understand and try to meet individual needs. Workers have to make skilled decisions minute by minute in order to help people. Further discussion of professional roles can be found in Chapter 1.

Professional relationships mean that we have to:

- work with people we don't know at first
- provide an equal quality of service for everyone
- provide an equal quality of service regardless of whether we like people or think they are attractive
- work with people whether or not we feel like it
- be prepared to learn about new people
- understand the idea of 'boundaries' in working with people (see Chapter 1).
- become involved with people sufficiently to care for them, but not become so involved that we worry
- behave responsibly as a member of a team (see Chapter 1).

DO IT

Describe four different types of relationships.

Select a day when you are at work or on placement. Keep records of the meetings and long conversations you have from early morning to late evening on that day.

Use your list of conversations and meetings to provide examples of at least four different types of relationships. Write a description of each one. Try to find examples of professional relationships, relationships with friends and family, and formal, informal, group and individual relationships.

Helping clients to maintain or develop relationships

When people are being cared for by others, their needs for relationships are still strong, but it may be difficult to develop or maintain them. For example, a young person may have lost touch with his or her parents; an elderly person may be in care away from his or her old home and friends.

Care workers can help people to develop or maintain relationships in the following ways.

1. Get to know the individuals you work with and build a sense of trust with them. This will involve good listening and conversation skills. Sometimes the care relationship becomes an important part of a client's support network – older people in the community may sometimes rely on their care worker for company and social support.

Figure 6.4 It is important to create a setting where friends and relatives feel welcome to visit

2. Organise activities and social events so that people have a chance to meet and develop new relationships. Planning and leading groups are important skills that care workers may need in order to organise activities.

3. Show respect and value for a client's family and friends. Many older people get a sense of purpose in life from contact with children and grandchildren, and parents are key people in the lives of many younger clients.

4. Create a setting where friends and relatives can visit or support the person you work with. It is important to do everything you can to keep people in touch with their support network. This might include providing a private setting where people can meet and talk confidentially. Relatives and friends need to be able to trust you and to feel welcome.

DO IT

Describe the role of a professional care worker in helping clients to maintain or develop relationships.

Think of a person you work with (at work or on placement). Draw this person's network of family and friends – being careful not to mention real names. In theory, what help can you provide to help this person to stay in contact with the network? You might prepare a chart and a three- to five-minute presentation that you could give to other students to explain what help you can give.

Loss or breakdown of relationship

When people lose relationships they may experience strong emotions such as grief, depression, anger and guilt. The loss of a partner or the loss of contact with friends or family can greatly reduce a person's self-confidence and self-esteem. Grief can sometimes make people feel that there is no purpose to their life – they can lose their sense of who they are through the shock of losing a close friend or partner.

If people lose touch with their entire network of friends and family, perhaps because of illness or disability, they can become socially isolated. Some older people can lose touch with relatives because their relatives live so far away, and a partner may die. Such an isolated person may feel vulnerable and threatened, and may experience anxiety or depression.

Do It

Explain how clients' rights, beliefs and preferences can be affected by relationships.

People have many different lifestyles, beliefs and preferences, but have a right and often a need for worthwhile social relationships. Design a poster that shows the importance of social relationships in helping people to live different lives with different lifestyles. You might present your poster to other students and give a brief explanation of its message about the importance of relationships.

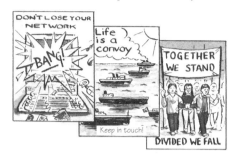

Figure 6.5 Some posters on the theme of social relationships

The importance of activities and interests

Young children might learn a range of practical and social skills from joining in activities like singing, playing musical instruments, drawing, painting and making things. Young children learn to develop their imagination with play activities like using a sandpit or using shapes to build structures.

Adults with learning disabilities may need the opportunity offered by activities and interests to mix with people and develop their relationships. As well as social activities, adults with learning disabilities might enjoy relaxation activities, and activities that develop independent living skills such as cookery.

Older people may be mainly interested in social activities, but these may include games and pastimes they have enjoyed in the past (for example, card games like bridge). Some older people may wish to take part in activities such as music and movement, which exercise muscles as well as providing social contact. Other older people may be interested in thinking and talking about their past. This activity is called 'reminiscence', and it may help some older people keep a strong sense of self-esteem.

Many types of activity can be relevant to social care work and different activities can meet different types of need. Some examples are set out in the table below:

Physical needs	Intellectual needs
Physical exercise can keep muscles working and joints moving. Exercise may help people to develop control of muscles and improve general fitness. Exercises might be linked with games, music or dance activities.	Some activities help people to learn new skills. Activities like shopping and cooking can help people to learn skills that will make them more independent. Sport or dance might help children to learn to co-ordinate their hands or their bodily movements. Social activities like a quiz might help some people to feel mentally fit and active.

Social needs

Activities like sport, card games, discussion groups, quizzes, gardening and cooking involve mixing with people and talking with them. Activity and interest groups can help people to meet others and perhaps make new relationships.

Emotional needs

If you can think 'I'm good at this', you may develop a feeling of self-worth. If you make good social relationships during activities it may help you to develop a higher level of self-esteem. Discussion and reminiscence activities may help some older people to keep a high level of self-esteem.

DO IT

Explain the value of three different types of activities for different clients in different settings.

On the next page are some sample lists of activities, of care settings and of client groups – you could add extra examples to the lists. Choose three client groups and three appropriate settings where you might meet them. Then choose three activities, and work out how these activities might meet the physical, intellectual, social or emotional needs of your chosen client group.

Who decides on clients' needs?

Activities can have many benefits, but not all activities are equally valuable to all clients. A young person might not find a reminiscence discussion very useful. An older person with poor eyesight and arthritis – who had never been interested in painting – might not find an art class very valuable.

Care workers can make some general guesses as to the value of an activity for certain groups of people, but they are unlikely always to guess people's needs accurately. The only person who really understands a client's needs in relation to activities is the client.

Imagine you lived in a country where you were required by law to walk or run five miles every day, to spend half an hour doing mental arithmetic, and to go to bed early. Imagine all this was checked by the secret police. The government might, quite rightly, point out that this lifestyle would be very good for you. Your mind and body would probably be much fitter than they are now. The government would be meeting your physical and intellectual needs!

But most people do not like being told how to live their lives. In a democratic society, we believe that people have a right to choose the interests and activities that make up their lifestyle. If people are pushed into doing things they have not chosen to do, they may feel that their opinions and views are of little importance.

Remember: clients should actively choose to join in activities or interest groups – if they don't choose to join in, the activities may do more harm than good.

Activities	Care Setting	Client groups
Building a house using boxes	School or day nursery	Children
Sand play	Home in the community	Adults
Cutting out shapes	Day centre	Adults with learning disability
Drawing or painting pictures	Residential home or rest home	Older people
Shopping for food		
Making masks		
Cooking		
Exercising to music		
Being part of a team playing a quiz game		
Using old photos to reminisce about the past		
Playing card games		
Using lighting and music to create a relaxation session		
Discussing shared interests with other people		

One elderly woman in a rest home was asked why she refused to join in activities. She explained that, at 85, she felt differently to the way she had earlier in life. 'I want to sit and think and rest – I don't want to do anything else. I've worked all my life, and I want some peace now. You may feel the same if you get to my age!'

Different people see their needs differently. It is a client's right to choose to opt in or out of activities.

Figure 6.6 Clients may have differing views about levels of activity

Planning activities

Most activities have to be planned, although sometimes you can just get talking to people or just show someone how to do something. If you are trying to get a group together to learn about cooking or to reminisce, you will need to do some planning.

Aims

The first thing is to work out the aim or purpose of the activity. What value will a game or an activity have for a group? Will it meet social needs? Is the activity intended to help people become more independent? Is the activity intended to give people a sense of achievement? Unless the aim of an activity is clear you can't be sure that it will meet people's needs.

Appropriateness

The next issue is to be sure that the activity is culturally and individually appropriate for the people you want to work with. If you want to lead a cooking session, you will need to check clients' views on food and food handling. Different cultures and religions have strict views on what may be eaten and how food should be prepared. In some cultures and age groups, men may feel that cookery is inappropriate for them. Some people dislike certain activities and certain foods.

Choice

Before starting any activity you need to know the background and views of the people involved. You must also check that they really would like to do the activity – it is a client's right to choose! Pressurising adults into doing things may threaten their self-esteem.

Safety

There are two aspects to safety – physical safety and emotional safety. Physical safety involves checking that people won't injure themselves. If you were showing people how to cook, the issues to check would include sharp objects like knives, hot things like boiling water and cooker hobs, and food hygiene.

Emotional safety means that the activity won't lead to individuals feeling upset, discriminated against or threatened. If you were going to lead a reminiscence session you might want to check that the pictures or objects you would show people were appropriate. Pictures of working-class children from long ago might offend an older person who saw himself as middle class! Some memories – perhaps of the war – might be upsetting for some people.

Environment

Next, you need to check you can have an appropriate room or setting for your activity and that all the equipment and materials you need are available.

You need to have a plan for how you will work with people. For example, you should decide how you will demonstrate cooking. Will you explain things step by step? How will you get people talking? What prompts or ideas will you use?

Finally, you should check all your planning with a supervisor or tutor before trying to lead any activity. If you are not experienced it may be important that there is someone to help you. Showing people how to do things or leading a discussion can look easy; but you can easily go wrong or forget what to do next. Having an experienced member of staff to work with you can create a sense of confidence for everyone.

Good practice: planning an activity

✓   set out the aim of the activity

✓   check that the activity is appropriate

✓   check that people want to be involved

✓   check for any physical safety risks

✓   check for any emotional safety risks

✓   decide which rooms/equipment/materials are needed

✓   decide on the methods or steps involved in the activity?

✓   check on the support and help available.

DO IT

Plan activities for two specific client groups.

At work or on placement, you will have observed clients taking part in activities. Choose two activities you have watched with different groups and work out what rooms, equipment and materials are needed in order to lead these activities. What steps and methods are needed in order to get the activity to work? Ask a supervisor or colleague at work to help you collect this information.

DO IT

Describe the factors which have to be considered when planning interests and activities for maintaining health and well-being.

If you have worked out how to organise two activities for the exercise above, you could use the whole planning list on this page to check whether it would be appropriate to lead each of the activities with clients you know – people you work with now or have worked with in the past.

You could share both these tasks with other students by swapping planning lists and discussing whether it would be right to go ahead with the activities.

The risk of isolation

Residential and day-care settings can help to meet people's social and emotional needs by providing a social atmosphere where care staff use conversation and activities to encourage people to get to know each other and perhaps to get on well with each other.

Without conversation and activities, a care setting may not be a sociable place to be. It is possible for members of a day centre or residential centre to live in their own 'bubble' of experience and not to communicate with others. If service users have lost touch with their friends and relatives, they may experience total isolation. Visits from friends and family may be very important for preventing a feeling of isolation.

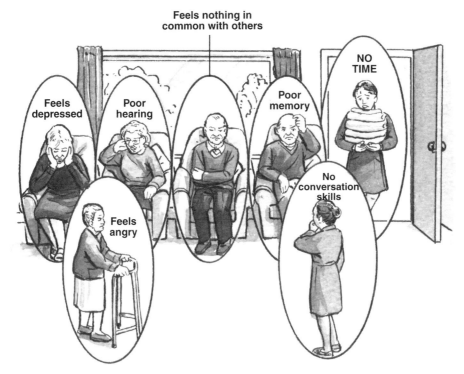

Figure 6.7   There is a danger in care settings that people will live inside 'isolation bubbles'

DO IT

Describe the possible isolation effects of a care setting.

Imagine a day in the life of a resident who lives in a large home where there is a low staff-to-resident ratio. The staff have time only to get the residents up, provide meals and help them with going to the toilet and other basic care. The residents all come from different backgrounds and have different disabilities. During the day, residents sit around in the lounge or wander about the home.

List the routine that a particular resident might experience from getting up at 7.30 am to going to bed at 8.30 pm. Describe how and why this person might feel isolated.

Conversation, activities and meetings with friends and relatives may be necessary to develop or keep a sense of self-worth. But activities can go wrong if they are not culturally and individually appropriate.

DO IT

Explain the need to respect clients' rights, beliefs and preferences when planning activities.

One of the most important principles of social care work is that we should understand that people have different beliefs, preferences and needs – people must not be treated as 'all the same' (see Chapter 1). Below is a list of activities, and a second list showing some differences between people. Explain what might go wrong if these activities were provided for everyone, and everyone was treated the same.

You could turn this exercise into a quiz, with one team asking another team 'What would go wrong if everyone had to . . . '. Why might certain people feel threatened, offended or excluded?

Activities	Differences
Learn how to cook bacon	Religions
Take turns in washing up	Beliefs about what it is right to eat
Sing Christmas carols	Beliefs about alcohol
Play bingo	Countries of origin
Go to a sherry or drinks party	Ethnic groups
Play cards, gambling for pennies	Gender and gender roles
Learn to paint	Social class
Do old-time dancing	Levels of practical ability and disability
Talk about photographs of England in the 1920s	

Supporting the client in a home setting

The place where you live is very important. It is your home. Imagine how you might feel if for some reason a stranger had to come and live in your home – or even your room. How would this affect you?

For people who need to be cared for in their own house it is particularly important for the carer to be sensitive to possible feelings of anger or fear.

Clients are likely to feel nervous when a care worker comes into their home, so it is very important that the worker is supportive. Carers should:

- develop a good sense of trust with the client
- build a relationship using listening and conversation skills
- show respect for clients and make them feel that their beliefs and preferences are understood and valued
- reassure clients that workers keep their information confidential
- explain their work role
- work within care plan guidelines
- respect clients' rights including the right to choose their own lifestyle, routines and standards.

When working with a new client, a care worker has to work hard to get to know the person. As well as being friendly, the care worker has to find out exactly what kind of help is needed and how the client would prefer things to be done. Care plan details are likely to explain only the general tasks that have been agreed. The care worker has to discover how to meet the client's needs in detail.

CASE STUDY MR WILSON

Mr Wilson's care plan simply states that he needs help with shopping and general household cleaning. When you meet Mr Wilson, you discover that his needs are not straightforward. Mr Wilson is lonely because he can't get out. He is a member of a local church; it seems a good idea for someone to contact the church to arrange visits or transport to church services.

Mr Wilson grew up in the Caribbean. He has a preference for certain fruits and vegetables, which can be bought at the local street market but not in the local supermarket.

Care workers may have to help clients with clothing, managing their own budget, making choices about food, with shopping or with cleaning. All these depend on the carer working in a supportive way.

Care of clothing and linen

Care of clients' clothing and linen involves:

- washing clothes
- ironing
- taking clothes to cleaners.
- drying and folding
- storing

Many clients will have their own routines for washing, ironing, folding and storing clothes. It is usually important not to take over and impose new ways.

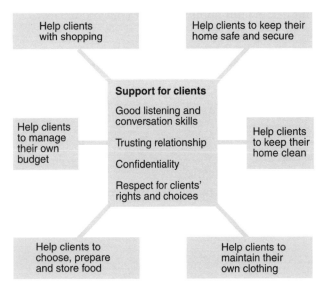

Figure 6.8 Practical help depends on using supportive skills

Clients may need help only with particular tasks. Perhaps a client may have difficulty with loading, setting and unloading a washing machine, but may be able to fold items of clothing. It is important to agree what work you can help with and how that work should be done.

Clients may have their own system for storing clothes in different drawers or cupboards. It may be very important to work within their system they have invented. If clothes are stored in new places, clients may become frustrated and confused.

Carers should discuss all procedures for washing, ironing and storing clothes with the person they care for. It is always important to show respect for client choice.

There may be laundry services for people who have problems with incontinence. These might be run by local or health authorities. Soiled laundry can be collected and cleaned, and then delivered back to the client.

Do It

Identify ways in which clients can maintain their own clothing and linen.

Work out in detail what your routine for washing, ironing, folding and storing clothes and linen is in your own home. Make notes and exchange your notes with other students. Are all your routines exactly the same? Do you all wash your clothes and sheets in the same way and as often. If you had to help another student, list how you would have to change the way you work, compared with the way things are done in your own home.

Choosing, preparing and storing food

Food is a very personal area of life. Many people express their individuality through their choices about food and food preparation.

Religion, culture, life experience and the amount of money available may all influence what a client will choose to eat and drink. Clients who are depressed or withdrawn may not want to eat. Encouraging clients to make choices is one way of showing you value them and helping to increase levels of self-esteem.

Case study Mrs Soros

Mrs Soros is 90 years old and has been on her own for nearly a year since her husband died. Mrs Soros has difficulty in preparing and cooking food because of breathlessness and partial sight. She says 'Everything tastes the same anyway!'

Mrs Soros has home care. Her carer, Jenny, encourages her to take an interest in food and cooking, but at first Mrs Soros would just ignore advice. She was happy to eat only sweets and fruit. After a few weeks Mrs Soros came to like and trust Jenny. They talked a lot and Mrs Soros started to take an interest in Jenny's life. Jenny decided to talk about the meals she liked to cook, and how they could easily be bought and prepared. Jenny suggested that Mrs Soros might like to try some of the new meals from the supermarket. Mrs Soros agreed – because she had become interested in Jenny's life, and because she trusted Jenny.

Relationships are often very important in motivating clients to make choices – especially if they have become depressed.

A home carer may often need to spend time finding out about a clients' beliefs and preferences connected with food. Many people have strong views about diet and the way food should be prepared. Carers may also need to spend time learning about different cultures' methods of food preparation so that they can understand client need. Carers must be careful not to push their own beliefs and preferences on to clients or to criticise a client's choices.

As with other activities, a particular client may need help only with one particular activity. Some clients can't get to the shops, but can manage their own routines for cooking at home. Some clients may need help with lifting heavy pots or pans, and others may need help to choose appropriate food if they have developed problems with memory. Each person will be different and the care worker needs to work out how best to support each client with his or her chosen diet and routines.

Food safety

There are some important principles care workers should follow when preparing food or assisting clients to do so, because of the need for hygiene and safety.

Good practice: food preparation

✓ always wash your hands before touching food

✓ cover any cuts or sores with a waterproof dressing

✓ try not to handle food any more than is necessary

✓ keep raw and cooked food on separate work surfaces

✓ clean utensils between using them for different foods

✓ keep food covered

✓ keep food refrigerated or very hot

✓ get rid of waste food quickly and properly

✓ keep all equipment and work surfaces clean

✓ check 'use by' dates on manufactured food products

✓ do not sneeze or cough near food.

Healthy eating

Current advice on healthy eating includes:

- cut down on fatty foods, which include red meat, cheese and cream
- eat plenty of fresh fruit and vegetables, and cereals with a high fibre content
- try to avoid eating too much and becoming overweight
- if you drink alcohol, drink only moderate amounts.

It is important not to impose health education advice on clients, as some may feel that being given such advice is an attack on their dignity.

Do It

Describe ways to encourage clients to choose, prepare and store food safely.

You could try this in pairs. Wear a blindfold or use glasses that limit your vision, so that you can play the role of a client with a visual disability. Work with another student who will act as your 'carer' and who will help you to choose and prepare a sandwich or some other form of food. You could swap over, so everyone has a chance to experience being on the receiving end of care. Follow safety rules. You do not have to eat the food at the end!

At the end of the exercise write notes on how it might feel to be cared for. In particular, did your carer:

- check your beliefs and preferences – or just tell you what to do?
- talk you through things?
- respect and value you?
- try to find out what you could do for yourself?
- give you choices?
- help you to do things for yourself?
- follow food safety rules in relation to the storage and preparation of food?

Maintaining a clean, safe and secure environment

There is detailed advice on hygiene and safety, and the issues of health and safety at work, in Chapters 3, 5 and 7. Chapter 7 also addresses the issue of security.

Care workers often work with people who have different standards, beliefs and preferences to their own. It is important not to argue with clients or to insist that our standards are the right ones. Instead, you need to estimate the risk that may be involved in a client's behaviour. For example, does the client let strangers in or light fires? If a care worker feels there is a risk to safety or health, he or she, should discuss the problem with a manager.

Think it through

What should a care worker do if:

- a client hoards newspapers? Some people have been known to fill whole rooms with newspaper – never to throw them away, but save them 'because they could be useful'.
- someone has a dusty and dirty home but doesn't want it cleaned?
- someone refuses to put the heating on because he or she wants to save money to leave it to the grandchildren?

Hoarding

Hoarding newspaper always increases the risk of a fire starting, and of a fire spreading quickly. However, many people keep old books and papers, and people have a right to store things that they want in their own homes. If the client is at risk of setting the paper on fire, some sort of emergency action may be needed to reduce this risk. But the action may not necessarily be to remove all the newspaper!

Dirt and dust

Dirt and dust are not good for people, but individuals have different standards. If a property is a public health risk, it may be necessary to clean the house to remove the risk. Some dust and dirt may be acceptable, however, and it is important to respect clients' wishes unless there is a risk to the care worker or the public.

Cold

Under-heated rooms can be a serious risk to old people and it may be that something needs to be done. However, carers cannot force their views onto clients. It may be possible for a care worker to keep an eye on a client at risk and get the client to turn the heating on when the temperature falls below a mark on a thermometer placed in the client's living room. However, a carer can't argue that the client must not save money on heating.

Security and access

You need to ensure that any access arrangements you have to the client's home do not create a security risk. It is not safe to leave front door keys under mats or pots or on a string through the letterbox. Systems for securing access to a clients' property may have to be negotiated with managers. It may be that keys to clients' properties will be kept in a locked safe and that you sign them out and back in after you have visited a client. Keys should never have names and addresses attached to them in case they become lost.

DO IT

Explain how to encourage clients to maintain a clean, safe and secure living environment.

You have to work with an older man who has become a little depressed and neglects the house where he lives alone. The man has a limited ability to walk, and needs help with shopping and cleaning. He shows little interest in doing anything for himself or in preparing or eating food.

Discuss this situation with another student and make a list of ideas that would not threaten this client or take away his rights, but which might help him to increase his self-esteem and interest in life.

Shopping for household and personal goods

Clients may not be able to get out to the shops to buy food, clothes and household goods such as cleaning materials and washing powder. Care plans often state that clients need help with shopping.

Some people know what they want – which brand of washing powder, and so on. It is important to respect a client's choices even though we may make different choices. Some people may have a fixed routine and want a set list of shopping every week. Other people will like change and will like to vary what they eat and drink.

It is important not to make assumptions that people will always want a fixed lists of things to buy. Part of the carer's job is to help clients to plan their shopping, and people may want to try different things from time to time.

Budgets

Many clients have to be careful with their money, and some clients may ask for your help in working out their shopping bills. Clients may also welcome any advice you can give about how much things cost. You should always keep the till receipts when you go shopping; usually you will need to check them through with the client. Checking the receipts not only proves that you have been honest, but it may also help to give the client up-to-date information on shopping.

Think it through

You return from shopping and the client is so pleased with you that she says: 'Keep the change – it's a little present, no one will know.' It is very important that carers never accept money from clients. Care agencies will have strict rules that forbid accepting money. The reasons for these rules is to protect clients from financial abuse, and also to protect workers from complaints about money.

Financial abuse can happen when people are expected to offer gifts or extra payments for services. If you never accept money, you can make sure that you can't be accused of trying to win trust so as to get money out of people.

Storage

When you return with shopping, many clients may ask you to help with putting the shopping away. There are two important principles to think about here.

1. The **system the client uses** Some people have difficulty in seeing or remembering where things are kept. If they have a set place for things, it is important that the carer understands and stores things in the right place.
2. **Safety** Heavy things should be stored where they can't fall out and hit someone. Older food purchases should be moved to the front of a cupboard with new goods stored behind them so that food is used before its 'use-by' date. Many types of food need to be refrigerated. Care workers may sometimes be able to offer useful suggestions on managing storage – but the client has a right to manage this as he or she wants to.

Do it

Explain how clients can obtain household and personal goods.

1. Keep a list over two weeks of what your household needs in the way of shopping. Note what your own (or your household's) routine is for going shopping, and organising where and how things are stored.
2. Now imagine you had to have professional care – and that you couldn't go shopping. write down your shopping list and how you would explain your list and your storage plan to a care worker.
3. Work in pairs, take turns explaining your needs to another student and see if you can understand each other's systems.

The supportive role of the care worker

Professional care is not just about meeting physical and practical needs. People in the community who need care often feel threatened by having a stranger come into their home. Clients will have a need to feel 'safe'.

Some people will have lost touch with relatives and friends, and sometimes the care worker may be the main person a client talks to. The care worker may become someone who helps to give a client a sense of belonging or a sense of purpose in life.

Carers need to think about all the 'levels of need' that people have – not just their physical needs. Working supportively involves trying to meet social and emotional needs, as well as physical needs.

Do IT

Explain the role of the care worker in supporting the client in the home.

Keeping in mind a) the physical needs, b) the safety needs, c) the social and d) the emotional needs of clients, write down three ways in which a care worker can help a client with these activities.

1. Look after clothing and linen
2. Choose, prepare and store food
3. Keep the home clean and safe
4. Plan shopping needs.

You could start this exercise by working with a small group of other students to think of ideas under each heading. When you have gathered your ideas, you may like to record them on work cards as illustrated in Figure 6.9.

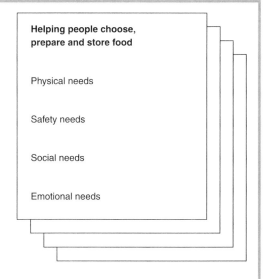

Figure 6.9 Work cards can record your ideas on the care worker's role

7 THE CARING ENVIRONMENT

A clean, safe and secure living environment

There are two main reasons for keeping clean the environment that we live in:

1. to meet people's social and emotional needs
2. to meet people's physical health and safety needs.

Social and emotional needs

People have different beliefs and values about how clean a home should be. Some people believe that everything should be neat and tidy, with a place for everything and everything in its place. Many people find dust or dirt offensive.

Someone used to living in tidy, spotless surroundings may become distressed if he or she can no longer keep to former standards of cleanliness. If you were forced to live in an untidy or dirty care setting you might feel that other people did not value you or think you deserve good treatment. Having to live in untidy or dirty surroundings could take away a person's self-esteem or cause depression.

Health and safety

Some people do not worry about how tidy or clean their environment is, and their self-esteem is not influenced by cleanliness. However, it is still important to clean the environment for health and safety reasons.

Controlling infection

Many illnesses and diseases are caused by micro-organisms such as viruses or bacteria. Once a person has an illness such as diarrhoea or a respiratory (throat or chest) infection it can spread to other people if they do not have sufficient resistance to infection, and there is a way in which the infection can spread.

How are infections spread?

Infection can be spread by:

- breathing in infectious viruses and bacteria
- taking in infectious organisms through the mouth
- infection through cuts, through mucous membranes, or just by skin contact.

Breathing in infections

When a person sneezes or coughs, infection can be carried through the air on tiny droplets of moisture. People may develop an illness if they breathe in these infected droplets. Droplets can settle and dry to particles that mix with dust. When the dust is disturbed it can mix into the air again – making it possible for people to breathe in the infection. Do you know the rhyme: 'Coughs and sneezes spead diseases'?

Good practice: protecting yourself and others

✓ Cover your nose and mouth if you cough or sneeze, to try to limit the spread of droplets.

✓ Ensure good ventilation. Fresh air circulation will help to remove infected particles. Closed, crowded rooms may make it easier for infection to spread.

✓ Do not mix with clients or colleagues if you think you have a serious illness such as flu.

✓ Prevent dust from building up by dusting or vacuuming domestic surfaces and floors.

Taking in infections by mouth

Putting unwashed fingers into your mouth may be enough to pass on an infection. Some infections are passed on through contaminated food, or food that has touched infected surfaces. Water and other drinks can also become contaminated.

Good practice: handling food

✓ Keep all food handling areas and equipment clean by regularly washing and wiping down.

✓ Follow food hygiene rules (see Chapter 5, page 151).

✓ Always wash your hands before touching any food or working in a kitchen. Always wash your hands after using the toilet.

✓ Do not prepare food for other people if you have a skin or stomach infection.

Infections through contact

Some infections can be spread by skin contact, or contact between harmful micro-organisms and an individual's mucous membranes (the thin membranes in your mouth, for example) or blood system.

Good practice: safe contact

✓ Take great care with knives and other sharp instruments. If you do cut yourself, encourage the wound to bleed and wash the wound as soon as possible. Report any injuries that happen, and cover all cuts.

✓ Wear protective gloves to provide a barrier against infection on any occasion where you have contact with body fluids including blood, vomit, urine or faeces, or with soiled linen or dressings. Take the gloves off by turning them inside out so that your skin does not come into contact with the outside surface of the gloves.

✓ Wash your hands before and after contact with other people's skin.

✓ Wear protective clothing such as a plastic apron for any procedure that involves bodily contact or deals with body fluids.

✓ Tie up long hair – to prevent contact with others.

✓ Clean all equipment and surfaces that come into contact with body fluids, using a disinfectant or antiseptic solution.

✓ Avoid sharing towels or other linen or clothing. Ensure that towels and other laundry are handled and washed according to appropriate procedures. Laundry should not come into contact with food preparation areas or be left on the floor.

✓ Clean all toilets, hand basins, showers, baths and bidets on a regular basis (usually at least once every 24 hours where different people use the same facilities).

✓ All waste material soiled with blood or other body fluids should be disposed of using yellow plastic bags to indicate that they contain hazardous material.

✓ Regularly clean play equipment or toys that are shared by children.

✓ Make sure you know the procedures for cleaning and for controlling infection within the care settings you work in. Make sure you have adequate protective equipment and that you know how to use the equipment provided.

Safety

It is vitally important that everyone who works in care checks for safety hazards. Safety hazards are explained in Chapter 3, and also later in this section.

Think it through

Look at the diagram in Figure 7.1. How many safety hazards can you spot? (Answers are given at the end of the chapter.)

Figure 7.1 How many hazards can you spot?

Security

If people are to feel safe there must be appropriate arrangements. In a care setting security arrangements can protect people from:

- loss or theft of personal possessions
- financial abuse or fear of losing money or possessions
- physical threat or attack
- loss of confidentiality.

It is important that equipment and materials within a care setting are not damaged or stolen. Staff should also feel safe and not at risk from intruders. Some security issues which may need to be checked are described below.

Access to care settings

Care settings should not be 'public places' where anyone can come or go. It is important to be able to check who people are and why they are in a setting.

Ideally, care settings should be organised so that visitors enter through a main entrance where they can be greeted and their identity checked. Many centres have a reception area where staff can record people entering and leaving a building. Doors and windows should have a locking system to prevent people entering without being noticed.

Knowing who people are is important in order to prevent theft and worse crimes such as assault. Clients have a right to choose who they see and who they do not see. If visitors are always met by staff, it will help to protect residents' rights.

Security of residents' property

Personal possessions can be very important to people. A wedding or engagement ring might have tremendous emotional importance. Losing a personal possession like a ring could create a deep sense of loss or pain; the ring might have much more value than just its monetary value.

There should be systems for recording witnessed accounts of the money and valuables that residents possess.

Personal security

Clients may sometimes be at risk of verbal or physical attack by other clients. It is important that staff can identify potential risks with respect to other residents' behaviour. Records of incidents and past behaviour can be important to help staff identify risks.

Where clients have poor memory or limited ability to understand where they are, it is important that they cannot simply wander out of the building to become lost or perhaps walk into dangerous traffic.

Security of records

Details of written or electronic records on clients must be kept confidential (see Chapter 4). Files and other records should be kept in locked rooms or cupboards and computer records should be protected by password security. It is important that staff follow appropriate procedures and do not leave files or records where they can be seen by people who do not have a right to read them. It is also vitally important that personal details, records of medication and so on do not become lost.

Do It

Identify the safety and security requirements of a care setting.

Make a list of what you can do to prevent infection in your work or placement setting. List the safety hazards that might exist in your setting. Next, list possible security risks that could exist in your setting. Check your lists with your placement supervisor. Share your ideas with colleagues on the course and consider their ideas before finalling completing your lists.

Supplies and equipment

Running a home or a care setting efficiently depends on keeping an adequate stock of food, cleaning materials, clean towels, clothes and linen.

Storage

It is important to store food separately from cleaning materials to help to prevent the spread of micro-organisms or the contamination of food. Certain foods such as cooked and raw meat should also be stored separately (see food hygiene points on page 192).

Monitoring stores

If you work with an individual in the community you may be able to monitor the person's needs by getting to know him or her and checking supplies in the fridge or cupboard. Even in this situation, however, it is important to organise fridge and cupboard space so that food is eaten in the order of its 'use-by' date and the stock of materials can be seen clearly.

In larger care settings, just leaving stock in cupboards would usually cause problems. Care homes have to **monitor** what is being used and how long different supplies last in order to:

- know how often to re-order supplies, so that they do not run out
- check best value for money (some cleaning liquids may work better or last longer than others)
- check that materials are not being used incorrectly, wasted or stolen
- budget and organise the finances of the home.

Monitoring supplies usually means that staff have to sign a book, data sheet or other list for materials such as protective gloves for personal use or for the transfer of materials such as toilet rolls. Some items such as drugs have to be monitored with total accuracy – every dose or tablet has to be checked and witnessed, for reasons of health, safety and security.

Cleaning

If you work in a client's own home it is important to find out about the client's routine and methods of cleaning so that as far as is reasonable you can work to his or her standards. If you work in a care setting there will be an established routine for regular cleaning in all areas. This is often organised in two ways: regular cleaning happens every day, e.g. for toilets, and periodic cleaning happens at longer intervals, e.g. for curtains and paintwork. You could ask your supervisor to clarify this routine for you.

Regular cleaning will take place in the following areas:

● **Kitchen**   Dirty cutlery, crockery and cooking utensils will be washed with an appropriate solution of detergent (washing-up liquid) as soon as possible. Detergent removes grease and food deposits which could otherwise provide a place for harmful micro-organisms to grow and spread. Dirty plates or glassware might offend clients.

Food preparation surfaces, floors and cooking equipment will be regularly wiped down with appropriate cleaning and disinfectant solutions. This helps to prevent the build-up of dirt in which harmful micro-organisms can grow, and to reduce the number of harmful micro-organisms that can come in contact with food. Cloths used for dishes and plates should be kept separate from those used on floors or other surfaces, to stop cross-infection from one area to another.

● **Bathrooms and toilets**   Hand basins, baths, showers, bidets, toilets and commodes should be cleaned on a regular basis using appropriate cleaning and disinfectant solutions. In a care setting this is likely to be done at least once a day, and more often if there is a need to control infection. Disposable cloths are ideal for this cleaning and all cloths and brushes should be cleaned with an appropriate cleaning and disinfectant solution.

Some infections can be spread by skin contact, so regular cleaning of washing and toilet facilities must remove the dirt that micro-organisms can live in. Disinfectants can kill harmful micro-organisms and help to prevent the spread of infections.

Towels should be provided on an individual basis and regularly laundered, or in more public settings disposable paper towels or other systems should be used to make sure that micro-organisms cannot be passed from one person to another.

● **Bedrooms**   Floor surfaces and furniture surfaces should be regularly cleaned to remove dirt and dust. This may involve vacuuming, wiping surfaces with a damp cloth and dusting with a cloth.

Bed linen, e.g. sheets and duvet covers, need regular laundering to prevent the build-up of micro-organisms. Soiled bedding must be removed and cleaned immediately, and should be treated as hazardous.

● **Halls, lounges and other general areas**   Floor and furniture surfaces should be regularly cleaned to remove dirt and dust. Dust can help the spread of harmful micro-organisms, and may also contain particles that cause allergies or asthma for some people. Furniture and equipment must be kept tidy to prevent the risk of tripping or other accidents.

Do It

Describe cleaning techniques and materials necessary to maintain a clean living environment.

Find out what the cleaning routine is for bedrooms, bathrooms, toilets, kitchens, lounge and hall areas in the care setting where you work or are placed. Make a list of specific cleaning materials and products used in this setting and how they are to be used. Note down the safety issues that are involved in this cleaning work. Check your list with your supervisor at work.

Creating a good impression for clients

Living in a clean environment with polished brass and sparkling glass, and a pleasant, fresh smell, is good for people's self-esteem. There may not be any value for physical health in polishing glassware, but it might have emotional importance for a client.

Assessing and developing abilities

In a great number of care situations, tidying and cleaning is an activity shared between care staff and clients. Clients's needs are assessed during the process of care planning, Often an agreement might be reached that a client will do certain tasks – perhaps washing and drying crockery in the kitchen while home carers clean the floor and food preparation surfaces.

In some care settings older children and adults are encouraged to learn independent living skills. In these settings staff will demonstrate the necessary cleaning routines and then help clients to learn how to take over these activities.

Where clients are agreeing or learning to look after their own home it will be important to keep care plan records and to understand how other team members may contribute to the client's learning and activities. It can be important that different members of staff do not teach different routines and activities.

The importance of a clean, safe and secure environment

People's well-being can be threatened in a number of ways:

- micro-organisms can attack a person's health
- safety hazards can cause physical injury
- intruders or other clients might physically or emotionally abuse clients
- dirty, unsafe or insecure care settings might make people feel emotionally threatened.

A setting that fits clients' expectations and standards might help clients to feel emotionally safe, and may contribute to increasing their self-esteem.

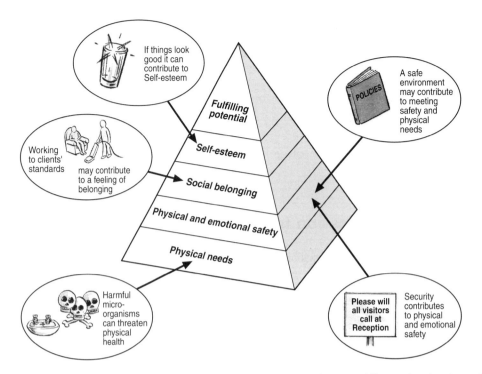

Figure 7.2   A clean, safe and secure living environment can contribute to different levels of need

---

DO IT

Explain the importance of maintaining a clean, safe and secure living environment.

Design a table listing the things your work setting does and the equipment it provides to ensure a clean, safe and secure living environment. What risks might exist for clients if these services were not provided? You might want to copy the outline below:

Cleaning

What the centre does, e.g. clean bathrooms every day	What could happen if this was not done?

Safety hazards

What safety hazards exist, e.g. in food hygiene?	What could happen if hazards were not checked?

Security

Security precautions	What could happen if there were not security precautions?

Working with other people

Working as part of a team

Being a care worker involves being good at making relationships and understanding other people. It is important to have good relationships with other staff. Usually this will involve working as part of a team, but also developing your role as an individual.

What is a team?

A team is a group of people who work (or pull) together to achieve a task. In some teams everyone works on exactly the same tasks, like a team of horses – everyone pulls their weight doing similar work. An example might be a team of care assistants who all work on the same unit with the same clients – but sometimes on different shifts. Some teams are more like a sports team where different people have different skills and abilities, but they are all working for the same general goal. An example of this might be a day centre, where the manager may spend a lot of time on administration, care workers provide most of the physical care and volunteers lead some activities with clients. People are all working together to improve life for clients – but different people do different jobs.

Think it through

In your own work or placement setting, how far does your team involve everyone working together on the same jobs, and how far do people in the same team do different work?

Working teams

The feeling of belonging to a team doesn't necessarily come about because people do the same work. But if teams are going to work effectively in care, individuals within the team have to:

- know who the other members of the team are
- share a common set of values with the other members
- respect and value the differences between team members
- communicate effectively with each other.

Sharing common values

When groups of people get together, they may go through a process of learning to become a working team. This process was described by a researcher called Tuckman, in 1973, as follows:

The forming stage: People introduce themselves and try to learn about others.
The storming stage: People compete with each other to control the group. People may disagree and have arguments. A team could breakup and stop working together at this stage.
The norming stage: People develop a set of beliefs and values about how the work should be done and how team members should behave towards each other.
The performing stage: Because people now have common values, they can work together and trust each other. The team can work effectively because there is a feeling of belonging together based on shared values.

In care work, teams are unlikely to work effectively unless staff share the values of respect for each other and concern about each other's rights.

The Care Sector Consortium defined a value base for care that can be used with NVQ standards (see Figure 4.4 on page 116).

Communicating effectively

When individuals get together to talk it is important that people feel a sense of belonging together and that they can discuss important issues. An effective working team will create the right working atmosphere. This will involve the following.

- **Showing respect and value for each individual**
  This might be done by welcoming each person by name, asking each person for his or her views, and being sensitive to the emotions and feelings that people express.
- **Creating a feeling of belonging to the group**
  This might be done by keeping a sense of humour and sharing jokes, encouraging people to speak openly, helping people to say what they feel, being friendly and responsive to others, and helping people to compromise.
- **Keeping people working on important issues**
  This might be done by organising an agenda for meetings, giving and asking for information during the discussion, bringing discussion back to the important issues, and putting ideas forward for other people to discuss.

Figure 7.3 Good team communication will involve a balance of issues

Good team meetings will involve a balance between meeting individuals' emotional needs, creating a feeling of belonging and keeping people working hard on the business of the meeting.

Develop your own role

Team roles are discussed in Chapter 1. Your role within a team will depend on the expectations that other people have of you, and how you wish to develop the way you work. Care work involves continual changes if you are to meet individual clients' needs. As you develop your skills and knowledge of clients, you may be able to discuss the work you do with other members of the team. You may be able to take on increasing responsibilites by negotiating with other members of the team.

Do it

Describe how people work as part of a team and develop their own role.

Get together with some other students and make a list of important factors that help people to work in teams.

Thinking about your own work or placement, give examples of good teamwork you have seen. List some ideas for developing your own role within the team.

Working with visitors

Many clients have a network of people who provide practical and emotional support to them. Visitors can be very important in meeting the social and emotional needs of clients in care. All the communication skills and care skills relevant to clients will also be relevant to clients' visitors (see Chapter 4 for discussion of communication skills).

There are some key issues to consider in relation to visitors. These are described below.

Learning about a client's support network

In order to provide a warm and friendly welcome to visitors, it can be useful to understand who is who in a client's network of friends and family. Learning to recognise faces and names can help to provide the right atmosphere. Knowing people also helps to maintain security. Information about a client's network of relatives and friends may be available from other team members or from care plan records. If you are a permanent member of care staff, you will usually have a need to know this information.

Clients' rights concerning visitors

Adult clients have a right to refuse to see visitors. It is important to remember that clients' needs are the first priority of a care service, not the needs of friends or relatives.

Sometimes visits will not go well. It may be that certain visitors seem to upset or distress an individual. If you notice problems, you should report what you have seen or heard to a manager as soon as possible. If an individual appears quiet or withdrawn after a visit, it may also be important to report these reactions.

Helping clients to stay in contact

Sometimes, care workers will take messages from friends and relatives to be passed on to clients. Sometimes, a client may ask a care worker to pass messages on to friends or relatives or request help in writing a letter. It is important to help people keep in touch with one another, but it is also important to maintain confidentialilty and not be drawn into giving information or opinions about a client.

Confidentiality

It is important not to talk about a client with relatives or friends unless you have checked with your client first. It is particularly important not to pass on details of medical matters, health or finances without permission. It is usually possible to suggest politely that friends and relatives discuss issues directly with your client rather than with you; say something like: 'I expect she would like to discuss that with you.'

Privacy

When visitors arrive it is usually important to have somewhere where they can talk with clients in private. Sometimes this might be the client's room, or in other settings there might be an office or side room. Having to talk with clients in an open setting causes problems in keeping information confidential, and can make conversation more difficult for clients and visitors.

Helping visitors with enquiries

Sometimes visitors may want to ask about the care services you provide. They may want to know about other services that might be available. Very often, working with visitors may involve suggesting where they might obtain accurate information. It is important, of course, not to give incorrect advice or information.

Welcoming visitors

Use your communication skills to make visitors feel relaxed and welcome. It is usually important to look interested in visitors and to smile. If you can remember visitors' names and who they are visiting, it will help to make them feel welcome. You may be able to develop particular ways of welcoming visitors by watching other staff and copying the good practice you see.

Coping with emotions

Visitors may experience a wide range of emotions when they visit. They may be anxious or worried about what is happening to a person they love. They may feel angry about things that have happened, or guilty because they feel they should be helping more. Care workers need to be sensitive to this and to recognise and understand the emotions that visitors experience. Skills that enable you to stay calm, listen, show concern and calm others are an important part of the work that carers undertake.

Do it

Discuss how to communicate with visitors in the care setting.

Make a list of the things it would be useful to know about a visitor before he or she arrives. List some ways you can make a visitor feel welcomed. Make a third list of some of the other key issues involved in working with visitors.

Abuse

Preventing abuse is a very important part of care work. Abuse can take the following forms.

- **Physical abuse**   Hitting, pushing, pulling, restraining or causing pain or distress by other physical actions.
- **Sexual abuse**   Sexually exploiting or humiliating others.
- **Emotional abuse**   Bullying, blaming, threatening and damaging others' feelings of self-worth and self-esteem (this is sometimes called psychological abuse).
- **Financial abuse**   Taking others' property or money, theft or exploiting other people's resources.
- **Neglect**   Not giving enough food or physical care, not giving attention.
- **Self-abuse**   Damaging or harming oneself. People who are distressed might cut themselves or seek to harm themselves in other ways. Self-abuse can sometimes happen when a person has been abused in other ways.

Abuse and the ways of identifying abuse are covered in more detail in Chapter 4.

DO IT

Identify potential forms of abuse in care settings.

Make a list of the possible types of abuse that could happen in a care setting. This will include the possibility of abuse between clients, abuse by visitors and by staff. Describe four possible examples of abuse, which might be physical, sexual, emotional or financial abuse, self-abuse or neglect.

Conflicts in care settings

People in care can become angry or refuse to co-operate with you, causing a 'limitation' to what you can do or achieve together.

Why do people become angry or refuse to co-operate? Some reasons include the following.

- **Illness** When we are ill it can become harder to control what we say and do. Conditions like dementia can mean that people are unable to control their emotions and responses.
- **Pain** When we are in pain it can be difficult to control emotions. We may get angry because of the pain.
- **Fear** Some people in care do not know what to expect. Not being able to understand a situation could make people feel afraid and angry.
- **Frustration** Some people become frustrated because they cannot do things as easily as they used to. This stress can lead to anger.
- **Feeling vulnerable** Some people may be afraid of losing their dignity. Others may become angry because they feel 'got-at' by others.
- **Past learning** Some adults and children may have learned that being angry is the way to get things they need. Some people may be used to arguments and fighting as part of their way of life.

What happens when people get angry?

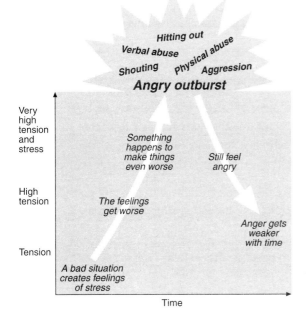

If oftens looks as if someone suddenly loses his or her temper. Perhaps a person who is learning to cook suddenly throws things across the kitchen. Perhaps an older resident who finds someone else sitting in what he sees as 'his chair' suddenly seems to explode with rage.

In many situations, a person already feels stressed before becoming angry. People may feel stressed because of pain or fear, or because they feel vulnerable. A person may be stressed because he or she is frustrated about not being able to do something. Feelings of emotional

Figure 7.4 How anger builds up and then explodes

tension can grow as the person feels more stressed.

When a person feels stressed it only takes a single remark, or some little thing that has gone wrong, to tip him or her into an angry outburst. People who feel stressed need a trigger to set off the explosion of anger that has built-up inside them.

After an explosion of anger, stressed people can still feel tense. Very often, they may feel that it is someone else's fault that they have been made to feel so angry. Anger can flare up again if the person is not given respect and encouraged to become calm. As time passes, tension may reduce if the stress can be relieved.

Not all anger follows this pattern. Some people learn to use aggression to get their way, and some can switch aggressive emotions on and off as they wish. Being angry can sometimes be a reaction that a person has chosen. But it is wrong to assume that all aggression and anger are deliberate. Most anger in care settings will involve the build-up of bad feelings described above.

Coping with anger and disagreement

If possible, try to prevent angry outbursts. If you understand the people you work with, it may be possible to spot when they are feeling tense. You may be able to calm people before an angry outburst happens, perhaps by using your conversation skills to get the person to talk to you. Talking may prevent anger if the person trusts you.

- Watch for things that might trigger anger in another person.
- Be careful not to make demands, or tell other people what to do. Try not to increase feelings of stress.

If an angry outburst happens:

- stay calm
- do not put yourself at risk
- don't blame the person, get angry, or try to 'get your own back'
- try to calm the angry person
- try to talk with the person if possible – but avoid arguing
- try to sort out differences and arguments after the other person is calm and willing to talk with you.

Staying calm

Witnessing anger, shouting, hitting out or abusive words will make a care worker feel stressed. The natural instinct in everyone makes us want to either run away or fight the person who is being aggressive. The ability to stay calm is a special skill that care workers need.

Like all skills, staying calm can be learned, but it may take time and effort to become good at it. An ideal way to learn to stay calm is to watch people who have this skill. Some ideas which may help are given below.

- Try to understand how stress can cause clients to become angry. Don't regard anger as a personal attack on you.

- Use assertiveness skills – know how to express yourself clearly and calmly without becoming aggressive or looking weak.
- Feel confident in your own skills and self-esteem. If you feel good, you are less likely to feel threatened.
- Know how to relax the muscles in your face, shoulders, arms and hands, so that you look and feel calm. It is possible to improve your calmness by practising muscle control.

Risk

If you don't think you can cope, or you think you might be attacked, then you should leave and report the situation immediately. If you are working with someone who you think may become aggressive, you should always check that you will be able to move out of reach and leave the room or house. It is important not to work alone with a client who may become aggressive; if you think you could be at risk, this should be discussed with your manager. Your health and safety are vitally important.

Getting angry

Any angry behaviour, insult or verbal abuse can be hurtful. If we feel hurt we may want to 'get even' by hurting the person who has caused these feelings. It is an important caring skill not to let this happen to you. If a carer does lose control, he or she might verbally or physically abuse a vulnerable person. Carers should not have to 'bottle up' their feelings, though. If you work with people with challenging behaviours, there should be someone with whom you can talk your feelings through. You should be able to talk to a supervisor or a manager during supervision, or perhaps talk to a counsellor.

Calming others

If you can develop your own skills of staying calm, you may be able to use these skills to calm others. Once again, calming skills are best learned by watching other people with the skill and copying what they do. Their skills may involve:

- keeping face, shoulder, arm and hand muscles relaxed
- showing respect and valuing the other person
- using a calm tone of voice
- speaking normally and clearly
- offering to listen to the other person
- keeping an appropriate distance from the other person
- avoiding fast or jerky movements
- keeping eyes, head and shoulders at a slight angle to the other person – rather than appearing to 'face down' the person.

Talking

When a person has thrown things across the room or shouted, it is natural to ask the person why he or she has done these things, and to discuss the issue. But it is best not to do this straight away, as it may lead to more stress and arguments. Carers should try to build a sense of trust before going on to discuss the reasons why a person feels angry.

Resolving conflicts and disagreements

It is important that an angry person becomes calm and begins to trust you before going on to try to sort out problems. Sometimes it may be important to leave the person for a short period before coming back to talk things through. Sometimes it may be appropriate to ask the person to sit down with you or agree something with you before trying to resolve the conflict. If the angry person agrees things with you, then you have probably developed a sense of trust, which may be enough to enable you to talk about the reasons for the anger. It is important not to argue with the person and not to demand things or threaten him or her. Try to see other people's side of the situation, and help them to see your side.

DO IT

Identify methods to resolve limitation or conflicts with clients.

Describe an example of anger or disagreement you have seen in a care setting. Imagine you had to deal with this situation, and list some skills and methods you could use to achieve a positive outcome for both yourslef and the client.

The role of family and friends in care

As well as having physical needs, people have social, emotional and intellectual needs. For many people, family and friends meet most of these social, emotional and intellectual needs.

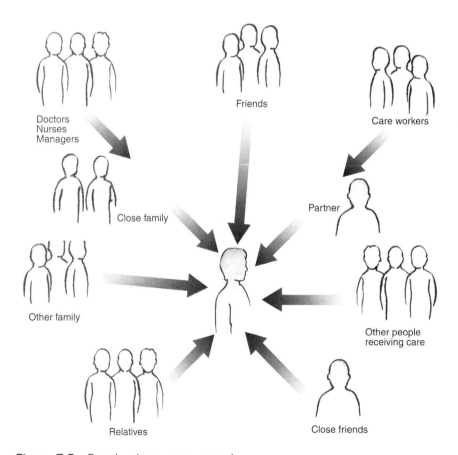

Figure 7.5 People who meet our needs

Close family and close friends may help us to understand who we are. When people go into care or receive a care service, it may be very important that they can keep in touch with the people who matter to them.

Helping clients to keep in touch

Care workers may be able to help clients stay in contact with friends and family by helping with:

- written communication
- telephone communication
- arranging visits
- getting to know friends and family during visits.

Written communication

A care worker may offer to write a letter for a person who finds this difficult. It is important to write what the person wants to say, and not to put in different ideas. Letters need to be read back to clients before they sign them.

Telephone communication

Some clients need help with making calls. This may involve taking a telephone to them, checking the number to dial and dialling for them, adjusting the volume of the telephone, or finding a private place to make a call.

Visits

Care workers may be able to send messages to help to organise visits. Working with visitors was discussed earlier in this chapter.

Getting to know friends and family

Care workers may learn to recognise friends and family when they visit, and something of their feelings and concerns. If friends and family feel welcome and understood, it may help them to maintain contact with relatives.

Involving friends and relatives in a client's care

Where clients enjoy good relationships, it may be possible to involve close friends and relatives with activities that take place in a care home. Sometimes friends or relatives may be prepared to help or join in with social activities or outings.

Where care is provided to people with a learning disability, it is often vital to explain activities and learning programmes to close family members who also provide care. Care plans for many clients may need to be jointly organised with family members so that the client's needs are fully understood by everyone, and to ensure that the client is not treated in different ways by family and carers. If close family are not involved in care it can be possible for a client to be treated inappropriately. For example, an Asian person may be used to

eating certain foods with his or her fingers when with the family. If a care centre failed to understand this, staff might try to encourage the client to use cutlery. Involving the family might help to prevent inappropriate care or teaching.

Dealing with emergencies

The settings in which you provide care are generally covered by the Health and Safety at Work Act 1974. This has been updated and supplemented by many sets of regulations and guidelines, but those most likely to affect care workplaces are:

- Management of Health and Safety at Work Regulations 1992
- Control of Substances Hazardous to Health Regulations 1988 (COSHH)
- Reporting of Injuries Diseases and Dangerous Occurrences Regulations 1985 (RIDOR)
- Manual Handling Operations Regulations 1992.

Health and Safety at Work Act

Many regulations, laws and guidelines exist to ensure health and safety, and you do not need to know the details of all of them, but you do need to know how the Health and Safety at Work Act is likely to affect what happens in care settings. The Act is the main piece of legislation, and all the guidelines and regulations either add to it, support it, explain it or extend it. See Figure 3.4 on page 95.

The effects of the law

The laws that govern health and safety place certain responsibilities on employers, and also on workers – you need to know what they are. For example, the employer must provide a safe place in which to work, but the employee (or student) also has to show reasonable care for his or her own safety.

Employers have to:

- provide a safe workplace
- ensure that there is safe access to and from the workplace
- provide information on health and safety
- provide health and safety training.

Workers must:

- take reasonable care for their own safety and that of others
- co-operate with the employer in respect of health and safety matters
- not intentionally damage any health and safety equipment or materials provided by the employer.

Each workplace where there are five or more workers must have a written statement of its health and safety policy. The policy must include:

- a statement of intention to provide a safe workplace
- the name of the person responsible for implementing the policy
- the names of any other individuals responsible for particular health and safety hazards

- a list of identified health and safety hazards and the procedures to be followed in relation to them
- procedures for recording accidents at work
- details for evacuation of the premises.

Control of Substances Hazardous to Health

What are hazardous substances? There are many substances hazardous to health: nicotine, many drugs, even too much alcohol! In this context, however, the Control of Substances Hazardous to Health regulations (COSHH) apply to substances that have been identified as being toxic, corrosive or irritant. This includes cleaning materials, pesticides, acids, disinfectants and bleaches. Each workplace may have other hazardous substances because of the nature of the work carried out.

Every workplace must have a COSHH file. This file lists all the hazardous substances used in the workplace, and should detail:

- where they are kept
- how they are labelled
- their effects
- the maximum amount of time it is safe to be exposed to them
- how to deal with an emergency involving one of them.

What to do in the workplace

If you have to work with hazardous substances, make sure that you take the precautions detailed in the COSHH file. This may involve wearing gloves, or protective goggles. It may involve limiting the time you are exposed to a substance, or only using it in certain circumstances.

The COSHH file should also give you information about how to store hazardous substances. This will involve using the correct containers as supplied by the manufacturers. All containers must have safety lids and caps, and must be correctly labelled.

Never use the container of one substance for storing another, and *never* change the labels.

The symbols in Figure 3.7 on page 100 indicate that these are hazardous substances – the signs are there for your safety and that of those you care for. Before you use any substance, whether it is liquid, powder, spray, cream or aerosol, take the following simple steps:

- check the container for a hazard symbol
- if it has one, consult the COSHH file
- look up the precautions you need to take with the substance
- make sure you follow the procedures carefully – they are there to protect you.

Do it

Explain the Health and Safety at Work Act and COSHH regulations.

Design and produce a poster or leaflet that could be given to a student on his or her first placement. It must give information about the Health and Safety at Work Act and include the symbols warning of hazardous substances, shown in the correct colours.

Emergencies that may arise in care settings

People who work in care have to be able to deal with a wide range of emergencies. They can include:

- health emergencies
- intruders or other security emergencies
- escape of chemicals or other hazardous substances

- fires
- explosions
- floods.

How to prevent emergencies

It is precisely because emergencies are unpredictable that they can be difficult to avoid, but following basic safety precautions and procedures will help.

Type of emergency	Actions to prevent it occurring
Health emergency	Trained first aider on duty Check for 'slip and trip' hazards Check safety of all equipment Check all drugs and medications are safely locked away
Fire	No smoking Check safety of electrical equipment Use all fire doors correctly Do not use naked flames
Intruders or security emergency	Have a system for checking visitors Ensure valuables are secure Have an alarm system and use it
Explosion	Regularly check gas appliances Be aware of unattended bags or packages
Escape of chemicals or hazardous substances	Store all chemicals and hazardous substances according to instructions Never put them in different containers Dispose of hazardous substances safely and correctly
Flood	Check the water system regularly Do not allow pipes to freeze Never leave plugs in baths or basins

What to do in an emergency

There are a few simple rules which apply in all emergency situations, no matter what the circumstances:

- keep calm – panic is infectious
- send for help, or get someone else to do so

- be clear if you are giving information or instructions – speak slowly and calmly using simple, short sentences
- act quickly but safely – speed is often very important in dealing with an emergency
- only attempt what you can safely do, not something you are unsure of – summon help and wait for it to arrive.

Do it

Identify types of emergencies that could happen in care settings and how they can be monitored.

In a group, choose an emergency situation which could arise in a health or care setting. Each person in the group must take on the role of one of the people in the emergency. The roles will vary depending on the emergency, and could include professional emergency workers such as ambulance crew or fire fighters, health professionals such as nurses or doctors, trained first aiders, people who offer assistance, victims of the emergency, bystanders, even journalists! You can either role-play the emergency and write an account of what happened in the role-play, or write down the details of exactly what the person in your chosen role would do, then get together with the rest of the group and put all your actions together. Write a short account at the end, showing how all the different roles worked together in the emergency.

Health emergency procedures

Summoning help

In the majority of cases, calling for help will mean telephoning 999 and requesting an ambulance. This will depend on the setting in which you work – clearly this is not required if you work in a hospital! But it may mean calling for a colleague with medical qualifications, who will be able to make an assessment of the need for further assistance. If you work in the residential sector, there may be a medically qualified colleague available. If you are the first on the scene at an emergency in the community, you may need to summon an ambulance for urgent assistance.

If you need to call an ambulance, keep calm, and give clearly all the details you are asked for. Do not attempt to give details until they are asked for – this wastes time. Emergency service operators are trained to find out the necessary information – let them ask the questions, then answer calmly and clearly.

Assist the person dealing with the emergency

A second pair of hands is invaluable when dealing with an emergency. If you are assisting someone with first aid or medical expertise, follow all that person's instructions, even if you don't understand why they are necessary. An emergency situation is not the time for a discussion or debate – that can happen later. You may be needed to help to move a casualty, or to fetch water, blankets or dressings, or to reassure and comfort the casualty during treatment.

Make the area safe

Often an accident or injury will have taken place in an unsafe area. At other times, it may be that the accident has made the area unsafe for others. For example, if someone has tripped over an electric flex, there may be exposed wires or a damaged electric socket; a fall against a window or glass door may have left shards of broken glass in the area; or there may be blood or other body fluids on the floor. You may need to make the area safe by turning off the power, clearing up broken glass or dealing with a spillage.

It may be necessary to re-direct people away from the area of the accident in order to avoid further casualties.

Fire emergency procedures

All workplaces must display information about what action to take in case of fire. The fire procedure is likely to be similar to the one shown in Figure 7.6.

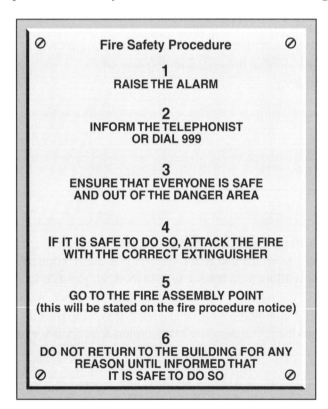

Figure 7.6 Action to take in case of a fire

There are specific fire extinguishers for fighting different types of fires. It is important that you know this, but you do not have to memorise them as each one has clear instructions on it. Make sure that you read the instructions before use.

Remember

- Read the instructions on fire extinguishers before tackling the fire – the extra few seconds will be well spent making sure you are using appropriate equipment in the correct way. This is even more important with the new extinguishers, which are predominately red.
- Check that you have the right extinguisher for the blaze you are tackling.

Red – water	Paper, wood, general fires
Cream – foam	Liquid oil, fat, petrol, oil, etc.
Blue – dry powder	Fuel oil, can be used on electrical fires
Black – carbon dioxide	Electrical, wiring fires
Green – BCF	Electrical and most others, but not used in most workplaces because of cost

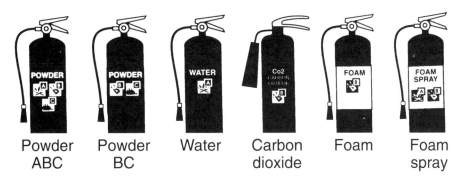

Powder ABC   Powder BC   Water   Carbon dioxide   Foam   Foam spray

Figure 7.7   Be sure to use the appropriate extinguisher

● Only tackle a fire if you can do so safely – otherwise leave the building and wait for help to arrive.

Evacuation procedure

Some other emergencies, such as explosions or the leaking of chemicals, may mean that a building has to be evacuated. Each workplace will have its own procedure, but they are likely to include the following points:

● stay calm, do not shout or run
● do not allow others to run
● organise people quickly and firmly, without panic
● direct those who can move themselves and assist those who cannot
● use wheelchairs to move people quickly
● if necessary, move a bed with the person in it.

First aid box

The essential items that should be in all first aid boxes are shown in Figure 7.8.

Do IT

Describe emergency procedures and equipment in a care setting.

Describe the procedures you would follow and the equipment, if any, you would use in the following emergencies:

a. fire
b. health emergency
c. escape of dangerous chemicals.

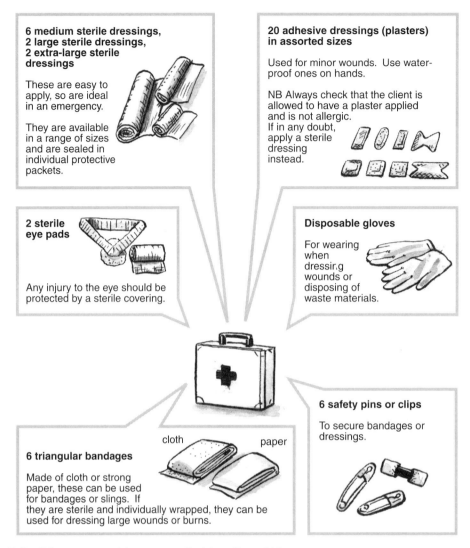

6 medium sterile dressings, 2 large sterile dressings, 2 extra-large sterile dressings

These are easy to apply, so are ideal in an emergency.

They are available in a range of sizes and are sealed in individual protective packets.

20 adhesive dressings (plasters) in assorted sizes

Used for minor wounds. Use water-proof ones on hands.

NB Always check that the client is allowed to have a plaster applied and is not allergic. If in any doubt, apply a sterile dressing instead.

2 sterile eye pads

Any injury to the eye should be protected by a sterile covering.

Disposable gloves

For wearing when dressing wounds or disposing of waste materials.

6 safety pins or clips

To secure bandages or dressings.

6 triangular bandages

cloth   paper

Made of cloth or strong paper, these can be used for bandages or slings. If they are sterile and individually wrapped, they can be used for dressing large wounds or burns.

Figure 7.8 What you would expect to find in a first aid box

Emergency conditions

It is important that you can recognise the major signs and symptoms of the main health conditions that may require emergency action.

Severe bleeding

Causes

Severe bleeding can be the result of a fall or injury. The most common causes of severe cuts are glass, as the result of a fall into a window or glass door, or knives from accidents in the kitchen.

Symptoms

There will be apparently large quantities of blood from the wound, and in some very serious cases the blood may be pumping out. Blood, even in small amounts, can be very frightening, both for you and the casualty. Remember that a small amount of blood goes a long way, and things may look worse than they are – stay calm. Severe bleeding requires urgent medical attention in hospital, because although people rarely bleed to death, extensive bleeding can cause shock and loss of consciousness.

Aims

- to bring the bleeding under control
- to limit the possibility of infection
- to arrange urgent medical attention.

Action

1. Apply pressure to a wound that is bleeding. If possible, use a sterile dressing. If one is not readily available use any clean, absorbent material, or even your hand. Apply direct pressure over the wound for ten minutes (this can seem like a very long time) to allow the blood to clot.
2. If there is any object in the wound, such as a piece of glass, *do not* try to remove it – simply apply pressure to the sides of the wound.
3. Lay the casualty down and raise the affected part if possible.
4. Make the person comfortable and secure.
5. Dial 999 for an ambulance.

Protect yourself

You should take steps to protect yourself while dealing with casualties where there is bleeding. Your skin provides an excellent barrier to infections, but you must take care if you have any broken skin such as a cut, graze or sore. Wash thoroughly in soap and water, and seek medical advice if blood comes into contact with your mouth or nose or gets into your eyes. Blood-borne viruses (such as HIV or hepatitis) can be passed only if the blood of someone who is already infected comes into contact with broken skin.

- If possible wear disposable gloves.
- If this is not possible, cover any areas of broken skin with waterproof dressings.
- Take care with any needles or broken glass in the area.
- Use a mask for mouth-to-mouth resuscitation if the casualty's nose or mouth is bleeding.

Cardiac arrest

Causes

Cardiac arrest means the stopping of a person's heart. Cardiac arrest can happen for various reasons, the most common of which is a heart attack. A person's heart can also stop as a result of shock, electric shock, a convulsion or other illness or injury.

Symptoms

- no pulse
- no breathing.

Aims

- to obtain medical help as a matter of urgency
- to start resuscitation to get oxygen into the collapsed person's lungs using mouth-to-mouth resuscitation, and stimulation on the heart by chest compressions. This is called cardio-pulmonary resuscitation – CPR. You will need to attend a first aid course to learn how to resuscitate – you cannot learn how to do this from a book, because you will need to practice on a special dummy.

Action

1. Check whether the collapsed person has a pulse or is breathing.
2. If there is no pulse or no breathing, call for urgent help from the emergency services.
3. Start methods of resuscitation if you have been taught how to do it.
4. Keep up resuscitation until help arrives.

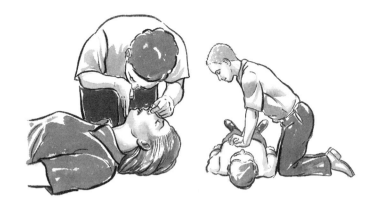

Figure 7.9 Mouth-to-mouth resuscitation (a) and chest compressions (b)

Shock

Causes

During shock, blood is not properly pumped around the body. This can occur as a result of the loss of body fluids through bleeding, burns, severe vomiting or diarrhoea, a sudden drop in blood pressure, or a heart attack.

Symptoms

The signs of shock are easily recognised:

- the person will look very pale, almost grey
- the casualty will be sweaty, and the skin will be cold and clammy
- the pulse will be very fast
- the person may feel sick and may vomit
- the breathing may be very quick.

Aims

- to obtain medical help as a matter of urgency
- to improve blood supply to heart, lungs and brain.

Actions

1. Call for urgent medical assistance.
2. Lay the person down on the floor. Try to raise the feet off the ground to help the blood supply to the vital organs.
3. Loosen any tight clothing.
4. Watch the casualty carefully, and check the pulse and breathing regularly.
5. Keep the person warm and comfortable – but *do not* warm the casualty with direct heat, e.g. a hot water bottle.

Do not

- allow casualty to eat or drink
- leave the casualty alone, unless it is essential to do so briefly in order to summon help.

Loss of consciousness

Causes

- Loss of consciousness can happen for many reasons, from a straightforward faint to unconsciousness following a serious injury or illness.

Symptoms

- reduced level of response and awareness
- this can range from being vague and 'woozy' to total unconsciousness.

Aims

- to summon expert medical help as a matter or urgency
- keep the airway open
- note any information which may help to establish the cause of the unconsciousness.

Action

1. Make sure that the person is breathing and has a clear airway.
2. Maintain the airway by lifting the chin and tilting the head backwards.
3. Look for any obvious reasons why the person may be unconscious, i.e. a wound, an ID band telling you of any medical condition. Many people who have medical conditions that may cause unconsciousness, such as epilepsy or diabetes, wear special bracelets or necklaces giving information about their condition.

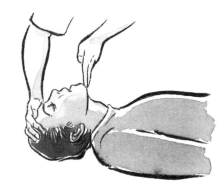

Figure 7.10   Open the airway

4. Place the casualty in the recovery position, *but not if you suspect a back or neck injury,* until the emergency services arrive.

Do not

- attempt to give anything by mouth
- attempt to make the casualty sit or stand
- leave the casualty alone, unless it is essential to leave briefly in order to summon help.

The recovery position

Many of the actions you need to take to deal with health emergencies will involve placing someone in the recovery position. In this position, the casualty has the best chance of keeping a clear airway, not inhaling vomit and remaining as safe as possible until help arrives. This should not be attempted if you think someone has back or neck injuries, and may not be possible if there are fractures to limbs.

1. Kneel at one side of the casualty, at about waist level.
2. Tilt back the person's head to open the airway, with the casualty on his or her

back and making sure that limbs are straight.

3. Pull the arm on the far side over the chest and place the back of this hand against the opposite cheek.

4. Use your other hand to roll the casualty towards you by pulling on the far leg, just above the knee.

5. Once the casualty is rolled over, bend the leg at right angles to the body. Make sure the head is well tilted back to keep the airway open.

Epileptic seizure

Causes

Epilepsy is a medical condition that causes disturbances in the brain, resulting in sufferers becoming unconscious and having involuntary contractions of their muscles. This contraction of the muscles produces a fit or seizure. The person does not have any control over the seizures and may come to harm by falling when he or she has a seizure.

Aims

● to ensure that the person is safe and not injured during the fit
● to offer any help needed following the fit.

Action

1. Try to make sure that the area in which the person has fallen is safe.
2. Loosen clothing.
3. Make sure that the person is safe – particularly try to prevent head injury.
4. If the fit lasts longer than five minutes, or you are unaware whether the casualty is a known epileptic, call an ambulance.
5. Once the seizure has ended, make sure that the person has a clear airway and place in the recovery position.

Do not

● attempt to hold the casualty down, or put anything in the mouth
● move casualties until they are fully conscious, unless they are at risk where they have fallen.

Choking and difficulty with breathing

Causes

Choking is caused by something (usually a piece of food) stuck at the back of the throat. It is a situation that needs to be dealt with quickly, as people can rapidly stop breathing if the obstruction is not removed.

Symptoms

● red, congested face at first, later turning grey
● unable to speak or breathe, may gasp and indicate throat or neck.

Aims

- to remove obstruction as quickly as possible
- to summon medical assistance as a matter of urgency if the obstruction cannot be removed.

Action

These guidelines apply to adults and children over eight years old.

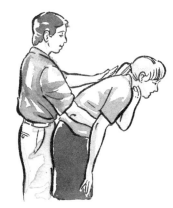

1. Try to get the person to cough, but if that is not immediately effective, move on.
2. Bend the person forwards, slap sharply between the shoulder blades up to five times.
3. If this fails, stand behind the person with your arms around him or her. Join your hands just below the breastbone. One hand should be in a fist and the other holding it.
4. Sharply pull your joined hands upwards and into the person's body at the same time. The force should expel the obstruction.
5. Alternate backslaps and abdominal thrusts until you clear the obstruction.

Fractures and suspected fractures

Causes

Fractures are a break or crack in a bone. This is usually caused by a fall or other type of injury. The person will need to go to a hospital as soon as possible to have a fracture diagnosed correctly.

Symptoms

- acute pain around the site of the injury
- swelling and discoloration around the affected area
- limbs or joints may be in odd positions
- broken bones may protrude through the skin.

Action

1. The important thing is to support the affected part – help the casualty to find the most comfortable position.
2. Support the injured limb in that position with as much padding as necessary – towels, cushions or clothing will do.
3. Take the person to hospital or call an ambulance.

Do not

- try to bandage or splint the injury
- allow the casualty to have anything to eat or drink.

Burns and scalds

Causes

There are several different types of burn; the most usual are burns caused by heat or flame. Scalds are caused by hot liquids. People can also be burned by chemicals or by electrical currents.

Symptoms

- depending on the type and severity of the burn, skin may be red, swollen and tender, blistered and raw or charred
- people are usually in a great deal of pain and may be in shock.

Aims

- obtain immediate medical assistance if the burn is over a large area (as big as the casualty's hand or more) or if it is deep
- stop the burning and reduce pain
- minimise the possibility of infection.

Action

1. For major burns, summon immediate medical assistance.
2. Cool down the burn. Keep the burn flooded with cold water for ten minutes. If it is a chemical burn, this needs to be done for twenty minutes, and you must ensure that the contaminated water used to cool the burn is disposed of safely.
3. Remove any jewellery, watches or clothing that are not sticking to the burn.
4. Cover the burn if possible, unless it is a facial burn, with a sterile or at least a clean dressing. On a hand or foot, a clean plastic bag will protect from infection until it can be treated by an expert.
5. If clothing is on fire, remember the basics: *stop, drop, wrap* and *roll* the person on the ground.

Do not

- remove anything that is stuck to a burn
- touch a burn, or use any ointment or cream
- cover facial burns – keep pouring on water until help arrives
- allow anyone with burning clothes to go outside or run around.

Remember

Stop someone with burning clothes from running around.

Get them to *drop* on to the ground – push them if you have to and can do so safely.

Wrap them in something to smother the flames – a blanket or coat, anything to hand. This is better if it is soaked in water.

Roll them on the ground to put out the flames.

Poisoning

Causes

People can be poisoned by many substances: drugs, plants, chemicals, fumes or alcohol.

Symptoms

The symptoms will vary depending on the poison.

- The person could be unconscious.
- The person may have acute abdominal pain.
- There may be blistering of the mouth and lips.

Aims

- to remove the casualty to a safe area if he or she is at risk, and it is safe for you to do so
- to summon medical assistance as a matter of urgency
- to gather any information that will identify the poison
- to maintain a clear airway and breathing until help arrives.

Action

1. If casualties are unconscious, place them in the recovery position, which should ensure that the airway is clear, and they cannot choke on any vomit.
2. Dial 999 for an ambulance.
3. Try to establish what the poison was and how much has been taken – this information could be vital in saving a life.
4. If a conscious casualty has a burned mouth or lips, he or she can be given small sips of water or cold milk frequently.

Do not

- try to make the casualty vomit.

Electrical injuries

Causes

Electrocution occurs when an electrical current passes through the body.

Symptoms

This can cause cardiac arrest and burns where the electrical current entered and left the body.

Aims

- to remove the casualty from the current when you can safely do so
- to obtain medical assistance as a matter of urgency
- to maintain a clear airway and breathing until help arrives
- to treat any burns.

Action

There are different procedures to follow, depending on whether the injury has been caused by a high-voltage current – such as overhead power cables or rail lines. In this case:

1. Contact the emergency services immediately.
2. *Do not* touch the person until all the electricity has been cut off.
3. If person is unconscious, clear the airway.
4. Treat any other injuries, such as burns.
5. Place in the recovery position until help arrives.

If the injury is caused by a low-voltage current, such as those that power kettles, computers, drills, lawnmowers, etc. the steps to follow are slightly different.

1. Break the contact with the current by switching off the electricity at the mains if possible.
2. It is vital to break the contact as soon as possible, but if you touch someone who is 'live' you too will be injured. If you are unable to switch off the electricty, stand on something

that can insulate you, such as a telephone directory, rubber mat or pile of newspapers, and use an object such as a broomhandle to move the casualty away from the current.

3. Do not use anything made of metal, or anything wet to move the casualty from the current. Use a wooden pole or broomhandle, even a chair.

4. Alternatively, drag the casualty with a rope or cord, or, as a last resort, pull by holding any dry clothing that is not in contact with the body.

5. Once the casualty is no longer in contact with the current, follow the same steps as with a high-voltage injury.

Figure 7.11 Move the casualty away from the current

DO IT

Identify signs and symptoms of different emergency conditions.

Demonstrate basic first aid procedures.

Each member of your group should choose at least two emergency conditions. Describe to the rest of the group how to recognise the condition and the basic first aid procedures to follow. You can do this by demonstrating what to do using a dummy or another member of the group, or by preparing a handout or visual presentation. After you have listened to all of the presentations, write about one other procedure, saying what you learned from the presentation.

Answers to Think it Through on page 199

Safety hazards in the kitchen

Crockery is left unwashed, with particles of decaying food around.

Electrical safety – the kettle lead is near water, creating a risk of electric shock. The electrical point might be overloaded with too many connections. The toaster is too near the sink and water supply.

Fresh food is left uncovered – flies can land on it and spread micro-organisms from the decaying food in the sink and bin. Micro-organisms from the air can also contaminate the food.

Bleach can be hazardous – it should not be stored near food. Here the lid is off and there is a risk of spillage or even food contamination.

Food preparation surfaces have not been cleaned, allowing microorganisms to build up and transfer to fresh food.

Knives are not stored in a safe way.

Decaying food is left in a broken pedal bin, encouraging flies and the spread of micro-organisms.

Fresh food is placed near decaying food, encouraging the spread of micro-organisms.

The dishcloth is contaminated with micro-organisms from the (dirty) floor area – separate floor and dishcloths should be used.

The dirty floor might create a hazard of slipping and falling, as well as encouraging the spread of micro-organisms.

The mop and bucket might be tripped over.

PROMOTING ACTIVITY

This chapter is about helping clients to remain active. This involves supporting clients' mobility, and helping them to participate in activity programmes. The focus throughout is on maintaining good practice when supporting mobility, and when choosing and supporting development programmes and activities.

Clients' mobility

This section deals with the factors that can affect clients' mobility. Being mobile is an important part of life for all of us, but we tend to take our own mobility for granted. Unless we have experienced periods when we are less mobile than usual, it can be hard to appreciate just how important it is. Being able to get around can be the key to being able to participate in a range of activities and pursuits that we all find enjoyable and enriching.

Clients whose mobility is restricted are likely to need our help and support to be able to take advantage of the activities that are available. To help them effectively we need to be aware of the legislation and policies that must be considered, the services and products that are available to help, and the need to maintain good practice when assisting clients.

Legislation and policies

The legislation and policies that are discussed in this section have different aims. We will be looking at aspects of them that are relevant to the themes of mobility and safety. This means safety for the client, for other people and for yourself.

The legislation and policies include:

- Health and Safety at Work Act (1974)
- moving and handling policies
- risk assessment
- Infection control policies
- Community Care Act (1990)

Health and Safety at Work Act

The Health and Safety at Work Act 1974 is a collection of regulations and guidelines that are designed to make everyone's place of work a safer place to be in. There are updates and additions to the Act which extend its range, and define the rules covering situations at work that are likely to be potentially dangerous. These were discussed in Chapter 3, page 95, and are shown in the table on page 231.

Name of regulations	Purpose
Control of Substances Hazardous to Health Regulations 1988 (COSHH)	To ensure that hazardous substances are stored and used safely
Reporting of Injuries, Diseases, and Dangerous Occurrences Regulations 1985 (RIDDOR)	To identify notifiable diseases, and to make sure that injuries and dangerous occurrences are reported and recorded
Manual Handling Operations Regulations 1993	To minimise the risk of injury due to carrying and handling at work
The Management of Health and Safety at Work Regulations 1992	To ensure that employers assess any risks that are associated with work activities

If you are helping clients to make journeys and visits, the requirements of the Act go with you, in the sense that you are still at work and have responsibilities towards yourself, the clients and the public.

Manual Handling Operations Regulations

Helping clients with mobility can mean helping them physically. This means that the Manual Handling Operations Regulations 1993 are likely to affect you. These were discussed in Chapter 3, page 98. The most important thing to remember when faced with the need to lift or handle a client is that you should avoid doing it manually. Guidance published by a variety of bodies, including the Royal College of Nursing and the European Commission, advises people to avoid manual lifting at work. The regulations require employers to avoid manual handling where there is a risk of injury, 'so far as it is reasonably practical'. Employers must provide aids to lifting, such as hoists, and these should always be used.

Think it through

The biggest cause of injuries at work for health and care staff used to be the lifting and handling of clients. A quarter of care workers took time off due to back problems created at work, and it was the greatest cause of people having to give up a career in care.

Risk assessment

Under the Management of Health and Safety at Work Regulations, employers have a duty to assess the risks associated with work activities, and to provide safeguards and equipment. This includes the need to move and handle clients in health and care situations.

Though this may provide a general protection in the workplace it is up to you to assess the risks in any particular situation. You need to make sure that you have thought through the procedures that will be carried out before you begin, and if you have any doubts, stop and get advice from senior staff.

Infection control policies

Infection control also needs to be considered when supporting clients' mobility. You need to find out whether individuals are known to have infectious conditions, and take appropriate precautions to prevent the spread of infection to yourself and others. These precautions could include wearing gloves and protective clothing, using clean equipment, and following the workplace procedures for the safe disposal of waste materials. Clients who have infectious conditions should not normally be taken on journeys and visits. Check with your supervisor if you are in doubt about this issue when trips are planned.

Community Care Act 1990

Care at home has been developed since the government passed the Community Care Act in 1990. This Act had two main aims:

● to allow people who need nursing care or help with daily living, but are not acutely ill, to be cared for in their own home
● to keep down the national costs of long-term care.

This was a marked change from previous practice, where people requiring high levels of care needed to go into residential homes. In residential situations specialist services can be bought in, and services like hairdressing and dental care can be provided since the number of clients being served at once makes it worthwhile. In a home care situation, the client is expected to travel to use these services, and to take advantage of social facilities the client needs to travel to a day centre.

This shift to home care has therefore meant that many clients need to travel more than in the past. Community transport schemes have been set up, and vehicles with adaptations are used to assist people with severe mobility problems. Generally, the Community Care Act aims to help people to live as normal a life as possible as members of the community, and supporting mobility is part of this.

DO IT

Identify the relevant legislation and policies that need to be considered when enabling client mobility.

Your supervisor has asked you to create a wall poster for the staffroom, listing the policies and legislation concerned with client mobility. List the main points. You could include the health and safety policy of the workplace, procedures to follow in case of an accident, lifting and handling guidelines, and risk assessment.

Services and products to help with mobility

A range of services and products are available to help clients to become more mobile. We will look at the modes of transport that clients can use to get around, personal mobility aids and equipment, and prostheses for those who have suffered the loss of a limb.

Modes of transport

The ability to get from place to place is something that we all need for shopping, going to work, visiting family and friends, or taking advantage of the variety of leisure pursuits that are available. The methods of transport we use include cars, taxis, buses and trains. But disabled people could be faced with problems in using any of these methods.

Ordinary cars

Some disabled people may find it difficult to get into and out of a normal saloon car. Frail clients can be helped into and out of cars, but there are issues of safe handling to be considered. A risk assessment if needed before this should be attempted.

Adapted cars

Figure 8.1 Vehicles can be adapted to meet the needs of individuals

Some disabled people are quite capable of using cars, and have cars of their own. Vehicles can be adapted to the needs of an individual both in terms of getting in and out, and in methods of control. Adaptations can be made to allow total hand control, so that there is no need for foot pedals. Wheelchairs can be stowed in the rear seat area, or on the roof, and special equipment is available to hoist them into place. There are schemes to help disabled people to buy and adapt cars, such as the Motability scheme. There are also organisations, such as The Disabled Drivers Association, who offer support and advice on matters like insurance and vehicle adaptations.

Taxis

Taxis may be used for transport. Black cabs are spacious inside and some have adaptations to accept wheelchairs, including ramp facilities. Some taxi firms have a policy of providing transport for disabled people and contracts with local health authorities and social services departments to provide this service. But many taxis are not appropriately fitted, so check before using one. Another problem is cost, as taxi fares are not cheap.

Buses

Most local bus services are difficult for disabled people to use. There is often a high step to climb in order to get onto the bus, and sometimes more steps inside. Seating may be cramped, and there could be none available on crowded routes. Generally, there is no access or support for wheelchair users. The need to get to the bus stop and queue could also be a problem. Some local bus services do have special provisions, however. Some buses are designed to be lowered to kerb level when stopped at a bus stop, so that people can get on and off easily, and some have wide aisles and an open space for wheelchairs near the front.

Trains

Trains may have arrangements to accommodate wheelchairs but this is not always the case. For wheelchair users, getting around some stations and changing platforms often involves getting help, and may be difficult. Train carriages have narrow aisles and wheelchair users may be confined to less comfortable parts of the train.

Special transport

Many disabled people rely on the transport provided by social services departments. Mini-buses are often used, with special adaptations for the needs of the clients, such as ramps, lifts and handrails. There is also the advantage that they are driven by experienced staff who can offer assistance to passengers in getting on and off. The disadvantage is that there is usually a high demand for social services transport and it needs to be booked in advance.

Think it through

Look at the design of the buses used by your local bus service. Do they have any features that would make it easier for a disabled person to use them? What features would make them hard or impossible to use? Also look at the facilities at bus stops. Is there any shelter or seating?

Mobility aids and equipment

A wide range of equipment has been designed to help disabled people to keep mobile. The list includes:

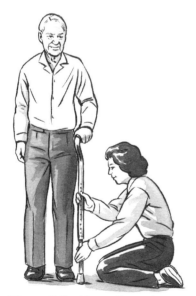

Figure 8.2 You will need to measure each individual for a walking stick

- walking sticks
- walking frames
- crutches
- wheelchairs.

Walking sticks are the most common form of mobility aid. They can be made of wood, metal or plastic, and handles can be curved or straight. They are fitted with a rubber end cap to prevent slipping, and this is an important feature that is prone to wearing out. For people who have a lot of difficulty in walking on one side, there are walking sticks with three feet, called tripods, or four feet, called quadrupeds. These are useful if a person has considerable disability on one side only, such as may occur after a stroke. On these sticks, each foot needs to have a rubber end cap. Many sticks, particularly the metal type, are adjustable in length.

Crutches are used when a person cannot put any weight on one leg, but is otherwise fairly fit. They are not usually seen as a long-term aid to mobility but are used when a person has a temporary disability while an injury is healing, or while they wait for a prosthetic limb to be fitted.

Walking frames, sometimes called Zimmer frames, provide a lot more support than a stick. They are used when a person needs constant support to walk safely, and is too unsteady to use a stick. Most walking frames are made of lightweight metal and have four feet. They are adjustable in height, so as to suit a range of clients. Some designs can be folded to allow storage, such as when travelling on a bus. Others have attachments from which to hang shopping bags, or deep trays to allow objects to be carried around. There are models with wheels fitted in place of the front pair of feet, for clients who are too frail to lift the frame forward between steps.

Wheelchairs are used to help people who cannot move around using their legs. There are many different designs, including chairs that have to be pushed, chairs that people can move by themselves, and motorised chairs. Chairs with small wheels are designed to be pushed by a carer. They are used in situations where the client cannot propel the chair safely, such as a very frail client or one who is very confused. They are also found in hospital wards, where patients are not expected to move themselves around. Clients who are more able will be supplied with a chair that they can propel. These chairs have large rear wheels with pneumatic tyres, like a bike, with a slightly smaller pair of wheels attached that the user grips to move along. Wheelchairs are available in a wide variety of colours and styles, including specialised chairs for sporting and athletic activities.

Motorised wheelchairs use an electric motor to power the rear wheels, and have batteries on board. They are steered using a small joystick mounted on one of the arms. Very little strength or mobility is needed to steer a motorised wheelchair safely, and they are ideal for clients who are unable to turn the wheels by hand.

Prostheses

Prostheses are items that are artificial replacements for natural parts of the body. They include substitutes for teeth, eyes, breasts or limbs. So far as mobility is concerned, prosthetic limbs are the important kind. Clients who have recently had limbs fitted may need additional support initially as they learn to walk steadily. Some people with prosthetic limbs regain nearly full mobility.

Do It

Identify the range of services and products available to enhance and maximise client mobility.

Take the care setting that you work in, or one that you are involved with, and identify the range of services and products that are used to help clients with their mobility. Use your observation skills, and talk to clients and staff about transport and personal mobility. Make a list of the results using the two headings 'Transport' and 'Aids and Equipment'.

From the comments of clients and staff, did it seem that all mobility needs were being met? Add a comments section to your list showing your findings on how well the mobility aids available are meeting the needs of the clients who use them.

Good practice when helping with mobility

Promoting independence and autonomy

CASE STUDY JOHN

John is an elderly disabled person who has moved into residential accommodation following the death of his wife, who used to care for him at home. He has been using a small wheeled chair at home for two years, and has become used to being moved around by his wife and other carers.

Following an assessment of John's needs and abilities, the physiotherapist suggests that he is given a large-wheeled chair that he can propel himself. At first, John is resistant to the suggestion, fearing that he will not be strong enough to move far by himself. Staff suggest an activity programme that will gradually help John to develop his strength and confidence in using the chair, and he agrees to give it a try.

A few months later, John is using his wheelchair regularly to get around the home, and he is now able to choose where he spends his time without having to ask for help.

I can manage this by myself!

Promoting the independence and autonomy of clients is about helping them to do things for themselves. This could be through a formal process such as the development programme described in the case study above. Perhaps more importantly it includes the ways in which care is carried out at a day-to-day level. In this sense it is a principle that should guide our judgement whenever we assess how to help a client.

There are many occasions when it would be quicker and easier for the carer to take over a task that a client finds difficult. It can be frustrating to watch a person struggling to perform a task when you could easily do it for them. But you need to hold back unless the client asks you for help. This policy means that you must often expect things to go at the pace of the client. Accompanying a client who is using a stick and walking fairly slowly may take longer than pushing him or her in a wheelchair, but it is allowing the client to be independent.

People being cared for may tend to become accustomed to being dependent on others – this is particularly the case in residential care. Clients will have been admitted to residential care because of their level of need, and their feelings about themselves may change because of their new situation. They can begin to see themselves as more dependent than they really are. Carers need to counter this by helping clients to do things for themselves. Successes need to be built on, and encouragement regularly given.

Clients who are getting used to unfamiliar new equipment, such as a walking frame or sticks, should be supported by encouragement and reassurance. Holding on to the client to make him or her feel more secure is not likely to help, however. You can be most helpful by making sure that equipment is adjusted to the exact needs of the client, such as by checking that aids like walking frames and sticks are set at the correct height.

Record keeping

Keeping records is important in care situations. It is one of the key ways of ensuring continuity of care. In other words, records help carers to find out about work done by other carers and how the client is progressing.

For clients who are being helped to become more mobile, carers should record progress in a form that allows other carers to access it easily. As with all written records, the issue of confidentiality should be considered. If it is considered to be sensitive information, the record should be kept securely. Different care settings will have their own rules about how records are kept and you need to become familiar with the methods operating in the setting where you work.

The type of information to be kept will depend on the particular needs of the clients and the mobility programme that clients are following. This should be agreed by the caring team so that the right information is recorded.

There are some rules of good practice that apply to any records, and these are shown below.

Good practice: record keeping

✓ Handwriting needs to be legible. Most of the records we are discussing are hand-written and they are only useful if they can easily be read. Take your time filling in records, however rushed you feel.

✓ Information needs to be clear. Use short sentences and simple language to make your point.

✓ Include all important points. Make sure that you record everything that is necessary, but don't ramble off the point.

✓ Use bullets if you need to make a list of points, as they can make information easier to read.

Assessment of clients' needs

Part of good practice is the assessment of the needs of clients as they are helped with mobility. Along with accurate record keeping this is a key process in a programme to improve a client's mobility. Initial assessment of need may involve professionals such as physiotherapists, and a programme to improve mobility. The carers carrying out that programme need to maintain an ongoing assessment of the client's progress.

Clients who are beginning to get used to new aids need to be listened to and observed so that their progress can be assessed. Carers can adjust the level and type of support offered in line with their assessment of clients' level of need.

Client choice

An important aspect of good practice is the recognition that clients can make choices about the care they receive. There may be occasions when carers feel that a particular course of action would be for the best, but the client does not wish to go along with it. This may happen when a client does not feel ready to try a new mobility aid, or has a particular fear of using it.

Situations like this can be frustrating for care staff who may feel that they are serving the client's best interests. There may be a temptation to keep on trying to convince a client, but this could lead to distress and damage your relationship with the client. Carers need to show sensitivity and judgement, and give the client room to say no. If it is seen as important, a strategy might be developed to help the client realise the benefits of the recommended procedure. For example, the client could be introduced to other users, who may be better to reassure and convince the client than an able-bodied carer. Whatever the outcome, remember that clients have a right to choice and that they must never be bullied into doing something they don't want to.

Client health and mobility

The client's state of health and level of mobility place limitations on the help that can be given. Clients who have severe illnesses or very debilitating conditions may have serious restrictions on their mobility. This places limitations on how much support carers can offer to improve mobility and independence.

Carers may wish to discuss the issue of mobility with medical staff, to assess whether limited improvements in mobility can be planned and worked towards. There may be ways that very disabled people can be helped to be mobile, for instance motorised wheelchairs can be operated by very light hand movements, though they need co-ordination skills for control. In some cases, however, the health of a client makes it difficult to promote independence.

Do it

Describe how to ensure that good practice is maintained when assisting clients with mobility.

Make a list of the factors that influence good practice when assisting clients with mobility.

This could include:

- promoting client independence and autonomy
- assessment of needs
- assessing client health and mobility
- record keeping
- client choice

Look at how the factors on your list are dealt with in a care setting where you are working or are involved. Make comments under each item on how good practice is maintained, and note any difficulties that may occur and how they are solved.

Development programmes and activities

This section is about assisting and supporting clients during development programmes and activities. Development programmes are important for the improvement of clients' quality of life. Through development programmes, clients are helped to retain their existing skills and to develop new ones. The aim is to help clients to cope better with their disability or impairment and to enable them to do as much as possible for themselves.

Policy and good practice

It is important that carers are aware of how to ensure good practice when assessing the needs of clients in development programmes, and when supporting them during the programme's delivery. To maintain good practice you need to be aware of:

- the role of activity within care plans
- assessment
- offering feedback.

- client involvement and choice
- monitoring progress

The role of activity within care plans

Care plans are statements of how a particular individual's needs are to be met. These needs may be physical, intellectual, emotional and social, and a programme of activities may be planned to meet some of these needs.

A development programme can take many forms, depending on the needs and abilities of the client and the resources carers can use to help meet these needs. Development programmes are structured, monitored approaches to improving clients' skills, health, or abilities. They include specific goals so that progress can be monitored. For example, a person who has suffered a heart attack may benefit from a programme of physical development as part of the recuperation process. A programme of supervised exercises could be devised so that the client can improve fitness, and reduce the risk of further heart attack. This is likely to involve regular visits to a gym or fitness centre over a period of several weeks. The client would be assessed bfore the programme and guided to exercise at a safe level for his or her physical condition, and monitored during the exercise programme to ensure safety and to record progress. Other types of development programme may be very different – a programme to develop a client's communication skills could involve meetings with a speech therapist, together with regular support from care workers during normal daily activities.

People with physical needs may benefit from a programme of activities designed to maintain and increase mobility and dexterity. Activities may involve becoming used to using aids, such as walking frames or wheelchairs. They could be aimed at clients developing skills in dressing or bathing themselves.

A care plan can include a programme of activities designed to encourage intellectual and social activity. Activities that stimulate the imagination or encourage conversation might be included, such as looking at a newspaper, doing a crossword, or taking part in discussions. Clients who are suffering from a mental impairment may need a lot of help to overcome their confusion or disorientation. A programme of activities designed to provide mental stimulation could form an important part of their plan of care.

Client involvement and choice

For any activity it is important that clients feel a part of the process and fully committed to it. This means that they need to be involved in the planning and carrying out of the development programme, and that their choices are listened to and respected. There are two good reasons for this to be included as an element of good practice. First, clients have a right to be consulted and involved in the planning of activities that they are to carry out and this includes the right to choose not to participate in an activity if they so wish. This leads on to the second good reason, which is that it is no use planning a programme of activity if the client doesn't want to participate in it. Even if they go along with it to please you, it is unlikely that they will get much benefit from the programme unless they are really committed to its success.

How do you help clients to become involved in their development programmes? First, you need to make sure that the programme leads to goals that the client recognises as useful to him or her. The best way to make sure of this is to discuss the activity with the client at the planning stage. If an individual is reluctant or is worried about any part of the programme this will be revealed at an early stage. It could be that the programme needs to be altered to accommodate the client's wishes, or perhaps some worries could be eased by explaining the potential benefits and the support that will be available. Clients could be shown the possible advantages by being introduced to people who have benefited from similar programmes in the past. Talking to people in a similar position may have more influence on them than the views of a fit young carer.

During the course of the activity, it is important to involve clients in what is happening to them as far as possible. What you are trying to achieve is a feeling in clients that they 'own' the programme, and that it is for their benefit. One way to help this process is to allow the client to have a role in recording progress. If simple measurements are made, such as the distance walked or the number of repetitions of an exercise, they can be recorded on a chart by the client – of course the carer should discreetly check that accurate records are being kept. Also simply asking the client how a session went can help to keep the client involved in the activity. If a client expressed the wish not to continue with a development programme, accept that and don't try too hard to persuade the client to change his or her mind.

Assessment

Assessment of need is one of the first stages of the care planning process. A care manager will be responsible for the assessment process, and for the organisation and delivery of the care package agreed. There are basic principles of good practice upon which an assessment should be based, and these are shown below.

Good practice: assessment

✓ The client must give consent before an assessment is made.

✓ The client should understand what the assessment is for.

✓ The views of carers and family should be taken into account.

✓ Clients should be given as much choice as possible in the services they are offered.

✓ Assessment should be seen as a partnership between the professionals carrying out the assessment and the client.

The professionals involved in the assessment will vary depending on the needs and history of an individual client. People with specialised skills such as a physiotherapist, speech therapist, social worker and GP are likely to be involved. The care plan that emerges from the assessment process will usually include a variety of services and provision. One part of this may be a development programme, which is likely to have been set up by a physiotherapist, possibly with input from medical specialists.

Monitoring progress

Assessment is not a once-and-for-all process, but one that is part of the cycle of care planning. The care planning cycle begins with assessment, from which a care plan is designed. Next the plan is put into practice and during this stage the progress of the client needs to be monitored. This means that the people carrying out the care must make regular checks on how the client is responding to the care being offered. Monitoring involves making a judgement about the progress made by the client and keeping useful records of the results.

Since providing care is a team effort, it is important that the records of the monitoring are usable by other carers. These records of progress will help in the reassessment of need which takes place at a later stage of the care planning cycle. It is likely that a physiotherapist or other professional responsible for designing a development programme will have specified the things that need to be measured and recorded as part of the monitoring process. The carers who carry out the monitoring need to keep records that can be easily read. In most care situations, standard methods of record keeping will be in use, and these should be followed.

Feedback

The purpose of monitoring and record keeping is to help both carers and clients see just how well the care plan is working towards its goals. This means that the results need to be fed back.

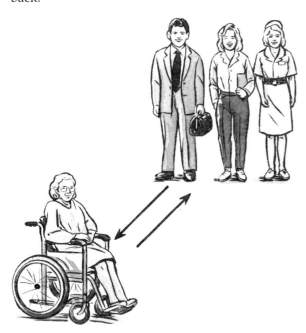

Feedback is important to carers as it contributes to the process of reassessment, an important part of the care planning cycle. Feedback is important to clients as it is important that they can see that progress is being made. If the process made is less than expected, the revision of the care plan will suggest different activities, or a change of approach. Feedback to clients can help them to understand the reasons for these changes, and encourage them to come to terms with them.

Figure 8.3 Feedback is important to both carers and client

┌───

DO IT

Explain good practice in the assessment of clients and delivery of activities.

Make a list of the features of good practice when supporting clients during development programmes and activities. You could use headings to separate the different sections of your list, including: activity care plans, client involvement and choice, assessment, monitoring progress, feedback.

Against each item in your list, note down the main reasons for this aspect of good practice.

└───

Equipment and materials

This section is about using materials and equipment safely. We will look at the safe use and storage of equipment and materials, and at the implications of using dangerous and defective equipment.

Safe use and storage of equipment and materials

Carrying out activities with clients means using equipment and materials, and this in itself leads to safety issues. A wide variety of types of equipment could be used in a development programme. This could include mechanical devices such as mobility aids or exercise equipment, and it could also include electrical or motorised equipment. Each piece of equipment will have been designed to do a particular job and will have correct methods of operation. In institutional settings, equipment will also have a place for storage.

To make sure that you use and store equipment safely, follow this 'do and 'don't' list:

Do
- make sure that you know exactly how a piece of equipment is used safely – this means that you need to know how and when to make adjustments if necessary.
- make sure that the client knows how to use the equipment – this means passing on your knowledge about the equipment to someone else, which is possible only if you have a good understanding yourself
- use equipment only for the purpose that it was designed for; any equipment can become dangerous if it is used in the wrong way
- talk to your supervisor if you feel unsure about the use of a piece of equipment, because it is far better to seek help than to carry on without understanding what you are doing
- store equipment in a safe way – make sure that equipment is folded away correctly, and that items such as electrical leads are safely stowed
- replace equipment in its normal storage area, remembering that others may need to find it later. If you are not sure where things go, then ask.

Don't
- ever use any equipment until you have been shown how to use it safely
- ever let electrical leads trail across the floor or become wrapped around furniture – this could be dangerous for passers by, as well as you and your client
- leave equipment lying around after use – make sure you store it away safely.

These rules also apply to materials you may use. In addition, you should bear the following points in mind.

- Some materials are dangerous. Make sure you are aware of any dangers presented by materials you use. Read the labels, and ask a supervisor if you are not sure.
- Some materials have a limited shelf life. Check the age of materials if they need to be fresh.
- Materials often run out. Make sure that you report it when stocks are running low.
- Materials need to be stored safely. Never stack things too high if they are likely to overbalance, and never put heavy items on top of fragile ones.
- Dangerous or hazardous materials require specialised storage. Make sure that you follow the system operating in your workplace.

Implications of dangerous and defective equipment

Equipment that is broken or damaged presents a real risk to safety. The type and level of danger depends on the nature of the equipment, and on the use to which it is being put. Some faults, such as damage to electrical equipment, can be life threatening.

It should be obvious from this that faulty or defective equipment must never be used. It presents dangers to yourself, the client and others. If you use faulty equipment knowingly, you are breaching health and safety regulations, and if an accident does occur it would be impossible to defend this way of working.

It is important to be able to spot when a piece of equipment is faulty. You should check any equipment before you use it and examine it for damage or defects. This does not mean carrying out a battery of tests, but you should be sufficiently familiar with the equipment you use to be able to assess its condition quickly. Remember that it is not your job to repair any faults you find, and if you try to do so you could make the situation even more dangerous. If there is a problem that involves more than making a few regular adjustments, the equipment should not be used.

Another aspect of your responsibility is to report any faulty equipment that you find. Your workplace will have a procedure for the reporting of faults and you must make sure that you follow it. Reporting faults is also a responsibility covered by health and safety legislation. Make sure that equipment found to be faulty is stored so that it is not used unwittingly by others – your workplace should have a system to ensure that this happens.

- Always check equipment before use. If you are in doubt about its condition, don't use it.
- Don't try to repair faults yourself.
- Always report faults. Make sure that you know the procedure for reporting faults in your workplace, and follow the rules on labelling and storage of defective equipment.

Do IT

Identify the uses and dangers of equipment and materials used in activities.

Take a piece of equipment that you use as part of your work. Write a brief list of the safety issues that affect this piece of equipment. Your list could include details of how the equipment is used, adjustments that can be made, checks to be made before it is used, and how the equipment is meant to be stored.

Add a section to your list which outlines the steps to be taken in case a defect is discovered. You should include details of the defect reporting procedure that operates in your workplace.

Factors affecting good practice

The role of staff

Offering support and encouragement is vital to ensure that clients are committed to the development programme and benefit from it. Clients need to feel that the programme has a point to it, and that they are getting benefits from it. Staff need to be sensitive to the feelings and reactions of clients, and able to respond to them. It is important to spot when a client is becoming frustrated or disillusioned through an apparent lack of progress. Doubts need to be worked through with them, without pressure being put on clients to continue unwillingly. An important feature of support is praising and recognising success, and client commitment may be improved by recalling things that have gone well in the past.

Another part of the role of staff is to offer guidance and instruction in how the activities of the programme are to be carried out. Staff need to be confident in their knowledge of the activity and able to help clients to carry it out successfully and safely. This means that staff must have the training and experience to help clients effectively, and an understanding of what the programme is setting out to achieve.

Facilitating the programme means making sure that the physical resources needed are ready for the client, and that suitable staff and space are provided. This organisation may be carried out by a senior member of staff, or it may be set up initially by a specialist such as a physiotherapist and then administered by a carer.

Staff also need to monitor and record progress, as noted above. Keeping records is part of the role of caring and it is vital for the co-ordination of the caring process. Review of the care plan involves looking at the progress made by clients, and this means that records must be available.

Clients' needs and interests

Another factor that affects the outcome of a development programme is the client's needs and interests. As already stated, clients need to be involved in the programme if it is to be really effective. The client's attitude to the programme will have a big influence on its success.

The programme will have been devised in response to needs identified for the client. The level and type of need will partly determine the nature of the programme and the goals it sets. The interests of the client also play a part in the choice of activity planned – the activity needs to be appropriate in terms of the things that the client likes to do. Good practice involves making sure that clients' needs and interests are reflected in the activities chosen for a development programme.

Desired outcomes

A number of factors are important in determining whether development programmes achieve their desired outcomes. These include the assessment methods and equipment used, the co-ordination of the activities, the preparation of clients, and the level of client satisfaction achieved.

Assessment methods and equipment

The methods and equipment used to assess client progress need to be appropriate and adequate. Assessment can take many forms, and the methods and equipment used to measure progress are just as varied. There may simply be a logging of the time taken to complete a task, or technical equipment may be used to measure results. The important thing is that the methods and equipment fit the activity being carried out, and with the client's needs and expectations. The choice of methods and equipment used should be made at the same time as the programme is devised. Choice may be restricted by the availability of equipment and of staff with appropriate training and experience. If problems occur during the programme, such as assessment methods that are difficult to implement or equipment with which the client feels unhappy, they should be reported as part of the monitoring and review process.

Co-ordinating activities

To ensure that continuity of care is taking place it is important that activities carried out with clients are well co-ordinated. Care is a team effort and it is vital that the input of an individual carer blends smoothly with that of the others.

Responsibility for co-ordination usually rests with the care manager who oversees the care plan of a client, but all staff have a part to play in ensuring that things run smoothly and tasks fit together. Sharing information is one aspect of this. All carers who work with a particular client need to keep the others informed about developments that are relevant to the activity. This means making sure that record keeping systems are used, and that information is available to those who need it. There are confidentiality issues to bear in mind here, and only relevant information should be passed on. Also, information should only be made available to people who need to know it.

Preparation of clients and environment

For the desired outcomes to be achieved, clients need to be properly prepared for the activity taking place. This means that clients should have an understanding of the process they are taking part in, and be prepared for what is to happen. It also means that they should be physically prepared for the activity. If the development programme involves mobility or exercise, clients should arrive in suitable clothing. Loose-fitting, comfortable clothes are best if movement is a part of the activity.

Figure 8.4 For activities involving excercise, loose-fitting, comfortable clothes are best

Programmes may require the client to bring aids and equipment that they normally keep with them. For example, a client who normally wears a hearing aid may need to bring it when attending a development programme session. It is important that clients are forewarned if they need to bring along any equipment.

The preparation of the environment is also important. If an activity requires an open space, it should be cleared before the client arrives. Any equipment that needs to be located, assembled or adjusted also needs to be prepared in advance. Another aspect of preparation is to make sure that any relevant information is consulted. This could be records of progress, or notes made during previous sessions by other carers. Being aware of the current situation of a client is as important as making sure that equipment is prepared.

Client satisfaction

Client satisfaction with the development programme and its results is the main goal. It would be hard to claim that a programme had succeeded if the client were dissatisfied with the outcomes.

It may be hard to measure client satisfaction, and perhaps the best way is to talk to the client and try to gain an understanding of his or her feelings. Some clients will be able to explain precisely how they feel about their experiences, while others may find it hard to convey their feelings. This may be due not to illness or disability, but to a desire to seem helpful or uncritical. Many clients feel grateful towards carers and do not want to bother or upset them. This can lead to misrepresentation of their true feelings about the care they are receiving, or the situation they find themselves in. In these cases it is important that carers use their communication skills to find out the truth as best they can.

DO IT

Describe factors that could affect the activities of good practice in ensuring maximum benefit to the client.

Make a list of the factors that could affect good practice in ensuring the maximum benefit to clients during development programmes and activities. For each item in your list, make a note of the things you could do to ensure that good practice is taking place. For instance, your list may include 'preparation of the environment' as a factor affecting good practice. Against this item you could write 'make sure that equipment is in place and adjusted'.

When you have finished, look through your list and think about a care setting with which you are familiar. What problems do you think you might have in ensuring good practice in this care setting? How could these problems be overcome.

Recreation and leisure activities

This section is about assisting clients in participating in recreation and leisure activities. It includes:

- the requirements of legislation that may influence the choice of activity
- elements of good practice in helping clients to take part in activities
- factors that influence the choice of activity
- factors that influence the achievement of outcomes in leisure activities.

Legislation

Recreation and leisure include an extremely wide range of activities, in fact practically anything that people take up as a hobby or spare-time interest. In practice, the range of options open to clients is restricted. A number of factors limit the choices of activity available, and one of these is the health and safety legislation that applies to situations where professional carers are helping clients to carry out an activity.

One of the main legal influences on activity is the Health and Safety at Work Act 1974 (HASAWA). The details of this Act have already been discussed, but we can recap the main points. Under the Act employers must provide:

- a safe workplace
- safe access to and from the workplace
- health and safety training and information
- a named person who is responsible for health and safety
- a list of identified health and safety hazards and procedures for dealing with them
- procedures for recording accidents at work.

Also under the Act, employees must:

- take reasonable care for the safety of themselves and others
- co-operate with their employer in matters relating to health and safety
- follow workplace procedures for reporting injuries and dangerous occurrences.

The HASAWA is a broad umbrella (see Figure 3.4 on page 95) and includes a variety of different legislation. It is intended to apply to a huge variety of work situations. To assess the implications of the Act for helping clients to participate in recreation and leisure activities, it is necessary to think about the particular activity and the client who will be carrying it out. The relationship between these two factors is important. For example, a client who is unsteady on his or her feet may face more risk when carrying out some activities than one who is more stable. People with co-ordination problems may face more risk than those with steady hands when using craft tools and equipment.

An assessment of risk needs to be made when considering the activities that may be appropriate for a particular client. This sort of assessment should be carried out by a senior carer who has the skills to take the different issues into account. These will include:

- the client's needs and abilities
- the demands that the activity will place on the client
- whether the activity can be safely carried out with the resources available
- possible hazards from materials and equipment used in the activity.

This last point relates to the Control of Substances Hazardous to Health (COSHH) Regulations 1988. A surprising number of items contain substances that are potentially dangerous. Some items contain hazardous solvents, such as certain types of paint, adhesive, and varnish; and some materials are highly flammable. All such products should carry warnings on the label. Be sure to read the labels on any materials you are providing for clients doing craft work.

Do it

Identify the requirements of appropriate legislation that may influence the choice of activity.

Choose a recreation or leisure activity that takes place in a care setting with which you are familiar. Write a brief description of the activity, and of the type of clients who take part in it. Now think about the aspects of health and safety legislation that are relevant to this situation. Write a list of the aspects of the legislation that are relevant to the activity being carried out with this client group.

Helping clients take part in activities

Good practice in helping clients to take part in activities includes taking into account their personal beliefs and preferences, discussing activities with clients and recording their responses.

These elements are essential in supporting clients' rights to choose and to have their ideas and feelings respected. Clients need to feel that they have been involved in making decisions about the things they do – when planning an activity this means that you need to talk carefully with the client.

Helping clients to express their ideas and feelings may not always be easy. You need to use your skills in communication, including listening skills and showing interest and support. Planning an activity may not be as sensitive as other more personal areas of discussion, but you should nevertheless be aware of possible barriers to good communication. A way to help make the communication more effective is to record the responses of clients. This could be done as part of a structured approach to finding out clients' preferences and interests.

A structured approach involves planning the questions, or the topics, that you intend to discuss. Writing down questions could make the discussion seem too formal and restricted, making it hard for the client to relax and open up to you. But you could make a list of topics to be discussed, writing down a description of the areas you want the discussion to cover. When the discussion takes place you can use your own words to introduce the topic, so that the communication feels more like a natural conversation. Responses can be written down in a space under each topic heading.

You may wish to talk to a client about such areas as previous interests and hobbies, views on different activities and the sorts of people who do them, the client's own ideas for activities, and activities that have been tried in the past but disliked by the client.

You will need to make notes and record the responses of the client during the discussion, even though this may stop the flow of the conversation. Making notes shows clients that you are genuinely interested in what they are saying and may encourage them to consider their answers more carefully and give more accurate responses.

Of course, it is important that the activities you plan for clients reflect the beliefs and preferences they have expressed in their discussions with you. If they have told you that they hate to watch competitive sport, don't take them to watch a football match! Respecting a client's right to choose means following his or her wishes as far as possible.

Do it

Identify appropriate elements of good practice in helping clients take part in activities.

You need to find out the beliefs and preferences of a client in your care as part of the process of supporting him or her in carrying out recreational and leisure activities. Prepare a list of the questions that you would ask, or the topics you would cover in a discussion with the client. Make notes alongside each question or topic, explaining what information you expect to get from it.

The choice of activity

We have already looked at how health and safety legislation can influence the choice of a recreation or leisure activity to be carried out with a client. Other factors will have an influence on the activity chosen, and these include: the role of recreation and leisure, the potential difficulties and dangers of activities, the resources available, and therapeutic effects.

The role of recreation and leisure

Recreation and leisure has a part to play in everyone's lives. We all use our leisure time to follow interests and activities, and get a variety of benefits from doing so. These activities help us to relax. We may find that they help us to forget day-to-day problems as we become absorbed in what we are doing. They allow us to feel we are doing something for ourselves, and they often give us a sense of achievement and accomplishment. Our recreation and leisure pursuits are part of our view of ourselves, and they can help to reinforce our self-confidence and sense of identity.

People receiving care are likely to have restricted opportunities for leisure and recreation pursuits, but it is important to remember that they are able to get similar benefits from recreation and leisure. The role of recreation and leisure as part of a care plan should reflect these benefits. It is not just a matter of keeping clients entertained or preventing boredom – positive emotional and social developments should be the aim.

Potential difficulties and dangers

Whether a particular activity is dangerous or difficult depends partly on the nature of the activity and partly on the needs and state of health of the client carrying it out. An activity may be safe for one client but hazardous for another. The conditions under which the activity is carried out also affect how difficult or dangerous it is likely to be – the support of specialist equipment and staff can turn potentially hazardous activity into one that is safe to carry out.

When you are considering the potential difficulties and dangers of a particular activity with clients, it is best to carry out an organised assessment. First, write down a description of the activity and list any equipment needed. Next, think about what a client has to do when carrying out the activity. This means being specific about the physical demands made by the activity. For example, these demands could include the need to lift or bend, or move quickly. Now you can list the physical demands of the activity below your description of it.

You need to consider the needs and abilities of clients in relation to the demands that will be placed upon them by the activity. Look at the notes you made when you analysed the activity and check this against the abilities and state of health of the clients you intend to work with. This process should help you to gauge the danger that an activity may present. Your analysis of the demands of the activity, set against the abilities of the client, is a form of risk assessment. This assessment should help you to make an informed choice about the suitability of a particular activity with a client group.

Available resources

Another factor that can influence the choice of activity is the availability of the resources necessary to carry it out. Some activities may be a lot easier to resource than others, and many can be carried out with a few, easily obtained materials. Activities like drawing, painting, and writing don't need specialised equipment or a lot of space, but other activities may be less easy to provide for. Some, like computing, need specialised technological equipment. Other activities, such as sports, need space.

Resources also include human resources – people. Many activities need more than one person to run them safely, and this may mean other carers will need to be available. Some activities require the support of people with specialised skills. For instance, some craft activities may need the help of a person with skills and experience in order to be run effectively, and some sporting activities may benefit from the help of skilled specialists, both in terms of getting the most out of the activity and in terms of safety.

You will need to assess the level and type of resources that are available, and take this into account when planning an activity. Remember that most resources have a financial cost, including the cost of your own time. Though you may be able to identify where you can obtain the equipment and materials that you need, you still have to find a budget to pay for them. Often, with a little ingenuity and imagination it is possible to assemble the resources you need.

Figure 8.5 Taking part in a creative activity can be an absorbing experience

Therapeutic effects

An important part of the value of recreation and leisure activities to clients is the therapeutic value that it has for them. At the beginning of this section we looked at the value of recreational activities to everyone. For people with restricted opportunities for leisure and recreation pursuits, the activities you help to provide are likely to be even more welcome and beneficial. Carrying out an activity can help people to feel more capable and confident. It reminds clients that they have skills and abilities, and taking part in an activity can be an absorbing experience that helps to distract clients from their daily worries and concerns.

Clients may also be able to gain specific therapeutic benefits if the activity chosen helps to support their medical needs. Maintaining mobility and co-ordination is an important part of the care offered to many clients, and recreation and leisure activities can help to promote these skills. Many craft activities involve co-ordination skills, and mobility can be supported by sporting activities.

The possibility for therapeutic benefits will depend on the needs of the client. Think about the activity being considered and assess the skills it calls for. These should then be matched with the therapeutic needs of the clients, and it should be possible to decide upon an activity that has a therapeutic effect for the client group.

Do It

Describe factors which influence choice of activity by the carer in assisting clients.

Make a list of the factors to be taken into account when choosing a recreation or leisure activity to be carried out with a client group.

Now think about a client group you are familiar with and write a brief description of their situation and needs. List some leisure and recreation activities that you think could be carried out with that client group. Try to pick a variety of activities. For each of the activities, compare the factors that need to be taken into account. Note down how these factors affect each activity.

Look at your results and try to decide which activities are likely to be the most suitable. Justify your decision by referring to the factors that should be influencing it.

The achievement of positive outcomes

Effective communication

Effective communication is important in all your work as a carer. You need to be able to communicate with clients, supervisors and other staff verbally, and to be able to communicate in writing when making notes and completing records.

Communication is also important when assisting clients to participate in recreation and leisure activities. Your communication skills will be needed at all stages of planning and carrying out an activity.

- **During the planning stage** you will need to explain to clients what the activity entails, and what they will be doing. You also need to listen to their responses, and to interpret their views in the context of the planning you are doing.
- **During the activity** you need to be able to communicate to the clients what is expected of them. Helping clients understand what is expected of them is important if they are to get the most out of their participation. You also need to use communication skills to help you to understand how clients are responding to what they are doing. If a client is

finding the activity difficult or not enjoyable, you need to be able to understand that this is happening. You may decide to discuss the client's feelings, and perhaps offer encouragement to continue.

If you do not communicate effectively with clients the outcomes expected of the leisure activity may not be achieved. Activities might be badly chosen, and clients may be unsure of what they are expected to do or what benefits they could gain.

Communication with fellow carers and other people might also affect the success of an activity. It is often necessary to make arrangements with outside agencies, such as transport providers or the staff who work in the facilities you hope to use. It is vital that these arrangements are made properly, and your skills in effective communication will help with this.

Dealing with conflicts of choice

In practice, people are fairly flexible and conflicts of choice are usually resolved fairly easily. Sometimes, though, you may find that members of a group have strong ideas about what they want to do and these could conflict with the choices of other group members.

Dealing with conflicts again calls upon your communication skills, as well as your skills in showing sensitivity to the feelings and needs of others. Do your best to allow the conflict to be solved within the group, by participating in a discussion and helping to keep it structured and under control. Your aim is to provide an activity that as many clients as possible want to do and can benefit from. This means helping all clients to express their feelings effectively, and helping clients to understand the views of other members of the group.

If the majority of people are in favour of a particular activity and one or two don't like the idea of it, try talking to the minority and explaining how they could benefit from participation. If they are unconvinced, you could remind them how important they are to the other group members, and how much their presence would add to the occasion. The argument that 'it won't be the same without you' can often win people over and persuade them to join in.

As the provider of the activity, you must make the final choice. You have to balance the need to respect the wishes of clients with the need for the whole group to do things together. If you find you have to choose an activity that some clients don't want to do, make sure that you talk to them individually and explain how you came to your decision. It may be possible to compromise and offer to arrange an activity that they would prefer in the future.

Evaluating activity

An important part of offering recreation and leisure activities is to evaluate how things went. All activities should have been planned with a particular set of goals in mind, in other words there should have been goals that the activity set out to achieve. An evaluation is the process of looking at how successful the outcome has been.

There are different ways in which an evaluation could be done, and a range of sources of information could be used to help it. The type of information you use to evaluate an activity will depend on the goals you expected the activity to achieve. An evaluation can be an informal process or a more structured one. In practice, an evaluation often has both formal and less formal components.

One way of evaluating is to write down your own impressions of how things went. Your observations can be important in gauging the overall success of an activity. Talk to other staff who where involved and record their views also. Any evaluation should of course include the feelings of the clients who participated. How you go about collecting this information will depend on the particular group you are dealing with and your relationship with them. It could be appropriate to hold a group discussion, where clients can make their views known.

It may be more appropriate to carry out your discussions on a one-to-one basis, speaking with each client in turn. This would be better if some clients have difficulty communicating and need help and time to express themselves. It could also apply in situations where one or two group members usually tend to dominate group discussions, making it difficult for others to make their views heard.

Other criteria may need to be included in an evaluation of the activity. If there were therapeutic goals, it may be possible to make measurements, which can then be taken into account.

An evaluation is important with any activity, as it helps to inform everyone's planning for future activities. Things that went wrong can be avoided next time, and successful aspects can be built on. An evaluation also helps to demonstrate the value of the activity to others who may question whether it was worthwhile. It is a way of ensuring that your work is achieving its goals, and that clients' needs are being met.

Do IT

Describe factors that may affect the achievement of outcomes in leisure activities.

Think about a group of clients that you are familiar with, and an activity that they take part in. What factors affect the achievement of the outcomes expected of that activity for that group? Make a list of these factors. Can you think of ways of doing things differently that will help the objectives of the activity to be achieved more successfully in the future?

POST-NATAL CARE

For a variety of reasons, often health related, a mother sometimes needs assistance to provide some or all of the care for her newborn baby (neonate). It is vital that she and the rest of the baby's family are in control of the care given by health and care workers. After a period of time, the mother or other members of the family will be totally responsible for the care, without your assistance. The key principle, therefore, is to avoid taking over entirely, even for a mother who is very ill or unable to perform tasks. This chapter provides the knowledge you need to develop the necessary skills.

Development in the baby and mother

The neonate

New babies are born totally helpless, requiring support and protection from caring adults. This care starts well before delivery, with a series of antenatal procedures and checks. The delivery period is carefully monitored, with the mother receiving care from a midwife, and occasionally an obstetrician if there are complications.

Careful observation of the baby at birth is essential to provide a baseline of its state of health, to measure against in the future. As soon as a baby is born the midwife scores it against an APGAR score. This means that five vital signs are observed:

- heart rate
- muscle tone
- skin colour indicating oxygen distribution.
- breathing
- reflex response to stimulation

A score is given for each point, to a maximum of 10 in total as shown in the following table.

Sign	0	1	2
Heart rate	Absent	Slow (below 100)	Fast (above 100)
Breathing	Absent	Slow, irregular	Good, crying
Muscle tone	Limp	Some movement of hands and feet	Active
Reflex response	No response	Grimace	Cry, cough, sneeze
Colour	Blue, pale	Body oxygenated, hands and feet blue	Well oxygenated to extremities

A score of 10 shows the baby is in prime condition.
A score or 8–10 is good.
A score of 5–7 gives some cause for concern, particularly about the breathing condition.
A score of 4 or less suggests a poorly baby, requiring urgent care.

The majority of healthy babies have a score of 8 or above at birth, rising to 9 about five minutes later, with the extra point often reflecting a tendency to have slightly blue extremities at birth.

A baby's APGAR score is carefully recorded, as it is a good indicator of future developmental progress.

Normal variations

If you compare a number of newborn babies they may seem very different in outward appearance. This is despite the widely held view that all new babies look the same. They do have many features in common, however.

Babies are measured and weighed to determine their basic length, weight and head circumference and to test future progress.

- **Weight** Most babies fall within the range of 2.5 to 4 kg, a weight under 2.5 kg suggesting a baby is of low birth weight and may need special care.
- **Length** Most measure around 50 cm, though it is difficult to make an exact measurement.
- **Head circumference** The average is around 35 cm.

Primitive reflexes

Babies are all born with 'primitive reflexes' – they appear to be capable of some quite extraordinary skills that disappear in the first months of life. The primitive, involuntary movements are replaced by voluntary responses as the brain develops. If a baby does not have these reflexes at birth, or they persist too long, this may be an indication of problems.

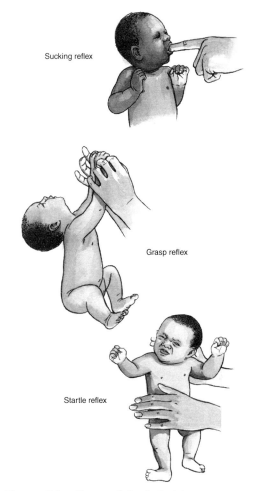

- **Rooting reflex** Gently stroking a baby's cheek will make him or her turn towards the finger to try to suck.
- **Sucking and swallowing reflex** A finger gently placed in the mouth will be sucked, and the baby will make swallowing actions.
- **Grasp reflex** A finger placed in the palm of the hand or under the big toes will be grasped tightly.
- **Stepping or walking reflex** Held upright with the feet on a firm surface, the baby will make forward stepping movements.
- **Asymmetric tonic neck reflex** Turning the baby's head to one side results in the arm and leg on that side straightening, and the opposite limbs flexing.
- **Startle reflex** A sudden noise or bright light will make the baby fling out the arms with fists clenched.
- **Moro reflex** Gently releasing support of the baby's neck results in arms being thrown out with open hands, followed by the arms folding back over the chest.

Figure 9.1 Some of the 'primitive reflexes' of newborn babies

New babies appear helpless, and until recently it was thought that they had few skills at birth. Research has shown this is not the case, and in fact a neonate can possess many skills.

- **Sight** The newborn can focus his or her eyes within 20 to 25 cm, the distance of the carer's face during feeding. Colour and three-dimensional objects attract interest.
- **Hearing** Very soon after birth, babies learn to recognise their main carer's voice. They respond to sounds by blinking or jerking their limbs.
- **Smell and taste** By ten days, a breast-fed baby can identify his or her mother by smell, and shows a preference for sweet tastes.
- **Touch** A new baby is very sensitive to touch and enjoys close physical contact. The mouth is the focus of these tactile sensations.
- **Motor skills** A new baby lies prone with the head to one side. If pulled up to sitting, the baby's head lags, the back curves and then the head falls forward. Eyes and head turn towards the light. Hands are tightly closed.
- **Emotional and social** New babies need close physical contact to follow on from their time in the mother's uterus, and to develop their emotional attachments to their carers. Cuddling and feeding are a neonate's main activities.

Do it

Explain the development of the neonate in the first ten days of life.

A friend who is 36 weeks pregnant is keen to find out what to expect from her newborn baby. Produce a poster or leaflet explaining the development of a baby in the first ten days of life.

Factors affecting early development

Development throughout life is affected by influences before birth and during delivery. At birth and in the first ten days, these effects are usually apparent and fall into the categories shown in Figure 9.2.

Factor	Example	Possible effects
Genetic	Extra or missing chromosomes, mutations Combining of two recessive genes	Down syndrome Congenital heart defects Cystic fibrosis
Environmental	Macro-pollutants in the atmosphere, living near chemical works Micro-pollutants in the home	Range depending on stage of pregnancy at time of exposure – e.g. limb deformities
Maternal illness in pregnancy	Rubella, toxoplasmosis Sexually transmitted diseases	Deafness Heart problems
Drugs taken in pregnancy	Alcohol Nicotine Prescription drugs Illegal drugs	Foetal alcohol syndrome Low birth weight Limb deformities Addicted baby
Radiation	Routine X rays Atmospheric radiation	Limb deformities Physical deformity
Diet and nutrition	Lack of essential nutrients Presence of harmful bacteria, e.g. listeria	Spina bifida (lack of folic acid) Nervous system problems, low birth weight
Emotional stress in the mother	Relationship problems Worry about managing with baby	May be 'jittery', irritable baby
Delivery	Delayed birth causing lack of oxygen to brain Umbilical cord round neck Forceps delivery Foetal distress	Developmental delay Cerebral palsy Paralysis of limbs

An important focus of antenatal care is to try to avoid or minimise the risk of any of these factors. Screening tests and advice to expectant mothers from a wide range of health professionals aim to ensure that babies are as healthy as possible.

A newborn baby has several examinations and checks to identify any concerns in the first few days of life. The APGAR test referred to above is the first of these. Sensitive handling of the

Figure 9.2 Factors affecting babies' development

parents is essential if problems are discovered, and any concerns you have should be passed immediately to your supervisor, not communicated to the parents by yourself.

The way that any infant is handled in the first ten days can influence how that child develops in the future. In the first few days, a welcoming experience for a baby can be provided by remembering the following:

- always speak in a gentle voice
- ensure a baby is never left exposed without any clothes for longer than a few seconds
- keep bathing to a minimum
- feed on demand
- ensure there is frequent cuddling and holding, especially by the mother
- temperature of the environment should be kept at approximately 20°C.

DO IT

Explain the factors affecting development in the first ten days of life.

Your elder sister is considering starting a family. Produce an information leaflet showing the factors that affect a new baby's development, and things to avoid during pregnancy in order to promote the development of a healthy child.

Anatomy and physiology of breast feeding

Breast feeding produces the ideal food for a new baby, and milk is automatically produced by the majority of new mothers in a production system that starts before delivery.

Many women feel they may not be able to breast feed because they have small breasts, inverted nipples or breasts that are too large. Breast size, shape or appearance rarely prevent successful breast feeding, however. Large breasts are usually an indicator of a greater amount of fat deposit, not of the size of the milk production equipment.

Breast milk is produced in the lobes, travels into the milk reservoir and then leaves via one of 15–25 lactiferous ducts. Montgomery tubercles (small glands in the areola) produce a fluid that helps to keep the nipples lubricated and soft.

A mother who is breast feeding should be encouraged to have a good fluid intake, as well as a balanced diet, to encourage milk production. Milk is produced on demand – the more a baby feeds, the more milk the mother will produce.

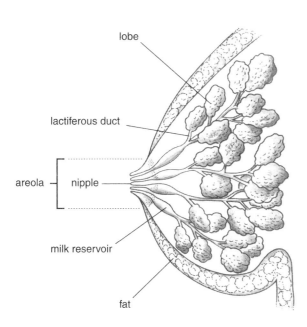

Figure 9.3 How the breast produces milk

Milk is released to the baby through the 'letdown' reflex:

1. Sucking at the nipple stimulates messages to the brain from the nerve endings.
2. The pituitary gland in the brain releases hormones on receiving the message.
3. The action of hormones on the breast muscles causes the release of milk from the lobes into the ducts.

Some mothers feel the letdown reflex as a strong sensation, while others hardly notice it. Sucking is not the only stimulus for the reflex – a crying baby, the approach of the usual feed time, or just holding the baby can stimulate it in many breastfeeding mothers. In the first few weeks of feeding it is the letdown reflex that can cause breasts to leak, until the supply and demand situation is sorted out.

The composition of breast milk changes in the first few weeks of feeding. For the first few days a substance called colostrum is produced. Colostrum has a very high protein content, packed with the mother's antibodies for protection against illness. It looks very rich and creamy. By the third or fourth day milk is produced and mixes with the colostrum, with the balance changing so that by ten days the milk does not contain colostrum and appears thinner and watery. However, all the required nutrients for the baby are produced.

Support from an experienced midwife and/or health visitor, and the mother's family, is important to establish breast feeding. For a mother who is unable to care for her baby by herself, this support is even more vital. Rest, adequate diet and demand feeding will help to establish good production of milk.

Do it

Describe the relevant anatomy and physiology related to breast feeding.

Your elder sister is pregnant and is now asking you about breastfeeding. She is curious about how milk is produced. In order to explain this, draw a labelled diagram to show the structure of the breast. In short sentences, describe how milk is produced in the breast.

Difficulties experienced in the first ten days

After the delivery of a baby, a woman's body needs time to return to normal. The uterus that previously held a 3–4 kg baby returns to about the size of a fist in six weeks. Breasts adjust to feeding, or not feeding, and hormone levels return to a pre-pregnancy state, or support breast feeding.

It does not take much imagination to see that many mothers will experience some degree of difficulty in the first weeks after delivery. Many of these difficulties are minor, but there may be significant difficulties that require more than just support and encouragement by her carers. The huge responsibility that has been taken on can seem overwhelming to some mothers. After the effort of delivery, her body is returning to normal, with rapid alterations in hormone levels, so it is not surprising that many mothers experience both physical and emotional difficulties. The table below shows some of the potential problems.

Type of problem	Cause	Possible solutions
Breast feeding difficulties	Engorgement – overfull breasts Blocked milk ducts Cracked or sore nipples Mastitis or infection Poor milk supply	Demand feeding Correct positioning of baby Exposing breasts to fresh air Attention to fluids and diet Support and encouragement
Tender or infected perineum	Difficult delivery Sutures (stitches) to area near vagina	Cushions to sit on Frequent use of bidet and warm baths Attention by midwife or doctor
'Baby blues' within 10 days – lasts up to 48 hours	Hormonal changes Sore breasts Family or external pressures Worry about baby or self Poor initiation of bonding	Reassurance that this is normal Support, listening, explanations to family Dealing with physical issues that need attention Usually stops, but health workers should be informed if continuing beyond 10 days – risk of developing into post-natal depression
Failure to return to pre-pregnancy body weight	Normal progress of post-natal period	Explanation to mother that it takes six weeks for body to return to normal, and that much of the weight gain is not just the baby, but general

The post-natal period is an emotionally demanding time. Mothers often feel out of control of their bodies, and can find the changes alarming. Care is needed, therefore, in supporting mothers and their families in the first ten days. Always pass on concerns to the midwife responsible for the family – midwives can support the family until 28 days after birth, with the health visitor having responsibility from ten days.

Do it

Describe the difficulties that mothers may experience in the ten days after birth.

Talk to several new mothers and/or women who have recently had babies. What minor problems did they experience in the first two weeks? Produce a booklet alerting parents to these difficulties. Ensure you identify sources of help and advice.

Key principles of infant care and feeding

Assisting the mother

The key feature of assisting the mother is to help and support without taking over. Wherever possible, the mother or other family members should be carrying out the care of the baby. If this is not possible, then all care of the baby should be done in front of the mother, with her directing operations in terms of choices.

The most important principle is that care should wherever possible be based on the requests of the baby's parents. In the first ten days, any baby needs:

- regular feeding
- keeping clean and dry
- to be kept safe.

- frequent physical contact with the mother
- adequate warmth

When the baby is awake or even when he or she is asleep, encourage the mother to hold and stroke her baby if possible. This is vital component of the bonding process, which will be considered further, later in this chapter.

Physical care

Physical care should be kept to the necessary minimum to ensure the baby is clean and comfortable. New babies do not get particularly dirty, other than in the nappy area. Often a new baby will feel very insecure if given a bath, not enjoying the procedure at all. If this is the case, advise the mother that all that is needed is the washing of the hands, face and nappy area. Cotton wool should be used for the hands and face, dampened in warm water. Soap should not be used on a new baby. Always use one piece of cotton wool for each eye, cleaning from the inner eye outward. Never be tempted to poke in a baby's ears or up its nose. The nappy area should be cleaned with cotton wool and warm water. Female babies should have soiled faeces cleaned from the front to the back, to avoid contaminating the genitals. Clothing for a new baby should be light, preferably made from cotton, with several thin layers, rather than one thick layer of clothing.

If a mother is unable to carry out any of the care for her own child, she will appreciate seeing daily tasks done for her baby. However, very few mothers are so ill or incapacitated that they are unable to perform some of the tasks involved in care. At the very least, they can hold the baby after you have done the practical jobs. By being as involved as possible, the mother will be getting to know her child and ensuring that her ideas are valued.

Chapter 15 gives a detailed explanation of nappy changing and bathing a baby.

DO IT

Describe how to assist the mother in the care of the neonate.

Imagine you are assisting in the care of a new baby, whose mother has very limited use of her limbs (due to severe arthritis). How would you help her to participate to the maximum extent in the care of her baby?

Safety of the neonate

New babies are perhaps the most vulnerable members of our society. They are exposed to a range of potential dangers as soon as they emerge from the uterus. Babies need help with all the factors shown in Figure 9.4.

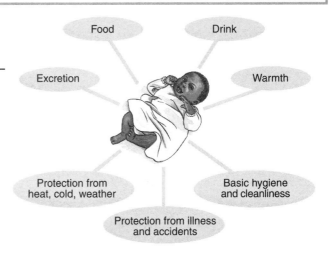

Figure 9.4 *Newborn babies need help and protection in many ways*

Physical safety

Aspects of a baby's physical safety include the following.

- Correct feeding procedures – how and where the baby is fed. Always have all equipment ready and ensure the person feeding the baby is in a comfortable position.
- A safe place to attend to hygiene needs – nappy changing, bathing and washing. These are best done in the baby's cot to avoid any risk of falls from beds or tables. Thought may be needed to improve access to the cot for someone in a wheelchair, for example.
- Safety of the baby's mother when caring for her child – if the mother has some health or mobility difficulty that makes her unsteady on her feet, look for ways to encourage her to protect the baby from falls.

Protection from other people

In recent years there have been several cases of babies being taken from maternity units by unauthorised people. *All* staff in a maternity unit are responsible for challenging someone claiming authorisation to take a baby for 'tests' or 'check ups'. Ideally a baby should not go anywhere without his or her mother, or another member of the family. Check the procedure in your placement or workplace relating to this.

Another aspect of protection from others relates to people with illnesses. Babies are vulnerable to infection, and visitors with infectious illnesses such as coughs and colds should be discouraged from visiting. As a carer, you should think carefully about being in close contact with babies if you are ill yourself.

Mistaken identities of babies

Very occasionally, babies have been 'mixed up' and the wrong baby has gone home with the parents – you may have read about these cases in the press or seen them on TV. Procedures to prevent this happening are in place in all maternity units. The usual procedure is that every baby is tagged with a wrist and ankle name tag at birth, in front of the parents. This happens before there is any possibility of the baby being removed from the delivery room for treatment, tests, etc. The tag should have the mother's details – name, record number, sex of the baby and time and date of delivery. These tags should *never* be removed before the baby goes home, and then only by the parents. Find out the procedure for this at your placement.

Health and safety issues

Every employee at any place of work has a duty of care under health and safety legislation. This is particularly important where babies are concerned. You should always be on the alert for any possible risks to the babies in your care, for example from:

- slippery floors where someone could slip when carrying a baby
- faults in equipment
- incorrectly functioning fridges that hold baby formula milk
- blocked fire exits.

> ## *Do It*
>
> **Explain the importance of ensuring safety of a neonate in the care environment.**
>
> Produce a poster or booklet explaining to an expectant mother how the safety of her baby will be ensured in hospital.

Advantages of breast feeding

Breast feeding is the natural feeding method for any infant. Whenever possible, a mother should be encouraged and supported in choosing it. Occasionally, a mother may not wish to or find it difficult to breast feed, and will require support in that choice, too. Breast feeding is the best method for several reasons:

- breast milk is easily available and is at the right temperature
- the constitution of breast milk is exactly right for a baby, in terms of protein, sodium and sugar
- there is no risk of contamination, leading to gastroenteritis
- the formation of a bond between mother and baby is enhanced by the physical closeness of feeding
- most of the mother's antibodies are passed to the neonate through breast milk, giving protection against illness
- the onset of allergy-based reactions such as eczema is delayed or minimised.

Further details about the advantages of breast feeding, and when formula feeding may be necessary, are given in Chapter 15, page 404.

> ## *Do It*
>
> **Identify the advantages of breast feeding.**
>
> You have been asked to give a short talk to a group of expectant mothers who are keen to breast feed. Plan your talk giving a balanced view of the advantages of breast feeding.

Planning and delivery of feeds

It is obvious that babies need feeding to help them to grow and develop. Food provides:

- energy
- nutrients for growth and repair of body tissues
- nutrients for the growth of bones
- nutrients for the development of the nervous system
- fuel for maintaining body temperature and metabolism.

The choice of a method of feeding is one for the baby's parents. Breast feeding is nutritionally and healthwise the best for a baby, but the most important factor is the contentment of the mother with her choice. An unhappy and stressed breastfeeding mother will not be helping her baby. A happy, bottlefeeding mum is far better. However, you can play an important role in supporting a mother in breast feeding. Whichever type of feed the baby has, there are several important points to consider in the planning and delivery of feeds.

Amount of feeds

Babies vary in the amount of feed they need. If you think about the range of birth weight, it is obvious that a 4 kg baby will need more food for fuel than a tiny, 2 kg baby. Even though new babies do not appear to do very much, they use a lot of energy in sleeping, breathing, excreting, crying and feeding. The basal metabolic rate is the amount of energy we use merely to be alive.

For a bottle-fed baby, there is a formula to calculate the amount of feed required. The packets of infant feed show this formula. As a guide, however, you will need 75 ml or reconstituted feed for every 500 g of a baby's weight every 24 hours. The total is then divided into the number of likely feeds – usually eight per 24 hours for a new baby, or one every three hours.

Breast-fed babies cannot be given a neat formula – they need feeding whenever they are hungry, for as long as they need. 'Experts' used to dictate figures such as five minutes per breast every three to four hours – which is fine for some babies, but not for all.

The important points to remember are:

- all babies are individuals – and some may be hungrier than others, or hungrier at different times
- a baby should not go any longer than four hours without a feed during the day in the first few weeks of life.

Careful attention to hygiene is essential – both in the process of making feeds, and the hygiene of the person making and/or giving the feed. Unused bottles should never be kept for later, even if only a small amount of feed has been taken.

All babies should enjoy close physical contact with the person giving their feed. For this reason it should ideally be the baby's parents who do the feeding. Babies need to hear talking, singing or cooing when they are being fed, and need to enjoy eye contact with their feeder.

Preparing formula feeds

The principles of preparing formula feeds are described fully in Chapter 15, page 405. This chapter also describes the equipment you will need, and the important principles of hygiene.

Figure 9.5   Before preparing formula feeds, always read the instructions on the container carefully, and wash your hands thoroughly

DO IT

Describe the main principles involved in the planning and delivery of feeds to a neonate.

Make up a formula feed using appropriate sterilising procedures.

You have been asked to help a mother organise her feeding schedule for her new baby. She is using formula feeds. Explain what she needs to know about the principles of feeding, so that she can correctly prepare her baby's feeds.

Relationship with the child's mother

Limitations of the carer's role

Imagine you were unable to care for your newborn baby. Perhaps you had a very difficult delivery that resulted in your being too weak to do so. Or you might have some illness or disability that will require you to have support in caring for your baby when you get home. Although you require support, you do not want the care of your baby to be totally removed from you. You can certainly hold your baby and you have very clear ideas on how you want to bring her up. However, you are a new mum, and you welcome advice and ideas on the best way to do certain tasks such as bathing, dealing with nappies, feeds, etc.

Think it through

Faced with someone else having to do much of the practical care of your baby, what would concern you? Think about it and discuss it with a colleague.

The following concerns may be going through the mother's mind.

- Will the carers be taking over my baby?
- Can I discuss my ideas with them?
- Will they follow my cultural preferences?
- Will they try to change my mind about breast feeding?
- Will they try to do everything for the baby and not let me try to see which aspects I can manage?

As a carer you must always remember the fact that the baby will probably be going home with its mother at some stage. The baby belongs to his or her family – their choices about ways of caring are the important choices. If you are constantly involved in the care of a baby it is easy to become attached to that child. Continuity of care, allowing you to develop a relationship with the mother and family, is an ideal situation in many respects, but it can be difficult for the carer when the time for the baby to go home arrives.

As a carer, in any situation it is important to establish the boundaries of your care relationship. This can be made easier by:

- ensuring that the parents plan the baby's care, and that you follow their plan – remember that different individuals and cultures have different ideas about baby care

- always asking the baby's parents for permission before you do anything, even picking the baby up
- always asking how the parents would like things done for their child, and checking that you are doing the right thing
- always doing tasks for the baby in front of the parents
- whenever possible, encouraging the parents to perform the care, or part of it, themselves
- never assuming that it will be all right to give an extra feed, or give the baby a bath, without following the guidelines above
- reminding yourself that you are there only for support, and for a very short period of time – whereas the parents will be there for life.

Do it

Identify the limitations of the carer's role in the care of a neonate.

Imagine that you are in the situation of needing help with the care of your newborn baby. What are the boundaries that you would expect the carer to observe in helping you to care for your baby?

The importance of the family in bonding

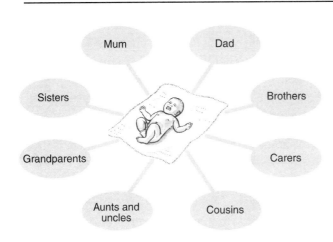

Figure 9.6 Babies develop close links with several different people early in life

Research has shown that babies need to develop close links with at least one important adult, and that this is the best way to help a child to mature into a person with emotional security. Usually, we develop close emotional links with several people early in life, as shown in Figure 9.6.

The first and most important link a baby will form is usually with his or her mother. Before birth, the baby has been listening to her mother's voice, hearing her heart beat, and becoming familiar with the rhythms of her body. In a normal delivery the mother may hold the baby while the placenta is being delivered, and she may start breast feeding straight away. Even if the birth has presented problems, it is usually made a priority that the mother holds the baby as soon and as often as possible, even if the baby has to be cared for in an incubator.

The process of bonding is strengthened by skin contact, eye contact and the sounds of voices. Bonding does not have to be with the natural mother, however. A baby can develop strong bonds with several people, but what is important is that babies have consistent carers. Ideally a baby needs just one or two constant caring figures.

If a mother cannot look after her new baby completely by herself, it is even more important to ensure that close bonds are formed with other members of the family. Whatever the reasons for other people being involved in the care of the baby, it is vital to the psychological development of the baby that there is a consistent carer in his or her life.

In the first ten days of life, family and friends are often frequent visitors to the new baby and parents. Rather than just viewing them as visitors bringing flowers and chocolates, you should involve some of them from the start in the care of the baby. If the support required by the mother is a long-term issue, the involvement of others will probably have been discussed at some earlier stage. Maternity units should actively encourage families to start this process in the hospital, rather than waiting until the baby goes home.

DO IT

Explain the importance of involving the baby's family to assist with the bonding process.

Consider the ways in which you could encourage members of a new baby's family to become involved with his or her care. List your ideas, and add a note about the importance of bonding with at least one constant carer.

Plans of care for the neonate

When planning care for a neonate the first priority is to draw up the plan with the baby's parents. Different cultures have different views on the care of the newborn. Some cultures do not believe you should bathe a baby in the first weeks of life. There are many different religious rites surrounding new babies, and you should always discuss these with the parents – never assume that your ideas are the same as theirs. By asking, you will learn a lot about other cultures, and avoid giving offence to the parents.

If asked for advice, you can suggest that care should be arranged around feeds. There is little point in waking a baby for a wash in between feeds, for example.

A neonate needs:

- regular nappy changes – bowel movements are very frequent in the first few weeks, as the intestines automatically contract every time the baby feeds; for the first few days stools are dark and sticky, made up of the meconium that has been in the bowels before birth
- hands, face and bottom to be cleaned on at least a daily basis
- clean clothes daily, to avoid rubbing from sweat or dried milk
- regular feeds – every three hours on average, but this may be every two hours in some babies or as little as every four hours
- close physical contact with parents – especially the mother
- a lot of sleep – many neonates sleep from 18 to 22 hours a day, waking only for feeds.

This pattern of needs fits in quite well with the needs of the mother. She has had a period of hard work, and also needs to rest and recover from the birth.

A useful plan of care could look like the one in Figure 9.7. The important point about the care plan is to ensure that the mother is fully involved wherever possible. If she is breast feeding this will be much more obvious – but remember, encourage her to perform as many tasks as possible. In between feeds, encourage the mother to rest, depending on her state of health.

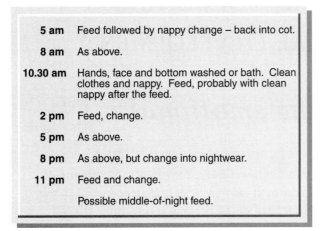

5 am	Feed followed by nappy change – back into cot.
8 am	As above.
10.30 am	Hands, face and bottom washed or bath. Clean clothes and nappy. Feed, probably with clean nappy after the feed.
2 pm	Feed, change.
5 pm	As above.
8 pm	As above, but change into nightwear.
11 pm	Feed and change.
	Possible middle-of-night feed.

Figure 9.7 An example of a plan of care

Your role in this care could be as simple as ensuring that the mother can reach the cot, and has all the necessary equipment to hand; or it could involve you doing all the activities yourself, with the mother present. Of course you will be constantly talking to her, and checking all your actions with her.

Do It

Describe a plan of care for a period of time for the baby, ensuring parental wishes are met.

You are to plan a period of care for a new baby. Outline your plan, explaining how you would involve the parents.

10 PHYSICAL, SOCIAL AND EMOTIONAL DEVELOPMENT

Physical, social and emotional development

How does a tiny newborn baby grow from a helpless bundle into an active child full of energy and intelligence? This chapter and the next examine that question. Although the subject of development is divided into topic areas it is important to remember that all aspects of development are linked together.

Children's development

Huge changes occur in a child in a very short space of time – especially from birth to eight years of age.

- Weight increases from 3–4 kilograms to about 25 kg.
- From being relatively immobile, the child becomes able to walk, run, skip and climb.
- From not being able to talk, the child becomes an able communicator.
- From being fully dependent, the child learns to dress, feed and think for himself or herself.
- From automatically grasping everything that is put into the hand, the child learns to pick up and use a pencil.

The stages of development are often split into five areas, the names of which can be remembered by recalling the word PILES:

P Physical development	refers to the body increasing in skill and performance.
	• **Gross motor development** is about using large muscles.
	• **Fine motor development** includes precise use of the hands and fingers.
I Intellectual development	involves learning the skills of understanding, memory and concentration.
L Language development	refers to communication skills.
E Emotional development	is about a child's identity and self image, and the development of feelings about the self and the other people.
S Social development	is about learning the skills to live in society with other people.

You might see the word SPICE also used for the five areas of development. It stands for Social, Physical, Intellectual, Communication and Emotional development.

Basic principles of development

There are three basic principles of human development.

1. **Development starts from the head and works down the body.**
    A new baby cannot hold up his or her head alone. Yet within a few months, the baby will be able to sit alone. This is because control of the spine and central nervous system develops from the top of the head down to the base of the spine. You can see this control developing in a baby as he or she starts to hold the head without support. Similarly, a newborn baby waves his or her arms around vaguely, yet in nine months' time will find the tiniest crumb or piece of Lego easy to pick up with the thumb and finger. This is because the nervous system develops from the spinal cord out to the extremities (hands and feet).

2. **All development happens in the same order, but many aspects occur at different rates.**
    A baby has to hold the head up, learn to sit with support, and then without support, before he or she can stand by holding on to furniture and then eventually walk alone. No baby can learn to walk before sitting up. But it is perfectly normal for one baby to walk at ten months and another not to learn this skill until the age of 18 months old.

3. **All areas of development are linked together.**
    A baby cannot start to finger feed until he or she can sit up and is developing the ability to pick things up between the fingers and thumb. Similarly, speech patterns are affected if a child has difficulties in hearing clearly.

Think it through

Write down the three headings 'Physical development', 'Social development' and 'Emotional development'.

Put the activities shown below under the appropriate type of development. Do any fit under more than one heading?

Crawling	Tying shoelaces	Making friends	Distress when goldfish dies
Riding a bike	Using a fork	Sharing toys	Walking upstairs
Starting school	Recognising main carer	Threading beads	Using a pencil

The 'normal' milestones of development

Child development experts have carried out a lot of research and observation with young children to study what children can do at different ages, and the rate at which they grow. From this research, milestones of development have been identified. These show the age at which most children have reached a certain stage of development. Many children will have reached that stage of development much earlier, but what matters is whether a child has reached it by the milestone age. You will also read about average ages for developmental stages, and these will be different. An average age is in the middle of the range of ages when all children reach a certain stage.

One important aspect of development is that of physical growth. Children grow very quickly – ask your own parents. Growth allows the development of many of the skills we will be looking at.

Growth occurs in four phases.

- From birth to two years there is a rapid gain of up to 30 cm in height, and a tripling of body weight.
- From two years to puberty is a slower stage – with a gain each year of 6–8 cm in height and 3 kg in weight.
- Adolescence sees a rapid growth spurt, with gains of 8–16 cm per year.
- Slow growth continues until adult size is reached at about 18–20 years of age.

With this growth there is also a dramatic change in body proportions – look at the size of a newborn baby's head in proportion to the rest of the body. Compare this with a child of seven or eight years.

All children develop at different rates and may be earlier in achieving some aspects of development and later in others, but the following table shows general milestones.

Some important milestones for development		
Age	**Physical**	**Social/Emotional**
Birth to 4 weeks	Lies on back with head to one side Head lags when pulled up to sit	Imitates facial expressions Stares at bright shiny objects
1 month	Head control unsteady Hands in tight fists Head and eyes move together	Gazes intently at carers
6 weeks		Social smile at carers
4 months	Uses arms for support when lying on stomach Turns from back to side Holds onto and shakes small items	Smiles, engages and vocalises with carers
9 months	Sits alone without support Uses index and middle fingers with thumb in pincer grip to pick up small items Will take and hold a small brick in each hand	Very interested in all around Recognises familiar and unfamiliar people Shows stranger anxiety
1 year	Stands alone Enjoys self-feeding	Shows definite emotions and is aware of emotions of others Will play alone
18 months	Can walk alone Can walk upstairs with hand held Tries to kick a ball Squats to pick objects from floor Builds tower of 6 bricks Assists with dressing and undressing Can use spoon	Stranger shyness Dislikes changes in routine Starts toilet training Start of tantrums when upset Has separate sense of self Little idea of sharing and strong sense of 'mine'

3 years	Stands and walks on tiptoe Can kick a ball confidently Builds tower of 9 bricks and builds bridge with bricks Threads large beads Undoes buttons	Strong sense of gender identity Less anxious about separation Plays alongside others
4 years	Builds large tower Draws a person with head, body and legs, and a house if asked Can brush own teeth Cuts round an object with scissors and copies a square Can catch a large ball Walks backwards	Enjoys co-operative and dramatic play Understands co-operation and competition Responds to reasoning Can take turns Enjoys independence but still needs comfort and reassurance
7 years	Builds intricate models Controls pencil in small area Enjoys board games Enjoys hopping, bike riding, roller boots, skating	Becomes engrossed in activities Develops fears of ghosts, things under the bed Concerned about being disliked

Do it

Identify the 'normal' childhood milestones for physical, social and emotional development.

Find a family with at least one, and preferably two young children under eight. One with a baby will be even better! Ideally you should know the family personally, but ask your tutor to help you to find a suitable family if necessary. Arrange to visit the family and ask if you can interview them and observe the children. Make sure that you go at a time that is convenient to the family. Have a list of questions ready about the development of the children in physical, emotional and social areas. If possible, spend time observing the children and write down in detail what you see. Did the children all reach the milestones at the same ages?

Record your findings in the form of a log of your visits and discussions. (It will be useful also to look at the next chapter and record details of the children's intellectual and communication development).

The relationship between areas of development

At six weeks most babies will smile socially – not because they have wind, or are practising using muscles, but because they have been talked to and smiled at by parents and other carers. Sadly, not all babies have loving carers, and for all sorts of reasons may not be smiled at and talked to. These babies will probably not smile at six weeks. A baby who has experienced lots of talking and communication will smile much earlier than six weeks, and will vocalise with the carer.

At nine months, a baby will sit without support, and can hold a small brick in his or her hand and pass it from hand to hand. As well as being able to play with bricks, babies can now sit up in a high chair and start to share family meals.

Achieving progress in nearly all aspects of development is dependent on a child having opportunities to practice the skills. Although the human body is designed to move onto the next stage of development, without practice the next stage may be delayed.

If one aspect of development is not as expected for the age and stage of the child, for example sitting alone, then another aspect will be affected, such as the ability to finger feed.

Communication is an essential feature of social living. It is not difficult to see the benefits to a baby of learning to communicate with his or her family. While a young baby has only very basic needs, crying and smiling may be enough. As the child grows and has increasingly complex needs, talking becomes more necessary.

Imagine trying to make friends when you started school if you could not talk, or join in games with your peers. If you have ever been to school in a new country or even part of the country where people have spoken in different languages or dialects, you might have some idea of how that feels.

Adults and children communicate in a two-way process. Babies are skilled at influencing the way their family and carers behave with them. Watch a small child trying to attract attention from parents who are engrossed in conversation.

Do it

Identify the relationship between areas of development which enable a child to function normally in a family setting.

Observe two children of different ages, if possible, in your placement, or one in placement and one in a family setting. Look at the skills and tactics they use to gain attention from adults. Note down the differences between the younger and older child. What does this tell you about their development?

Basic routines of care for a child's needs

Most people have various fixed tasks and practices that are part of their daily routine. These include washing, dressing, eating, travelling to work or school, relaxation time, watching TV, study, etc. Young children and babies also need a routine. Their routine will fulfil the basic needs for human existence. Look at the two routines shown opposite for children at different ages.

Both of the routines provide for the children's basic needs, but the baby spends far more time asleep, doing little more than sleep, feed, and interact with carers. The three-year-old has more time for the development of intellectual and social skills in his or her routine.

Fitting in with family life

Routines are not developed for a child in isolation. Children belong to some type of family group, and part of social development is learning to fit our needs in with other people's

Baby aged 4 weeks		Girl aged 3 years	
6 am	Nappy change, morning feed	7 am	Wake, to parents' bed for cuddle
6.30–9 am	Sleeping	7.30	Breakfast with parents
9 am	Bath, playtime	8 am	Shower and dressed
9.30	Feed	8.30	Travel to nursery
10–12	Sleep	9–12 noon	At nursery school – play in sand, paint, listen to story time, take snacks at 10.30
12 noon	In baby chair close to carer	12.30	Lunch at Grandma's, watch TV
1 pm	Nappy change, feed	1.30–2.30	Afternoon sleep
1.30–3 pm	Asleep in pram during walk and shopping	2.30–5 pm	Shopping and baking with Grandma
3–4 pm	In baby chair playing with carer	5.30	Home with parents, playing with toys
4.30	Change and feed	6 pm	Supper
5–7 pm	Awake, grumbling, playing with carers	7 pm	Bath, storytime, bed
7.30	Change, feed		
8 pm	Bed		
Midnight	Feed		

needs. All families are different, and so their routines will be different. Look at the comparison of family routines given in the table below.

Activity	Family A	Family B
Getting up	All have shower in arranged rota.	First come, first served in bathroom.
Breakfast	All together in the kitchen, sitting at table.	Various times, Mum leaves first for work, Dad watches Breakfast TV.
Getting to school and nursery	Older children take younger ones, walk to school. Baby goes to childminder.	Dad takes children to school and nursery in car. Looks after baby at home.
Lunch	School/nursery meals.	Packed lunches at school and nursery, baby fed at home.
Teatime/ hometime	Children have snack, flop in front of TV.	Older children do homework in bedroom. Baby and nursery-age child have tea.
Early evening	Homework, more snacks.	Older children and parents sit down to meal together.
Bedtime	Whenever children are ready. Younger ones go with parents into family bed at parents' bedtime.	Strict bedtimes in order of age. All children in bed by 9 pm in their own rooms.

Think it through

Compare your daily routine with that of some of your friends. How much time do you spend in bed, in the bathroom, and eating, for example? Discuss the reasons for your different answers.

When you are planning routines for children, it is important to remember that young children are all different, and will have slightly different needs. Carers need to pay attention to all areas of development when planning daily and weekly care for children, making sure that each child is treated individually. To meet their physical, social and emotional needs, children need a mix of exercise, rest and sleep, and they need toileting and washing, play time and story time.

Do it

Illustrate basic routines which can be used to care for a child's daily needs.

When you go to see the family you are studying, ask if you can arrange to interview the parents about the family routine. Plan your questions and ask about bedtime, bathtime and mealtime routines. Compare your findings with those of other students. What differences have you found? Can you think of any reasons for the differences?

Physical requirements of good health and development

Figure 10.1 Germs and physical dangers are always lurking

Children, especially very young children, cannot protect themselves, so it is the responsibility of all involved in their care to think about all the dangers lurking in everyday life that could harm a child.

As a childcare worker you have an important role to play in protecting young children – but it is important not to be over-protective. If you protect a child from every single potential source of infection, for instance, he or she will never develop natural immunity or protection from illness.

To protect against dangers, you need to:

- keep dangerous substances out of reach, or locked away in cupboards
- keep the environment tidy – no trailing flexes or toys on the floor
- use safety equipment, for example socket covers for electric sockets; safety gates for stairs
- check equipment and toys regularly for loose parts, which could cause choking or injury
- keep toys and equipment clean
- supervise children closely at all times.

Think it through

Good practice in hygiene is your responsibility. Complete the chart below, putting in the solutions – the first has been done for you.

Topic	Hazard	Solution
Your own personal hygiene	Dirty hands, or hands contaminated from use of toilet Long hair dangling loose	Regular hand washing after 'dirty' activities
A child's personal hygiene	Poor toilet habits Not washing hands	
Hygiene in a child's surroundings	Sour milk in bottles Dog allowed to foul play areas	
Hygiene in a child's diet	Leftover food not thrown away Food spills on kitchen surfaces Food left in warm kitchen	

Health

If you stayed at home every time you felt slightly ill, you would probably not be at work very often. Reliability is an essential part of childcare work. It is important, though, not to go to work if you are a source of infection, for example if you have flu or gastro-enteritis.

Likewise, children should not be going to nursery or school if they are infectious and could pass on an illness to the other children. Different childcare settings have various policies about attendance. If there is an outbreak of an infectious disease, often a child is more likely to pass it on to others before the symptoms develop, so it could be argued that there is not much point in excluding a child from nursery when the infection has already been passed on.

Do It

Describe the importance of health, safety and hygienic practice in a childcare setting.

Check the routines in your placement that are related to health, safety and hygiene, for example how often the toys are checked and washed.

Produce a booklet for parents aimed at reassuring them that all necessary attention is given to these very important areas.

Encouraging healthy eating

Food is a fuel – it helps children to grow and develop, and gives them the energy they need for the hard work involved in playing and learning. When they are small, children need help to ensure they have the right amount and balance of food – they are incapable of providing food for themselves, and to begin with they are unable to eat without help.

Everyone needs to eat a balanced diet, to help to maintain health. The important parts of the diet are shown in the table on page 276.

Nutrient	Function	Sources
Carbohydrates	Energy for growth and activity Aid digestion of other food	Potatoes, pasta, rice, pulses, sugar, fruit
Fats: Saturated form from animal sources Unsaturated from vegetable sources	Energy, body heat Contains vitamins (A, D, E and K)	Butter, cheese, meat, olive, vegetable and fish oils, nuts
Proteins	Growth and repair of the body	Meat, fish, soya, pulses, cheese, eggs, nuts, cereals
Vitamins: Fat soluble (A, D, E and K) Water soluble (C and all Bs)	A – promotes good vision and healthy skin B – aids blood formation, nerve and muscle function C – promotes healing D – encourages growth of bones and teeth E – protects cells from damage K – allows blood to clot	Fat soluble – oily fish, cheese, tomatoes, carrots, milk, liver, egg yolk, green vegetables Water soluble – fruits, juices, meat, leafy vegetables, beans, eggs
Minerals: Calcium, sodium, potassium, magnesium, sulphur, flouride, trace elements	For healthy bones and teeth, balance of fluids, energy production, control of nerves and muscles	In nearly all foods in differing amounts. Sodium in salt, meat, fish and bread Fluoride in water
Fibre	Adds bulk to food to keep bowels functioning Thought to help in protection against heart disease and cancer	Oats, wholewheat bread, beans, leafy vegetables, prunes, apples
Water	Maintains fluid balance Helps in waste elimination	All foods and drinks in varying amounts

Certain proportions of each food group are required for a healthy diet. We need to be sure that food is eaten in balanced quantities, as shown in the following table.

Food groups		Nutrients	Portions per day
1.	Bread, potatoes, cereals, pasta and rice	Fibre, vitamins, minerals, carbohydrates	3 to 4 portions – one at each meal
2.	Fruit and vegetables	Fibre, vitamins, minerals, carbohydrates	5 portions
3.	Milk and milk products	Proteins, fats, vitamins and minerals	2 to 3 portions (a portion is 200ml milk, 1 small yoghurt or 1 oz cheese)
4.	High-protein foods – meat, eggs, fish, pulses, nuts	Proteins, vitamins, minerals, fats	2 to 3 portions
5.	Fats and oils	Essential fatty acids	Small amounts, infrequently

Think it through

Keep a record of your diet for two or three days, writing down everything you eat. How does your pattern of eating meet these requirements? Should you be making some changes?

Good eating patterns

How do children move from being totally dependent on milk to eating a balanced family diet, containing the correct levels of all these foods? The process is called weaning. Foods other than milk are introduced usually between the ages of three and six months – Chapter 15 looks at weaning in more detail.

Eating can quickly become a battleground for parents and children if undue fuss is made about what a child will eat and what he or she needs both in terms of amounts and a balanced diet. Children will not starve themselves, and if they have the chance they will eat a variety of foods over a period of time that contain the nutrients they need.

As a childcare worker you have a big part to play in encouraging positive eating habits. One thing to remember is that there will be as many different eating routines as there are families. The many ways of encouraging good eating habits include:

- not fussing if a child isn't hungry
- keeping sweets and snacks for after meals
- offering small portions of attractive food
- avoiding over-filling a plate
- accepting a dislike for a food – it may be accepted at a later time
- not using food as a bribe
- offering different eating experiences – with friends, in a café, picnics, etc.
- setting an example by eating healthy foods
- introducing changes to diets slowly, with one new food at a time
- involving children in choosing, cooking and serving their own food as much as possible.

'Junk' food is often dismissed as not providing a healthy diet, yet a burger, a pizza or fish and chips can provide a useful contribution to a child's diet. The secret is variety – just as a constant diet of shepherd's pie or curry and rice would not meet all dietary needs, eating nothing but burgers is unlikely to give you a balanced diet.

Do It

Identify the essential components of a healthy diet in young children and describe ways to encourage healthy and positive eating habits.

Plan a weekly set of menus for a child of four or five years. Ideally, this could be a child you know, and who attends nursery or school, and who enjoys the occasional pizza or burger. Match the menus against the essential components for a healthy diet. How could you make mealtimes enjoyable for a child?

Rest, sleep and quiet periods

We all need to have rest and sleep as part of our everyday routines, not only because we get very tired, but because sleep and rest have several functions – not least allowing the body to recuperate.

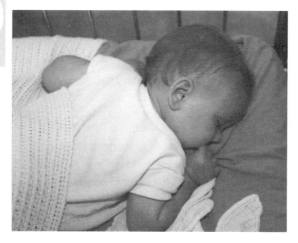

If we are deprived of sleep, we soon start suffering from memory loss, irritability, and even hallucinations. Parents often describe a child who is very tired as behaving irritably.

How much sleep do children need?

There is no fixed answer to the question of how much sleep children need. Some babies sleep 18 out of every 24 hours, others only 12. Some toddlers can cope on ten hours at night and a nap in the day, while others will sleep for 12 hours at night and then need two hours' sleep in the afternoon. Sleep patterns will change with changing routines and events in a child's life.

The body does not recuperate only by sleeping – rest will serve the same purpose. Very few children will spend all day running around, actively playing – they will sit down sometimes and watch the world go by, or ask to be read to, or watch TV for a short time. These are all resting or quiet periods.

Most nurseries and reception classes have a designated 'quiet' time in their daily routines to allow for children to recoup their energy. A skilled childcare worker will build these times into the routine with children.

CASE STUDY BEECHWOOD NURSERY, ZAK AND HASSAM

Beechwood Nursery has places for 24 children aged two to five years. Many of the children stay for the full day, from 8.30 to 5.30 pm. At mid-morning the children have a quiet half-hour, sitting in small groups while a story is read to them, then watching a short TV programme. After lunch the children lie down on mats with quilts for an hour to rest and recoup their energy.

Lizzie is a nanny for Zak, who is nine months old, and Hassan, who is three. Hassan attends playgroup each morning. Zak is awake all morning now and has a sleep from about 1–2 pm. By serving lunch for both children as soon as the three-year-old comes home from playgroup, Lizzie can enjoy a quiet hour with Hassan while Zak is asleep. This hour also gives Hassan a chance to rest, and occasionally he falls asleep on the sofa.

Providing the right environment for sleep

Just as important as time in a routine for rest and sleep is providing the right environment for the child. Children enjoy having familiar objects and routines when they are settling down to sleep, perhaps including

- bath before bed
- a ritual of goodnights to the entire family, toys, etc.
- story time or songs
- warm drink

It is essential to be sensitive to the changing needs of children. Sleep, rest and appetite needs may change in some situations, for example:

- during and after illness
- after changes in family circumstances
- at the time of starting school.

- after the birth of a new sibling
- before and after exciting events, e.g. a party or outing

You should be alert to the changing needs of children you care for. Sometimes these changes can be the first signal that something is happening in their lives.

Do It

Describe the importance of rest, sleep, quiet periods and eating regularly as part of a child's daily routine.

Ask a family you know about the patterns of rest, sleep and mealtimes. What bedtime routines do they follow? How do the parents feel the routine developed, and are they happy with it? Record the patterns as a chart or table, adding your comments following your discussion with the family.

If you cannot ask a family for this information, imagine you are caring for a family of three young children, aged four months, two years and six years, for the weekend. The parents have had to go away and asked you to care for the children. Plan the weekend, paying particular attention to eating, sleeping and rest for all the children. How will you make sure you are not altering their routine too much?

Exercise and healthy development

Figure 10.2 Exercise helps to develop skills and confidence

You would be right to think that young children hardly need encouraging to exercise, as they are constantly on the go. However, recent studies have shown that many children do not have enough exercise, possibly as a result of parents transporting children everywhere by car, parents fearing to allow children to play far from their home, and increasing use of TV and computer games.

Children may need some direction to gain the opportunity to develop skills through exercise. Carers can help by suggesting and providing opportunities. Exercise is an excellent way to encourage the use of newly gained skills, or to help further development of skills a child may be struggling with.

Here are some of the benefits of taking exercise.

- Older children learn social skills such as turn-taking, and experience winning and losing, through energetic games and races. You can help less active children with example and encouragement.

- Adventure playgrounds with climbing frames, rope swings, etc. are ideal for children to learn from one another and are usually designed so that there are levels of climbing, swinging and so on to suit different abilities.
- Energetic play can be an ideal way for children who are angry or upset to work off their aggression. Ask any teacher about the effect of bad weather, resulting in enforced indoor play – a group of young children may react badly to not having the chance to work off their energy in the playground!
- Exercise uses the energy provided by the food a child eats. If exercise does not burn up enough energy in the food eaten, a child will gain excess weight.
- Exercise helps to develop muscles. You can see how important this is if you examine an arm or leg that has been in a plaster cast after a fracture for six weeks – it will be very much thinner and weaker than the other limb, as a result of not having any exercise for that short time.
- The immune system is strengthened through exercise, and so can help a child to be less vulnerable to illness.

What type of exercise is best, and at what age? The table below shows some examples of exercise and how they can help children to develop.

Type of exercise	Effect on health and development
Baby on changing mat without nappy – kicking freely, rolling for toys	Nappy area exposed to fresh air – healthy skin Physical stretching, building muscles in legs Development of mobility
Baby bouncing on knee of carer	Social interaction Developing strength in legs, practising standing
12–18-month-old child using push-and-ride toy	Practising walking with support Manoeuvring skills Independence Muscle movement
Two-year-old in the park, running playing on the swings and slide Rough and tumble play in a safe environment – with foam mats, cushions, etc.	Developing gross motor control by physical activity Social interaction with other children Fresh air, sunshine – benefits for building the immune system
Swimming Gymnastics Dancing Football (any age)	Help to promote healthy development of bones, muscles and the immune system Social skills developed, team skills, self-esteem by achievement Co-ordination skills Learning about rules and turn-taking
Music and movement (any age)	Co-ordination of body to music Creativity, imagination

For exercise to occur, it may need only the child and his or her imagination, or some suitable space may be needed, or extra equipment and support. As a childcare worker, you will need to consider indoor and outdoor exercise, and appropriate equipment for both settings. The requirements could include:

- space
- swimming baths
- music
- balls of various sizes
- tricycles, sit-and-ride toys
- naturals features – trees, streams with stepping stones
- skipping ropes
- swings, slides, frames, benches
- tents, play houses.

The best resources to enable children to enjoy and benefit from exercise are their own imagination, space and someone to help them to use those resources and their bodies.

Do it

Give examples of three types of exercise and describe how they promote health and encourage development in children.

Over a period of a week, write down all types of exercise you see children taking part in. Try to observe a wide age range, and a variety of activities. Remember that exercise does not have to be formally organised – children exercise as they are playing.

Choose three separate examples, and write about the activities in detail. Describe the number of children involved, how it was organised, the equipment needed if any, the safety implications and so on. Explain how each type of exercise is promoting health and encouraging development in the children involved.

Exercise for children with physical disabilities

When you are planning an activity of any sort, you should always consider *all* of the children who may be joining in.

To a child who is timid about large groups, a boisterous game of chase or playing on the climbing frame may be very daunting and you should think of ways of helping him or her to join in. You may need to think about providing two parallel activities, if staffing and numbers allow, in order to meet all the children's needs.

The climbing frame will not be suitable for a child who is a wheelchair user, without having a helper with the child at all times. Padded matting may be needed underneath the frame in case of falls. A child with reduced vision could enjoy using the frame if paired with another suitable child or assisted by you.

By using your imagination and thinking about the safety issues, you can help most children to enjoy most activities and equipment. They can usually be adapted to suit all children without losing the aim of the exercise. Careful thought must be given to make sure that no one is discriminated against in his or her play and exercise.

There are many ways to avoid excluding a child with a disability. Many manufacturers make suitably adapted play equipment, for example tricycles with bucket seats. Equipment specifically designed for children with disabilities can usually be used by all children. The manufacturers of 'ball pools' and huge foam wedges in different shapes originally intended them for children with disablilities, but they now feature in most adventure playgrounds for younger children. Careful use of foam mats can take much of the risk out of physical exercise for all children, so that falls do not have hard landings.

Do It

Identify exercises suitable for children with physical disabilities and how indoor and outdoor play equipment can be adapted.

You are in charge of a group of eight energetic five year-olds, five girls and three boys. Samir is slower than the others in walking, due to a condition affecting his muscles. Paul doesn't like rough games and is reluctant to join in groups. Lucy likes any game that is noisy and rough, but she broke her arm last week and has it in plaster. The weather was wet and windy all morning and now the sun has started to shine. The class teacher asks you to take this group outside and organise some exercise for them in the grounds of the school for half an hour.

Plan your half-hour to include all of the children. What exercise would you provide, and what would the benefits be for the children?

Now imagine it has not stopped raining all day and you are asked to help the children have some exercise indoors. Again, plan half an hour for all the children.

Emotional development

Variations in children's social and emotional needs

Just as adults vary in their nature and temperament, so do children. A child may be sociable and outgoing, or shy and reserved. You will see many other variations of character among children in your care. These variations have several possible causes:

- genetic – inherited from one or both parents
- primary socialisation – learned behaviour
- position in the family
- experiences in early childhood – positive or negative.

Are you similar to one of your parents in character, and in the way you deal with feelings, or are you totally different from both of them? If you have brothers and sisters, does this apply to them?

Social and emotional development starts at birth and continues throughout life. The general stages are described in the table below.

Age	Stage of social and emotional development
Birth	Responds positively to main carer
6–9 months	Starts to show interest in other babies, smiling. Becomes more interested in social interaction, depending on amount of time spent with other children and their personality. Fear of strangers and distress at separation from carer. Interacts differently with various family members. Uses comfort object – blanket, etc. Seeks attention.
12–18 months	More demanding and assertive, emotionally volatile. Temper tantrums may start. Unhappy at changes in routines, expresses rage at being told 'no'. Distinguishes between self and others, but still egocentric – only concerned with his or her own view of the world.
2–3 years	Enjoys other children's company but reluctant to share toys. May show concern when another child is upset. Engages in parallel play (alongside others). Remains egocentric. Becoming emotionally stable, but still prone to mood swings. Learning to separate from carer for short periods – e.g. while at nursery. Knows own identity.

Age	Stage of social and emotional development
3–4 years	Greater social awareness. Will play in twos or threes, sharing ideas. May have close friends. A lot of mixed play of the sexes. Stable and emotionally secure. Friendly to other children. Increasing independence, but still needs support from adults. Fears loss of carers.
5–8 years	Able to form firm friendships. Very supportive of each other, playing complex games. By the age of six or seven, playing in separate sex groups. Fairly independent and confident. Increasing sense of morality – right and wrong.

This chart outlines only the 'normal' expectations of social and emotional development. These are the aspects of development that are most dependant on a child's experiences and family life. Many children do not achieve these stages of social and emotional development as quickly as expected. There are many possible reasons for this.

● Children may have delayed language development, affecting their communication with others.
● Children may not speak the same language as the setting where they spend time.
● Children who are physically unattractive may be shunned by their peers.
● Children may be immature, unfriendly, or aggressive.
● There may be prejudice and discrimination from other children against those who are of a different racial group or have a disability.
● There may be poor primary socialisation.
● Serious illness may have occurred in the first years.
● The death of a parent, or a traumatic separation, may have occurred.

Do It

Identify variations in children's social and emotional needs at different stages of development.

The best way to demonstrate your understanding of this topic is by describing children you work with, who display variations from the normal expectation of social and emotional development.

They could be exceptionally shy, or too rough and boisterous, or perhaps slow to speak. If possible, choose at least two children and explain how these aspects of their development vary from the expected. Give your ideas as to why this might be so. How are these children treated by their peers?

Strategies to help children to cope with their feelings

Young children live very much in the present, and an explosive outburst will often pass very quickly, with the child returning to his or her previous activity – possible leaving other children and adults feeling exhausted. Dealing with outbursts can be challenging. A two-year-old child who is frustrated by something or someone can be like a whirlwind of anger, and it can be very difficult not to react to this with anger yourself.

Hugh Jolly, a childcare expert writing in the 1970s felt that if you ignored temper tantrums and walked away, while providing the child with easy access to you, the outburst would soon burn out and the child would approach you for a cuddle. Recent guidelines suggest that you gently hold children to prevent them from hurting themselves or others, and be ready to cuddle when the fury is over. In these circumstances a child cannot start to feel ashamed of the outburst and find it difficult to approach the carer. You might see this practice referred to as 'holding therapy'. It developed from being used for children with special educational needs when they had bouts of temper and tantrums.

As a child grows, tantrums become more unacceptable – in a five- or six-year-old, for instance. Through the socialising effect of home, nursery and school, children learn that tantrums are unlikely to achieve the desired result – and other children may shun them.

Children should be encouraged to express their feelings in ways that are acceptable to society. As a society, we find it easier to accept expressions of happiness, rather than of sorrow. Part of your role in working with children is to encourage the expression of all feelings, including feeling:

- happy
- proud of work well done
- sad that a friend has been hurt
- angry if property is spoiled.

- pleased to see a friend
- sorry about something done wrong
- unhappy that the pet rabbit has died

Most children are spontaneous and wholehearted in their expressions of emotion. This means that children who are not so open will be obvious in a group – a child who is inhibited in expressing emotions at home may stand back and not join in open laughter with a group of children.

It is usual for a child below the age of five or six years to express anger spontaneously. For instance, if one child takes a toy from another, the wronged child may hit out or start to cry. A child who just accepts the theft and turns away or fails to express feelings should give cause for concern. Studies of children in hospital or residential care whose parents were not regularly present found that the children soon stopped all outward displays of distress. At first this was regarded as the child accepting his or her situation. In fact the child was giving up in the face of feelings about being abandoned, and had realised that crying was not going to bring the parents back. When the parents returned, such a child often rejected them. Serious emotional damage occurred to children who were separated from their familiar carers for long periods. As a result of this research, parents have been actively encouraged to stay with their children in hospital.

It is easy for a child to pick up the message that expressing emotion is not acceptable. But if children are unable to express their emotions directly, all that happens is that they are expressed in another way – through unwanted behaviours, regressing to wetting, ill health, etc.

How can you help children to cope with their feelings? Look at the example in the case study below.

CASE STUDY LOIS

Lois is aged three and a half and has been at nursery for five months. Staff have been worried that she is very slow to join in with other children, despite all their best efforts. Her mother appears to be concerned as well, and reports that Lois is reluctant to go to bed at night, and often wakes with nightmares.

Last week Lois bit another little girl for no reason, and has started to burst into tears very easily. Her mother came into the nursery for a discussion with the supervisor, and it emerged that Lois's father left home 18 months ago. As Lois was only two at the time, her Mum didn't think it had bothered her – she saw her Daddy every week. However, Lois's father has a new partner and she met a new stepsister last month. Visits have been reduced to once every two weeks, and Lois does not like her stepsister.

Lois is clearly a little girl in distress. She has had to deal with many changes in her short life, but has not been able to express her feelings. It is doubtful that Lois would be able to speak about these intense emotions, and they have been emerging in other ways. Lois and her mother obviously need a lot of understanding and support. Her mother could be very upset about the situation with her ex-husband, and transfer some of her emotions to Lois. Support for the mother is not within your scope, but a supervisor should talk to her about counselling or seeing a health visitor or doctor, for instance.

As a worker with Lois, you have a vital role to play. Lois needs acceptance. She already feels she has been 'rejected' by her Daddy and replaced with a new daughter. If you are cross with her for biting and leave her alone when she doesn't want to join in, all her feelings of rejection will be magnified.

Taking time to discover what Lois likes to do, playing on a one-to-one basis with her, and gradually introducing her to other children will help. Paying full attention to Lois, trying to prevent battles occurring and offering distractions when necessary should avoid biting incidents in future. Rather than punishment, Lois needs a lot of praise and attention for her self-esteem, and activities to encourage her to express her anger and distress. Home corner activities can help, allowing her to vent her anger on dolls, teddies, etc. and use them as vehicles of expression. Outdoor play using a lot of energy can also help to relieve anger.

A note of caution

When you are working with children, it is important to be aware of the feelings a child or group of children may produce in you. A child expressing extreme anger may bring out feelings in you related to how your own parents reacted to you as a child. If you were shouted at for showing anger, or even smacked, or if you witnessed anger in others, it may be uncomfortable for you to deal with this type of situation.

Sometimes a response may come to mind that is a reflection of your own experiences, and it may not be appropriate in the situation. It is important to recognise this, and accept that recognising your responses is an excellent step on the path to being a professional worker. You may be able to work it out for yourself, or you may have a supervisor or colleague with whom you can share your feelings.

Do IT

Identify the range of feelings a child may experience and suggest strategies to enable children to cope with their feelings and express them appropriately.

Produce a poster for your placement on the theme of children's feelings. Make sure that you cover as many different feelings as possible, both positive and negative, with the possible causes for them, making it clear that these are all normal. How do you think you might introduce these ideas to the children in your placement?

Promoting self-esteem, self-reliance and self-confidence

Adults involved in caring for children sometimes forget that children need to make mistakes in their drive for independence. All children are working towards the ultimate goal of full independence in all areas of life. As early years workers our role is to support them in reaching this, to a level appropriate to their age and stage of development.

By encouraging independence, we automatically encourage self-reliance, self-esteem and self-confidence. I am sure you can think of people you know who claim not to be able to look after themselves in basic tasks such as preparing a meal or washing clothes. Such people might have a reduced amount of work to do, but is this good for their self-esteem?

Feeding a child is much faster than encouraging self-feeding, but this tactic will not be appreciated when the child starts school and still needs help. Self-reliance is needed in a child when he or she starts school – a child has enough to deal with in adapting to all the new demands of school without the worry of not being able to use the toilet alone, or not being able to cope with changing his or her clothes when it is time for PE.

Think it through

Look at the picture in Figure 10.3 of the child ready for school. Some skills she needs are named – add as many more as you can think of. How can these skills be developed in the nursery setting?

can go to the toilet alone

plays group games

dresses herself

cuts up and eats food

Figure 10.3 Some of the skills a child needs when she is ready for school

Do It

Describe the role of the adult in promoting self-esteem, self-reliance and self-confidence in the child.

Write notes reflecting how you think the named child will feel in each of the following situations. How could the adults behave in a more positive way?

1. Sarah spends an hour finishing a model of a castle from cereal packets. When her mother collects her from nursery, she throws Sarah's model in the nearest waste bin.

2. Ali's mother has picked him up from nursery with his junk model, and she goes round to Grandma's to show her Ali's work.

3. Miss Singh asks parents to come in and look at *all* the children's work on the wall, including Ben's.

4. Instead of putting on her coat to play outside, Shuli goes and sits on the mat for story time as she has not heard the instructions. Mr Jones tells all the other children to look at Shuli being silly and not listening properly.

5. Every time Miss Glory chooses the order for children to go for snacks, Sam is last, because he is always the slowest finishing his work.

6. Kate's chart of stars is growing as a reward for good work and behaviour.

Attachment, bonding and socialisation

The development of the deep feelings between parents or carers and their children comes about through a process of bonding and attachment.

This attachment is helped in the early months by:

- skin contact
- talking, and listening to parents' voices
- bathing
- play
- eye-to-eye contact.
- smell
- feeding
- changing nappies

The researcher John Bowlby described 'bonding' and 'attachment', and confirmed the idea that all children need consistent carers to allow them to develop attachments and start to form loving relationships with their carers. If the period following birth is interrupted by illness in mother or baby, or many different carers, a child may have difficulty in forming close relationships in later life. Other children can have difficulties in this process due to visual or hearing problems, or because of severe learning difficulties. Parents of children who have problems affecting the bonding process need extra support and encouragement.

It used to be thought that a baby could form a close attachment only to his or her mother, but this has been shown to not be the case. Children can and obviously do form strong bonds with a wide range of people – grandparents, siblings, friends and others. It is regular and frequent contact that is important, and even where a child has a normal attachment to parents and family, it is important that in a nursery setting he or she is allowed to develop attachment to at least one regular carer.

A child who has formed close bonds with several important people will be far more secure than a child who has not done so. Where there is a strong sense of security in a child, there is likely to be less emotional trauma caused by future separations from the main carers. Often a very clingy child will have had some difficulty in the early years in forming a close bond with carers.

Socialisation

Socialisation is all about learning to cope in the family and society we live in. The socialisation process will by its definition vary from family to family, and in different societies. You will remember from Chapter 2 that **primary socialisation** is the socialisation that takes place within the family, in the first years of a child's life.

Secondary socialisation starts when children come into regular contact with people and settings outside their home. This includes playgroup, nursery and school, and continues throughout life. Secondary socialisation teaches children about:

- society's views of gender roles
- how to interact with peers
- the 'rules' of society – what is acceptable and what is not.
- how to interact with other adults
- the views of peers

Your role as a childcare worker is part of the process of secondary socialisation – children will learn a great deal from your behaviour, both obvious and hidden behaviour.

Do IT

Define attachment, bonding and socialisation.

Make notes explaining the importance of these processes in the lives of young children. Give examples from the development of children you have worked with or know well.

Play to help expression of feelings

Play is work to children. Huge amounts of energy are spent in play of all types. Much of this play develops or teaches new skills and helps with social development – it can be plain fun, but it can also be **therapeutic**. Therapeutic means that it helps to heal. The healing may be needed because a child is angry, upset, frightened or worried – any one or a combination of negative feelings are possible. Nearly all types of play can help a child to express feelings, but especially:

- painting
- playing in the home corner
- acting out roles – pretend play
- playing with dolls
- physical games involving running and shouting
- dough and plasticine.

Hospital playworkers have done a lot of valuable work in developing play with children who are about to have an operation or treatment, to explain what is going to happen to them. Dolls are made or adapted to show operation sites, injured limbs, etc.

Social workers engage abused children in playwork, to allow them to express what has happened where words may not be available. Again, they may use adapted dolls, such as anatomically correct dolls for dealing with sexual abuse cases.

Recognising a distressed child is very important. Having recognised the distress, you should have some ways of helping the child to express that distress. Physical play with clay is a good way of bringing out anger, as is whizzing around on a tricycle. Big foam cushions on which a child can bounce are useful – the list is endless.

When you are encouraging expression and the working out of feelings, you need to make sure the child is physically safe, feels comfortable in the activity, and will not feel silly afterwards. Protecting other children is important too, especially if the activity is very physical. Seeing a child acting out anger on a pile of cushions may upset other children.

All different types of play are useful means for children to express themselves. It may not be necessary to set up play situations deliberately to allow expression. Your role is to be alert to situations and to be ready to support a child as necessary.

Think it through

If you are working with a child who is playing in the home corner and taking out her emotions on dolls, you may hear verbal descriptions or role play of incidents that worry you. An example would be an uncle doll getting into bed with a little girl doll. You would be quite right to be worried, and should always report anything you are not comfortable with to your supervisor. This is not breaking confidence; it is your professional responsibility.

Do it

Describe play activities which enable children to work out their feelings.

You and a friend on your course have been asked to look after your neighbour's two children, aged three and five, for the day on Sunday. Their grandmother has just died and the parents are going away to organise the preparation of her house for sale. Both girls were very close to their Granny, and their mother thinks they are upset, but are not showing it. You have noticed that both seem very quiet and withdrawn. How will you plan the day? What activities would you provide that might allow them to express their thoughts and feelings? How will you support them?

Encouraging and supporting good behaviour

Good and inappropriate behaviour in children

All children need attention, and all children thrive on praise from their carers. These two statements may seem very obvious to you, and are sentiments that you can empathise with.

The definition of good behaviour is relative – relative to time, place, the age of the child and the relevant culture. What is perfectly acceptable behaviour in one family would be condemned as unacceptable in another. You may have experienced this in your parents' attitudes to staying out late, friendships, helping at home, etc. as compared to the attitudes of other parents. All childcare establishments have an accepted code of behaviour, which is explained to children and parents, but within each establishment there will be individual differences of interpretation among staff.

It is important to remember a few basic rules when considering and dealing with children's behaviour.

You should **always**

- be specific when describing a child's behaviour – e.g. Shanaz nipped Poala on the arm, rather than Shanaz was cruel to Poala
- consider causes behind inappropriate behaviour
- beware of listening only to one side of a dispute between children, and be sure you have the full facts before intervening
- remember that children will repeat behaviours they have experienced
- make sure that a child knows that it is the behaviour you do not like, not the child.

You should **never**

- use physical force or violence towards a child
- belittle a child who has behaved inappropriately
- make threats or promises that you will not keep.

Factors contributing to behaviour

Behaviour is a vague term. Do you remember being told as a child on a special occasion to 'be on your best behaviour', and wondering what on earth it meant?

Children are often described as being very good or naughty, with no definition of these terms. As we have already seen, behaviour is relative, and it is particularly relative to the age of the child.

Think it through

Imran sat on the floor turning the pages of a book for two minutes. Then he noticed some big fat crayons his sister had been using, and went over to pick up the red one. He looked around for a second, and then started to scribble on the wall. At that moment Imran's mother came into the room.

Was Imran being 'naughty'? That depends on how old he is. If you knew he was 18 months old, would your opinion be the same as if he was five years old? At 18 months, we would not expect a child to concentrate on an activity for much more than two minutes. The incident with the crayons would be annoying to Imran's parents, but an 18-month-old would have no conception that he was not using the crayons in an appropriate way. At five years of age it would be reasonable to expect him to crayon on paper, and to understand that the wall is not a suitable place.

This is an example of age and stage of development being an important factor in judging appropriate behaviour.

Whenever you consider whether a child's behaviour is appropriate, it is important to look at the child's age. Parents often have unrealistic expectations of a child, not recognising that very young children will not have a sense of good and bad. If a toddler is told not to touch something, within minutes he or she will have forgotten this instruction if the desired article is very attractive.

It is important to be specific in describing appropriate and inappropriate behaviour. Look at these two statements.

A   Joel was annoying his friend; he kept distracting him and stopping him working. Then he started to draw attention to himself.

B   Joel repeatedly jabbed his pencil into his friend's side, and snatched his book from him. Then he started to rock on his chair and scrape the legs on the floor.

Statement B is much more precise than A – we have a very clear picture of Joel's behaviour. As a student in Joel's class, you would be giving the teacher a much better description if you wrote down B.

Think it through

In pairs, think and write down specific examples of what the following descriptions mean to you, in

a) a child of two years and b) a child of six years.

- naughty
- sulking
- being disruptive.
- bad tempered
- being a nuisance

Compare your ideas with those of another pair. How many different ideas do you have for each word or phrase?

Inappropriate behaviour

Inappropriate behaviour can be a symptom of problems and issues in a child's world. Think about the times when you felt out of sorts because of an argument with a friend or parent before leaving home in the morning. For a while afterwards you feel snappy and grumpy with everyone, and may slam a few doors. Young children are no different. There are all sorts of factors – some minor, some major – that can affect a child's behaviour.

CASE STUDY ELIZABETH

Elizabeth had seemed very quiet at nursery, and did not join in easily with the other children on Monday. The staff were surprised as this was unusual for her. When they were playing in the sand, Elizabeth pushed Tracy hard when she tried to take the funnel. Tracy fell over and started to cry. Elizabeth ran into the home corner and burst into tears. When her mother came to collect her, the staff mentioned the incident. Elizabeth's mother told them that the family dog had died at the weekend.

This is a typical example of upsetting incidents affecting behaviour. Other potentially upsetting incidents include a new baby in the family, moving house, parents separating or rowing, access visits by absent parents, a poor night's sleep, minor illness, a parent losing a job, a new teacher or class, moving schools, and so on. Any change in routine can upset a child, and it is your responsibility to be alert for changes in a child's behaviour and report these to a senior person.

DO IT

Describe examples of good and inappropriate behaviour in children and identify factors which contribute to them.

Observe examples of good and inappropriate behaviour at your placement. Try to give at least six examples of each. If possible, note what caused the behaviour, and how the staff involved reacted to the incident.

Behaviour policies and procedures

Children need security to thrive and develop. Going for the first time to playgroup, nursery or school are momentous events in any child's life. They should not have to cope with inappropriate behaviour in the form of abuse, racism or sexism, and it is the responsibility of every childcare worker to make sure this does not happen. Childcare settings therefore need to have clear policies and procedures relating to many things, but in particular to behaviour. This does not mean to say that a long list of rules should be drawn up in nursery that children have to learn. Children as young as four or five will understand simple rules related to caring for others, not being unkind, and not taking items belonging to others.

A **policy** is the statement of what is expected or is provided in a setting, e.g. *all children will be treated with respect.*

The related **procedure** would state something such as: *Cases of children taking items not belonging to themselves must be reported to the member of staff in charge of that group. Parents must be informed.*

The related **'rule'** might be: *All children are expected to look after their own and other people's property. Children should not bring their own toys into nursery.*

All childcare settings have stated policies and procedures dealing with issues such as bullying, stealing, deliberate damage, etc. and these are known and understood by staff. Children and parents should be aware of the associated rules where appropriate – in some cases this will be only the parents where the children are very young. Clearly, policies will depend on the age of children who attend.

A very important point is that policies and rules must be fair, consistently applied, and all consequences followed through. Children should understand as soon as possible what the result of breaking a rule will be, and why the rule exists.

DO IT

Explain the need for behaviour policies and procedures.

In placement, ask if you can see the policies, procedures and rules relating to behaviour. If possible, copy them down. How are they related to the ages of the children at your placement? Do you think they are reasonable? Are any rules missing? Imagine you had to amend them for children either two years older or younger – what changes would be needed?

Strategies to deal with common behaviour problems

Inappropriate behaviour does not happen without reason. Think about teachers you may have had yourself, or seen in placement. Have you ever been in a classroom with a teacher who shouts all the time? Or seen a parent who seems to shout and tell the children off all the time? In comparison, think of a quietly spoken parent or teacher who seems to have well-behaved children. A carer's behaviour can greatly influence the behaviour of the children.

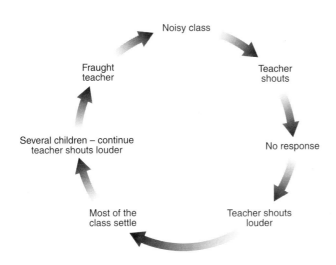

Figure 10.4   Inappropriate behaviour can set up a 'vicious circle'

The way staff deal with issues that arise in the classroom or nursery can have a huge impact on the response of the children. Ignoring bullying, racism, or disruption passes all the wrong messages to children, and encourages equally bad behaviour. In contrast a fair adult, who deals with issues promptly and fairly and shows respect for all the children, will encourage a calmer, happier setting.

The best way to encourage a child to continue with inappropriate behaviour is to make a fuss about that behaviour and pay a lot of attention to it. The best way to stop the behaviour is to ignore it. Pay attention and give plenty of praise to a child when he or she is behaving in an appropriate way.

Ignoring bad behaviour can at times be hard, if not impossible. You might manage to ignore the behaviour, but your colleague perhaps can't, and stands the child in the 'naughty' corner.

Rewards

Working on a child's inappropriate behaviour requires a lot of co-operation and teamwork, with both parents and staff involved. Observations are needed to decide on the exact nature of the problem behaviour, and targets must be set to improve it through positive behaviours. Through a series of rewards for good behaviour, targets are gradually raised. This method is called 'behaviour modification'. Even as a student, you can use some of the skills developed from this method.

Imagine never being the object of positive attention, but only of negative – in other words being shouted at, told off, punished. This is not ideal attention, but it is attention and for some children it is better than none. For many children with behaviour problems, this is the cycle they have got into. From their first entry into nursery some children become known as the 'naughty one', and their reputation sticks. I am sure this sounds familiar to you.

The next time you are working with children, try to listen to other staff and yourself to see if you and they spend more time praising children or telling them off. It is important to try to look for something to praise, even if it is only that a child has sat still for a few moments, or done a good painting, or shared something.

Most schools have a merit or reward system, with children being given small rewards such as stickers. An example of a merit chart is shown in Figure 10.5.

Merit chart for Zoe One smiley face for each time span of sitting still. 5 stickers to choose the book for story time.						Stickers
Monday 2 mins	☺☺	☺☺	☺☺	☺☺	☺☺	✓✓
Tuesday 3 mins	☺☺	☺☺	☺☺			
Wednesday 3 mins	☺☺	☺☺	☺☺	☺☺		
Thursday 3 mins	☺☺	☺☺	☺☺	☺☺	☺☺	✓✓
Friday 5 mins	☺☺	☺☺	☺☺	☺☺	☺☺	✓✓

Figure 10.5 A merit chart may be used to help children earn small rewards such as stickers for consistently good behaviour

---

Do IT

Suggest strategies to deal with common behaviour problems and how to support children who are suffering from inappropriate behaviour of others.

Describe the methods of dealing with behaviour issues at your placement – this may be in a group setting or a home situation. Do the methods work? You might like to discuss using a merit chart for a particular child or group of children you are working with, if staff are in agreement. How did it work?

Child protection laws

The main legislation aimed at ensuring children's rights became law in 1989: **The Children Act 1989**.

Until 1989, laws protecting children were numerous, unco-ordinated and confusing, even to people working with them. There were many loopholes in all the different laws. Often, children and families were visited by a host of different professionals, operating to different guidelines and often working against each other.

The Children Act co-ordinated all these and introduced the legal concept of 'parental responsibilities'. Previously, parents had had rights, but now they had responsibilities to meet the rights of children in their care.

- People who are not natural parents can have parental responsibility – this may be aunts or uncles, grandparents or even non-relatives.
- Parenthood is for life – parents are encouraged to share parenting even if it is not in the same household
- Parental responsibility can be shared – e.g. between divorced parents, or foster and natural parents.

In order to make sure that children's rights are given priority, statutory services are based on five principles.

1. Services must be provided for all 'children in need'. The needs of these children must be co-ordinated and known by the local authority.
2. There should be partnership with parents.
3. Services must take a child's race, culture, religion and language into account.
4. Services should be co-ordinated to support the family.
5. The individual needs of an individual family must be recognised.

The Children Act has led to a new approach in protecting children from abuse, based on the belief that in most cases children are best brought up with their natural family. Child protection is based on:

- prevention, by identifying and supporting families under stress
- intervention on a voluntary agreement with the parents
- formal intervention only where a child is at risk of 'significant harm' from sexual, physical or emotional abuse – the tools available for this include
  - a child assessment order
  - an emergency protection order
  - a recovery order
  - a police order.

The key feature is that all professional bodies – health visitors, social workers, police, teachers, etc. – work together to help support the family and protect the child.

Underlying the Children Act are several basic beliefs:

- children should be listened to
- children's wishes should be identified and taken seriously
- children should be treated with respect
- children should play a part in decisions taken about them
- children should be protected from harm
- children should be loved and cared for.

The laws relating to children are very complex in their full form. It is important that you understand the basic principles behind them, however, and are aware of how these laws are applied in childcare settings. Every childcare setting has to have an equal opportunities policy, and has to have policies relating to child protection. There will certainly be rules about how you deal with incidents relating to these policies. As you progress in your childcare career, there will probably be additions to the Children Act 1989. You must make sure you are aware of them.

Do IT

Summarise the key points of child protection law that early years workers should be aware of.

Ask your placement supervisor if you can see a copy of the placement policies and procedures on equal opportunities, child protection and safety. Read them carefully and write down your understanding of them.

When you are back in college, pair up with a friend and compare notes. Now produce a guide for parents explaining these policies in easy-to-understand language. You might want to give examples of how your placement carries out their policies in practice (e.g. featuring cooking from different cultures, or celebrating Diwali and Eid as well as Christmas).

Do IT

Identify and give examples of factors which contribute to good and inappropriate behaviour in a childcare setting.

Consider the factors and issues we have discussed in this chapter. Describe how your placement creates an appropriate atmosphere for encouraging good behaviour. List examples of practice you may have seen in all your different experiences that have encouraged inappropriate behaviour.

11 INTELLECTUAL AND COMMUNICATION SKILLS

Sensory and intellectual development

This chapter describes how children develop some very important skills – those of using tools (fine motor skills) and communication.

The patterns of development for fine motor skills and communication are the same as for other areas of development:

- development is a process that happens in stages
- skill development has a predictable order
- children need to practise their skills to develop competence in them.

The table below shows the milestones of fine motor skill and intellectual development.

Age	Milestone
Birth	Grasps objects when they touch the palm of the hand Blinks in reaction to bright light Turns to soft light Stares at carer Cries when basic needs require attention
1 month	Stares at soft light Gaze caught by and follows dangling ball
3 months	Follows movements of large and smaller objects Watches movements of own hands, plays with own hands Holds rattle for a few seconds if placed in hand
6 months	Very curious, easily distracted by movements Immediately fixes sight on small objects close by and reaches out to grasp them Uses whole hand in palmar grasp, passes toy from one hand to another Puts everything in mouth Watches toys fall from hand within range of vision
9 months	Can hold a toy in one hand and take a second in the other Lifts block but can only release by dropping Pokes at small item with index finger Will pick up small item between finger and thumb – this is called the inferior pincer grasp Looks in correct direction for falling toys

Age	Milestone
12 months	Neat pincer grip – picks up anything tiny from the floor Drops toys deliberately and watches them fall – this is called 'casting' Looks in correct place for toys that have rolled out of sight Starting to show hand preference Clicks two cubes together Puts cubes in box when shown Recognises familiar people at 6 metres
18 months	Uses delicate pincer grasp for tiny objects Holds pencil in primitive tripod grasp and scribbles Builds tower of 3 cubes when shown Turns pages of books, several at a time, enjoys picture books Points to interesting objects outside
2 years	Builds tower of 6 cubes Holds pencil in normal grip and will copy lines and V shape Turns single pages in book
3 years	Threads large beads, builds bridges with blocks when shown Copies circle and cross, draws man with head Matches 2 or 3 primary colours Paints with large brush, cuts with scissors
5 years	Threads large needle Copies square, and range of letters – some spontaneously Draws man with head, body, arms, legs and features, and will draw house Colours pictures neatly Names 4 primary colours and matches 10 or more colours
6 years	Ability to write developing – able to write some words and copy others Reads simple books Increasing sophistication in drawing and painting Fine motor skills allow finer manipulation of building bricks, jigsaws, etc.
7–8 years	Able to understand concept of conservation – e.g. the amount of playdough remains the same if you make a ball of dough into a long, thin snake Developing the ability to think about several things at once Enjoys games and rules Understands the use of symbols in maths, writing, etc. Great curiosity in relation to workings of his/her environment.

DO IT

Describe the milestones of sensory and intellectual skills development.

Tom is aged three months. His parents are keen to give him a head start in his intellectual and communication skills development. Describe the stages and milestones through which Tom will progress to achieve his potential in these areas up to 18 months of age.

Give a summary of the other main milestones up to eight years of age.

Encouraging fine motor skills and sensory development

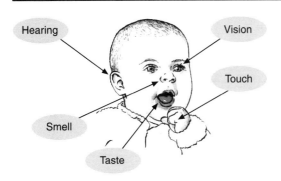

Figure 11.1 All of the senses work together

Many skills depend very much on how much practice and experience children get in using them. Sensory development and the development of the fine motor skills involves all of the senses linked together.

The gathering of sensory knowledge starts from birth. Even a very young baby will enjoy watching the branches of a tree blowing in the wind, or a bright mobile suspended over the cot. Different sounds will soon be recognised, with some noises being enjoyed more than others.

Hand–eye co-ordination is closely linked – from watching his own fingers at close quarters, by three months a baby will be putting those fingers in his mouth to explore what he has been watching. Until around 18 months, a child explores as much as possible of the world through the mouth. A baby's first experience of touch and taste is the breast or bottle, so this is understandable.

With a little imagination, you should be able to think of endless ways of encouraging sensory and hand–eye development. Encouraging curiosity in babies and very young children brings great rewards as they grow older – they should be full of curiosity about the sensory world. The table below gives some ideas – can you think of more?

Activities to develop understanding and curiosity

Sense or skill	Possible activities
Sight	Mobiles and cot/pram toys Posters with different images/colours, frequent changes of some Rolling balls/toy in view Setting a mirror by the baby's chair, cot, etc. Bright picture books Selective use of TV Pointing out moving objects inside and outside Using photographs of familiar people
Touch	Using different textured fabrics in clothes, covers, etc. Offering safe objects of different textures Putting the child's hands on different textured surfaces Using the language of texture when talking to children – rough, smooth, soft, spiky, etc. Encouraging massage and stroking by appropriate adults Encouraging messy play – with playdough, finger painting, 'slime', etc. Making a feely box or bag – several different textures and objects Using the outdoors as much as possible – crunchy leaves, splashy puddles, wet rain, soft and hard snow

Sense or skill	Possible activities
Smell	Offering different smells – soap, flowers, food as appropriate Using the language of smells whenever possible – mealtimes, cooking, outdoors Games with different smelling objects – smelled 'blind'
Taste	Offering different tastes – using foods Encouraging experiences of different tastes, but introducing them gradually
Hearing	Lots of talking to a child from birth Limited use of TV and radio Using different noises at varying levels close to, further away from, at the sides and behind a child Alerting to noises outside and inside Using tapes recordings of different sounds Using different kinds of music and encouraging singing and dancing
Hand–eye co-ordination	Over-the-cot toys encouraging reaching out Use of play centres with range of activities Using squeakers, rattles, etc. Encouraging reaching for objects after baby is 3 months of age Encouraging self finger-feeding with bread, apple, etc. Offering smaller items to hold as pincer grasp develops Using range of activities to encourage development of skills, bricks, lego, pencils Playing finger games and rhymes – e.g. Incy Wincy Spider Use of games such as yoyos, cats cradle, hand and finger puppets

DO IT

Identify types of activities which encourage gross motor skills, hearing and vision.

You have the care of two children, Lois aged 11 months and Paul aged three years, for an afternoon. Their mother is keen to develop their sensory skills. Plan the activities you will offer them for the session, and list the resources you will need. Write down which skills each of the activities will develop. You could do this by creating a chart with three headings: Activity, Resources, and Reasons for choosing.

Encouraging creative and intellectual development

With support and help, children will be very curious. We need to provide children with a stimulating environment to encourage them to try out their own ideas. Even before they are mobile, babies visually explore their surroundings, and they test out objects through their senses as much as possible. Once they are mobile they can test even more by going to all the interesting objects on display.

In early childhood, the imagination soars as children can play and explore – they do not have preconceptions of adulthood. What to you might appear to be a simple cardboard box could represent a house, car, cave, spaceship – whatever the child's imagination wants it to be. Given a range and variety of play materials – which can be everyday household objects – a child will try out ideas and develop creativity and imagination. It is important to offer a child the opportunity to work with as many materials as possible.

The only barriers to a child's imagination are those put there by carers. Good quality play with children can extend their imagination even more. When a child explains to you that he or she is in a boat, sailing on the sea, going to a land where trees grow everyone's favourite sweets, ask how long it will take, or what teddy (who is also in the boat) will find on the trees!

Try leaving a selection of empty cardboard boxes of varying sizes with a group of children and observe their play. Painting is also an excellent medium for a child's imagination. Depending on the paint and paper available, a group of children will each produce a totally different picture. Asked about the painting, children will give you a wide range of explanations.

A golden rule to remember when asking a child about his or her work, of any creative nature, is never to ask a closed question, e.g. 'Is that a painting of your brother?' It is far better to ask an open question, e.g. 'Tell me about your picture'. Try it.

As a child develops language skills he or she will be bursting to find out the names of objects or activities. The 'what is it?' stage can be very tiring for parents, but is a child's natural response to the surroundings. It is no coincidence that speech and full mobility develop in parallel. To a two-year-old who can run around, climb and explore, the obvious question to ask is 'what is it?' Once sense has been made of the surroundings, and names given to everything, the next question is 'why?' At around three-and-a-half, a child wants to find out what something does, or why there are trees or why is it windy or why we have to go to bed.

Simple, clear answers are needed to encourage and stimulate intellectual development. Ignoring, brushing off or giving incorrect answers to questions is not helpful, and will discourage questions in future. If you can extend your answers, so much the better – you are giving more fuel for the fire of intelligence.

Think it through

A Lewis, aged three, is busily playing with some bricks when he notices a big box being brought into nursery. He rushes over and asks what is in the box 'Nothing for you', says the nursery nurse, and carries on pushing it into the storeroom. Lewis stands and looks uncertainly at the box and then wanders back to his bricks.

B Lewis's nursery nurse tells him that the box he has noticed being brought into the nursery contains some new books that have been brought in a van. If Lewis goes to the window quickly, she says, he will see the big red van which is going back to Manchester. 'Where's Manchester?' asks Lewis. The nursery nurse says they will find a book with a map in it to show Lewis, and she also looks at all the new books with him, making a mental note of the ones in which he shows particular interest.

Which scenario do you think stimulated Lewis' imagination?

Books, painting, clay, playdough, walks in the woods or fields, storytelling, pictures of unfamiliar scenes and settings – the list of activities that can be used to encourage intellectual and creative development is long. In Chapter 13 you will be learning more about these.

An excellent way to encourage children's development is to pick up on a subject they are already interested in. Look at the example in the case study below.

CASE STUDY JENNIFER

Jennifer noticed that the children at her placement were fascinated by the wind, running around in the playground laughing at their hair blowing around, and watching the washing blowing on the line. She asked her supervisor if she could plan some activities with the children later in the week. By using windmills, a hairdryer, kites, stories about the wind, pictures of waves and tornadoes and games using air movement, the children's natural interest was expanded to enlarge their understanding.

Simple, everyday activities such as baking can be used to encourage intellectual development. How do eggs, flour, butter and sugar change to make a cake mix? What happens in the oven to make it rise and turn brown?

DO IT

Describe ways to encourage creative and intellectual development.

Choose one of these everyday activities or events: the wind, going shopping, a trip to the park, springtime. Compile a resource file around that theme. List activities you could help a child with, songs to sing, rhymes, and stories. Collect samples of materials that would be appropriate, with notes as to their potential use.

Different types of play

Children use play to make sense of their lives – they can work through emotional upsets, express their feelings, practise relationships, learn about how things work, and above all enjoy themselves. Play uses a lot of energy and can be hard work – above all it needs a lot of time. Asking a child to play for ten minutes is not very helpful – meaningful play can take a considerable amount of time to develop. Play is now actively encouraged where children are in unfamiliar settings, for example hospitals and social services units, and increasingly in doctor' and dentists' surgeries. Quality play can help a child to express fears about procedures in hospital, or be used to explain what is going to happen.

In order to help children play effectively, you need to have experienced using the materials yourself. Ask your tutor if you could have a practice play area, or ask in placement if you can try dough, plasticine, painting, lego – anything you have not used before.

Adults have an important role in encouraging play. They should facilitate play, not organise it. This means that the adult provides resources if necessary, ensures a safe environment, allows time for play and does not interfere or direct the play. Of course, for some play, the adult might be needed or wanted by the children – but as a participant, not an organiser.

Forms of play

Play can take many forms, and it can be helpful to use a system of categories to describe different activities. Very often, a play activity will fall into several categories, so do remember that there are no clear-cut divisions between the types.

Type of play	Examples	Some benefits
Physical play	Running, skipping, cycling, rough and tumble	Encourages and promotes physical and social development. Understanding of concepts such as area, energy, etc.
Creative play	Painting, modelling, cooking, puzzles, junk modelling	Hand–eye co-ordination, creativity, self-expression, emotional release, learning about colour, shapes
Pretend play	Role play, domestic play, dressing up, puppets	Coming to terms with their world, release of stress, communication, countering gender-role stereotyping
Exploratory play	Exploring new ideas and objects, e.g. magnets, old telephones	Intellectual development and creativity
Constructive play	Using Lego bricks, Meccano, K'nex	Fine motor skills, imagination, sense of achievement, early numeracy skills
Messy play	Cornflour and water, sand, water, playdough	Exploring textures, colours. Release of stress and inhibitions

Children of all ages and stages of development can experience play of all types, appropriate to their level of skills.

Play can be a group activity – often called **social** or **group play** – or children can play by themselves in **solitary play.** Solitary play is the first type of play a baby experiences. A toddler will often play alongside another child, without sharing the activity – this is known as **parallel play.**

Figure 11.2 Many items found at home can be used as a resource for play

Resources for play

Toys do not have to be expensive, complex items with only a short lifespan in terms of interest and durability. Media advertising bombards children with the images of the latest inventions of toy manufacturers, many centred on the latest craze or pop group. At Christmas you will hear parents giving accounts of the time they have spent looking, often in vain, for the latest desired toy. All this is not a necessary part of providing toys and play experiences for children.

You have already explored the idea of using seemingly ordinary items, such as empty cardboard boxes, for play. A look around your home would reveal many resources for a child to play with: kitchen pots and pans, packets of food for playing shops, furniture for making dens, dressing up clothes, water in sinks with plastic utensils – the list is endless.

Many of these items can be used in the nursery or classroom. Most children have a selection of toys available for play, ranging from the most simple to highly technical – paper and crayons, dolls, bicycles, construction toys and technical computer equipment and games. There are a few basic rules for choosing a successful toy. It should be:

- right for the stage of the child
- safe to play with
- strong enough to be used
- suitable for a range of play – imagination, learning new skills, etc.

Children should be encouraged to try all sorts of toys without gender or culture bias. Boys can enjoy the home corner, and cooking or doll play as much as girls can enjoy construction, climbing or car play. As an early years worker you have an essential role in encouraging equal opportunities in all areas including play. Many useful books have been written about play, and some toy manufacturers produce catalogues that are worth studying.

Do it

Explain the different types of play.

Observe at least three children playing throughout a session at nursery or school. Try to watch them on at least three separate occasions. Write down what they are doing on each occasion. Devise a chart showing the play you witnessed, resources used, which type of play you think it was, and the benefits to the children.

Cultural variations

In your childcare career you will encounter carers from many different backgrounds. You would not expect everyone to have the same ideas or preferences about food, leisure activities or religion, so you should not expect all adults to have the same expectations about children's behaviour and development.

Examples of different cultural backgrounds include:

- religion
- gender
- age
- race
- education
- social class.

Behaviour is one clear example of cultural variation. Compare the following accounts.

Child A, aged four, appears to be a 'model' child. At home he is expected to play in his own room. At mealtimes he eats everything that is put in front of him, and is allowed a dessert only if he has eaten all his main course. Bedtime is 7 pm sharp, after a bath and a story read by his father. He already understands that he has to fit in with the routine of his parents.

Child B, is also four, and would be regarded as a very unruly child by A's parents. Her play takes place wherever she feels is best at the time. She is always asked what she would like to eat, and meals may be eaten while she is playing on the floor or occasionally at the table. There is no pressure to eat more than she wants to of any particular food. She usually goes to bed when her parents go, and often shares their bed.

Think it through

In a small group discuss how you feel about these two different ways of child rearing described above. Do you think one is preferable to the other? Which fits most closely with your own experiences? How do you think the cultural backgrounds of the children affects people's expectations of them?

In the 1950s, childcare experts would have been horrified by Child B, but very approving of A. Today's 'experts' tend to be more relaxed, and recognise that within certain boundaries it is more important that patterns of care and behaviour fit comfortably with the family. Those boundaries are matters that affect a child's health, safety and well being. Within these limits, parents should feel free to develop a pattern of routines and behaviour that they are comfortable with.

Children are not pre-programmed into acting in one particular way. A child whose parents work at night could easily develop a routine of sleeping all day and being awake at night. Problems might arise, however, when that child starts to go to nursery or school.

Expectations of intellectual development, too, can reflect wide cultural variations. In certain communities, four- and five-year-olds are expected to be making rapid progress towards fluent literacy. In other communities, they would be expected to be developing skills through free expression. Different theories of nursery and primary education, such as the Steiner or Montessori system, reflect different cultural expectations.

As a childcare worker it is your responsibility to recognise cultural differences in expectations, and to respect these. In addition to respecting them you should ensure that these differences are reflected in activities in the care setting.

Do it

Review cultural variation in adult expectations of children's intellectual development and behaviour.

After discussion with your supervisor, choose three or four children who you feel reflect cultural variations in expectations about their behaviour and intellectual development. Try to identify six areas of behaviour and intellectual development, and compare the children in the light of these. If possible, talk to some of the parents to ask about bedtimes, mealtimes, etc.

Language and communication skills development

Milestones of language development

The following table summarises the milestones achieved by most children in developing their language and communication skills.

Age	Milestone
Birth	Cries when basic needs require attention
1 month	'Freezes' when a bell is rung gently close to the ear, moves head towards the sound Stops crying at sound of human voice (unless very upset) Coos in response to carer's talk
3 months	Becomes quiet and turns head towards sound of rattle near head Vocalises when spoken to and when alone
6 months	Makes singsong vowel sounds, e.g. aah-aah, goo Laughs and chuckles and squeals aloud in play Responds differently to different tones of voice Starting to respond to noises out of sight with correct visual response
9 months	Vocalises for communication, shouts for attention Babbles loudly and tunefully – dual syllables in long strings, e.g. dad-dad, baba, mam-mam Imitates adult vocal sounds, e.g. coughs, smacking lips Understands 'no' and 'bye-bye' Instant response to hearing test 3 feet slightly behind child, out of sight
12 months	Knows own name Jargons loudly in 'conversations', includes most vowels sounds Understands words in context, e.g. cup, dog, dinner, and understands simple messages, e.g. 'clap hands', 'where are your shoes?'
18 months	Growing number of words – uses 6 to 20 recognisable words, understands many more Echoes prominent or last word in sentences Tries to join in with nursery rhymes Responds to simple instructions – 'fetch your shoes', 'shut the door'
2 years	Uses more than 50 words, makes simple 2-word sentences Refers to own name, talks to self during play
3 years	Large vocabulary, can give full name, sex and age, holds simple conversations Asks many questions, of the type: what? why? and how? Enjoys repetition of favourite stories Counts to 10
5 years	Speech is fluent and correct, using descriptive language Gives full name, age, birthday and address Enjoys jokes, singing, rhymes, etc.

Age	Milestone
6 years onwards	Rapidly expanding vocabulary
	Recognises new words and asks the meaning of them
	Will accurately copy accents heard
	Can be bilingual
	Produces most sounds, with some residual difficulty with some letter groups

Children communicate even before they are born. A baby in the uterus will respond to loud noises or distress by moving. A newborn baby communicates through crying and quietening with increasing sophistication. It does not take long for a carer to recognise the meanings of different cries – hungry, tired, cold, fed up, needing a cuddle, etc.

Non-verbal communication is as important to children as it is to adults. Indeed, children probably use it more than adults do. Observe a group of young children playing and try to work out what is happening without listening to their speech.

Figure 11.3 Children probably use non-verbal communication more than adults

Speech is an aspect of development that can vary widely without any relationship to other developmental aspects or to the child's intelligence. Parents often become very concerned that a child is late in talking compared with an elder sibling. This can be simply because the older child is anticipating all the younger one's needs, removing any urgent need for the child to talk.

DO IT

Identify milestones of language and communication skills development.

Record the communication attempts of children of different ages and stages. Aim for at least three, spanning babyhood to the age of five or six years. The baby may of course be babbling only. Describe the differences in their communication skills; include communication that is non-verbal, as well as speech or babbles. Does their development of communication match the milestones chart above?

Encouraging language and communication skills development

Communication is the area of development that most dramatically shows the effects of input by carers. A baby as young as two or three months who regularly is talked to, sung to and experiences general communication will vocalise far more than a baby who has little one-to-one communication. From birth, babies learn patterns of speech and are absorbing them ready for when they start to reproduce all the sounds. The vocalisations of babies and toddlers are part of the pre-language skills that prepare a child for speaking fluently.

Some element of repetition is involved in learning a language. This is clearly demonstrated in children with 'glue ear' (a blockage of the tubes in the inner ear which stops sounds travelling to the auditory nerve). They cannot hear consonants at the beginning of words, so they hear 'bus' as 'us', 'car' as 'ar', and they repeat them as they hear them.

The main activities that help a child learn to talk are for a child to:

- listen to voices
- practise making sounds
- learn the meaning of sounds and words.
- hear other people talking to him or her
- copy sounds made by others

Activities to encourage language development

You can engage a child in a wealth of activities to encourage language development. Some examples include:

- singing songs, especially with clear, easy-to-follow words
- talking about events in the child's life, e.g. what happened at the weekend
- relating nursery rhymes with accompanying actions
- reading stories, especially those with interesting pictures that can stimulate conversation
- gentle repetition of words that have been mispronounced, and encouraging the child to repeat them.

As a carer, you should always try to:

- ask open-ended questions – for example, ask 'could you tell me about your painting?'
- listen to a child and respond with a fair and true answer
- give a child time and attention, getting down to the child's level and looking at him or her
- check for hearing difficulties
- encourage exercises given by speech therapists, etc.
- allow time for the child to express feelings and reactions – try to avoid rushing a child's attempts at communication
- show that you value a child's communications.

These 'rules' apply to any child, but are particularly important for children who find communication challenging – for example, children who may have hearing impairment, speech difficulties, a second language, or emotional problems.

Very often a child who seems delayed in language development will make rapid progress after starting nursery or playgroup, because the constant contact with other children and adults helps to stimulate speech.

A child may, of course, require professional intervention to help him or her to make progress, and this is explored further below.

DO IT

Describe ways to encourage language and communication skills development.

You are asked to keep an eye on a new child at nursery – Jay, who is four years old and seems very shy. He has never been to any pre-school group before, and his health visitor and family are concerned about his lack of speech. How will you help Jay to develop his communication skills?

Songs, music, rhymes and stories

From birth, many children hear a carer singing lullabies and rocking songs. As children grow they delight in songs and rhymes – the constant repetition makes it possible for them to join in these familiar, sing-song types of communication. New songs and rhymes introduce new words and phrases, which are quickly learned.

Once a child is attending any sort of group, from toddlers to school, songs are an important activity. Used with actions or puppets, group songs allow a child to try joining in without being singled out. For a child for whom the language is a second language, or who is very shy singing, there is the safety of play.

Songs and rhymes can fit very easily into themes and topics in the nursery or school. Figure 11.4 shows some examples.

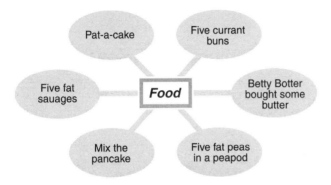

Figure 11.4 Some songs and rhymes on the theme of food

Music

Music is a medium to which most children respond. A piece of music can serve many functions including soothing children, allowing them to express themselves in movement, promoting dance and providing inspiration for a painting. All these are forms of communication, and are especially important when a child has difficulties in verbal communication. Apart from listening to music, children love to make music, and again this can be used for communicating. Clapping hands is the simplest form of music making.

Have a look at the range of musical instruments in your placement – do they include any of those shown in Figure 11.5? Try them out to see what type of noise they make.

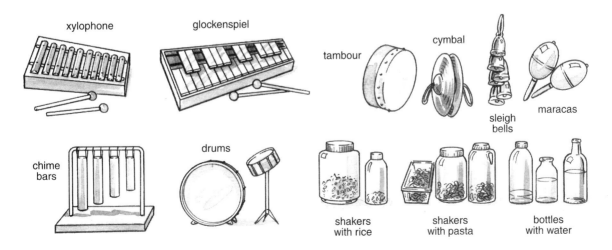

Figure 11.5 A range of musical instruments for children

You should develop your own library of songs, music, rhymes and stories that encourage communication and language development. Every time you hear or see a new example in a book, in placement, etc., write down or copy the details. Create a resource file with various headings.

Do IT

Identify songs, music, rhymes and stories to encourage language and communication development in children of a range of ages.

Choose a theme, for example autumn or animals. An ideal theme would be one that is in current use at your placement. Collect as many relevant songs, rhymes and examples of music as possible and file them in your resource file. Choose one of each and try them out with a few children in placement, making notes on the success of the activities.

Books

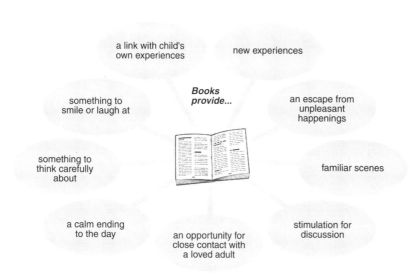

As with music, you should look at the range of books available to seek out ones suitable for helping language and development.

Reading stories to children is an important part of communicating – very few children, if any, do not enjoy hearing a story, either as part of a group or on a one-to-one basis.

Figure 11.6 Books help in many ways to promote intellectual and language development

Reading promotes all of the aspects of intellectual and language development shown in Figure 11.6.

Choosing the right book is important. The choice of book has to be related to the child's:

- age
- ability to understand the story
- stage of development
- interests and cultural background.

However, the same book can serve different age groups. A storybook with bright, attractive pictures will provide stimulation to a toddler who enjoys the pictures, and an older child who enjoys the story.

Books that open up discussion are an excellent medium for promoting language development. Examples include books that show familiar scenes – say of a shopping street.

The book will help you encourage children to talk about their local shops and the goods inside, or about lorries or vans.

Books also can be central to developing a theme for further activities. *The Very Hungry Caterpillar* is an excellent example. This book describes the growth of a caterpillar into a butterfly, showing what the caterpillar ate on its way to forming a chrysalis. Work on food, growth, change, insects, numbers and colours can all develop from reading this one book. It is a book with a story that is easy to remember, so it can help in memory development with children.

Having heard a story from a book, children can be stimulated to produce paintings, models, collages or, with older children, to develop their own related story. Children will enjoy verbally extending the story they have heard, or 'writing' their own story in pictures. These activities all help in development of communication.

Do it

Review books to identify key points in their use to promote language, intellectual and communication skills.

Choose at least two different books and briefly describe them. Make a list of all the extra activities that can be linked to the books, and how the book and the activities will help to promote language and intellectual development.

Overcoming barriers to language development and self expression

Those who can communicate well do not give much thought to the skills they use. They wish to say something, open their mouths and say it.

For some children this is not always easy. For a range of reasons, their communication skills may be impaired, or there may be barriers preventing them from making themselves understood.

A child may simply be delayed in speech development in relation to his or her peers, but will eventually catch up. There are several possible causes for the delay of speech development:

- genetic – there may be a history of a late start in speech
- deafness – a child has to hear before he or she can speak
- lack of opportunities to be spoken to – some children rarely have the pleasure of one-to-one communication
- lack of encouragement – a baby must be responded to when he or she is making attempts at communication
- a child may be concentrating on other aspects of development, such as walking, and will start to talk when other skills have been mastered.

Barriers

Some barriers to communication are shown below.

- **Physical barriers**   There may be damage to the parts of the body involved in speech production, e.g. the ears, vocal cords or parts of the brain.
- **Emotional barriers**   Shyness, fear or lack of confidence may be preventing communication skills from developing.
- **Cultural barriers**   Different languages, accents, or backgrounds, or being the child of deaf parents, can cause problems.
- **Communication problems**   Stammering may be hampering the development of speech.

In order to overcome communication barriers, it is important to find the reasons for the barriers, and if possible take steps to remove them. This is not always easy, but some possible approaches are shown in the following table.

Barrier	Intervention needed
Deafness	Hearing test and investigation as to cause Possible surgery to drain glue ear Hearing appliances for nerve deafness Use of alternative communication modes, e.g. Makaton
Cultural – different language	Use of adult who speaks the appropriate language Input to help the child learn the new language – bilingual assistants Use of games, activities that allow a child to learn the new language
Physical causes	Referral to speech therapist to help the child to develop speech mechanisms Use of Makaton, electronic speech synthesisers
Stammering	Referral to speech therapist to develop strategies to overcome stutter Giving a child time to speak, not interrupting or attempting to finish off the sentence
Emotional cause	Investigate underlying cause of speech difficulties and try to address Try to gain the child's confidence – use of books, communication by other means such as non-verbal, through painting, etc. Referral to speech therapist
Lack of individual attention	Lots of one-to-one attention, mixing with other children and adults

As a childcare worker you can be of great help to a child with communication problems by:

- giving a lot of one-to-one attention
- reading stories
- talking clearly to the child
- encouraging communication by asking open-ended questions about things the child understands
- encouraging social and emotional development
- learning how to use alternative methods of communication, e.g. Makaton, electronic speech synthesisers
- responding to the child as an individual

● working with other professionals who are involved with the child – checking with the speech therapist how you can help, reporting on progress or otherwise, and above all liaising with parents and carers.

Do it

Identify ways to overcome some of the barriers to language development and self expression.

Liam, aged four, is a very shy child who lives in an isolated village with his single mother. His contact with other children has been limited, and he seems to have a serious degree of speech delay. He often seems to have difficulty in hearing what you say to him.

Zak is also four and is the eldest of three children. His parents came to England from Pakistan just before he was born. Although his parents do speak some English, they speak in their mother tongue of Urdu at home.

Consider the two cases. Which other professionals do you think might be involved with the children? How could you help these two boys to overcome their barriers to communication?

Activities to promote sensory, intellectual and communication development

Safe practice in the delivery of activities

Chapter 12 explains the checks that are necessary to ensure the health, safety and wellbeing of children in early years settings. Every time you plan to do something with children, you must think through the safety aspects first. A checklist should include the following questions.

● Is there a suitable space for this activity? Is there enough room? Is the surface safe (e.g. for water or sand play)?
● Is all the appropriate safety equipment in position (e.g. mats under large play equipment, guards on the cooker)?
● Are all materials used safe, especially for very young children – e.g. paint, dough?
● Will I need to control the numbers of children? There may need to be maximum numbers in force for using the sand tray, or running around outside.
● Is another activity going on that will clash with it? There may be another class in the playground at the same time.
● Are there enough adults to ensure adequate supervision? If scissors or some other potentially dangerous equipment or tools are being used, numbers of adults may need to be increased.
● Can I make sure that the children will not be harmed by equipment being used – e.g. a cooker when baking?
● Is help available if a child is harmed by the activity? A child may get paint in his or her eyes, or fall off outdoor equipment.

It is your responsibility to think through every activity you provide for children, and every outing you make with them. Almost all accidents that occur could have been prevented. Prevention is far better then cure. You should automatically think through every stage of everything you do, in advance, and think of what might happen. Some events you cannot predict, and others you cannot do anything about – e.g. the weather, or outside events – but you do need to carry out what is called a 'risk analysis'. This means asking yourself whether you have done everything reasonable to ensure that the children in your care will not be at risk from injury.

Do it

Describe safe practices and identify common hazards in health and safety and hygiene when planning and undertaking activities with young children.

Choose three different types of activity which you have provided for children during your work so far. Make a safety checklist for each activity. When you have finished, evaluate the activities. What risks were there for each one, and should you have done anything to try to minimise them?

The early years curriculum

Until 1996 there were no national standards suggesting what children should be learning in their pre-school years. For older children, the National Curriculum for compulsory education (that is from the age of five onwards) has been in operation since the 1988 Education Reform Act. It states the minimum requirements for a curriculum in schools. The core subjects are English, mathematics and science. Foundation subjects include design and technology, history, geography, art, music, languages and physical education.

In 1996 the Desirable Outcomes Curriculum was introduced for the under-fives, laying down these six areas of learning:

- personal and social development
- maths and numeracy
- physical development
- language and literacy
- knowledge and understanding of the world
- creative development.

The desirable outcomes are to be revised in 1999, but are likely still to cover the same broad areas of learning.

Most childcare workers naturally provide opportunities for young children to cover all these areas of learning, but it is important that you consider the outcome of all your activities in relation to the desirable outcomes. Check that your plans meet the needs of all the children, and that you are providing activities to support all areas of development.

Think it through

Look at the plans at your placement – you should be able to see how the staff have planned to meet all of the desirable outcomes. Talk about some of your activities with your supervisor, and ask for feedback and suggestions for developing them further.

Below are some examples to show how activities can be linked to the pre-school curriculum.

- **Music, song and dance**   Listening and moving to music, and physically using the body, covers physical development, language, maths (if there are numbers in a song or the counting of steps in a dance), and creativity in movement, sounds and interpretation.
- **Meal times**   Personal and social development is involved in talking about food, passing things, saying please and thank you, and sitting down for a length of time.
- **Painting and model making**   Activities may be solitary or in a group, and use different materials such as paper, card, dough, paints, glues and glitter. The needs for creativity, maths, language, and personal and social development may be met.
- **Water play**   Using a range of containers, funnels, sieves, coloured water, and learning about temperatures all helps in understanding of the world, maths and creativity.
- **Story time**   Using a range of different books and relating them to other activities could cover all the areas.
- **Baking**   From simple non-cook or 'cold-cook' items to quite complex baking, cooking is an activity that most children enjoy. The transformation of flour, eggs, sugar, etc. into edible buns will encourage their language, practical maths, understanding of the world, creative development, and physical development.
- **Outdoor play**   Ranging from the use of large equipment, climbing, and running around, to games such as hopscotch and hide and seek, outdoor play offers potential for all the areas of development.

Early years settings usually plan their activities a number of weeks ahead to allow time for preparation. The planning often starts with a theme or idea – such as movement, spring time or the colour red. From this central theme, all aspects of the early years curriculum are considered in order to provide suitable activities and opportunities for the children.

Creative development
Creative activities around spring theme, e.g. chickens
flowers, farms – wall displays
Use of natural materials to dye cloth, etc.
Drawings and paintings about spring
Listening to music, e.g. Vivaldi's 'Spring' – dancing,
drawing, paintings linked to this
Looking at pictures on spring topics

Language and literacy
Many story and picture books on the
theme of spring – growing and changing,
e.g. *Hungry Caterpillar*
Peter Rabbit
Sleepy Bear
Talking about spring

Physical development
Outdoor play
Link with external visits, walking,
exploring woods, tree hugging

SPRING

Maths and numeracy
Measuring growth of plants
Recording numbers of animals and chickens
Shapes of plants, trees, leaves
Use of stories with number games
Measuring, matching, sorting
Puzzles, growing sequences

**Knowledge and understanding
of the world**
Visit to farm, country – watching
lambing, seeing planting
Walk to woods, local park – looking at trees, plants
Listening to bird song, watching nest building
Planting seeds, bulbs in nursery

DO IT

Select activities and state how they meet the needs of the early years curriculum.

Choose a different theme from the one in the example. It might be a good idea to ask your supervisor what the next theme is likely to be in your placement. Plan the use of that theme, ensuring you have the activities to cover all of the desirable outcomes.

Games and activities to develop new skills

In a group childcare setting, most activities are planned with the early years curriculum in mind, and by their very nature these activities will develop new skills. If you are working in a child's own home, or with one child in a group setting, you may need to plan your activities to develop particular skills.

In order to develop new skills, a child must have reached the stage in development where he or she is ready to do so. This may sound obvious, but a child will not be able to read, for instance, until he or she has mastered letter and word recognition. One theory is that all the major skills will develop at an optimum point in a child's development – that there is a right time to learn a skill. If this time is missed, then the skill will prove much harder to learn later. In practice, when a child is asking questions such as 'why is the sky blue?' or 'where does rain come from?', it is an ideal time to start some work on those topics.

DO IT

Describe games and activities to develop new skills in children of a range of ages.

The theme in your placement is 'creativity', and it has been decided to aim to help children develop interest in a new creative skill. Choose one of the areas of development (physical, intellectual, emotional or social) and think of as many ways as possible to assist development of relevant skills in children aged between three and five years. Describe two of the activities in detail.

Activities for children with specific needs

Whenever you are planning an activity you should consider the needs of all the children in the group you are working with. Chapter 12 includes a section dealing with children with special needs, and you should refer to that for more information. However, you may wish to help a child to improve skills in an area that is giving him or her some difficulty.

When you are thinking of an activity to help skill development, break it down into the steps involved in the relevant skill. Then look at activities that use two or three of those steps together. For example, taking off trousers involves:

1. unfastening the button
2. unzipping the zip
3. pulling down the trousers
4. stepping out of the trousers.

If the child's problem is with fine motor co-ordination, try devising something that will help with that. Using a task toy that has different sizes of buttons, or fastening a toy scarecrow coat will be a fun way to practise button fastening. A zip could be incorporated into the same task toy.

Children who have a specific problem, such as a visual impairment, will miss opportunities for learning in that specific way. Think what you learn visually – colours, shapes, what things look like, and how things fit together.

Hearing-impaired children miss out on sound recognition, and different inflections of speech. Children who are unable to walk cannot enjoy the sense of running around freely, or of dancing to music in the same way as another child can. It is your role with children who have some form of disability to help them to discover the missing aspects.

CASE STUDY AHMED, SUSIE AND LUCY

Ahmed is three years old and has a visual impairment. To make toys more useable they should be big, bright and colourful to help him make the most of any sight he may have. A bigger area of a bright colour, hung in a window area, illuminated with a lamp, is one example.

Home-made jigsaws, with shiny colours in very big pieces will help in the development of fine motor skills. Touch can replace vision – jigsaws with different textures can be used to learn matching. A different texture can represent a different colour for playing picture dominoes. Raised surfaces will help in number or picture recognition.

Susie, aged five, is profoundly deaf, yet she loves music. One reason is that she has had a lot of percussion music played to her – drums, piano played in a room with a wooden floor so she has picked up the vibrations of music.

Story time is as enjoyable for her as any other child as lots of pictures are used, her carers have all learned Makaton, and they always make sure that the story is accompanied by gestures and mime.

Lucy, aged four, spends most of her time in a wheelchair. She is quite limited in her physical skills, but has developed her sense of space and the outside world through time at the swimming baths, through big movement activities on soft foam on the floor, by going out in her wheelchair and experiencing new sights, and by getting out of her chair to lie and roll in snow, and fallen autumn leaves.

DO IT

Identify activities that may be used for children with specific needs.

You are told at a staff meeting that a new child will join the nursery in a few weeks' time. Amira, aged three, has a severe hearing impairment and, because of loss of function in her leg muscles, she has some difficulty walking. The Christmas holidays are approaching and all the children are starting to practise for the end-of-term concert. How would you involve Amira in the activities?

Ensuring the success of activities

Children need support and help to encourage their development in all the areas we have been looking at. The role of the carer is to support the children without interfering in play. To do this the carer needs to:

- allow plenty of time for play
- avoid over-organising, and allow children to lead their own play
- provide a wide range of materials and show ideas of how to use them
- test out new ideas first before introducing them to children
- make sure that activities and equipment are safe to use
- ensure that all equipment is in working order, and suitable for the activity
- make sure there is enough of all materials for all the children involved
- use as many opportunities as possible for children to meet people and see examples of creativity
- avoid the use of templates, pre-drawn outlines, colouring books, and tracing
- be a helper in play or activity, not a leader.

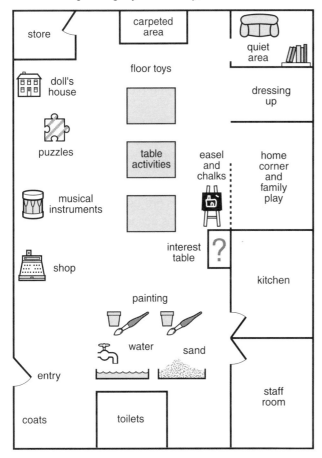

Figure 11.7 One layout used in a well-organised nursery

The layout of a room is important for ensuring the success of an activity. There must be enough space for all the activities that are going on, or the children and adults may both become frustrated, little may be achieved, and accidents may occur. However, even a small room can support a number of children and allow a range of varied activities. Well-designed and well-planned storage is the first priority. Storage boxes should be clearly labelled, and easily accessible so that children can help in the setting out and clearing away. In a small room it may be possible to have only one or two activities going on at the same time.

A larger room needs just as much organising as a small one. Lack of planning and organisation will result in disorganisation and lack of progress. Again, storage and clear labelling are essential.

In any setting a clear plan for the day, of which all staff are aware, is a necessity. Staff who know the routine and the position of all equipment will ensure the smooth running of a nursery or classroom.

A well-organised nursery or class never appears to be *too* organised. Careful organisation and structure can give the impression that the children have control over their own activities.

Do It

Describe the role of the adult and the effects of the accessibility of materials and the layout of an activity on the success of an activity.

Observe a well-structured and well-organised nursery or classroom for part of a session. At the end, ask the person in charge how the session was planned and organised. Make notes and write down an example of how to improve the running of a session of activity with children. Think about aspects of the adult's roles or the use of materials that particularly impressed you, say if anything surprised you, and indicate if you feel there were areas for improvements.

Evaluating activities

Evaluating activities is discussed in Chapter 13. In this section we shall cover the main points.

Why evaluate activities?

Every action you carry out in your work with children has an important effect on them. You have a duty to ensure that at all times you are working as effectively as possible in your role as a childcare worker. The only way of checking that is to evaluate your actions.

It should become second nature to you with experience, but in your early times as a care worker you should be asking yourself the following questions.

- Was that an enjoyable experience for the children?
- If so, what features made it enjoyable?
- If not, what made it less enjoyable, and what could I have done to overcome this?
- Did I meet the needs of all the children involved?
- What changes are needed to make sure all children get full benefit?
- If I were doing this again, what would I do differently?
- What sort of feedback have I had from the children and from other staff?

Everything can be improved – even something that has worked really well and has met all your aims. Never be complacent and think that you have already done your best – there is always potential to make something even better.

Do It

Evaluate the activities carried out.

Look at one of the activities you have recently carried out with a group of children. Using the checklist on this page, carry out a written evaluation of your activity.

The role of the early years worker

Duties and responsibilities of early years workers

When you are caring for children, you carry a great responsibility. When you are caring for someone else's child, you have been entrusted with that child's safety and wellbeing. Never underestimate this responsibility, because failing to meet it could have tragic results. The skills needed by all care workers, described in detail in Chapter 1, are equally applicable to childcare workers. In practising these skills, you can meet the responsibilities outlined below.

Commitment to the needs and rights of all children

The needs and rights of all children, regardless of any personal preference or prejudices you may have, must be respected. Working within equal opportunities guidelines is a vital part of your responsibility, and it includes challenging others who do not operate within them. You should treat all the children in your care as individuals, meeting their specific needs, rather than working to group needs alone.

In protecting children's rights, you have a responsibility to report any bad practice that you may see – this is called 'whistleblowing'. It is not tale-telling, but is vital in protecting the rights of children in your care.

CASE STUDY JANE

Jane was a student in a private day nursery. While she was working in the toddler room with the owner's daughter, she was horrified to see the young woman smack some of the toddlers on the legs on several occasions. At first, Jane did not know what to do. She knew that it is against the law for a care worker to smack a child. She spoke to her tutor at college, who then went to see the owner. As a result, the owner sacked her daughter for the offence.

Witnessing bad practice puts you in a difficult situation. While you are a student, your tutors in college are always a good source of help. They will have a knowledge of the local situation and will know how to handle the problem. Once you are qualified, you should speak to your line manager or his or her own manager if necessary. Ultimately, you may have to report a problem to the social services department or the education authority. Never ignore bad practice – you have a responsibility to the children not to do so.

A responsibility for the safety of children also means that you should always challenge any stranger who appears in the childcare setting. If a person has a right to be there, he or she will not mind providing proof of identity. If a person should not be there, a challenge may make him or her leave quickly.

Respecting confidentiality and trust

In any area of care, you will hear and see a lot of confidential information about children and their parents. Remember that confidential information is not to be discussed with your friend on the bus, or told to your family at home. It could be that the person sitting behind you on the bus is linked to the family concerned.

Sometimes, however, you have to share information with colleagues. As a student or a junior worker remember: 'If in doubt, shout!' But rather than shouting, have a quiet discussion with your supervisor. This is called 'professional confidentiality' – sharing information for the good of the children in your care.

Think it through

Jolene, aged seven, tells you that she and her mummy are going on holiday to Spain next summer, but that it has to be kept a secret in the meantime from her little brother, aged four.

Javeed, aged six, tells you that his uncle has been showing him his penis – but it's a secret and no one has to know.

Do you think you should keep both of these secrets to yourself, or should you share either of them with your supervisor? You don't need to share Jolene's secret with anyone, but clearly Javeed could be in need of protection, and it is your responsibility to share that secret. You should always tell a child that you can't promise to keep everything he or she tells you a secret – if you don't say so, you may lose a child's trust.

Respecting parents and other adults

You will come across many differing types of childcare practice and opinions on good practice. Life would be very dull if everyone had the same views. Provided that these diverse ways are all safe practice, that is absolutely normal. Different practices develop for all kinds of reasons – cultural, religious, geographical, or social class. Your role as a carer is to respect other people's views, especially the views of parents whose children you care for, and to support them.

Communicating with colleagues and professionals

Good communication skills are your best working tools. You need to communicate with many different people, as shown in Figure 11.8.

Teamwork is all about communicating. Planning an activity with a group of children, and not telling other members of the team, could lead to conflict – someone else may have planned a similar or conflicting activity.

You should always communicate the results of your observations. If you see a child being sick or sitting very quietly when he or she is usually very active, this

Figure 11.8 Childcare workers need good, two-way communication with many different people

information must be passed on. Parents may need to be contacted, the child will certainly need some attention, and other children may be at risk.

In order to communicate effectively in a team, it is important to know the procedures for doing so. There are usually lines of communication, or reporting must be done through line managers, in a large organisation. In a small one it may be appropriate to speak directly to the owner, manager or class teacher. Make sure you know who you should report to.

Other duties

Apart from these rather heavy responsibilities, there are several duties that you have towards children in your care. If you are a committed childcare worker, the wellbeing of the children will be foremost in your thoughts. The following list shows some of your duties towards children you are caring for.

- Care for the children by showing you are pleased to see them, and expressing concern if they hurt themselves.
- Respect children as individuals and enjoy the fact that some children will enjoy playing rough and tumble outdoor games with you, while others will prefer time in the story corner with you.
- Try to view the world through the eyes of a child. Suspend your own adult view of why the world is as it is, and you will get a lot of enjoyment from listening to a child's view.
- Try to enjoy yourself when working with children. If you are miserable at work, then the children in your care will be miserable as well.
- Aim to provide stimulating, enjoyable activities for children, but also to recognise when they need gentle, relaxing times.
- Help and promote children's activities, without taking over and running their lives for them.
- Remember that the children have parents and families who want to be kept in touch with events in their child's day.

DO IT

Identify the duties and responsibilities of an early years worker in a childcare setting.

Devise a charter of the duties and responsibilities of a childcare worker, applicable to any setting. You could work in pairs, and produce a poster for your placement or college.

Parental consultation and involvement

Always remember that children have parents. Stop and think why children attend their playgroup, nursery or school. Some of the reasons are:

- parents are working
- a child needs playmates
- a need for intellectual and social stimulation
- to encourage delayed speech development
- the legal requirement to attend school
- parents need some space apart from their child
- the chance to play with toys and equipment that are not available at home.

Parents have a right to be involved with their child's education and care. They are the main carers in their child's life, and may be the main people the child has spent time with in the past. Remember that starting nursery or school can be a traumatic event for the parents as well as the child.

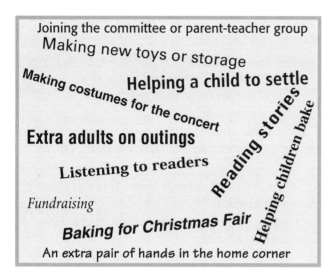

Parents, grandparents, aunts – in fact any member of a child's family – can enrich a nursery or school by contributing. There are many ways a parent can contribute (see Figure 11.9).

Parental involvement benefits both parent and child – parents may see alternative ways of helping their child, they will gain new ideas for activities, and children who are slow to settle in may be happier with a familiar adult around.

Figure 11.9 Ways in which a parent can contribute to a nursery or school

Even if parents cannot or are unwilling to come to school or nursery, it is still important to work with them. Do not assume that parents who are not in contact or helping in nursery or school are not interested in their child. Very often, parents feel intimidated by schools.

Parents are very important when a child is moving to another room or class. They can help in preparing a child for the change by talking about it at home, or reading appropriate books to their child.

DO IT

Identify the need for parental consultation and involvement.

Consider your current work placement. Discuss the level of parental involvement with your supervisor, and make a list of points about this. Now think of any ideas as to how parents could be involved to a greater extent.

Communicating with parents

Communicating with parents is no different from communicating with other adults. Think about how you would communicate generally, and use those skills.

- Use the names parents wish you to use. Never assume that Jane Smith's mother is called Mrs Smith. Different cultures have different formats for family names. If in doubt, ask what you should call someone.
- Acknowledge when a parent is there. You may be busy with a child, or talking to someone, but a brief turn of your head and a welcoming smile shows you have seen the parent.
- Give parents feedback about their child – 'Lia did a lovely painting today'.
- If you do not share the same language with parents, make sure that information is

translated for them. You may both speak English, but it is very easy to use technical jargon that outsiders do not understand – *you* know that DLOs means desirable learning outcomes, but a parent may not.

- Make sure parents receive regular written information – letters, posters displayed in the setting, etc.
- Always make sure that written information is in a language the parent can read. If you are not sure if parents can read, it is better to speak to them to make sure vital information is received. Do not rely on a child to pass on written information – sometimes using the postal service might be a more reliable way.
- Be sensitive about conversations that may be embarrassing. If a parent is uncomfortable talking to you in the corridor, take him or her into an empty classroom, staffroom, to ensure privacy.
- Try not to appear shocked if you hear information that surprises you. You will alienate the parent, and you should not be making judgements.
- Remember that as a student you should not be dealing with difficult situations with parents – pass them on to a more senior member of staff.

Do it

Identify appropriate ways of communicating with parents.

If possible, ask some parents of children about communications they receive from their child's nursery or school. Write down the details of letters and discussions they may have had, and ask if they were happy with them. If so, why? If not, what do they feel should have been said or written?

If this is not possible, describe how you would communicate with the parents at your nursery in the following situations:

a There is to be an outing to the local park for a teddy bear's picnic next week. Children need to bring something to eat, and of course a teddy.

b Lizzie, aged two, has bitten another child, leaving teeth marks in his arm. Both sets of parents need to know about this.

Describe how you would communicate with the parents, and note the points you would have to take into account and be careful with.

12 GOOD PRACTICE IN CHILDCARE SETTINGS

This chapter looks at issues you should always be aware of in your work with children, including equal opportunities, health and safety and meeting specific needs.

Equal opportunities issues in a childcare setting

Legislation to ensure equal opportunities

All children have a right to be treated fairly and with due attention to their particular needs. The United Nations Convention on the Rights of the Child recognises this. The UK became a signatory to this agreement in December 1991, agreeing to recognise that:

● the views of children should be listened to and carry weight
● all children have a right to parental care and family life
● parents have the right to appropriate help in child rearing
● children have the right to protection
● children have the right to be treated as individuals who have feelings and ideas, and who need to be listened to and respected.
● children need to be with people who show them love and affection – usually their family
● children's development needs should be met and protected.

We cannot take it for granted that all children live in an environment that meets all these needs, so laws are necessary to protect and support these basic rights. The relevant legislation follows two main strands:

● general legislation that applies to everyone
● specific legislation that applies to children.

General legislation involves everything you have considered in relation to equal opportunities. The most important laws affecting equal opportunities are the following.

The Sex Discrimination Acts 1975 and 1986

It is illegal to discriminate against anyone because of his or her sex:

● in employment
● in their education
● in selling or renting property
● when providing goods or services.

The part that applies to child care workers in particular is the education section. You already know how important it is to treat all children as individuals, and not deny them something because of individual characteristics. The Equal Opportunities Commission was set up as a result of the 1975 Act and investigates alleged discrimination.

The Race Relations Act 1976

This Act makes it illegal to discriminate against anyone on the grounds of his or her colour, race or nationality. Racial discrimination is often thought to be targeted at ethnic minority groups with a visible difference, e.g. skin colour. Often unrecognised targets are people with white skins who are refugees from European countries.

Discrimination can be:

- **direct** – such as refusing to carry out services for or sell something to someone because of race
- **indirect** – when rules are made that are impossible for someone of a different race to follow. For example, it is impossible for a girl who is a Moslem to comply with a rule that girls may not wear trousers in school.

The Commission for Racial Equality (CRE) performs a watchdog function for this Act, and like the Equal Opportunities Commission it can prosecute offenders.

The Disability Discrimination Act 1995

This recent piece of legislation finally gives people with disabilities some protection of their rights under the law. The Act covers access and provision for disabled people in the following areas:

- employment
- letting or selling land or property
- public transport vehicles.
- access to goods, facilities and services
- education

The Act's implications for education are particularly relevant, and it is important that you are familiar with the intentions of the law in this area. Essentially, all children with special educational needs have the right to be educated in mainstream schools. Schools must publish their policy and procedures related to this provision.

The National Disability Council is charged with advising the government about the operation of the Act, and eliminating and reducing discrimination. As yet, it has no legal powers to prosecute offenders.

It is important that you are aware of the legislation that forms the basis of equal opportunities practice. Legislation is not enough, though – what is important is how you work with children to ensure that those from all backgrounds are recognised and their cultural needs met.

Your behaviour is a role model for the children you work with, so you have a responsibility to act in a non-discriminatory way and to promote equal opportunities. Sometimes this is not easy; you may observe practices and actions that are discriminatory.

Think it through

What would you do in these situations?

1. You are asked to line up the children ready for outdoor play with the girls in one line, the boys in another.
2. Mrs Smith complains because her daughter has been playing with a little girl with cerebal palsy.
3. A boy in the reception class uses abusive racist language.
4. The owner of the nursery insists that all children wear shorts in nursery, although there are many children who are Moslem.

These are all incidents that have occurred in childcare settings, and all are discriminatory. Think about how you would feel if you witnessed these incidents, and what you should do about them.

In all aspects of your contact with children you need to ensure that you are working in a non-discriminatory way, with the needs and rights of all children in your care uppermost in your thoughts. You can use the following checklist to help you do this.

Good practice: equal opportunities

✓ Always be a good role model – mix girls and boys evenly in a group, ask a child who may be slow in moving to help you set out an activity.

✓ Always challenge racist behaviour, especially from other children. You can do this by making it clear there are words and actions that will not be tolerated.

✓ Put yourself in the shoes of someone who has been the subject of offensive remarks.

✓ Be ready to question your own attitudes and beliefs, challenging them if necessary.

✓ Use any opportunity to extend your own knowledge about cultures and groups other than your own.

✓ Be clear and consistent about what is acceptable and unacceptable behaviour.

✓ Double-check plans to ensure you are not inadvertently excluding or offending anyone.

✓ Be prepared to report incidents to your supervisor.

Do it

Identify aspects of the equal opportunities legislation and the United Nations Policy on the Rights of the Child which are relevant to working in a chosen childcare setting.

Look again at the United Nations Rights of the Child, and the equal opportunities legislation. Produce a section for the brochure of a local nursery school, or a poster for the entrance, to show how the nursery ensures that it respects the rights. Under each heading give an example of activities or policies in the nursery that show its commitment to equal opportunities.

Activities to encourage diversity

Learning about, and participating in, different cultural activities helps to prepare children to live in a multicultural society.

You should investigate the customs and practice of the different cultural groups to which the children you work with belong. It is important to remember also that not everyone who feels that they belong to a particular religion, for instance, follows exactly the same practices. To assume they do is to stereotype a person, and stereotyping leads to discrimination.

There are many cultural differences that distinguish different groups of society. These differences can be based on culture, race, or social class, but it is important to remember that not everyone from each group will strictly follow a certain code of behaviour. However, you will find it useful to be aware of some of the major cultural differences, as shown in the table below.

Respecting cultural differences	
Food and diet	Muslim people do not eat pork, and all meat should be halal. Hindu people do not eat beef. Buddhists are vegetarian. Jehovah's Witnesses will not eat blood products like black pudding.
Religious observances	All adult Muslims must pray at five specific times each day. Jewish people observe Saturday as their holy day.
Religious festivals	Nearly all religions celebrate special festivals. These may vary in date according to the lunar calendar. Examples of festivals include the Hindu festival of lights (Diwali), Muslim Eid, Christian Easter, and Jewish passover. Some religions, such as Jehovah's Witnesses, do not celebrate festivals at all.
Family traditions and values	Muslim families have strict views about separation of the sexes after puberty.

Children should be made to feel that their way of life is valued, no matter how different it may be from the rest of the group. Children are usually very curious about other people's lives and this can be used to advantage by encouraging them to learn.

Ways of raising awareness

The home corner is an ideal setting in which to raise awareness of different cultures. If a childcare setting has many different cultures represented in its group, parents can be encouraged to help in the home corner on a rota system, representing their own culture. Cultures that are not represented

Figure 12.1 Home corners can display items that help children learn about other cultures

amongst the children in a group should be included also – you will have to do some research for these. It should not take too much imagination to think of all the aspects that can be covered.

Games from different cultures can be included – if there is a mix of cultural groups among the staff this will be easy, otherwise you could ask some of the parents or do some research.

Displays could focus on a different country or culture at different times. One idea is to link these into specific festivals, e.g. Diwali, or to a country in the news. You can do a lot to show children the positive side of other cultures. For instance, a country that is in the news because it has suffered from some natural disaster like a flood or famine could be the subject of a project to show the children how life usually is in that country.

Use a **'news'** or **'carpet time'** slot for children to bring in objects from their culture, or others they have read about or travelled to.

Different items and techniques you can use to show children about other cultures and ways of life include:

- pictures and posters
- artefacts such as statues, chopsticks, pots, items of clothing, small pieces of furniture
- asking parents to come into school or nursery to talk to the children
- videos, slides or photographs
- visits to areas nearby if possible, e.g. a Chinatown district.

Considering children's needs

Equal opportunities is not about treating everyone exactly the same. It is about making sure that all children are treated with respect and according to their own specific needs. Some children need more help with some activities than others if they are to gain the most from them. Planning activities for a group of children means thinking very carefully about the needs of the group. Look at the example in the following case study.

CASE STUDY ZARHA

Zarha planned an activity around the book *The Very Hungry Caterpillar*. She planned to read the story, discuss it with the children and then help them to make a wall display based on the story. The children are aged from three-and-half to five years. Three of the children are from families from Bangladesh, and speak very little English. One girl, Jane, has difficulty with activities requiring fine motor skills. One boy has a severe hearing impairment.

Zarha's choice of book is a good one as it is a very visual book, so it can help with language and hearing difficulties. By making sure that the children from Bangladesh and the child with a hearing impairment were sitting at the front, Zarha helped them to see the pictures. An interpreter helped with the discussion. Asking the children to draw pictures of the story also helped. While the children were drawing, Zarha talked to Jane about her ideas for the wall display, and both of them then put these ideas to the rest of the class. As the display took shape, Jane and Zahra directed the tasks.

If you are organising a game that relies on recognising colours and you have a child in your group who has a visual impairment, talk to him or her about the colours, or perhaps you could attach a noise or texture to each colour. A game using a ball and involving running around will need to be adapted for a child in a wheelchair – you may need to push the child in the chair, or change the game to avoid the running around.

DO IT

Prepare an activity which takes into consideration the diversity of individual children within a group.

You have been asked to plan a display with the children with the theme of 'celebration'. This could be a wall display, a table display, or even a small play performed by the children which you could video. Develop your plan, including at least six different types of celebrations that reflect different cultural groups.

Positive images of gender and race

One of the ways that children learn is through identifying with pictures and images that are familiar to them. All children have the right to see in stories and on posters adults and children who are like themselves and their carers, as this gives value to that child and his or her family. Material showing stereotypes should have no place in society, least of all in childcare settings. Examples of stereotyped images include:

- mother always caring for the children
- people with disabilities being looked after
- men and women in 'typical' jobs, e.g. male car mechanics, female shop assistants
- female nurses, male doctors
- police officers always with a white skin
- father doing home repairs
- black people as bus conductors or shopkeepers.

As an effective childcare worker you should aim to provide positive examples to children. Many posters and books are available that show adults of various cultural backgrounds and people with and without disabilities in a range of jobs and situations.

Think it through

Does your placement have posters, books, and pictures that provide positive images of different people? If not, what could you do to redress the balance?

Toys and books supporting equal opportunities

Stories that you read to the children should have girls as heroes as well as boys, and children with disabilities as central, active figures. Books in dual languages are essential to children for whom English is a second language. Learning to read involves the parents at home. Having a story in Punjabi, for example, will encourage a child to start reading in his or her language as well as English, and possibly help adults at home.

Books and posters reflecting the range of diversity in society help children become aware of people and settings outside their immediate family experience, as well as ensuring that all children have the opportunity to identify with familiar images and settings. All good bookshops have these types of books in stock, and your placement should certainly have them.

DO IT

Describe toys/books which provide positive images of gender and race.

Choose ten books from the story-reading stock in your placement. Devise a chart briefly describing each story, its 'hero', the racial mix of the characters, and whether there are any images of people with disability.

Of the ten, choose one that has a limited range of types of characters and produce an outline showing how you could reflect a more balanced view of racial, gender, or disability issues.

As childcare workers, we need to ensure that the whole range of racial and cultural groups are used in the planning of activities, even if people at the particular nursery or school come from only one or two cultural groups. Sometimes you might find people expressing surprise that this is necessary, but it is important to take this responsibility seriously. If a nursery puts up just one poster with positive images of diversity but does nothing else, this is **tokenism.**

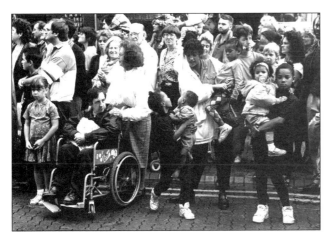

If you look and listen in the street, at work, on the bus, at school, in college, and watch television, you will see evidence of the rich variety of cultures that exist in every community. Valuing diversity in society and learning about it will enrich everyone's life. Unfortunately, this diversity can be viewed in a less positive light, resulting in stereotyping and prejudice, where there is a lack of knowledge and understanding. By helping children to develop an awareness of different cultures you can help to prevent such misunderstandings. Ways of widening the experience of the children include:

- cookery sessions from different cultures
- songs and dances from other cultures, perhaps on video
- storytellers from a range of ethnic groups, perhaps telling stories in their own languages
- displays of items from other cultures, such as eating implements, arts and crafts
- celebrating different festivals, appropriate to children in the setting and to others
- a theme week based on a particular culture.

DO IT

Plan a visual display which demonstrates understanding of gender, race or non-stereotyping.

Choose a cultural or racial group other than your own. Find out about its particular customs, stories, food, etc. to help you to plan a visual display. Produce a flow chart of your ideas and say how the children can be included.

Meeting specific needs in a childcare setting

Most people have a special need of some kind. If you are shortsighted and use spectacles, you have a minor disability that can easily be dealt with. Special needs range from a mild disability to a profound physical disability and/or learning difficulties.

It is important that you approach the task of meeting specific needs with the right attitude. For more on this topic, turn to Chapter 2. There are many different causes of physical and learning disabilities, and different ways of viewing them. Which of the following two models reflects your view?

- A **social model** recognises that any problems of disability are created by society and its institutions. If someone is a wheelchair user, problems are caused not by the wheelchair but the fact that some buildings do not have ramps and that buses are difficult to access. The solutions to problems of disability are therefore in society's hands, and involve changing the attitudes of the able-bodied.
- A **medical model** views the disability as the problem. Disability is seen as a tragic, incurable fact leaving the sufferer with little chance of a normal life. It focuses on the disability the person has, rather than his or her abilities. Under this model, people with severe disabilities are cared for in institutions with little hope of independence.

Think it through

Look at these two examples of children with a disability.

Sam, aged seven, was born prematurely after a pregnancy of 30 weeks. As a result of problems during his delivery, Sam has cerebral palsy. He uses a wheelchair to move around and a voice synthesiser to communicate. Although he cannot play sports Sam loves watching football, and enjoys playing games related to football. Sam and his friends spend a lot of time together playing games at weekends. School swimming sessions are his favourite time. With the support of a personal assistant, Sam attends a mainstream primary school and is looking forward to moving to senior school with his friends.

Lorna, aged six, was also born with severe cerebral palsy and relies on her wheelchair to move around. Her parents were never encouraged to hope that Lorna could attend a mainstream school. She attends a special school with children who all live a long way from Lorna. Lorna's parents are not happy to let her visit the one friend she has nearby, as they worry she will not cope without them. Although Lorna loves shopping, her parents do not take her very often as it is hard work, and they find it difficult to cope with people staring at her. They are thinking that Lorna will eventually live in a residential unit with care assistants looking after her.

Compare these two children, both with similar physical difficulties, and think about why they have different lifestyles – which would you prefer?

Causes of physical or learning difficulties

Special needs can be grouped into several categories, as shown below.

- **Physical impairments** cause problems with co-ordination and/or mobility. An example is cerebral palsy.
- **Chronic (long-term) diseases** and **terminal illnesses** include conditions such as cystic fibrosis or serious heart defects.
- **Learning difficulties** may be moderate to severe, or specific (e.g. dyslexia).
- **Communication difficulties** are caused by speech or language problems.
- **Loss of sensory abilities** includes the impairment of vision or hearing.
- **Emotional difficulties** include mental illnesses or severe family disruption.
- **Behavioural difficulties** include hyperactivity and, attention deficit disorder.
- **Giftedness** is an extremely high level of academic, artistic or musical ability that sets a child apart from his or her peers.

Some children may have needs that fall into two or more categories. A child who has cerebral palsy may have a physical impairment, communication difficulties and also be a gifted child. A child who has a long-term illness may also be affected by dyslexia.

Within all these categories there are several possible causes for the presence of special needs, as indicated in the table below.

Cause	Example	Effects
Genetic-chromosome abnormality	Down's syndrome	Heart problems, low intelligence
	Haemophilia	Bleeding easily into joints, soft tissues
	Brittle bone disease	Bones break easily, causing deformities to limbs
	Cystic fibrosis	Lack of vital enzymes in digestive and respiratory system, causing problems with breathing and digestion
	Achondroplasia	Very short arms and legs, resulting in small stature
Drugs taken during pregnancy	Thalidomide	Missing and shortened limbs, facial deformity
	Alcohol	Foetal alcohol syndrome
	Heroin	Addicted baby, small for its dates
	Nicotine	Small for dates, chest problems
Environmental, e.g. radiation, pollution (often difficult to specify cause)	Spina bifida	Lower limb paralysis, hydrocephalus
	Early childhood cancers	Variable
	Toxocaris (from dog and cat faeces)	Blindness
Illness of mother in pregnancy	Rubella	Heart malformations, blindness and deafness
Birth injury	Lack of oxygen to brain, trauma to limbs from forceps	Cerebral palsy – gross motor skill and sensory delay, poor fine motor skills
		Learning difficulties
		Weakness of arm or leg
		Damage to the optic nerve
Illness of child	Meningitis	Severe learning difficulties
	Polio	Paralysis
	Otitis media	Deafness
Accidents and injuries	Home or motor accidents, or abuse	Brain injury, paralysis
		Delayed development, physical injury
		Emotional and behavioural difficulties

The cause of the disability does matter to the child and his or her family. As a childcare worker, you should be more concerned with how a child's development is affected by a disability, and how you can support the child so he or she can lead a full and active life.

DO IT

Describe reasons why a child may have a physical or learning difficulty.

List as many reasons as possible for physical or learning difficulties. Group the possible causes into the following groups:

- hereditary and congenital
- developmental in the uterus
- caused through accident or illness.

In a small group, discuss how you think that these could be prevented or their effects could be minimised.

Meeting particular requirements of children with special needs

It is important for childcare workers to ensure that a child is not discriminated against in terms of the opportunity to reach his or her full potential. Look at these three examples.

1. Jodi has hearing difficulties and as a result her speech has been delayed. She experiences communication difficulties unless alternative methods of communication are considered. When her group at nursery has story time, the nursery nurse always makes sure that Jodi sits at the front and that the story has a lot of visual appeal, using puppets, pictures and miming.
2. Samir has cerebral palsy, which means he has difficulty in controlling his movements without shaking. Playing in the home corner was difficult because it was a small area, and Samir tended to knock things over. His teacher has resited the home corner so that it is in a bigger area and Samir can now play safely in it.
3. Wheelchair users may have difficulties in playing outside with other children, unless ways are found to overcome obstacles. Rajeet has difficulty getting into the playground as access is up two small steps. However, he can move very quickly once in the playground in his lightweight wheelchair. With the help of one of the staff, Rajeet's friends have invented a new form of football that allows him to use his arms instead of his feet.

There are many other ways to overcome difficulties. It is essential to structure activities and opportunities for the entire group of children in your care, taking needs into account. All children can benefit when activities are adapted – for instance, making story time a wider experience, and learning new ways of playing traditional games.

Adapting equipment for children with special needs

Sometimes special equipment may be needed to allow children with special needs to practise and develop all their skills.

- A child who has poor fine motor skills and difficulty with fine hand and eye co-ordination may benefit from the use of thicker pencils and other tools.
- Children with delays in developing gross motor skills (large body movements such as

walking or running), or sensory problems (vision, hearing, etc.) may enjoy large-scale toys such as ball pools and soft foam cushions.

● A child with a visual impairment may be able to read large-print books, and will enjoy listening to stories recorded on tape.

Some centres are equipped with multi-sensory rooms that provide opportunities for children with a wide range of specific needs. These rooms feature a range of lights, sounds, smells and touch sensations that stimulate (or in some cases soothe) the senses.

Any activity, game or toy designed to develop an aspect of a child's skill should aim to allow the child to use the skills that already exist, and encourage him or her to extend them. For example, when a child reaches the stage of being able to turn the pages of a book, make sure he or she has books with thick pages, showing pictures of interesting objects.

Sometimes there is no need to adapt equipment, but to change your methods of promoting an activity. A child who has difficulty sitting still for long will struggle to take part in a modelling activity lasting 15 minutes. Think about how you can adapt – you could sit with the child and keep up the encouragement, or ask to look at progress at frequent intervals. You could give a child some responsibility for drawing all the children's efforts together, say for a display. This may help to prevent a child's behaviour becoming unacceptable.

Maintaining self esteem

You must never forget the importance of maintaining a child's self esteem. Offering a child an activity usually aimed at much younger children could make the child feel inadequate and frustrated. The best person to consult is very often the child involved. For example, a child who has some delay in development of fine motor skills may have difficulty with small Lego bricks. Using larger bricks may be easier, but ask the child first and let him or her make the choice. This will help to maintain the child's self-esteem.

Children sometimes act in a cruel manner by mocking others who are struggling to keep up in games or activities. Your role is to stop such mockery and steer conversations or activities so that the emphasis is placed on children displaying their skills.

Do It

Create an activity/toy which is designed to meet the particular requirements of a child with a specific need.

Choose a popular game or activity that you have used with children.

If you had a child with visual impairment and another child with difficulties in gross motor skills, how would you adapt the activity to meet the needs of both? If you feel the game or activity cannot be adapted, design a toy or game that would be suitable to allow both children to gain full benefit from it.

Children with restricted mobility

Children may find that their mobility is restricted for a variety of reasons, including:

● physical disability causing full or partial loss of function of the legs
● visual impairment

- hearing impairment that also affects balance
- cerebral palsy
- brittle bone disease – the child is at risk of fractures
- frequent seizures or fits.

Think it through

Look at these three examples.

1. Millie has cerebral palsy. She may see and recognise an obstacle and know that she needs to avoid it, but the message from the brain to her legs is not effective, so she tends to appear clumsy in her movements.
2. Jawed has a visual impairment – he cannot see outside a narrow tunnel of forward vision. He often falls over objects that are outside this limited visual field. Crossing the road safely is difficult, as he cannot see all the vehicles around him.
3. Danny is a wheelchair user and becomes very frustrated when he cannot move around the classroom because of thoughtlessly placed furniture. Sometimes he finds it difficult to get close enough to work he is doing if tables do not allow his wheelchair underneath.

How could you help Millie, Jawed and Danny to take part in normal class or nursery activities?

A number of mobility aids can be used to assist children with restricted mobility, such as:

- wheelchairs, which can be self-propelled or electric
- walking sticks or elbow crutches
- walking frames or tripods
- trolleys
- calliper splints.

| Self-propelled wheelchair | Electric wheelchair | Tripod | Quadruped |

An able-bodied child can see obstacles and has the body control necessary to avoid them. A child with restricted mobility may not be able to do so. How can the environment be adapted to suit children with restricted mobility?

- Sometimes it is simply a question of avoiding leaving items lying around on the floor, and making sure equipment is kept in its proper place.
- Adaptation may be as simple as placing large foam pads and cushions around a slide, or providing a play area made up of shaped foam blocks to allow a child to roll, jump and fall in safety.
- Equipment such as slides, climbing frames and bicycles may need to be adapted to suit the needs of a particular child. Usually when a child has a special need of some type he or she will have had an assessment by an Occupational Therapist – a professional who specialises in adapting everyday equipment and recommending specialist equipment. If you have worked with a child who has cerebral palsy, for instance, you may have experience of electric wheelchairs, possibly with special extension to support the head.

- Children who tend to fall over and injure themselves may need to wear some form of protection to allow them free access to indoor and outdoor play space, such as helmets, knee and elbow pads.

Although the safety of all children in your care is of paramount importance, you also need to strike a balance so that children are allowed the freedom to enjoy their activities. Occasionally it may be necessary to support a child in play if he or she cannot play alone. In this situation you should respond to the child's wishes as far as is practical, not stop the child exploring and developing his or her skills.

Do it

Create a checklist of the adaptations necessary within a play area so that a child with a mobility aid can safely take part in the activities.

You may have a child with restricted mobility in your placement. If so, take him or her as your case study and explain what has been done or needs to be done to allow the child full participation in all activities. Draw a plan of the area showing necessary changes. Do you think anything else is needed to help this child in nursery or school?

If you do not know such a child, imagine that Louise, who is aged four and has limited mobility, is starting at your placement. Louise has difficulty walking far, and occasionally uses a wheelchair. Her mother wants her to experience everything available at your nursery, both indoors and outdoors. What adaptations will be needed to allow her to participate fully in all activities? Draw a plan of the area and write a checklist of the changes you would make.

Health and safety in a childcare setting

Local authority registration

Local authorities' social service departments have a duty to satisfy themselves that children are being properly cared for outside their own homes. By doing this they can offer some reassurance to the children's parents and encourage care providers to maintain high standards of safety. All registered child care providers must be inspected at least once a year, and extra visits will be made if the local authority feels there is a need. Inspectors have a legal right to enter any registered premises, or premises that should be registered, at any time.

The Children Act 1989 requires inspectors to carry out checks before the person in charge, the owner or the setting can be registered, and again at least at yearly intervals.

There are slightly different requirements for different kinds of childcare settings. Local authorities are responsible for registering nurseries, playgroups, child minders, crèches, after-school clubs and play schemes. Requirements for ratios of staff to children vary – a good rule of thumb is that the younger the children, the more staff required.

Full day care 0–2 years, 1 adult to 3 children
2–3 years, 1–4
3–5 years, 1–8

Some of the issues that owners or managers of childcare settings need to address in order to be registered are shown below.

● There must be an equal opportunities policy to show commitment to non-discrimination.
● All persons employed to look after children must have passed a police check to ensure they do not have a criminal record.
● Staff must make a health declaration or produce a statement from their GP.
● Personal references must be provided by all staff, and checks must be carried out on them.
● Staffing ratios must conform to legal requirements.
● Consultations must be carried out with the planning authority, fire authority, building inspector, and environmental inspectors to ensure that all legal requirements are met.
● Premises for children should be large enough for the numbers of children. No room should hold more than 26 older children or 16 younger ones. Babies and toddlers should be in a separate room.
● Safety issues must be addressed. Low-level glass doors or cupboards should be safety glass or boarded up. All sharp corners at low levels should be padded. Electric sockets should be covered. Floors should be clean and free of splinters. Access for prams and pushchairs should be provided.
● There must be adequate, safe, hygienic kitchen facilities, with enough storage space.
● There must be enough outside play areas or access to them and they must be free from hazards.
● There should be separate areas for quiet, noisy and messy activities, and an area where children can rest.
● A clear policy on supplying, maintaining and replacing toys has to be provided.
● Facilities should be available for making snacks and meals.
● Observation, assessment records and reports are needed, keeping a careful log of all children, staff, the reports of the management committee, and the progress of the children.

Do It

Identify the local authority registration requirements for registering childcare settings.

You and your friend are planning to open a nursery for 20 children between the ages of two and five years. You have planned the nursery and had advice from all the appropriate authorities. Write a report for your local social services inspection unit showing everything you have done to meet inspection requirements. You may do this task in pairs.

Health and safety

The Health and Safety at Work Acts lay down basic ideas and principles to ensure health and safety at work, imposing duties on both employers and employees. This means that when you are working in a childcare setting (or anywhere else for that matter) you have the right to expect that you will not be exposed to any dangers to your health and safety – it is your employer or placement's duty to protect you and everyone using the building, its surroundings and equipment.

The legislation covers all of the following:

- buildings and services – design and maintenance
- cleanliness of the environment and of food preparation areas
- safe storage and use of equipment
- working practices that promote health and safety
- provision of a safety policy.

As an employee, even if you are in an unpaid placement, you have a duty to make sure that you do not expose anyone to any danger to health and safety. This obviously includes yourself as well as the children in your care.

If you notice anything that could be a source of danger you must report it immediately and/or take steps to protect other people. You must also co-operate with your employer on health and safety issues, for example not using unsafe equipment or ignoring warning notices. Blocking fire exits with toys or uncovering electric sockets, for example, are very serious offences because they go against safety regulations.

Whilst the general principles of health and safety legislation, as discussed in Chapter 7, apply to everyone, there are also codes of practice and standards that give guidance for specific places of employment. There are special ones for child care settings – children often do not have the ability to protect themselves, and as in all other aspects of child care we have a duty to protect them.

Buildings and maintenance

- Doors opening into entrances and exits from the building must not be capable of being opened by young children.
- Floors should not have any loose rugs or pieces of carpet.

Cleanliness of the general environment

- There should be a high standard of cleanliness throughout the buildings.
- Spillages should be immediately cleaned.
- Toilet areas should be regularly cleaned and checked.

Food preparation areas

- All staff dealing with food should have a food hygiene certificate.
- All regulations relating to food storage should be followed.

Safe storage and use of equipment

- Cupboards at 'child level' should not contain cleaning items, knives, tools or any other potentially dangerous items.
- Toys with very small parts should be kept well away from children under three years of age.
- Children should not be able to touch heaters and radiators.
- Outdoor slides, swings, etc. should have safe, impact absorbing matting provided.

Working practices that promote health and safety

- Adults must not leave bags or coats containing medicines within reach of children.
- Adults must not bring hot drinks into the same room as children.
- All stairs should have fixed guards at the top and bottom.
- Children using babywalkers, bicycles, etc. should be supervised at all times, wearing helmets where appropriate.

If you talk to a nurse or doctor who has worked in an accident and emergency department, you will hear a catalogue of examples of incidents where children have been seriously injured, scarred for life or even killed as a result of adults not being fully aware of possible dangers to the children in their care.

Think it through

In a small group, work through the lists of possible hazards given above, and write down your ideas of the sort of accidents that could happen if good practice was not followed in each case. Think about babies and toddlers, as well as older children aged three to five.

Creating a safe environment

It would be impossible to think about every possible danger and avoid it – children are notoriously good at finding things that could injure them – but it is possible to eliminate the majority of risks and protect the children in your care. The skill of protecting children from injury involves a thorough knowledge of child development. Children can move onto a new stage of development before carers realise it, and can be at risk of injury.

So far we have looked at dangers in 'official' childcare settings, from childminders' homes to playgroups, nurseries and schools. Do you think the same considerations apply to private homes where children are cared for? Obviously, childminders are subject to the requirements, but what about a child's own home? You may in the future be employed as a nanny in a private home, or even just to babysit.

Think it through

Look at the picture in Figure 12.2. How would you make the room safer for a young child?

Figure 12.2 How many dangers can you spot in this picture?

Being aware of potential dangers to a child's health and safety is not enough – you must plan procedures and routines that ensure safety. Every person working with children is responsible for monitoring their safety. Some of the necessary procedures are listed below.

● Equipment should be regularly checked for broken parts and sharp edges.
● Arrangement of large equipment and toys should allow safe use by all children.
● Outside play areas should be checked daily for broken glass, syringes and other dangerous litter.
● Toilet and washing facilities should be regularly checked, and you should ensure that children use them at all appropriate times.
● Locks, catches, etc. that stop children leaving the building alone should be operating.
● Cupboards and shelves that are accessible to children should not contain dangerous items, e.g. knives or bleach.
● Outings from the placement should be carefully planned, with all possible dangers being considered and strategies introduced to deal with them.
● Written parental permission must be given for outings.
● There must be strict use of procedures to deal with spillages of urine, faeces, blood and vomit.
● Procedures must be in place to deal with visitors to the setting – reporting, signing in, etc.
● Food must be prepared and served in safe, hygienic conditions.

Do It

Create a checklist of routine procedures which must be followed to ensure the health, safety and hygiene of children in a range of early years settings.

You have been given the responsibility for the daily safety checks in the toddler room at the nursery where you are working. Your supervisor has asked you to write down your checklist of points for safety in the room. Make your list showing the checks you would carry out to ensure the safety of all the children in your care.

Childhood illnesses

All children pick up infections, and become ill from time to time, as they are developing their immunity. Immunity is the ability of the body to resist infections. All of us are in constant contact with bacteria and viruses, but we do not develop an illness from each one because of our immunity. There are several ways that children become immune to germs. In the uterus (womb) and during breast feeding, the child develops immunity to all diseases to which the mother has immunity, with protection passing from mother through the placenta and later through breast milk. In the first year of life and later, immunity is built up as a result of experiencing illness such as colds and stomach upsets. Immunity can also be gained from immunisations, e.g. for polio, diphtheria, mumps and whooping cough.

You should be familiar with the immunisation pattern for children. Ask at your doctor's surgery or health centre for a leaflet. You will see a chart similar to the one shown below.

Age	Immunisation	Age	Immunisation
8 weeks	Diphtheria Tetanus Pertussis (whooping cough) Hib (viral meningitis) Polio	4–5 years	Diphtheria Tetanus Polio
12 weeks	As for 8 weeks	10–14 years	Rubella BCG (tuberculosis)
16 weeks	As for 8 and 12 weeks	15–18 years	Diphtheria Tetanus Polio
12–18 months	MMR (mumps, measles, rubella) as one injection		

Childcare workers should be sure that they are protected against diseases, and should talk to their doctor about the need for boosters of immunisations – particularly rubella or polio. If workers are ill, they should not go to work in case they spread their illness to colleagues and the children.

You should be familiar with the signs and symptoms of childhood illnesses in order to care for a sick child and to protect other children. The following chart shows some of the common signs and symptoms, the treatment of action needed, whether an immunisation is available, and the incubation period – the time before the child shows signs of the illness after catching it.

Illness	Signs and symptoms	Treatment or action needed	Immunisation available?	Incubation period
Common cold	Sneezing, sore throat, runny nose, headache, temperature.	Treat symptoms with rest, plenty of fluids. Encourage child to blow nose.	No	1–3 days
Gastro-enteritis	Vomiting, diarrhoea, dehydration.	Replace fluids, seek medical help.	No	1–36 hours
Tonsillitis	Very sore throat, fever, headache, aches and pains.	Rest, fluids, medical attention as antibiotics may be needed.	No	Varies
Scarlet fever	Fever, loss of appetite, sore throat, pale around the mouth, 'strawberry tongue', bright pinpoint rash over face and body.	Rest, fluids and observe for complications.	No	2–4 days
Dysentery	Vomiting, diarrhoea with blood and mucus, abdominal pain, fever and headache.	Medical attention, rest fluids. Strict hygiene measures.	No	1–7 days
Chicken-pox	Fever, very itchy rash with blister-type appearance.	Tepid bath with soda bicarbonate, and calamine applied to skin to stop itching. Try to stop child scratching to avoid scarring.	No	10-14 days
Measles	High fever, runny nose and eyes, later cough, white spots in mouth, blotchy red rash on body and face.	Rest, fluids, tepid sponging. Medical attention to check for complications.	Yes	7–15 days
Mumps	Pain and swelling of jaw, painful swallowing, fever. May be swollen testes in boys.	Fluids, may need a straw to drink, warmth to swelling, pain relief.	Yes	14–21 days

Illness	Signs and symptoms	Treatment or action needed	Immunisation available?	Incubation period
Rubella (German measles)	Slight cold, sore throat, swollen glands behind ears, slight pink rash.	Rest, treat symptoms. Avoid contact with pregnant women.	Yes	7– 21 days
Pertussis (whooping cough)	Snuffly cold, spasmodic cough with whooping sound and vomiting.	Medical attention. Rest, fluids, feed after a coughing attack.	Yes	7–21 days
Meningitis	Fever, headache, drowsiness, confusion, dislike of light, very stiff neck. May be small red spots.	Immediate urgent medical attention. Take child to hospital.	Yes for some strains	2–10 days

In nearly all cases a child is most infectious to others before the symptoms appear. Many illnesses have a cold or fever as their first signs – it would not be possible to exclude all children with these symptoms from nursery, nor would it have much effect on the spread of a disease. Different settings have different rules about excluding children with common illnesses, ranging from excluding all children with symptoms, to excluding only while the child feels unwell.

Your role

Your role includes encouraging parents to have their children immunised wherever possible, and to make sure that routines in the nursery, school, etc. help to protect children from illness. For example, good practice involves careful hand washing, blowing of noses, covering up coughs, and cleanliness of toilet areas. You should also be sensitive to the needs of a child who has been ill. Even when fully recovered from an acute illness, a child may need activities that are usually more suited to a slightly younger child, or more reassurance and attention.

Parents may ask you for advice about their children when they are ill or appear unwell. Always suggest they take their child to the doctor if they are uncertain what to do. Family doctors prefer to see a child, even if for a minor illness, rather than miss a serious illness such as meningitis.

When a child is taken ill in your care, the parents or guardians must be informed. As a student or junior worker you should always check with your supervisor. You can provide support to a child who is ill while his or her parents are coming by sitting quietly with the child, perhaps reading a story.

Often after a visit to the doctor a child may need to take medicine whilst at nursery or school. Most settings have a policy that parents must give written consent for their child to have medicines administered by the nursery nurse or teacher. Childcare workers are not allowed to give medicines to children without this written permission under any circumstances.

DO IT

Describe common childhood illnesses.

Find out about the policy at your placement on the exclusion of children who are ill. Design and make a booklet for parents at your placement describing the common childhood illnesses and how they and you can help protect their child. Include a section on the policy of the placement on exclusion during illness.

Accidents and emergencies

Young children are prone to having accidents and injuring themselves. Even a simple banging of heads when two children run into each other could be serious if the carer failed to notice symptoms that something was wrong.

All childcare settings must have at least one person qualified in first aid. As a childcare worker it is your responsibility to take a first aid course if your tutors do not provide it. You should keep your first aid knowledge up to date.

Everyone working with children should be able to deal calmly with an accident and decide when it is necessary to call for additional help.

What is an emergency?

An emergency is whenever someone is injured or seriously ill, or in danger of being so.

Examples include:

- choking
- severe bleeding
- convulsion
- broken bones

- swallowed poisons
- allergic reactions
- head injuries
- unconsciousness

Before you do anything, you must follow the AABC code.

A – Assess the situation It is no use trying to deal with an incident if there is danger to yourself or any other person. Other children should be moved away from the scene as quickly as possible, and someone should be asked to look after them. Assess the scene for dangers – e.g. electricity, broken glass or spillages. Then you must give attention to the casualty's:

A – Airway
B – Breathing
C – Circulation

The aims of first aid are to:

1. Preserve life
2. Stop the condition getting worse
3. Promote recovery.

Chapter 7 gives examples of common emergencies and how to deal with them until qualified help arrives. See pages 216 to 228. The following table shows further examples of emergencies that may affect children in your care.

Emergency	Treatment
Head injury	Control any bleeding by applying pressure with a pad Lay casualty down Take or send to hospital Monitor level of consciousness, vomiting, etc.
Convulsions Often the result of a high temperature in a child.	If hot, cool child by removing clothing Protect from injury – clear surrounding objects Sponge with tepid water Place in recovery position Dial 999 for an ambulance
Back injury Always suspect after fall from swing, slide, tree, etc.	Do not move or attempt to move Steady and support neck and head Dial 999 for an ambulance
Allergic reaction To stings or medicines – red blotchy skin, swelling of face and neck, problems with breathing	Dial 999 for an ambulance Put into comfortable position Monitor condition (ABC)
Choking in young children (see Figure 12.3)	Give 5 back slaps between shoulders – lean an older child forward, put a baby over your knee face downwards Remove any obvious obstruction from mouth Next, give 5 chest thrusts: stand behind the child, make a fist against lower breast bone, grasp with other hand, and press sharply into chest – for a baby, press two fingertips on lower half of breast bone Check ABC Dial 999 for an ambulance
Asthma attack	Make child comfortable, seated in position most comfortable for the child Let child use inhaler – usually a blue reliever Encourage to breathe slowly If attack does not subside, call for medical help

In the case of an accident, in addition to taking action to help the casualty, you must:

- send for a qualified first aider if you are not qualified yourself
- call for your supervisor
- calm the other children
- inform the child's parents
- record the incident in the accident book.

Consideration and thought about the children in your care can help to prevent potentially serious emergencies. For example, very young children learn a lot from putting things in their mouths and exploring taste and texture. Unfortunately this can lead to accidents, so

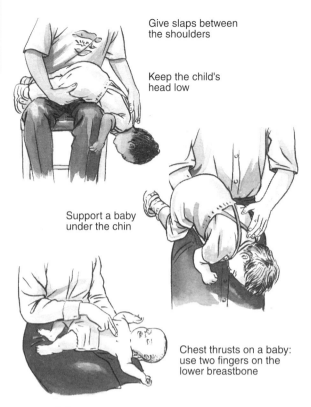

Give slaps between the shoulders

Keep the child's head low

Support a baby under the chin

Chest thrusts on a baby: use two fingers on the lower breastbone

Figure 12.3 Treating a child or baby who is choking

always be careful about giving a child a drink or food whilst playing, because innocent items can be lethal when combined.

Ambulances

When dialling 999, always have ready the details of the accident and injury, the age of the child and of course where the injured child is. In serious incidents involving breathing difficulties or severe bleeding, an ambulance should be summoned as soon as possible – preferably while first aid is being given.

First aid boxes

Always make sure you know where the first aid box is kept, and what is in it.

A good first aid box should have the following items in it:

- a range of plasters in different sizes
- sterile eye pads
- safety pins
- crepe bandages
- tweezers
- non-alcoholic cleansing wipes.

- medium and large sterile dressings
- triangular bandages (slings)
- disposable gloves
- scissors
- cotton wool

Many of these items are illustrated in Figure 7.8 on page 220.

Think it through

The next time you are in placement, find out where your first aid kit is and have a look inside. Do the contents match the list above? Is anything missing? Are there any extra items, and if so what are they for?

Procedures after an accident or emergency

Dealing with the immediate situation in an accident is only part of the procedure for the nursery or school. The next important action is to inform the child's parents or carers.

The child will have a record card in the office giving emergency contact numbers. This may not be the child's parents, because work commitments may make it difficult for a parent to be contacted. The number may be the child's grandparents or aunt for example – it should be someone who is usually easy to contact, and who in turn can contact the parents.

The person in charge must get in touch with the emergency contact as soon as possible and inform the relevant person of the incident, and where the child is being taken. Obviously someone the child knows well should go to the hospital with him or her until the parents or other carers arrive. This will help to reassure the child, and be a point of contact for the parents when they arrive.

Even with a minor accident that does not need hospital treatment, an entry should be made in the accident book. Under certain circumstances the accident may need to be reported to the Health and Safety Executive, particularly if the child is seriously injured. A full report is needed, and in any incident the person in charge should examine the circumstances to see what could be done to prevent a similar emergency occurring.

Preventive measures may be as simple as having more adults to supervise the children at outdoor play, or there may be the need for changing equipment or putting more safety protection in place, such as more matting under swings.

A review of the policy on accidents may be needed, but at the very least some type of preventive action is likely to be taken. Accidents are less likely to happen when:

- potential dangers are seen – kettle flexes are kept well away from worktop edges, ponds are properly covered or filled in
- children are not over-protected and are allowed to develop skills to keep themselves safe
- adults are good role models and set a safe example
- children are never left alone
- wherever possible toys and equipment purchased have the kitemark or safety mark on them to show they are of a good standard. The British Standards Institution gives kitemarks and safety numbers to approved products. The Lion mark is put on British-made toys that meet British safety standards, and the CE symbol means products have met both British and European standards (see Figure 12.4).

Kitemark of the British Standards Institution (BSI)

BSI safety mark

Lion mark

CE mark

Figure 12.4   Look out for these safety marks on toys and equipment

---

Do It

Explain procedures followed when dealing with a minor accident.

Describe how to inform carers of the action to take in an emergency.

You are in charge of two small children, aged two and five years, at their home. Their parents have gone shopping for the afternoon. At 2 pm, during a game with a ball, Iqbal (the five-year old) trips and falls heavily on his left leg. You see that his leg is swollen and it looks a strange shape.

Describe what you would do, in the appropriate order. You should include contacting his parents, and remember his little sister.

Now imagine this incident had happened at school; describe anything else that you think would have to be done.

13 CHILDREN'S ACTIVITIES AND PLAY

You have looked at children's development in detail, and at some specific activities to promote areas of development. You are now going to explore the range of activities that you can do with children. The chapter looks at planning, preparing and finally delivering activities. These are some of the fundamental tools of an effective childcare worker.

Practical activities for use with children

Language activities

Language development is a crucial part of a child's progress. Without communicating through language, reading and writing, it is very difficult to progress in life. Children learn language skills from before birth, by hearing the sound of the mother's voice in the uterus. This continues through adults' constant communication with children, and you have a vital role to play in this. Reading stories, repeating rhymes and singing are an important part of your job as a childcare worker.

When you are reading a story to a child or group of children, you need to give careful thought to the type of book you choose.

- Does it have a theme that will interest them, and that they can relate to?
- Are there attractive pictures to look at?
- Is the length appropriate to their age? Very young children need short stories that hold their attention, while older children may enjoy a story that can be read in a few instalments.
- Can you develop other activities from the story – rhymes, songs, paintings and so on?

Look in a good bookshop or the children's section of the library. You will see a selection of the following types of books:

- pop-up and flap books
- feely books
- dual-language books
- joke books
- books based on TV programmes and characters
- factual books about events such as the arrival of a new baby, or starting school.

Before selecting a book for use, make sure that it does not portray stereotypes of particular groups, e.g. always shows girls playing with dolls, or older people in rocking chairs. Books should reflect a mix of cultures, both ones that are familiar to the children and ones that offer new experiences.

Music activities

Music is a language common to all children. All children are exposed to music in some form, even if it is only on the radio or television. Music can be a very useful way to soothe a distressed baby, and in their first year babies will enjoy joining in by clapping hands and imitating the singing, accompanied by body movements. From the age of two, they enjoy singing with other children and can learn the words and tunes of songs.

Music can allow children to explore their feelings and ideas, to develop their physical skills and co-ordination through dance, and their manipulative skills by playing instruments.

Young children will enjoy music when:

- it has meaning in relation to things they know about, e.g. weather, time of year, festivities
- they can choose some of the music
- songs have accompanying actions
- they can accompany songs with instruments.

Musical instruments come in many types, and can be purchased or home-made. Simple instruments are those that involve:

- banging, e.g. drums, triangles, xylophones, tambourines
- shaking, e.g. maracas
- blowing, e.g. whistles.

Some of these are easy to make, for example shakers can be made from an empty container filled with a few dried beans or lentils, and drums can consist of a bowl with several layers of greaseproof paper or cling film, or a simple wooden box. Children can begin to learn simple scientific principles if they are shown the use of different-sized instruments, fillings, materials, etc.

Older children respond to the use of more sophisticated instruments such as recorders and keyboards. Children as young as five can begin learning to play instruments in which they are interested. Parents may need to be careful not to push them too hard, or they may lose interest.

Plastic bottle containing pasta or beans for shaking

Blocks of wood to rub or knock together

Empty biscuit tin and wooden spoons make a 'drum'

Figure 13.1   Some home-made musical instruments

Carrying out music and language activities

If you are reading to just one or two children, a quiet corner with comfortable seating is all you need. Ideally, you should be free from interruptions. Reading, singing or playing music to a group requires a little more thought to be given to the arrangement of the room.

- All the children should be able to sit comfortably, and see what you are doing.
- Make sure there is adequate lighting.
- Try to use appropriate body language and expression to add interest to the book or songs. You may find it amuses the children if you use props such as hats and glasses, or different voices.
- Find points where the children can join in or repeat lines, to add to their interest.
- After you have finished, try to develop a discussion about the story or song, asking for the children's opinions or experiences.

Do it

Select appropriate materials and carry out music and language activities for use with young children.

Select two different stories with linked songs. One should be suitable to use with a group of children aged four to five, another for a few children aged two to three. Describe each story and song; explain how you would use them. If possible try using one pair with the children in your placement and write a short report on the project.

Prepared and improvised games, physical activities and role plays

Games are an excellent way of developing children's social skills – even young babies playing peek-a-boo are learning valuable skills. Older children learn about turn-taking and rules through games.

When you choose games to play with children, remember that a child under three cannot sit still for very long, and does not understand rules. A visit to a toy shop will show you a wide range of games, many of them expensive to buy, but it is possible to play games that cost very little or nothing.

Types of game	Examples of games
Table-top	Snap, pairs, lotto, matching games, counting games, Kim's game, Monopoly, Jenga
Physical games	Hide-and-seek, musical statues, football, rounders, hopscotch, obstacle races
Party games	Oranges and lemons, hunt the thimble, pass the parcel, musical chairs, sleeping lions

If you are playing games with children, especially younger ones, make sure that all the children have a go, and discourage serious competitiveness. Once they understand the rules, children are usually fiercely defensive of them and do not react well to 'cheats'.

You will need to unobtrusively organise the games for younger children, as they will need help to take turns and understand what they have to do. Children will often enjoy playing with an adult an individual game such as snap, especially if they occasionally win.

Role play

Role playing can all be part of a game, involving dressing up and pretending to be someone else. Children can explore and express their feelings through role play. It can use:

- everyday materials such as dressing-up clothes and items found in the home corner
- pre-prepared resources, e.g. a shop or café set up in the school or nursery
- resources from outside the children's experience, e.g. from other cultures, from history, etc.

Care should be taken that materials conform to health and safety requirements, and they should be monitored to check whether they need cleaning or repair work.

With role play, as with any game, it is essential that you give careful thought to the children who are going to participate. Can they all take part? Do you need to make any changes to the organisation of the activity to suit the children's needs?

Do It

Use prepared and improvised games, physical activities, and role plays.

Explore the games and role-play materials at your placement. Ask if you can plan and use a game with a group of children. Write a description of how you planned and arranged the game, how it worked, and any changes you had to make to suit the needs of the children involved.

Materials for creative activities

Creative play allows children to express themselves, and to discover the physical properties of the materials they are using. The role of the adult is to provide a range of materials and encourage experimentation. With creative activities, the process is far more important than the end product. Most creative play is potentially messy, and good preparation is necessary to avoid children spoiling their clothes or their surroundings – this takes away any anxiety from the activity. Consider safety aspects carefully, especially with young children who may put everything in their mouths. Be careful that dyes and colours are not poisonous. Some children may need encouragement to get their hands wet, dirty or covered in paint.

Activity	Materials and preparation
Painting and drawing	Tables, easels, or the floor with adequate covering Different paints – poster, acrylic, ready-mixed, finger paints Chalks, pastels, wax crayons, glitter, felt tip pens Paper, card, brushes, rollers, sponges, potato shapes for printing
Junk modelling and collage	A wide range of boxes, containers, papers, materials, pasta, sawdust and shavings, sweet wrappers, sequins Scissors, glue, aprons.
Sand and water	Both can be indoor or outdoor, and need attention to safety Purpose-built trays, mix of wet and dry sand Water with different coloured dyes, soapy suds, bottles, jugs, funnels, sponges, objects that sink and float Sand scoops, sieves, spades, buckets, toy cars
Clay, dough and	Home-made or bought dough of different consistencies, colours plasticine and smells Plasticine and clay Rolling pins, cutters, scissors, boards, plates, modelling tools

Most creative activities will stimulate all areas of a child's development. Hand–eye co-ordination is promoted, along with manipulative skills, language in talking about the work, emotional expression, pride in seeing work displayed or completed, and social skills in turn-taking. When you are selecting activities for children, make sure that they will all be capable of carrying out the activity. If you have to help them with everything, there will be little sense of achievement and they will soon lose interest.

Always recognise a child's efforts at creative activities, and ask the child to tell you about what has been made or done. If possible, write a short statement of this to attach to the work. Make sure that the child's name is on the work, and that unless it is going on display it is given to the child to take home.

DO IT

Select appropriate materials and carry out creative activities.

Spend some time looking through the resources in your placement, and reading catalogues to find out about the wide range of creative materials available. Ask if you can have small samples, and make notes on their uses. Put your findings into a file, to make a personal catalogue of resources for creative activities. Every time you develop a creative activity, put a sample in your file, with a note of the materials needed, and instructions for use.

Indoor and outdoor play equipment

Large and small play equipment can be used to encourage children's physical development. Large-scale equipment will enhance gross motor development and co-ordination, while small play equipment encourages manipulative and fine motor skills.

Large equipment

Which of the following equipment is in use in your placement?

- climbing frames
- swings
- play tunnels
- slides

- trampolines
- ropes and rope ladders
- bicycles and tricycles
- seesaws
- sit-and-ride toys
- large balls, hoops, beanbags.

All large equipment needs plenty of space if it is to be used safely. Children will enjoy using it either indoors or out of doors, but wherever it is used you must think about:

- protective matting for the floor in case of falls, and avoiding the risk of falls onto dangerous objects
- adequate adult supervision
- avoiding too many children trying to use the equipment at once
- adaptations and support for children with physical disabilities.

If your placement has a wide selection of equipment, try to find out how the adults decide which item is to be used. Children enjoy variety in activities, and keeping a piece of equipment for occasional use will make it a treat. For example, a trampoline needs close supervision, so it can be used only at certain times. Large-scale equipment needs careful checking before use for loose parts, broken sections, and cleanliness.

If it is kept outside, covers should be put over it. If possible, equipment stored indoors to prevent spoilage.

Small equipment

Small equipment has fewer potential hazards, and requires less space. It offers great potential for children to develop their self-esteem, as results are almost instantaneous. An important rule about selecting suitable small equipment is that smaller children need bigger pieces, while larger (older) children enjoy smaller pieces. The safety issues are obvious – small children can and will put small items in their mouths, and may choke.

Smaller children should also be kept away from older children's construction and modelling work, to avoid the accidental destruction of their efforts.

Small play equipment includes:

- stacking beakers
- Duplo
- jigsaws of many types
- foam blocks
- construction straws, stickle bricks, Meccano, etc.
- posting boxes
- Lego
- interlocking train sets
- wooden blocks

Think it through

Chapter 11 described how children develop fine motor skills. For which age group might small equipment be suitable? Put an approximate age range against each type of equipment listed above.

As with large play equipment, you need to be selective in the amount of equipment you put out. Small play materials need to be carefully stored in boxes or trays, keeping different-sized pieces separate. Tables should be arranged to confine each type to a separate area. In this way, toys will be kept in good condition and not get mixed up or lost.

> ## *Do it*
>
> **Describe how to set up and use large and small play equipment and indoor/outdoor play equipment safely.**
>
> **1.** You have been asked to set up the small play equipment area for the morning session in a nursery for three- and four-year-olds. Describe how you would do this, and the types of toys you would put out. What safety considerations would you have to bear in mind?
>
> **2.** How does your placement provide opportunities for using large play equipment? What are the most popular items? How are safety issues managed?

Cooking activities

Most children enjoy cooking. Part of the enjoyment is creating something from a mix of items, and learning about the changes that occur – then there is the fun of eating your results! Some children may have experienced cooking with parents or carers at home, but many may not have done so. Adult supervision is essential, and because small groups are usual, there is an excellent opportunity to talk with the children about the task, where the food comes from or other issues. Let the children do as much as possible themselves, to encourage a sense of achievement.

Many parents feel comfortable about helping out with cooking activities in nursery or school. There is the added bonus that if you involve parents you and the children will learn about other cultures, or different recipes and ideas.

In choosing cooking activities, consider the following factors:

- the ages and size of the group
- equipment and ingredients that are available
- time available
- the level of involvement of the children
- learning outcomes (such as science or numbers)
- dietary considerations – cultural and health matters (e.g. nut allergies) as well as personal preferences
- trying the recipe out first at home.

You don't need to confine cooking activities to making buns or rice crispy cakes. Cooking can also be 'cold cooking'. Think about involving children in making snacks – sandwiches, toast, fruit, pizzas. Making jellies or milky whips involves changing textures and producing tasty results.

Preparing and clearing away cooking activities

You need to think about the following issues when you are cooking with children.

- The safety of the children – access to hot surfaces, knives, etc.
- Ease of access for the children to work comfortably and safely.
- Numbers of children who can work at one time.
- Hygiene – hand-washing, etc.
- Protection of clothing – aprons.
- Access to cleaning facilities – sink, washing up liquid.
- Safe storage of food.

Do it

Carry out cooking activities to cater for different ages, cultural groups and personal preferences.

Plan a morning of cooking with a group of five-year-old children. You have been asked to choose something with a theme, e.g. Christmas, or a country. Write out your plan, describing the items needed, how you will involve the children, and safety considerations.

Creating and using interest tables

Anything that can be put on a table or shelf can contribute to an interest table. Adults and children can provide items, and the main focus of an interest table is to allow children to touch and see objects of interest. Safety rules include the following.

Good practice: interest tables

✓ Ensuring that small children cannot pick up items they can swallow or chew.
✓ Place the table in a position where it will not be knocked over.
✓ Avoid food items that may spoil or present a health hazard if eaten.
✓ Discourage the presentation of insects, small animals, etc.

Interest tables usually have a theme – for example colours, toys, a country, or holidays. It is possible to create a 'growing' table by planting bulbs, seeds, or plants that can be observed in progress.

Think it through

With a partner, brainstorm as many themes for an interest table as possible.

Preparing an interest table

Displaying items to their advantage and stimulating discussion is a task that needs thought and preparation. The following steps will help.

1. Cover the table with a plain cloth or fabric. Choose a colour that complements the objects to be placed on it.
2. Use boxes and books under the cover to raise certain items above the level of the table.
3. Do not include precious objects that could be lost or spoiled.
4. Arrange objects so that children can see and touch them.
5. Label objects neatly, and make sure the names of their providers are on them.
6. Encourage the inclusion of everyday objects from home – contributions do not have to be exotic.
7. Beware of inadvertently encouraging the picking of wild flowers or plants from gardens.
8. Try to add additional material such as books or pictures relevant to the theme.
9. Take a photograph of the finished table.

Once constructed, the interest table is a focus of attention and can be used to:

- stimulate discussion about the objects – what they are, where they are from, what they are used for, etc.
- stimulate creative activities – paintings, stories, model-making
- promote learning in areas of science, literacy and numeracy, and interest in the world at large.

Do It

Create and use interest tables to extend learning and imagination, and communication skills.

Using an idea that fits in with the aims of your placement, plan and prepare an interest table. Write about your experience, including details of the items shown, the use made of the table, and any problems encountered. If possible, include a photograph of the finished display.

Activities to promote development and learning

The Early Years Curriculum

The National Curriculum for compulsory education provides guidelines for schools on what children need to be taught.

Since 1996, the government has also provided a set of guidelines for pre-school children, and up to the age of eight. These are called Desirable Learning Outcomes, or DLOs. Generally, the DLOs mirror what has been provided in most good pre-school settings for many years. They are concerned with helping children under eight years old to develop and learn.

Underlying the curriculum are some basic principles about how children learn. They are:

- children learn best when material suits the stage they have reached in their development
- attention needs to be given to the whole child – that is, to physical, moral and emotional needs as well as intellectual needs
- children learn in an integrated manner – they do not separate learning to speak from learning about numbers, for example

- children learn best when they are allowed to try things out and make mistakes
- children need to have their efforts recognised and valued
- you should always start with what a child can do, not what he or she can't do
- conditions for learning have to be positive to ensure the development of creativity and imagination – children need materials and encouragement
- there are particular times when a child is ready to learn certain skills
- a child's relationships with other children and adults are very important.

Chapter 11 introduced you to the Early Years National Curriculum, which covers six areas of learning, as shown below.

- **Personal and social development** outcomes focus on children learning to work, play, co-operate with others and function in a group. They cover important aspects of personal, social, moral and spiritual development.
- **Language and literacy** outcomes cover important aspects of language development and provide the foundation for literacy.
- **Maths and numeracy** outcomes cover important aspects of mathematical understanding and provide the foundation for numeracy.
- **Knowledge and understanding of the world** outcomes focus on children's developing knowledge and understanding of their environment, other people and features of the natural and made world.
- **Physical development** outcomes focus on children's developing physical control, mobility, awareness of space and manipulative skills.
- **Creative development** outcomes focus on the development of children's imagination and their ability to communicate and to express ideas and feelings.

DO IT

Describe the basic requirements of the Early Years Curriculum.

Produce a briefing sheet for parents at an open evening or for new entrants to nursery, explaining what the Early Years Curriculum is about.

Who should be consulted when planning activities?

As the children are the central characters in each activity you do, it is a good idea to consult older children, say over the age of three. There is little point in developing an activity, at much expense of time and resources, only to discover the children are not interested in it! But it is likely that in a group of say 20 children, you will not get agreement from all of them.

Working within the Early Years Curriculum, you are aiming for a well-balanced programme, facilitating all-round development. You will also have other aims in planning activities.

- Do they fit in with the overall plan or theme of the setting?
- Are they suitable for the time of year? There is little point in working on a theme of winter in March – far better to use spring.
- Are the materials you need easily available, and cost effective? Grandiose schemes using the entire materials budget for the term will not make you popular.

- Will there be enough or too many children for the activity? Think about timing at the start and end of terms, about holidays, etc.
- Are there any cultural implications? Be careful not to offend children, parents or other carers. An activity based on food during the Moslem fasting period of Ramadan would be rather insensitive.
- Is the activity planned for a suitable time in the nursery or school day? Try not to have a very boisterous activity just before rest time, or when the children have just come in from outdoor play.
- Does your plan conflict with anyone else's? Children need diversity, and a repetition of an activity they have already done will not be a great success.
- If appropriate, will it be possible to display the results for parents and visitors to see?
- Are there any other constraints – other activities in the building, outside visits, and so on?
- Can all the children join in? Some activities may exclude children with impairments, illness, allergy, etc.
- Are there any health and safety implications?
- Are any permissions required, especially for trips out of school or nursery?

If you look carefully at these points, the list of people you may have to consult should become apparent:

- head of your placement
- other childcare staff
- parents
- for outside trips, the organisations you might be visiting, people involved in transport, etc.
- social service registration unit to check on staff ratios for visits
- kitchen staff if food is involved
- cleaning or caretaking staff if any mess if likely to be made.

Do It

Explain who must be consulted when planning each activity.

Jason is planning a week of activities in the private nursery school where he works, around the colour red. He plans to read stories, set up an interest table, do some baking with the children, go for a walk in the park and the high street, and do some painting and modelling to be put on display.

Make a list, giving reasons, showing who he will need to consult before he finalises his plans, and add notes explaining how he might do so.

Activities suitable for different children in different care settings

Effective planning can make all the difference to the success of an activity. You may have heard staff using the phrase 'planning cycle'. The planning cycle is a very useful tool in your work with young children.

Planning cycle

Planning happens at a variety of levels in a childcare setting. It can be over a term, a month or a week ahead. The following flow chart demonstrates how a theme is developed, using the example of the theme of change.

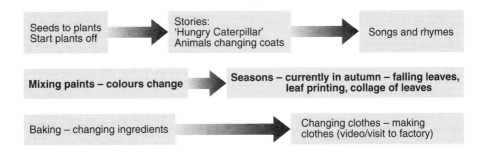

Within the framework of the overall plan, there will be small-scale planning of individual activities, to ensure that the needs of all children are met. See Figure 13.2 for an example.

Activity Planning Sheet

Group Blue group   **No of children 8**

Age range   4 to 4 and a half

Planning activity   Baking fairy cakes

Outcomes   Learning about transformation of ingredients – science
Finding out about why things happen – knowledge and understanding of the world
Numeracy – weighing, counting, time
Turn taking
Manipulative skills – mixing, spooning into cases

Room Kitchen   **Date and time** Monday 12 October 11am

Resources

250 g self-raising flour
2 eggs
250 g margarine
250 g sugar
milk

Icing sugar, cherries, hundreds and thousands

Bun baking tray, bowls and wooden spoons, aprons, scales

Plan of action

1. Explain activity to children
2. Divide group into two – Mrs Smith will work with other half
3. Take children to wash hands and put on aprons
4. Explain need to be orderly, keep away from the oven, and for hygiene
5. Start baking – ask each child to weigh one ingredient, allow each to stir
6. Let children fill three bun cases each
7. Bake
8. Clear away and wash up – children to take the lead
9. Allow buns to cool, while other group bake
10. Mix icing and allow children to decorate buns
11. Identify owners of buns
12. Allow eating of one bun – take the other two home.

Points to consider

Safety in the kitchen
Conversation to explain process, what they can see happening
Asking for experiences at home, with grandparent, etc.
Ask about preference for buns, favourite foods, where else they get cakes.

Activities such as baking lend themselves to being carried out in both group and home-based childcare settings. In fact, the close link between home and school or nursery can be valuable. Children of all ages usually enjoy baking, and the complexity and involvement can be increased with older children at different stages of development. Different cultures and dietary requirements can be explored with baking, often with the help and support of parents and other adults from the community.

Your planning sheet could include a note showing how you would use the activity with different age groups, and in different settings. Your review (see the next section) certainly should show these details.

Figure 13.2   An example of an activity planning sheet

Think it through

You have volunteered to do some baking with the children, to show how flour, eggs, margarine and milk can change into buns to eat. You need to give a lot of thought to the task to make sure it works well. Using a planning sheet such as the one in Figure 13.2 will help your thought processes.

Few if any activities can be enjoyed only by a narrow age range, or in only one setting. A well-thought-out plan, with attention to the skill level of the particular children you are working with, should ensure an activity is matched to the ability of the children.

If you are working with a group of children with a wide range of skill levels, greater care will be needed. You may have to adapt the activity within the group to allow for this. For example, in a baking activity, some children may not be able to weigh the ingredients, due to lack of manual skills. They could be asked to put out the bun cases, and be more involved in stirring the mixture. Some children may be able to recognise the required weight on the scales, while others pour the flour into the scale pan.

Do It

Plan a variety of activities suitable for children in different care settings at different stages of development.

You have been asked to provide a creative activity for a group of six children aged four. Choose and activity – it could be one you have already used – and complete a planning sheet, indicating how you will allow for different skill levels and interests.

Skills required to perform planned activities

All the planning and preparation involved in a successful activity will be wasted if you have not thought about a vital question: have the children reached the required stage of development, and do they possess the skills necessary to take part in and enjoy the activity? A good understanding of child development and observation of children playing and working will help you to develop the knowledge you need to decide this question. Most activities are planned with the aim of extending children's skill levels, but skills cannot be extended or developed if the child is not ready for that next step.

One example is the use of jigsaws. It requires quite a high degree of manipulative skill to put jigsaw pieces together, and children need to learn to use slot-in jigsaw boards first, where they can match the picture underneath. Next they move on to jigsaws with very large pieces, and gradually move to harder puzzles.

Think it through

Can you think of an activity you have prepared for which the child was not ready? What did you do in the situation?

The chart in Figure 13.3 below should help you to choose activities matched to the age and stage of development of the children you are working with.

Age	Play needs of the child	Indoor equipment	Outdoor equipment
1–2	The child is mobile and gaining gross motor and fine manipulative skills. The child needs plenty of opportunities to strengthen muscles and develop co-ordination.	Push and pull toys Toys that make music Dolls Trolleys Building bricks Posting toys	Paddling pool Baby swing Small slide
2–3	Children are starting to notice and play with other children. Their language is increasing and much of their play is pretend play. Children are gaining confidence in physical movements and enjoy playing outside. Children of this age can be easily frustrated and have a short consentration span – less than 10 minutes – so they need opportunities to be independent in their play and range of activities. There should be plenty of equipment as children find it difficult to share with each other.	Dressing-up clothes Home corner equipment – e.g. tea sets, prams, cooking utensils, pretend telephones Building blocks Toy cars and garages Dolls and cuddly toys Dough Paint Jigsaw puzzles Musical instruments	Paddling pool Sand and water tray Slide Climbing frame Swings Sit and ride toys Tricycles
3–4	Children are starting to co-operate with each other and enjoy playing together. Most of their play is pretend play. Pieces of dough become cakes; tricycles become cars! Children enjoy physical activity, gaining confidence in being able to use large equipment – e.g. climbing frames. They are also developing fine manipulative skills and beginning to represent their world in picture form.	'Small world' play – e.g. playmobile, Duplo figures Dressing-up clothes Home corner and equipment Dough and other malleable materials Water and sand Construction toys such as train tracks, building bricks Jigsaw puzzles	Climbing frame Slide Paddling pool Tricycles Bicycles with stabilisers Balls and bean bags
4–6	Children are more interested in creating things – e.g. making a cake, drawing cards and planting seeds. Children enjoy being with other children although they may play in pairs. Children are beginning to express themselves through painting and drawing as well as through play. Children are enjoying using their physical skills in games and are confident when running and climbing.	Materials for junk modelling Cooking activities Dough and other malleable materials Jigsaws Home corner Construction toys Small world play – e.g. Duplo people Simple board games	Mini gardening tools Skipping ropes Hoops Climbing frame Slide Tricycles Different-sized balls
6–8	Children are confident and can play well with other children. Children are starting to have particular play friends and are able to share ideas about their play. Games that involve rules are played and rules are added and changed as necessary! Most children enjoy physical activity and play organised games. Sometimes this age can be very competitive. Children are also keen on making things – either of their own design or by following instructions.	Creative materials – e.g. junk modelling, crayons, pieces of card and paper Board games Jigsaw puzzles Complex construction toys Books Collections – e.g. stamps, stickers	Balls Hoops Bicycles Roller-skates Skipping ropes Climbing frames Slides Swings

Reproduced from Child Care and Education *by Penny Tassoni, Heinemann Educational, 1998*

Figure 13.3 Activities and equipment suitable for children at different stages of development

DO IT

Recognise the skills the child requires to perform planned activities.

Choose at least three activities that you have carried out with children in your placement, all using different skills. Make a chart giving the age of the children you worked with, the skills the activities required, and notes on how the children coped with the activity. You should also indicate if you had to make any changes as a result of your observations.

Adapting activities to meet specific needs

Activities need careful thought to make them accessible to all. A child may have difficulty joining in because of:

Help !

- cultural issues, for example a Muslim girl may not be able to join in an activity requiring shorts to be worn
- religion – e.g. a Jehovah's Witness would not be able to join in activities that celebrate Christmas
- gender issues – boys may take over a construction activity, because of poor attention to gender issues in the setting, or be pushed out of cooking activities by the girls
- an activity being too boisterous for a timid child
- an activity requiring a skill level they do not possess.

Reassessing an activity to make sure that it is suitable for all the children is often only a case or remembering the basic principles shown in the checklist below.

Good practice: planning activities

✓ Make sure you have a thorough knowledge of the children in the group before you start planning.

✓ Is there enough room for children to move around?

✓ Is the equipment suitable for all children – have you provided a range of sizes of paint brushes, for example?

✓ Is there special equipment for particular children?

✓ Can equipment be reached by all the children, to promote independence?

✓ Do any of the children require practical assistance, e.g. putting on aprons, moving to the table?

✓ Ask children if they need help, rather than waiting for them to ask you.

When you are planning activities that develop a child's creative skills, do not make the mistake of basing your planning on your own cultural or gender identity. You will not meet all needs in this way. Look at the following examples.

- When baking it would be easy to limit your ideas to those you are familiar with – especially as you want to be comfortable with the activity. A simple way of broadening it is to ask a parent from a culture other than yours to be involved.
- Look for books that are in dual languages – e.g. English and Urdu – to appeal to all children in your nursery or school.
- When setting up an interest table, use the opportunity to focus on another culture or race.
- Choose a topic that is popularly viewed as mainly female or male, and deliberately widen the appeal and interest to both genders.

Do it

Plan an activity which has to be adapted to meet the needs of a child to include particular needs, gender, race and cultural differences.

You have been looking for a book to read to the children that can be developed into an activity and you have chosen *Cinderella*. As you read it, you realise that it is based on gender and ability. The wicked stepmother is pretty stereotypical, too. How could you adapt the story, and subsequent activities, to challenge these stereotypes?

Carrying out planned activities

Using equipment and space effectively

Children are cared for in a variety of settings:

- a childminder's home
- church halls and community halls
- adapted buildings used as nurseries
- parts of sports halls
- the child's home
- classrooms in schools
- purpose-built nurseries
- areas of shopping centres.

Some of these areas are easier to arrange for effective care and activities than others. A purpose-built unit will have tables, sinks, toilets, etc. all designed for children, and equipment will have suitable storage. Buildings that are used for other purposes, such as community centres, pose a challenge, as you will probably share storage space with other groups and have to adapt furniture and fittings. However, the size or quality of the space is less important than how it is used. Careful planning can make the most of the available space, and help to ensure that children's needs are met.

Always make sure that:

- entrances and exits are kept clear
- the room is well ventilated and at a temperature between 18° and 21°C
- there is enough space for the activities, and for the children to move around – if space is limited, it is good practice to set out fewer activities at a time
- there is room for wheelchair users to move around
- there are sinks near to 'messy' activities such as painting or dough, and the flooring and tables for these activities are protected or very easy to clean

- the book corner is well lit, with comfortable furniture or a carpet
- the room is easy to clean and is not cluttered with other equipment
- toys, games and equipment are stored effectively, and are easy for the children to access.

The layout of private homes will be affected by the needs of the rest of the family. There may well be babies playing in the same room as older children, so thought must be given to the safety implications of small toys, etc. Possessions that could be broken should be kept well out of reach of the children. Kitchen tables will serve several purposes:

- eating
- playing games
- painting and other creative activities
- cooking
- doing puzzles
- serving as the roof for a home corner.

All settings must have a quiet area where a child can go to relax, perhaps listen to a story or go to sleep. The range of facilities for this will vary from a carpeted corner, a sofa or chairs, to a separate room with cots or beds.

Preparing equipment

Children should never be presented with toys or games that are broken, dirty or have parts missing. They will not enjoy playing with them, they could be dangerous, and a child will be frustrated with a jigsaw that has a piece missing.

Your role is to check toys and equipment before the children have access to them. This should be done as they are put away and again as they are put out for use. Equipment that is broken should be attended to straight away, and broken toys should be thrown away. You should also ensure that everything that will be needed for a particular activity is available and ready for use.

Do It

Prepare equipment and use space effectively.

Draw a plan to scale of your placement. This could be of the room you work in, an overall plan of the building, or both. On the plan indicate the usual layout of the room, with a detailed explanation of the equipment that is regularly used, and where it is placed. Make sure you indicate windows, heating equipment, doors, storage space, toilets, sinks, etc.

Describe the type of building it is and any special features, such as other groups who use it and when.

Key points of health and safety

Health and safety issues were discussed in detail in Chapter 12. It is essential that you keep the principles of health and safety in mind when you are planning and carrying out activities. Remind yourself of the main points by using the following checklist.

> ## Good practice: health and safety checklist
>
> ✓ Is there adequate adult supervision? Are more adults needed for certain activities?
>
> ✓ Is the building secure, to prevent strangers from entering and children from wandering off?
>
> ✓ Are there any hidden dangers in the immediate area – tools, steep steps, badly protected pools?
>
> ✓ If outside, are there any poisonous plants or berries within children's reach?
>
> ✓ Are fire exits clear and extinguishers in place?
>
> ✓ Is the flooring safe – no frayed carpet edges, loose rugs, splinters in wooden floors?
>
> ✓ Is all basic furniture and equipment in good condition, and not liable to be pulled over?
>
> ✓ Are safety items in place – mats under climbing frames, safety gates, childproof locks, and so on?
>
> ✓ Are all toys and games safe to use, and clean?
>
> ✓ Are spills cleaned up immediately?
>
> ✓ Do adults understand they must not have hot drinks in an area where children are playing?
>
> ✓ Is there adequate provision for waste disposal?
>
> ✓ Is there a clear and practical routine for cleaning the setting and equipment?

Being constantly on the alert for possible dangers will help to prevent accidents and illnesses in children. As soon as you spot a potential hazard, do something about it. Remove a broken toy, mop up a spillage, and report anything that you cannot deal with to your supervisor. If you do not do so and a child is injured, you could be held responsible under the Health and Safety at Work legislation.

Do It

Recognise and act on key points of health and safety.

Devise a checklist for your placement to ensure points of health and safety are checked regularly. Your checklist should be divided into daily checks, weekly, monthly checks, and so on. Obtain the details from your supervisor, and write about the procedure for dealing with any risks that are discovered.

Providing guidance, support and supervision during activities

Children should not undertake any activity without the supervision and support of an adult. This is for many reasons, including the following:

- safety – to prevent accidents, to ensure safe usage of equipment
- helping children to start an activity, by explaining to them what the activity involves, perhaps demonstrating it
- providing help when they need it – when they encounter a difficulty or reach a natural pause in an activity

- to support children who need extra assistance
- to keep order in the group, facilitating turn taking and the sharing of equipment
- to help with the ending of the activity, displaying the work, and tidying up
- helping the child to move onto the next activity, game or break.

How guidance and support can be given

There is a difference between offering guidance and support to children and taking over and doing things for them. The best way to learn this skill is to observe experienced people. Guidance and support is about:

- asking if you can help
- offering plenty of praise
- suggesting easier or alternative ways, by asking 'have you tried …?'
- listening to children's thoughts and ideas, asking questions to prompt them
- being a quiet presence during activities
- observing from a distance to avoid intruding, but being ready to step in if needed.

Children need supervision so that they feel secure and protected. The presence of adults will give them the confidence to try activities that are new or difficult. Supervision of children in a care setting is a legal requirement, but it should also be common sense.

DO IT

Provide appropriate guidance/support/supervision of the children during each activity.

If possible, spend one of your sessions in placement shadowing an experienced childcare worker. Make notes on how the worker offers guidance and support to the children he or she is with, and how supervision is provided. Try to decide if the level of guidance and support is appropriate, or whether children sometimes seem 'lost' or over-supported. What are the skills the carer is using? Think about communication skills, practical assistance, demonstration techniques, etc.

Reviewing activity plans

Whenever you plan an activity for a child or group of children you should be completing a planning sheet that also has space to allow you to review it later. Why should you review activities? Because reviewing allows you to reflect on the following points.

1 The success of the activity in achieving your aims.
2 Why it was successful or unsuccessful.
3 Any alterations you need to make next time.
4 Why you needed to make alterations, for example if it was too easy or too hard, or did not suit a child with a physical impairment.
5 Whether the time allowed was long enough or too long.
6 Whether the children enjoyed the activity.
7 Whether the equipment was suitable and adequate.
8 Safety issues.
9 How the activity could be developed for older or younger children.
10 How you would use the activity again in the future.

You will find it helpful to use a form with these headings, perhaps kept in a notebook or file, for the purpose of reviewing activities.

Think it through

Liam planned a game of snakes and ladders with four children aged five. This well-known game offers opportunities for number work, turn taking and sharing. After ten minutes, the game was in uproar, and one little girl was pushed over. The game had to be stopped. In his review, Liam recognised several issues.

1. Four children were too many for the board size – a bigger board would have improved matters.
2. The table he was using was too small to allow space for the children to spread out. A larger table was needed, with the children sitting down.
3. There were long gaps between turns – two dice would have kept the pace moving.
4. The die he used was too small, and he only had one – a larger die would be easier to see, or a card twizzle die. Two dice would have been better.
5. He needed to have a better awareness of potential tensions between the children.

This example of the game of snakes and ladders above shows how even simple activities can be improved. Reviewing a creative activity might need thought about materials, or even the basic plan.

Do it

Review activity plan and identify any changes that would be necessary before repeating the exercise.

Choose an activity the next time you are in placement and write a detailed review of it, using the checklist on page 366. What lessons have you learned from the review?

Reporting on outcomes

Virtually everything children do in school or nursery will have an impact on their skill levels in some way. As a childcare worker you have a responsibility to report on the progress or lack of progress that you see in children, both to your supervisor and to parents or carers.

Schools and nurseries are expected to assess children's progress against attainment targets for schoolchildren and desirable outcomes for pre-schoolers. Senior staff cannot do all the observation and work involved in assessing these attainments, and rely on their support staff for help and information.

It is also important for individual children that you report on outcomes. A child may be making exceptional progress in reading, for example, and need more challenging material, or may be finding some difficulty and need easier material. A child may also need to be assessed for reasons other than academic progress, perhaps on behaviour or emotional reactions.

Make sure that you are aware of the feedback that will be required before you start an activity. If you are in doubt, ask. If a formal assessment sheet must be completed, make a copy of it and record your findings on the copy. You can then complete the sheet in a legible fashion. If there is no formal feedback form, you may find it easier to make notes in a small notebook as you work with the child, or immediately after the activity has finished. Always be factual in your reporting. 'Jolene has read very well today' is vague – it would be far better to say 'Jolene read to page 12, and did not make any mistakes'. Reports of behaviour should be specific – try to avoid terms such as 'disruptive' or 'naughty'.

Reporting to carers

Carers who have left their children with other adults want feedback at the end of the session, because they are genuinely interested in what their child has been doing. Most parents like to hear positive things about their child, so always tell them something positive, even if it is only that the child ate all of his or her lunch. Most children do some positive work – painting a lovely picture, or building a big bridge with bricks. Chapter 14 looks in greater depth at communicating with parents.

DO IT

Report on the outcomes to the supervisors/carers.

Ask your supervisor about all the different reporting methods used in your placement. Using one of them, write a report on the activity you reviewed in the last section. You should show what you will report to your supervisor and what you will report to parents.

Planning outings

Children enjoy and benefit from outings of all descriptions, ranging from going to post a letter, to a full day trip to the seaside or country. Trips and visits fulfil many functions for children.

- They provide new experiences.
- They develop new awareness.
- They build on skills and abilities.

Taking children out from school or nursery is potentially a hazardous occupation, however. The biggest potential for problems lies in being too ambitious. Choose a place to visit:

- that is not too far to travel
- that will not be too tiring for the adults or children
- with plenty of interest and at a suitable level for the age of the children.

Popular places for trips include the following:

- local parks
- museums – particularly hands-on types
- behind the scenes in large shops
- adventure playgrounds.

- farms
- fire stations
- a picnic in the countryside

A successful outing requires a lot of planning, and all those involved should meet to discuss and plan the trip. Parents will want to be convinced that their children will be safe with you. A visit to check the facilities and the potential of the locations should be made before children or parents are told about the trip. When you are planning an outing you must consider all of the factors shown in Figure 13.4.

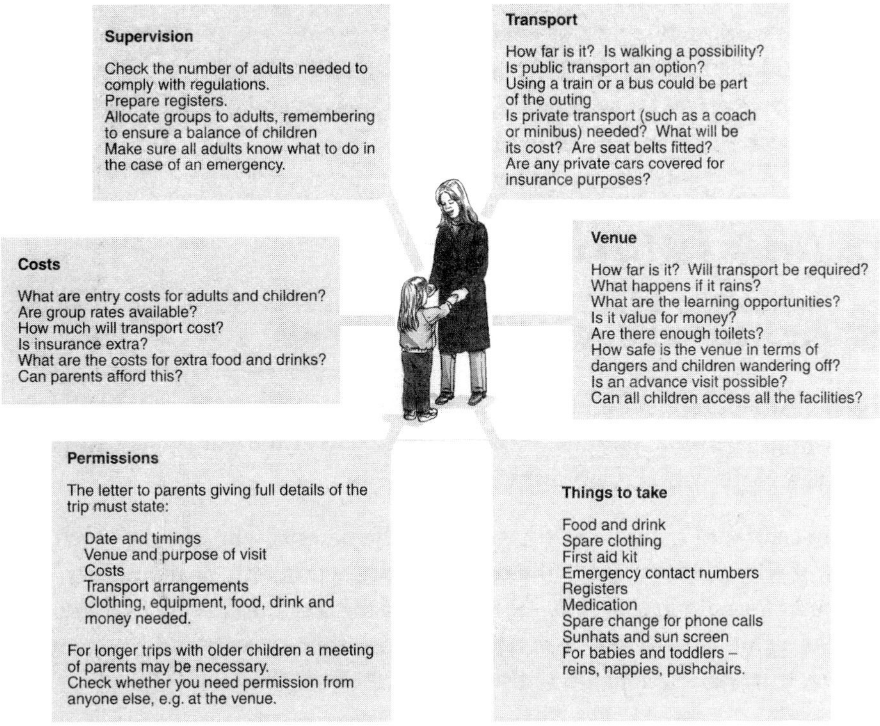

Supervision

Check the number of adults needed to comply with regulations.
Prepare registers.
Allocate groups to adults, remembering to ensure a balance of children
Make sure all adults know what to do in the case of an emergency.

Transport

How far is it? Is walking a possibility?
Is public transport an option?
Using a train or a bus could be part of the outing
Is private transport (such as a coach or minibus) needed? What will be its cost? Are seat belts fitted?
Are any private cars covered for insurance purposes?

Costs

What are entry costs for adults and children?
Are group rates available?
How much will transport cost?
Is insurance extra?
What are the costs for extra food and drinks?
Can parents afford this?

Venue

How far is it? Will transport be required?
What happens if it rains?
What are the learning opportunities?
Is it value for money?
Are there enough toilets?
How safe is the venue in terms of dangers and children wandering off?
Is an advance visit possible?
Can all children access all the facilities?

Permissions

The letter to parents giving full details of the trip must state:

Date and timings
Venue and purpose of visit
Costs
Transport arrangements
Clothing, equipment, food, drink and money needed.

For longer trips with older children a meeting of parents may be necessary.
Check whether you need permission from anyone else, e.g. at the venue.

Things to take

Food and drink
Spare clothing
First aid kit
Emergency contact numbers
Registers
Medication
Spare change for phone calls
Sunhats and sun screen
For babies and toddlers –
reins, nappies, pushchairs.

Figure 13.4 Planning outings

DO IT

Plan an outing for a child/children.

Plan an outing for 12 children aged three and four. Choose somewhere local to you, so that you can visit it and assess all the points you have read about.

Keep your plans in a file with all the appropriate paperwork – letters to parents, to the venue, briefing notes for staff, etc. Ideally you should carry out the trip – discuss this with your supervisor. If you do, write an account of the trip.

14 WORKING IN PARTNERSHIP WITH PARENTS

Working in partnership with parents and carers will be an integral and important part of your role as a childcare worker. By working together with parents, you can help to support the social, emotional and intellectual development of children, and help them to feel secure and happy. A friendly and professional relationship with parents and other carers is essential, and this chapter will help you work towards that aim.

Parents and families

Promoting a positive relationship with parents

Whatever type of family setting a child lives in, he or she will usually relate principally to the carers in that setting. The term 'parents' is used in this chapter to refer to the main carers of the child, regardless of the actual relationship.

A child's parents are central to a child's life. It is usually the parents who decide which playgroup, nursery or school their child will attend. You are acting only as temporary custodian of their child for a limited period – at the end of the day the child goes home with his or her parents. As a childcare worker you have a responsibility to work with parents and build up an effective, trusting relationship with them, for the benefit to the child.

Since the 1970s, parents' and children's rights have been enshrined in various charters and regulations placing a legal responsibility on childcare workers to co-operate with parents in the care of children. Some of the reasons behind this are shown below.

- A child needs the feeling of being at the centre of a group of concerned adults, all with his or her wellbeing at heart.
- A child may be cared for during the majority of the day be adults other than his or her parents. All those involved need to pass information to each other about the child's day and night.
- A child may require some intervention such as work on behaviour. This will only work if all adults collaborate.
- The childcare setting needs the co-operation and permission of parents for outings and activities.
- Some schemes such as home reading schemes will not work without parental involvement.
- Parents have a right to be involved in and consulted about their child's care setting, because they are responsible for their children.
- Parents can and do challenge decisions as a result of their rights under the Parents' Charter, which lays down a framework within which professionals involved with families must work in partnership with parents.

A positive relationship is crucial. Parents must feel they are part of the team caring for their child, never just tolerated. The rest of this chapter considers how the relationship can be made a positive one.

Do It

Identify reasons for the need to promote a positive relationship with parents in the care and education setting.

Does your placement have a clearly displayed charter? Ask to see it and obtain a copy of the Parents' Charter – your placement should have one, or your local education authority will. Read it carefully. Now devise your own version of a parent's charter, making it appropriate for the settings in which you work.

The benefits of parental participation

Parents can bring skills and experiences to a group that can greatly enrich your work with the children. Not only do they have detailed knowledge and understanding of their own child, but they may also have specific skills, for example playing an unusual musical instrument or carpentry skills.

Usually, the first involvement a parent will have is in helping their child to settle. A move to a new nursery, or even a new room, the change to primary school, or the very first start in group care, are all potentially traumatic for both parent and child. Parents should always be encouraged to stay with a child during a defined settling-in period, which will vary with each setting and the age and stage of the child. The benefits to children of a parent being with them at this stressful time include:

- a familiar and loved figure is present in a strange setting
- security
- the parents learn about the routine and activities in the setting, which is reassuring to them
- there is a focus for conversation at home to discuss the setting.

Many childcare settings have an active programme of parental involvement, including:

- regular parent volunteers in schools, assisting with reading, the home corner, putting up displays, routine tasks such as photocopying, or work in the school library
- occasional involvement, for example when baking, on outings, or special occasions such as the Christmas play, help to make the costumes and scenery.
- parents who are central figures in the organisation – in playgroups, or mother-and-toddler groups
- assisting a child who may have some disability or special needs with which the parent prefers to help, such as a child with speech difficulties
- fund-raising – through a support group, parent-teacher association or parents committee.

All parents can offer something to their own child and others – through listening to readers, helping with the painting area, reading stories, or just being a useful extra pair of hands.

Parents who have not always had a very positive experience of childcare settings can benefit from making valued contributions by building their own self-esteem. A child's self-esteem is also improved by the input of his or her parents. You should guard against the risk that children whose parents cannot participate, due to work or other commitments, may feel at a disadvantage.

By participating in their child's care, parents can often learn new skills and knowledge that will benefit the child at home. For example, they may learn:

- ways of initiating play
- new recipes for playdough
- more about child development.

- improved communication skills
- new ways of dealing with unwanted behaviour

Sometimes involvement had advantages for parents because they are spending time outside the home interacting with other people, as well as their child. This is especially the case for parents who are in isolated situations.

DO IT

Explain the benefits to a child and parent of parental participation in group sessions.

Find out the level of parental involvement in your placement. Do staff feel that parents are involved as much as they could be? How could this be improved? Create a booklet for your placement, written for the parents, to encourage parents to come and be involved with their child's care in the setting. Include the advantages to them and to their children. Remember to make it sound fun!

Respecting parents wishes

When parents take their child home at the end of the day, they will continue to care for the child in their way, not yours. If this is widely different, the child may be confused by the inconsistency. Differences may arise for a number of reasons, for example some parents may not mind if their children eat with their fingers or run around at mealtimes whereas you may need the children to sit down. There may be cultural differences concerning clothes, food and age of weaning.

Through effective communication, any potential difficulties about differences of approach can be prevented. A clear explanation of the childcare setting's policies and procedures, given before a child is admitted, will offer parents the opportunity to decide if the philosophy of the setting fits in with their ideas on caring for children. Meetings with parents before admission should encourage parents to provide details about care routines and specific issues of concern.

Some issues are not negotiable. If a parent holds religious convictions that involve dietary restrictions, you would be wrong to challenge them – many Jewish people do not eat pork, for example. Restrictions may also be based on medical conditions – it would be very wrong to allow a child who is diabetic to eat the wrong foods.

The only occasions on which you should consider contravening parents' wishes are those concerning health and safety. For example, allowing a child to play unattended near a pond, or on swings, is unacceptable – if the parents say it doesn't matter, that their child is 'sensible', tell them 'I'm sorry, but it's against health and safety regulations'. If you knowingly allowed a child to be injured by neglecting health and safety, you would be held responsible, even if you were obeying a parent's apparent wishes at the time.

It is also not possible to concur with a parent's wishes when they contravene equal opportunities policies. This is a serious issue that may make the parents reconsider their child's placement, but it is not negotiable.

CASE STUDY LEILA, LUKE, SARAH AND JOEL

Leila, aged three, is about to start at the nursery class in her local primary school. Her family are strict Muslims and Leila wears a shalmar chemise at all times. The head of the nursery likes all children to wear shorts for their time in the gym. Leila's mother is not comfortable talking to the male nursery nurse, as mixing with men other than those in her family is not allowed unless a male relative is present. She is concerned that Leila may not be given a suitable diet, avoiding pork and non-halal meat.

Luke is eight months old and is joining the baby room at a nursery attached to his mother's workplace. He is still fully breast-fed, and his mother intends to come in every four hours to feed him. One of the staff has already commented that he should be on solids.

Sarah, aged 18 months, is the only child of older parents. She is attending your nursery for a short period while her mother goes into hospital. When she came to look around, Sarah's mother was insistent that Sarah was not to be allowed out of the nursery on trips or outings. A regular feature of the toddlers' care is to go out at least once a week to the park or supermarket.

Joel is five and his best friend is Liam. Liam has some difficulty in tasks requiring fine motor skills, and also some degree of learning difficulty. Staff in school are distressed when Joel's father comes to school asking that his son should not be allowed to play with Liam, 'because he is handicapped'.

DO IT

Recognise the need to respect the wishes of the parents in the care of their child.

Work in pairs through the case studies above. For each child, make a list of the potential problems that may result from the parent's wishes. For each point, state why the parent's wishes should be respected and why the parents may feel that way.

Could you talk through any of these issues with the parents? If so, what approach could you take? Try role playing one of the situations.

Why parents may find it difficult to participate

Parents coming into a nursery or school for the first time may feel nervous or anxious before they start. Added to all the natural nervousness involved in a new experience, parents are concerned about the feelings of their child, and not wishing to appear inadequate in front of them or let them down.

There are many other reasons why parents may find it difficult to become part of the group.

- Parents may have had a bad experience of education during their own time at school, and find it difficult to go into a school or nursery to help in their children's education.

They will need reassurance that they are valued as partners in the care of their children.

- They may fear not having adequate skills to be of assistance in the childcare setting. Parents need encouraging to see that they have a wide range of skills and experiences that are of value, e.g. cooking, story reading, musical skills, or talking about their culture.

- Parents may feel intimidated by staff as a result of attitudes and the use of jargon. It is easy to forget that terms such as DLOs, SATs or assessments may mean little to parents, and indeed can make them feel shut out. Giving parents very unimportant tasks, not offering them a cup of coffee or showing them where to put their coats sends a message that can result in parents feeling very unwelcome.

- Parents can feel intimidated by other parents, especially if there is a clique of parents who are already involved in the setting and have developed working relationships with each other and the staff.

- Parents may lack time because of work commitments. This can be very difficult for a child to understand, especially if the parents of their friends spend a lot of time in the school or nursery. Often, there is not an easy solution to this problem.

- Care of other children can impinge on the time parents have available to help in school or nursery. With some thought this can be overcome, perhaps by allowing younger siblings to come into the setting while parents are helping. This can have the additional benefit of allowing the younger child to become accustomed to the group childcare setting.

- Language problems may prevent adequate communication between staff and parents, and may deter parents from offering their services. Bilingual parents can be very helpful to a school or nursery. They can interpret, provide information about their culture, tell stories, make music, and offer an alternative experience to that available from the staff.

- Sometimes cultural issues may prevent involvement – it may not seem to be appropriate to be involved. A lot of work must be done encouraging parents, breaking down barriers, and making parents feel they are partners. Hostility is often due to a lack of understanding of recent changes in education and care, and previous negative experiences at the hands of care professionals.

- If parents have a sense of being tolerated in school or nursery, rather than being welcomed as true partners in their child's care and education, they will soon stop offering their services.

- Parents need to feel a real sense of purpose during their time in nursery or school. Although parents are usually happy to undertake routine jobs, always doing menial tasks such as washing the paint pots will not help them maintain a sense that their time is valued.

Think it through

Think of a time when you have felt very nervous because you have found yourself in a new situation. It could be starting on your college course, starting school, or joining a new club. Do you remember the nervous questions, will I fit in, will anyone talk to me, where do I go, what do I do, will I understand what is going on, and so on?

Identify reasons why a parent may find it difficult to become part of the group.

Brainstorm a list of all the ways that you can think of to encourage parents to become actively involved in the childcare setting you are most familiar with. How many of these ideas are used in your placement?

Sharing information with parents and others

Before a child starts in nursery or at a school it is important that their parents have received all the relevant information. This includes practical details such as:

- address and phone number of the setting
- the staffing structure – names, roles, qualifications
- name of the child's main worker
- opening, closing and holiday times
- fees, and effects of absence on fees
- contact to be informed if the child is ill
- what parents have to provide – nappies, food, money.

Details of the way the setting is organised and the 'spirit' of its way of working should be included, for example:

- how play and learning are organised
- whether there are outings for children, and who is involved in them
- any rules
- how parents can become involved in the setting.

Parents have a right to receive information from the nursery or school once their child is established there. Information should always be given about:

- changes in circumstances – moving to a new class or room, a change in start or finish times.
- planned outings or trips away from school or nursery
- a child's progress or concerns about a child's behaviour
- holidays, teacher or staff training days
- schemes to promote children's learning, e.g. reading at home
- opportunities to view a child's work.

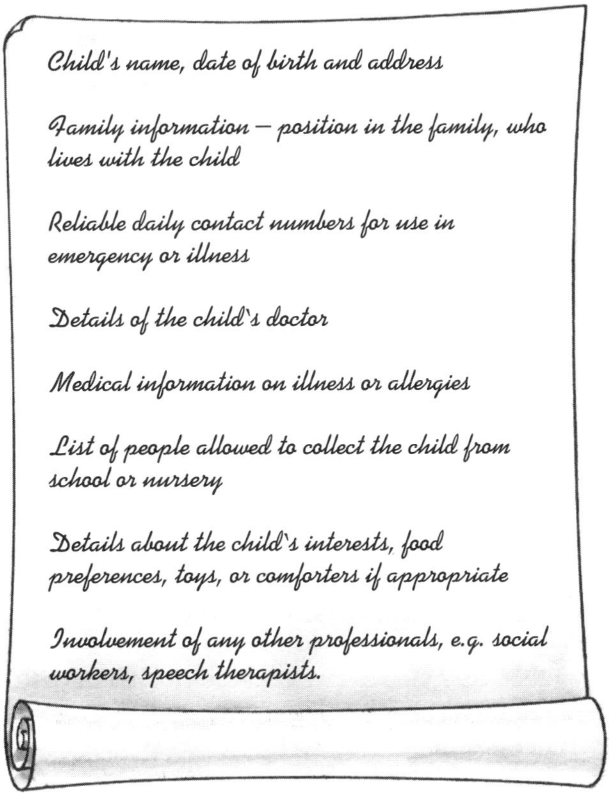

Child's name, date of birth and address

Family information – position in the family, who lives with the child

Reliable daily contact numbers for use in emergency or illness

Details of the child's doctor

Medical information on illness or allergies

List of people allowed to collect the child from school or nursery

Details about the child's interests, food preferences, toys, or comforters if appropriate

Involvement of any other professionals, e.g. social workers, speech therapists.

Figure 14.1 Information parents should provide

Equally, parents have a responsibility to provide the setting with information about their child. Before the child starts at the setting, parents should provide information to help you gain as full a picture of the child's life as possible. This information will include that shown in Figure 14.1.

Do It

Identify information that it is appropriate and right to share with parents and other team members.

Design a form that could be used to share information about a child. It should contain the information you and the parents need to share about the child. It could be designed to be filled in at a child's entry to nursery or school, with a copy kept by both parents and carers. Show it to a parent. Does it contain everything the parent wants included?

Boundaries of responsibilities when working with parents

Shared care

Both parents and carers are very important members of the team in a child's shared care. But remember that parents are usually the legal guardians of their children, and have to make the ultimate decisions about what is best for their child's welfare. Parents usually know their child best, and do not take decisions about their care lightly. But they may need and ask for your professional help and guidance about issues of childcare. Keeping the 'balance of power' steady can sometimes be tricky. Look at this case study to see what can go wrong.

Case study John

Week 1
John, aged two and a half, is to start at nursery. His mother is planning to return to work in a month's time. On his first visit, John stays very close to his mother, who looks around the nursery, asks a lot of questions about it and after half an hour of watching the activities leaves with John to consider if this nursery is suitable for her child.
Think it through – who does the balance of power lie with and why? What might John's mother decide?

Week 2
After a telephone conversation with the owner, John and his mother return with the aim that John will spend an hour at the nursery. He clings to his mother for about 20 minutes, but eventually becomes interested in the activities that are going on. He sits down to join in with story time and songs. His mother stays throughout. Later in the week, John returns with his mother. After about 20 minutes his mother goes out of the room and talks to the owner in her office about fees, etc. John plays quite happily.
Think it through – where does the balance of power lie now?

CASE STUDY JOHN

Week 3

John starts nursery full time. All the staff have been moved round, and no one knows John. He wails miserably as soon as his mother goes, and some days he does not stop crying for some time. It takes a lot of persuading for John to join in any activities. By the time his mother collects him in the evening he is often very tired, and falls asleep in the car. Whenever she asks how John is settling and whether she can come in to see him, his mother is always told he is fine and so does not need to visit. She puts his quietness down to tiredness and a change in routine.

Think it through – now who holds the balance of power?

John's mother begins to be concerned when he starts waking a lot at night and refusing to use his potty. Mentioning this to the nursery staff, she gets very little response. Whenever she asks what John has been doing during the day, all she gets is a vague answer that he has been 'playing', and she starts to realise that she knows very little about John's days. After careful thought John is removed from the nursery and temporarily spends time with his grandparents. His mother decides to look for another nursery where she feels that she will be able to share in her son's time.

DO IT

Describe the carer's role and that of the parent related to shared care.

In the case study above, at first the nursery seemed to be acting in an appropriate manner to share the care. What went wrong? Try to identify how the staff should have behaved to help him settle.

Consulting parents

In the previous case study, the staff had not given much thought to checking with John's mother about his favourite toys, comfort objects, or routines. Instead of just allowing his mother to sit in the room with John for a short time, the staff should have been active in seeking out information about John's routine and habits. Look at the table below for details of a possible day in the nursery for John.

Time/routine/activity	Information needed before child starts in the setting	Information needed on a daily basis
Arrival at nursery	Pet names for John, comfort object, how he reacts early in the morning, usual breakfast. Stage reached in potty training. Usual home routines. Level of independence in tasks such as hand washing, going to toilet, feeding.	How he slept last night, what he had for the previous evening's meal, breakfast. How potty training is going. Anything out of the ordinary in home circumstances or his routine.
Free play	Favourite toys, games, activities.	Any new activities, etc. at home.
Snacks and lunch time	Favourite foods, dislikes, allergies. Cultural influences on diet – vegetarian, religious influences. Way of drinking – cup, feeder cup, etc. Usual level of appetite.	Any digestive upsets, change in appetite.

Time/routine/activity	Information needed before child starts in the setting	Information needed on a daily basis
Story time, TV time	Interests, favourite stories, experiences.	New interests, current favourite book, favourite TV programme at home.
Rest time	Routine and timing for daily routine. Preferred type of bedding, any allergies to feathers, etc. Whether frightened of the dark. Comforters used at sleep times.	Any changes to rests.
Nappy changing, toileting	Type of nappy used, creams, potty routines.	Any nappy rash, changes in toilet habits, any diarrhoea.

If you regularly exchange information with parents they will feel that you have a genuine interest in their child as a whole person, and that he or she is not just another child who happens to be in your group in the nursery or class.

DO IT

Plan a routine day for a child/children in your care and identify the areas where parental consultation is required.

Choose two different children in your group at your placement. Try to choose two of a slightly different stage of development. Without breaching confidentiality, devise a chart similar to the one in the table above, personalising it with the information you have about each child and the consultations that you or your colleagues have with the parents on a daily basis. Do you think you are consulting with the parents as much as possible? If not, what is missing?

Seeking professional advice

Parents are usually committed to the best interests of their child. Often, they may ask your opinion about an issue of concern, for example their child's hearing, health issues such as a rash or failure to put on weight, or problems with their child's behaviour. Whatever your opinion, always advise a concerned parent to seek appropriate professional advice – e.g. take the child to the doctor, or ask a solicitor or health visitor.

If you are concerned about some aspect of a child's care or development, it is important that you pass this information on to the parents with a suggestion as to how to follow the matter up. Be careful about referring a child to a professional without the parent's knowledge – this is not within your responsibilities, except in very rare circumstances that we will discuss below.

Remember

Always check with your supervisor first before discussing a child with his or her parents.

Read the case studies below and think about what you should do next.

CASE STUDY ASHRA, SARAH AND JAY

Ashra is three, and has been in your group for three weeks. You are worried because he often seems to ignore you when you call his name or ask him to do something. His speech is not easy to understand, and he seems to have a constantly runny nose.

Sarah is five and in the reception class. Sarah seems to have few friends, and is often the cause of disruptions in the home corner. You have seen her thumping and nipping another child, and she seems incapable of sitting still.

Jay is six. He is very thin and withdrawn, and often comes to school smelling of urine and appearing dirty. At changing time for PE, you notice some very odd bruises on his back that seem to be in the shape of buckle marks.

What do you think you should do about each of these cases? Check below.

Ashra would appear to have a hearing impairment, and it would be helpful to ask his parents if they have noticed it, and suggest he should be taken to his GP.

Sarah's problems should likewise be discussed with her parents, and the carer might suggest that she is referred to a psychologist.

Jay's situation should be discussed with your supervisor and a referral made to social services, without discussing the situation with the parents first.

A simple rule is that if you are in doubt, you should advise parents to seek a professional opinion. The nursery or school may sometimes arrange the referral, but usually the parents need to do this.

In cases of suspected abuse, for example, strange bruises on the child, it is essential that immediate steps are taken to protect the child. As a junior member of staff you should speak to your supervisor, who will then follow local policy.

Most professionals associated with children are happy to give informal advice. It is very useful to build up contacts with speech therapists, social workers, health visitors, psychologists, etc. to whom you can turn for informal advice and guidance.

DO IT

Identify situations that may arise which would require the carer to seek professional advice.

Talk to your supervisor about the professionals who are involved in your setting. Find out about all their roles, and identify the types of issues you would refer to them. If you can, mention examples of issues being referred to professionals.

Sharing information

In Chapter 1 you looked at the importance of verbal and nonverbal communication skills. These apply to all types of communication in the childcare field. Remember the important points:

- maintain appropriate eye contact
- don't interrupt when the other person is speaking
- show you are listening by nods and smiles
- give feedback in summary form of what has been said
- if you are asked a question to which you do not know the answer, say so – don't try to cover up lack of knowledge
- don't shout back if a parent or child starts to shout at you – talk quietly and calmly, show you are listening, and try to move the conversation to a private place.
- think about your body language – don't stand talking with folded arms, or appear distracted by other activities
- be sensitive to communication barriers – for example, an accent that is difficult to understand or someone with poor hearing – have an interpreter present if needed, or use pictures and visual aids
- never belittle the other person
- if in doubt, refer to a person of higher authority than yourself
- never gossip – either to or about a parent, child or colleague.

Another important rule is always to tell the truth. Parents need to be informed, confidentially, if their child is behaving in a manner that causes concern. Think about how and where you talk to parents. Most settings have a staff room or interview room to which you can invite parents for a private chat.

Important information should always be easy to understand, clear, and if necessary repeated in some way.

Practical ways of communicating information

The following list shows some ways in which information can be given to parents and other carers.

- Posters in the collection area.
- Notes sent home with the children.
- Use of an interpreter to speak to parents.
- Discussions when parents collect their children.
- Booklets of information.
- A meeting.
- Articles in the local newspapers.
- Messages through community representatives.
- Information on the local radio or TV.

Do It

Demonstrate how to communicate information to parents, other professionals and children in an appropriate manner.

Gather details of all the methods of communicating information used in your placement.

Look at communicating with children, their parents and other professionals. You might like to make a list split it into these three sections. Try to include examples of leaflets, letters, etc. that have been produced in your placement. Evaluate the effectiveness of the information methods, and describe how you think things could be improved.

Information to pass on to parents

Young children learn and do something new every day. Even though their parents are not with them all day, they will want to know what their child has been doing. Has a little one taken a first step or said a first word? You have a valuable role in passing on information at the end of the day. Information that could be passed on to parents includes that relating to physical care, activities and achievements and any changes or new information.

Physical care information

- Any accident or illness that occurs to the child during his or her time with you.
- When a child is on regular medication, e.g. for asthma, how often it was used.
- Food eaten during the day, and any problems with food that might have occurred.
- The amount of sleep taken.
- Issues involving physical care such as nappy rash with a baby, or the success or otherwise of toilet training.

Activities and achievements

- Visitors to the setting, or outings.
- New achievements, such as a first step or being able to read at a higher level.
- Activities done by the child – painting, models, etc., which should be taken home if possible.
- Anecdotes about incidents during the day, such as how the child helped other children or staff.

Changes and new information

- Any changes in behaviour.
- Any concerns about the child.
- Information relevant to the next day in the care setting, so that parents can ensure children are prepared and suitably equipped.

This type of information transfer is particularly important in settings with the under fives. Their memory span and communication skills may not enable them to tell their parents everything. Even with older children, however, it is important to make sure that parents are kept fully informed.

DO IT

Identify the type of information which should routinely be passed on to parents at the end of a childcare session.

When you are next in your placement, make notes for three children on the information you will give their parents at the end of the day. Were you able to pass it on to them? Evaluate the usefulness of the information you gave and the way you gave it.

Building up trust with parents and teams

Confidentiality is essential in any care setting. When parents are in a school or nursery, they may confide personal information to staff. You would not disclose information about a child unless it was professionally necessary, and the same applies to confidential information about parents. Personal information about parents should not be the topic of gossip in the staffroom, and should never be repeated to other parents.

In an early years setting you have to exchange information with other members of staff to help each other operate effectively. Because life is busy in a nursery or school, this exchange of information may take place in the room with children. Ensure that parents are not able to overhear such conversations, or you will be guilty of breaching confidentiality.

You will often receive very personal information from parents. Some information has to be shared with others, even if the parent has indicated that he or she does not want the information to be passed on. Some examples of this situation are given below.

- If a parent confides that her partner is hitting their children, who are already on the child protection list, you cannot keep the information a secret. You must make it clear that you will have to pass it on to your manager.
- If a parent confides that she intends to leave her partner, this poses a different dilemma. This information may not involve the child being put directly at risk, but it will have an emotional impact of the child. You may feel that you have to discuss this confidentially with your manager.
- Information about health problems in a child that may affect his or her performance or give rise to a medical emergency in school or nursery must be passed on.
- Changes in the child's circumstances that may affect his or her behaviour, e.g. a death in the family or a parent losing a job, should also be communicated to the necessary people.

Consider the guidelines given below about confidentiality in a childcare setting.

Good practice: confidentiality

✓ Parents need to feel that confidentiality is respected when they are working in close partnership with carers.

✓ Everyone concerned must be aware of the rules of 'professional confidentiality' – that is, which information must be shared with a line manager, such as issues relating to child protection.

✓ Let parents know that you may have to share some information with your line manager, before they start to talk about confidential issues.

✓ Never gossip about parents, children or other member of staff.

✓ Never discuss one parent with another parent.

✓ Do not make value judgements about a child or a family, but always respect a person's culture and identity.

✓ Remember to share information about a child's dietary needs, allergies, who collects the child, and any concerns with the rest of the care team.

Most childcare settings hold a lot of personal information about their charges. It is important that everyone concerned is aware of the requirements of the Data Protection Act. This allows people to view the information that is held on file about them, or their children. Remember this when you are committing your thoughts to paper or computer – you must report facts and events objectively, factually and accurately. Parents should be made aware that they have rights under the legislation, and reassured that all files are kept in a secure environment.

Do it

Explain why confidentiality of sensitive information is essential to build up trust when working with parents and in a team.

Find out how your placement ensures confidentiality and the protection of information. Make notes, and discuss the matter with your tutor and supervisor.

Working as a member of a caring team

Local authority requirements

Chapter 12 discussed local authority requirements for the registration of childcare settings. You will remember that all childcare settings have to be inspected by local authorities, to ensure they are healthy, safe and legal. To help them meet the requirements of their inspections, all local authorities produce guidelines for childcare settings. The guidelines state what the local authority needs to find out about in the inspection, and cover these points:

- the principles of day care
- children's and parents' rights
- equal opportunities policies and procedures
- children with special needs
- behaviour policies
- precautions covering infectious diseases and illness
- storage and administration of medicines
- the fit person to care for children – personal qualities and grounds for disqualification
- discipline and child protection
- diet and food hygiene
- safety and first aid
- the importance of play and conversation
- partnership with parents
- child development
- reading lists for further study
- general registration criteria and principles
- required and relevant qualifications and ratios for staff.

Think it through

What do these guidelines really mean? In groups, choose some of them and discuss them. Report back to the whole group what you think they mean and give examples.

Detailed sections for each care setting are given covering:

- full day care
- sessional day care
- child minding
- private nursery schools
- open access facilities such as creches, etc.
- day care for school-aged children under eight.

The registration system is based on the concept of 'registered persons', and that all such registered persons are 'fit' to care for children. A local authority has to be satisfied that all people who are likely to come into contact with children under eight years old have:

- experience or suitable qualifications in working with children
- an ability to provide consistent and warm care
- an understanding of and good attitude towards multi-cultural issues and equal opportunities
- commitment to treat all children as individuals and with respect
- good physical health
- mental stability and integrity
- no known involvement with criminal cases involving abuse or other serious offences.

Do it

Describe the requirements of the local authority in a childcare setting.

Your placement should have a copy of your local authority requirements. Ask if you can read it or discuss it with the manager of your placement. Does anything in it surprise you?

Roles and responsibilities

The basic role of any childcare worker or parent is to help the children in their care to develop to their full potential. A prime responsibility of all such people is to ensure a child's safety and to see that all their basic needs are met.

Think back to the information on human needs given in Chapter 2. Children need help to achieve these, but the amount of assistance they need decreases as they grow and develop.

Parents

Parents' roles in a childcare setting have been discussed in the earlier parts of this chapter. Parents do not give up all responsibility to their child's carers when they leave the child at the door. They have a duty to inform the carers about issues relevant to their child and his or her safety and welfare. Parents have a responsibility to make sure, to the best of their ability, that their child is being cared for in a satisfactory manner.

General principles relating to roles and responsibilities

There are several golden rules that should underpin your work in the childcare field. The basic principles could be summarised into the following ten commandments.

Caring for children: the 10 commandments

1. You have a responsibility for the care of the children, shared with their parents. Always remember that all children have parents or guardians who are the final decision-makers about their child.
2. Always consult about care needs, with the child if possible, and always with the parents. Respect the wishes of parents and child.
3. Always behave in a manner that shows your respect for the child and his or her culture and background.
4. Always challenge discrimination and stereotyping behaviour.
5. Have a child's safety foremost in your thoughts when planning for his or her needs.
6. Always keep information that is given to you confidential, if that is the wish of the parents and it is appropriate to do so. Know when you must pass on information.
7. Be willing and ready to seek help, either from your line manager or outside agencies, especially if you see other staff behaving inappropriately.
8. Never force a child to do anything against his or her wishes.
9. Always try to praise a child's positive behaviours and minimise the negative.
10. Enjoy your work with young children – your enthusiasm will be infectious!

Being a nanny

Working in a child's home as a nanny carries a different responsibility from that of a childcare worker in a nursery, for instance. As a nanny you are likely to have sole charge of a child or children. Although there are no legal controls as to who can become a nanny, you have a duty to be realistic about your abilities. Being a nanny can be a very isolated job – you may be in someone else's home, alone for most of the day, and with little contact with the outside world. Working overseas as a nanny can be even more isolating, as you will be living in a different culture, even if it is an English-speaking one. You have a responsibility to be realistic about your role and its boundaries, and the personal skills and abilities you need to cope. It is also important to ensure that your contract is clear about your duties, pay and conditions, and that you are happy with them. Before accepting a post as a nanny, do a lot of research, asking other nannies about their jobs, talking to nannies previously employed by the family, and applying for jobs through reputable agencies who will back you if things do go wrong. You might like to think about cases that have been highlighted in the media when things went dreadfully wrong.

Childminders

Childminders have some similarities to nannies, in that they are based at home. However, they are in their own homes, and as you have seen they are covered by strict regulations. Very often, childminders care for a mixture of children, some of their own, and others from two or more families. There are several possible areas of conflict for a childminder:

- the risk of neglecting their own children in favour of the others
- the risk of favouring their own children
- resentment from their own children about lack of full attention
- refusal of their own children to share toys, etc.
- parents having opposing views on aspects of care.

Just like nannies, childminders may feel isolated, but they do have the advantage of being in their own home, in their familiar community with friends and neighbours nearby for support. Many local authorities encourage support groups of childminders, and many offer training groups.

DO IT

Describe the role and responsibilities of a nanny, of the parent, childminder and carers in a group setting.

Reconsider the roles and responsibilities of different childcare workers. Using the title of each role as headings, make a list of the responsibilities of each and identify incidents and issues that may make it difficult to fulfil these. Describe how a person in each of the roles might deal with such conflicts.

The childcare worker as a member of the caring team

If you work as a child carer in a group setting, you have different roles and responsibilities. You have a responsibility to:

- the children in your care
- your fellow team workers
- the children's parents
- the organisation that employs you, and pays your wages.

Sometimes it can be difficult to fulfil all these responsibilities, as there is potential for conflict of loyalties.

The following list shows the main responsibilities of a care worker in a group setting:

- to follow the organisation's policies and procedures
- to carry out instructions from supervisors and managers
- to report accurately on the progress of children
- to try to minimise conflict in the team by working effectively with other team members
- to adhere to rules about confidentiality and the boundaries of responsibility at all times
- to pass on all appropriate enquires to the relevant person
- to respect all parents and children
- to respect all other team members.

DO IT

Explore the role of a childcare worker as a member of the caring team.

Using the list of responsibilities given above, discuss with a colleague the best ways to promote good teamwork in childcare workers. Present your ideas to the rest of your group.

Improving your performance

Throughout your training as a childcare worker you will have been receiving feedback on your performance. This will have come from:

- college tutors, about your written work and practical performance
- supervisors in placements on a daily or weekly basis, both informally and formally
- a combination of both in the form of a report on your performance in placement
- parents and children, in the manner in which they respond to you
- yourself, as you have evaluated events and activities throughout your training.

It is important to recognise that no one is perfect, or ever will be! But it is very useful to develop the skill of constantly reviewing your performance. After a major activity, and at least at the end of every day, ask yourself the questions in the following checklist.

Good practice: recognising strengths and weaknesses

✓ What have I done today that went well?

✓ Why did it go well?

✓ What has gone less well?

✓ Why did this happen?

✓ Did I ensure that I met the needs of all the children I worked with today?

✓ How could I have improved this?

✓ Have I communicated effectively with everyone – other carers, professionals, parents and children?

✓ How could I have improved?

Following this checklist and listening to feedback from formal and informal reports should help you to identify your strengths and weaknesses. Admit that you have weaknesses, but even more importantly recognise and value your strengths.

Think it through

In a group of four (ask your tutor to divide you into groups according to personality, to achieve a balanced group) compare the qualities you feel you each have, and your weaknesses in relation to childcare. Does your opinion of your own weakness match that of your colleagues, or do they see your weakness as a strength?

It is useful to ask other people for their honest, objective opinion of your methods of working with children and parents. It is perfectly acceptable to ask a colleague in your placement what he or she thinks of planned activities – in fact, while you are training you should always be doing this, and afterwards asking what the person thought of your progress. Ask the children what they thought, too – but be prepared for some less-than-welcome answers.

Having identified your strengths and weaknesses, it is important that you do something with that knowledge. As a student, you should be drawing up an action plan to discuss with your tutor about ways you intend to overcome your weaknesses, and build on your strengths. Look at the example in Figure 14.2.

Area for development	Action needed	Where to get help	By when
Difficulty keeping interest when reading stories to a large group	More practice, and ideas to maintain interest	Observe class teacher. Ask to try with smaller group	End of the month
Ideas for working on themes	Read relevant material Attend planning meetings in nursery	Supervisor, head of placement	Before the end of term
Tend to run out of ideas to encourage children to tidy away at the end of a session	Observe experienced practitioners	Supervisor	Ongoing
Enjoy working with children with communication problems; seem to have a special skill in this.	Develop more methods of working	Read relevant material Observe other 'experts'	Ongoing

Figure 14.2   An example of an action plan

DO IT

Recognise own strengths and weaknesses and make positive suggestions about improving own performance.

Review all your reports, work, evaluations, etc. and draw up an action plan similar to the one in Figure 14.2. It will be helpful to brainstorm areas of strengths and weaknesses first, and ask your colleagues, friends and supervisors for their views. When you are developing your action column, be realistic, and don't try to achieve too much at once!

CARE OF BABIES

This chapter concentrates on the knowledge needed to help you work with babies under a year old. One of the best ways of learning how a baby develops is to observe a real one in action! If you know someone who has recently had a baby or there is a young baby in your placement, ask the parents if you could visit from time to time and ask questions about the baby as he or she progresses over the first year of life. Explain that you will keep all information confidential, and will share your notes, exercises, etc. with the parents. A log of your interviews and photographs can be used to create a guide to the baby's first year, and you might like to give it to the parents when you have finished your course.

If you do have this opportunity, all of the 'Do it' exercises in this chapter could be based on your study. Of course, using other examples too from time to time will enhance your work, and help you to understand the wide diversity seen in the growth and development of babies.

Care routines

Stages of development up to 12 months

Babies' growth and development in their first year is at a greater pace than at any other time of their lives. Weight will triple on average; length or height will almost double, and head circumference will increase by 50 per cent.

Most babies born at full term weigh between 2.5 and 4 kg and measure between 45 and 52 cm in length. Head circumference average 33 to 37 cm.

Age	Weight (kg)	Height (cm)	Head circumference (cm)
Birth	2.5 to 4.0	45 to 52	33 to 37
3 months	4.5 to 6.5	54 to 64	38 to 43
6 months	6.0 to 9.0	60 to 72	42 to 46
9 months	7.0 to 10.5	65 to 74	43 to 48
12 months	8.0 to 12.0	68 to 78	45 to 49

Try plotting the figures from the table on graphs to see the pattern shown by growth. Graphs have been made from the measurements of thousands of babies showing the average range babies should fall into if they are growing normally. These are called 'centile charts' and are a useful guide for childcare professionals. If you have a baby to study, start a chart for each measurement of growth and plot the stages as you receive reports of each.

In Chapters 10 and 11, you looked at the developmental milestones of all children from birth to eight years of age. Look again at the principles and rates of development on pages 269 to 271. The principles are the same for babies.

To specialise in the care of babies you need to know more detail about development in the first year of life. A thorough knowledge of development will help you to plan appropriate care routines for a baby.

Age of baby	Stage of development	Associated care routines
Birth to 4 weeks	**Physical** Lies supine with head to one side (tonic neck reflex) Large jerky movements of limbs Head lags when pulled up to sit All primitive reflexes present **Intellectual** Fixes on faces and bright objects Reacts to loud sounds **Social and emotional** Enjoys feeding and cuddling Needs to suck for comfort as well as food Quietens when picked up Sleeps most of the time	Needs firm but gentle handling, supporting neck Constant holding when awake Lots of cuddles, touch, talking and singing during and in addition to feeding, bathing, etc. Playing music Use bright colours and mobiles within 8–10 in of face Feed on demand, no set routine – this will provide emotional security through cuddling in addition to providing food
8 weeks	**Physical** Controlled movements starting to replace reflex responses Turns from side to back Starts to lift head when on front **Intellectual** Begins to respond to adult's voice, looks for sounds Smiles in response to adults, starts to coo and squeal with pleasure **Social and emotional** Cries can be identified for different needs Still enjoys sucking Recognises familiar face	Use baby chair or carry around to allow baby to watch everyday activity Put bright pictures near the cot, use mobiles and chimes Talk and sing to baby, allow time for response Still lots of physical contact, massage, etc. Feeding may have a pattern – probably still needing night feeds Starts immunisation programme
3 months	**Physical** Movements smoother and continuous Waves arms with hands open Kicks Head lag disappearing When placed on front, lifts head and upper chest **Intellectual** Visually very alert, moves head to gaze around Watches own hands and fingers Recognises feeding bottle Holds rattle placed in hand for a few moments Vocalises well Quietens to sound of bell or rattle **Social and emotional** Sucks in response to feed preparation Fixes gaze on person feeding Reacts to familiar situations with coos and smiles Enjoys bathing and care routines	Will enjoy freedom of activity now – on changing mat without nappy, or on blanket Enjoys baby gym activity Introduce new noises, visual experiences, e.g. through music, animal noises Change pictures by cot, plays with different mobiles, showing things around and outside the house, nursery Enjoys lots of conversation from carers and songs Starts to enjoy soft squeaky toys, range of textures and sounds from toys Starts to enjoy looking at picture books – adult pointing out names Will enjoy bathing, use of toys Still needs lots of physical contact, gentle rough and tumble games May start to sleep through the night, routine should be developing – daytime naps, evening bath, story time, etc. May start introduction of solid foods Second immunisation (third at 5 months)

Age of baby	Stage of development	Associated care routines
6 months	**Physical** On back, lifts head to look at own feet Sits with support and turns head to look around Lifts arms up to be picked up Pulls self to sit up when holding hands Kicks strongly with alternate legs Rolls over from front to back and starting to from back to front May sit alone for a few seconds On front, lifts head and chest well up, supporting self on extended arms Held standing, bounces up and down **Intellectual** Very curious, attention easily attracted Vocalises with sing-song and double syllables Laughs, chuckles and squeals Responds to different tones of voice Reaches for and grasps small toys Starting to use single hand Takes everything to mouth to explore Finds own feet interesting **Social and emotional** Pats breast or bottle with hand when feeding Reaches for offered toy immediately Passes objects from hand to hand regarding them closely Starting to show shyness with strangers – develops at about 7 months to stranger shyness. Not happy when main carer is out of sight	Attention to safety issues essential – start of mobility Look at safety gates, fireguards, plug covers, etc. Needs strapping into high chair, pram Development of physical play – activities to encourage rolling over Knee games – e.g. Humpty Dumpty Toys needing manipulation start to be enjoyed – activity centres Also enjoys play with everyday objects – pots and pans, empty boxes, rustly paper Bath best at night – starting to get grubby during the day from floor play and feeding Weaning well established eating wide range of mashed foods, losing dependence on milk Enjoys outings to the shop, park Routines firmly established – clear daytime nap times May sleep all night
9 months	**Physical** Sits alone for up to 15 minutes Leans forward to pick up toys and can turn body sideways without falling over Rolls or squirms across the floor, may try to crawl Pulls self to standing on furniture, but cannot lower self When held standing, moves feet in steps **Intellectual** Reaches out to grasp objects with one hand, passes them from hand to hand Looks at new object before grasping Points at distant objects with index finger Holds string on toys, etc. in scissor fashion to pull Picks up small items with finger and thumb – 'inferior pincer grasp' Releases toy by dropping, cannot put down voluntarily Looks in right direction for falling toys – start of 'casting' Vocalises as communication, shouts attract attention to Babbles in long strings of syllables – e.g. dad-dad-dad Understands no and bye-bye Imitates coughs, 'brr'	Safety aspects increasing in importance – very mobile Allow using feeder cup alone, offering spoon when feeding As many finger foods as possible Do not rush in practising activities Allow choice of activity, e.g. building bricks, post it boxes, play with safe household objects Give plenty of chance to copy activities – building bricks, finger and hand games Offer changing variety of items and activities to stack, bang, build, roll on, look at, listen to Continue to widen experience of the world – feeding the ducks, visits to farms, walks in the country Respect child's fear of strangers – don't force to accept new people Respect lack of concept of object permanence – has not yet grasped that if carer goes out of room he or she has not gone forever – will be distressed, so take child with you if possible Continue to widen range of foods, tastes in diet

Age of baby	Stage of development	Associated care routines
	Immediately locates sounds in hearing tests (3 feet from ear) **Social and emotional** Can hold, bite and chew on finger food Tries to grasp spoon when being fed Throws back head and body when annoyed Very wary of strangers, clings to familiar people Plays peep-bo, and tries to clap hands Holds out toy to adult but cannot let go yet Finds toy that is partly hidden while watching – very early stage of concept of object permanence	
12 months 	**Physical** Sits alone indefinitely, can rise to sitting from lying down Crawls or shuffles rapidly Pulls to stand and walks round furniture, side stepping (cruising) Can drop to sitting Walks with one or both hands held May stand, walk alone or crawl upstairs – at average age 13 to 14 months **Intellectual** Has neat pincer grip for tiny objects Drops and throws toys deliberately and watches them fall – 'casting' Looks in the right – place for toys that have rolled out of sight Points with index finger at items of interest Recognises familiar people from 20 feet Uses both hands freely, starting to show preference for one hand Holds cube in each hand and bangs them together Knows own name Jargons loudly in conversational tones – containing most vowels and many consonants Understands several words in context – dog, dinner, walk, and simple instructions with gestures, such as 'come to daddy', 'say bye-bye' **Social and emotional** Drinks from cup with little help, holds spoon and tries to use it Holds out arm to put in sleeve and foot in shoe when being dressed Mouthing becomes less frequent Puts bricks into box when shown, rattles spoon in cup without being shown Gives toys to adults on request Plays pat-a-cake, waves bye-bye on request and later without prompting Sits or stands without support when being dressed Likes to be within sight and sound of familiar adults	Keep thinking of safety Encourage walking skills – push-along toys, furniture for cruising Use of sand, water and paint with supervision Offer books with thick pages – will enjoy turning Continue to extend and explore language, music with stories, songs, rhymes Encourage displays of affection Encourage self-feeding using cup and spoon May start to lose interest in food with increasing mobility Distract wherever possible from undesired behaviour Use a firm 'no' if necessary Make a game of dressing Offer range of experiences through feely-type toys, toys that make things disappear, such as posting objects Lots of songs and action games, with singing and hand movements

---

Do it

Describe the stages of development of a baby 0–12 months.

Describe the main changes you would expect to see in a baby, from his or her birth to 12 months. You should look at changes from birth to three months, then to six months, then to one year. Base your observations on a real child if possible.

Care routines

In their first year, babies' routines are weighted towards their physical care needs. Providing for their intellectual, social and emotional needs is a natural development from providing physical care. It is almost impossible to think of feeding or changing a baby without interacting with the baby, playing games or showing him or her interesting things to look at.

A routine for a baby is not a fixed plan. In an average day a baby may eat, sleep, get rid of bodily waste, be kept clean, be dressed, have some fresh air, have an outing, go to the clinic for weighing, play, and have plenty of cuddles.

In Chapter 10 we saw that all children do not have the same routines. In the first year babies' routines will change dramatically, due to their changing needs. In the first few weeks of life a baby may need to be fed, changed and allowed to sleep. By 12 months, a baby spends more than 12 hours awake and is actively learning new skills, demanding entertainment, and socialising. The routine is likely to be very different from when he or she was a few weeks old.

When planning routines for babies, the following checklist will be useful.

Good practice: checklist for babies

✓ Feeding requirements

✓ Sleeping requirements

✓ Home-based, or at a childminders or nursery?

✓ Time parents go to work

✓ Family mealtimes

✓ Carer's routine – especially if with a childminder or relatives

✓ Visits to clinics

✓ Needs of other children

✓ Routine of nursery

✓ Time for play

✓ Bath time

✓ Nature of child – is he or she more lively in the morning or evening?

✓ Parents' wishes

✓ Changes, such as illness in the baby

Planning a routine may appear to be much easier if you are starting from the basis of the nursery where you work – nurseries have routines of their own. However, always remember that each baby is an individual. It is no use trying to make a baby fit into the routine of the baby room, if his or her needs do not match it. The result will be a miserable baby, and desperate staff.

Do It

Plan a safe and stimulating care routine for babies at three different developmental stages.

Plan a routine for a baby at birth, three months and nine months – highlighting the changes that have occurred in the baby's needs and requirements. You should include physical care, play needs and emotional and social care. Again, it would be ideal if you could describe the exact routine of a particular child.

Communicating with parents

The reasons a baby is receiving day care will vary, but very often the only parent or both of the parents are working. You will see and hear various 'authorities' stating their opinions on the issue of working mother or single parents, and you will have your own views. Part of your professional skill is to make sure that your own views, even if they conflict with the situation, are not made apparent.

Parents who use the services of childcare professionals to look after their baby may feel guilty that they are not caring for the baby themselves. You need to be sensitive to this and think of ways to involve the parents as much as possible.

Good practice: working with parents

✓ Before the baby starts in nursery, or before you start as a nanny, ask the parents for the baby's routine. Ask about feeding patterns, sleep times, favourite play activities, and so on.

✓ Check with parents about their views on diet if the baby is weaning, the use of TV for entertainment, and any cultural issues that may affect the baby, such as soya milk feeds for babies of vegan parents.

✓ Always ask permission for intended outings and visits before the event.

✓ Keep a chart or other record detailing everything the baby has done that day – feeds taken, sleep time, number of dirty nappies, outings, toys played with, and so on.

✓ Always record any change from the norm, particularly any sign of illness or unusual behaviour, however trivial this may seem, and tell the parents.

✓ At the start of your time with the baby, ask the parents what sort of night the baby has had, did the baby take all of his or her feed, seem comfortable, have a dirty nappy yet, etc.

✓ Before you finish your shift, give verbal feedback to the parents on the type of day the baby has had, of any changes in routines, etc.

✓ If possible, have a camera on hand to record anything that will interest the parents, such as activities in the nursery and outings.

Particularly in the early weeks of leaving their baby with a carer, parents may feel that they want to telephone during the day to ask about their child. This is perfectly normal and acceptable – never feel that you are being checked up on in any way. When parents are comfortable with the care arrangements, phone calls will reflect only their wish to keep in contact with their child's day.

When to contact parents

There are times when you should contact the baby's parents, for example:

- if the baby is ill
- if the baby is behaving out of character in any way
- if there is an unplanned outing, and the parents would be anxious if they telephoned while you were out.

Communication with parents is all about mutual respect. You will maintain respect for them as the main people in the baby's life, who must be kept in touch with everything happening in his or her life. They will respect you as a person important to their baby, who is concerned for his or her welfare, and as a childcare professional.

DO IT

Identify the importance of respecting parents' wishes and keeping parents informed about the activities experienced by their babies.

If you have a baby to study, ask the parents what information they would like to receive from their baby's carers, and what information they already receive. Devise a chart or booklet that could be used to communicate with the parents of a baby you were caring for, either at home or in a nursery.

Hygiene, health and safety procedures

Organising babies' environments

As a childcare worker you are responsible for the health and safety of babies and children in your care. Some basic, essential rules should always be in your thoughts when working with any child, but are particularly important with babies.

1. You must always wash your hands to avoid cross infection:
   - before picking up a baby
   - before preparing or giving feeds
   - after changing a baby
   - after taking older children or yourself to the toilet
   - after playing with pets.
2. Strict hygiene and care is essential with babies' feeds, and you must
   - never reuse a partly finished bottle of feed
   - never leave a bottle of feed out at room temperature
   - always keep bottle teats covered when not in use
   - never test the temperature of a bottle by tasting a drop yourself – check it on the back of your hand
   - not allow other children or pets to touch spoons or dishes that are for a baby's food

- never prop feed a baby – that is, leave a baby in a pram or seat with the bottle propped up on a pillow, etc. – the baby could choke
- never thicken a baby's bottle with rice or rusk – solids should be given by spoon, otherwise babies may choke
- always supervise an older baby when eating, particularly hard foods such as rusks or apple.

3. Always remember that young children, and babies in particular, have no sense of danger. They need protecting from:
   - animals, even family pets
   - dangers from heat, household objects, etc.
   - falls, as they become more mobile – a baby should never be left alone on a surface above ground level
   - other children, who may injure them through exuberance or jealousy.

4. You should try not to expose babies to known infections, although this is not always easy, as many conditions are infectious before symptoms appear.

5. Always put a baby to sleep on his or her back, with the feet at the bottom of the cot, and use blankets that can be tucked in and will not billow over the face. This will help to prevent sudden infant death syndrome (cot death).

6. Never smoke in the presence of any child, especially babies. Smoking is a factor involved in sudden infant death syndrome.

7. Never be tempted to leave any child alone in a house.

Preventing accidents and illness

The dangers to babies change as they move through their first year. The chart below shows the dangers they face and how to prevent accidents or illness.

Age range	Danger	Prevention
Birth until crawling or cruising	Injury from cold or overheating	Attention to room temperature and clothing Room temperature between 18° and 21°C
	Gastroenteritis	Strict hygiene and bottle care
	Injury from other children	Avoid leaving toddlers alone with babies
	Sudden infant death syndrome	Don't allow smoking anywhere near or in the same room as a child Put child to sleep on back Avoid overheating
	Choking	Care when feeding, milk only in bottles Attention to ribbons, etc. on clothing Avoid leaving small toys or other items in reach
	Illness	Avoid people with known illness Ensure child has appropriate immunisations
When a child becomes mobile – crawling, shuffling	*All the above, plus:*	
	Falls	Use baby gates, play pens, closed doors
	Injury from pulling objects onto self	Attention to wires, cords any dangling objects, tablecloths

Age range	Danger	Prevention
	Burns and scalds	Care with hot drinks, kettle flexes, and bath temperatures Use of fire and cooker guards
	Electrocution from plug sockets	Use plug covers
	Poisoning	All cleaners, chemicals, paints, medications, etc. kept securely locked or in high cupboards

DO IT

Describe how to organise babies' environment for hygiene, health and safety procedures.

Visit a selection of baby-care shops and, if possible, collect catalogues. Look at the equipment available in the safety section and re-read the information on safety in Chapter 12.

Produce a simple and easy-to-understand booklet describing how carers can protect children in their care at home from injury or ill health during the first year of life.

Selecting and dealing with clothing

All children's clothes shops and most department stores have a wide range of clothing suitable for all ages and activities. Prices range from inexpensive to designer label levels. Babies do not mind what they are dressed in, as long as they are warm and comfortable. The wide ranges of styles is aimed to appeal to carers, and for the manufacturers' profits.

A few basic points about baby clothes are important to remember:

- natural fibres are more comfortable to wear as they absorb perspiration
- two or three thin layers of clothing are better than one very thick layer – clothing can then be adjusted to suit the temperature
- overheating can be dangerous for a baby – more so than being a little cool
- clothes that are machine washable are easier to care for
- clothes should be loose and easy to put on and take off
- avoid ribbons and cords that could easily cut off the circulation around a finger or neck
- all materials should be flame resistant
- care should be taken with clothes that have feet in them – for example stretch 'babygro' suits. It is important to check frequently that there is enough room for the baby's feet to move, as wearing too tight a suit will damage the soft, growing bones of the feet.

Choice of clothing

Encourage parents to use second-hand clothes from other babies – often their appearance is new. The list of essential clothing for a new baby is quite short, and includes:

- stretch suits
- vests – with an envelope neck for easy application
- cardigans for cooler days

- mittens for cold days
- socks or booties for cold days
- hat or bonnet – essential for cool weather, and a sun hat for days when the sun is out
- shawl for extra warmth.

An older baby who has started to be mobile through crawling or shuffling needs very practical clothes. Dresses get in the way of crawling, and pale-coloured, delicate fabrics quickly show their limitation with a mobile baby. Dungarees or stretch trousers with a similar top are practical and easy to wear.

'Snow suits' or jackets are essential for cold weather when a baby is in a pushchair or papoose carrier. Remember that in cold weather a baby is not moving around in the same way as you are, and needs additional layers of clothing.

Caring for baby clothes

A daily change of clothes is usually necessary, as the baby will perspire and may posset (bring back up) small amounts of food. If clothes have been well chosen they should be easy to wash, preferably in a washing machine. It is important to be familiar with the fabric care symbols on clothing.

Choice of washing powder is an important factor. Babies have skin that is much more sensitive than that of most adults. Biological powders may irritate the skin and should be avoided. Fabric conditioners should be used with care, and they can cause serious irritation. This is a particular problem if clothing becomes soaked in urine, due to a leaking nappy. Urine reacts very badly with most fabric conditioners and can produce a serious rash. It is advisable to look for the special conditioners for babies that avoid this problem.

Clothes that have become soiled with faeces or vomit need to be soaked in cold water after the solid residue has been disposed of into the toilet.

> ## *Do It*
> **Describe how to select suitable clothes and deal with soiled clothing and napkins.**
>
> Design a poster showing the essentials of a baby's clothing requirements from birth to 12 months. Include information on how to care for the clothes.

Nappy changing and common skin problems

Ask your parents what type of nappies you used to wear. Were they disposable, terry towelling or a mixture depending on the activities for the day? If you ask your grandparents what type they used for your parents, the answer will undoubtedly be terry towelling.

Disposable nappies have taken over in the past 20 years, with the result that millions of dirty paper and plastic nappies must be destroyed daily. Disposable nappies are convenient, don't require washing or carrying around if you are out, but they are very expensive and present society with the big problem of disposal.

A move back to using terry nappies is slowly gaining ground. You may find yourself caring for a baby who uses them, so being able to change one is a useful skill.

Changing nappies

Whichever type of nappy you have to change, there are several important points to consider.

- Always gather all your equipment together first.
- Have some means of cleaning the baby's bottom – water and cotton wool, or baby wipes.
- Have a bin or bag ready to receive the dirty nappy.
- Immediately you finish the task, clear the rubbish away and then wash your hands thoroughly.
- Never leave the baby unattended on a changing table or at any height above the floor.

The best way to learn the mechanics of changing a nappy is to watch a competent person. The folding of terry nappies is almost an art form, and there are many ways to do it depending on the size and sex of the baby. This is one of their advantages, as the nappy can be folded to be thickest at the position of urination. The same sized terry serves a tiny 3 kg baby and a bouncing two-year-old. They need to be covered with some form of plastic outer to prevent wetness coming through, and are often used with a thin paper lining to make the disposal of faeces easier.

Disposable nappies come in many different sizes and shapes with a range of special compounds to absorb wetness, built-in cream to prevent soreness, etc.

The aim of changing a nappy is to put the baby into a clean, dry nappy with a clean, dry bottom. The following procedure is recommended.

1. Collect all your equipment first – nappy, water, soap and cotton wool or baby wipes, cream, changing mat, bucket or bag for the dirty nappy.

2. After removing the nappy, clean the baby's bottom. If the nappy is a dirty one this will need greater care than if the nappy is wet. When cleaning female babies, always clean from front to back to avoid introducing infection into the vagina. With boys, try to avoid soiling the foreskin area. Using clean water is fine, but baby wipes contain a solution to neutralise ammonia and so help to prevent nappy rash.

3. Apply cream if used. Be careful not to get cream on to the adhesive fixings of a disposable nappy – if you do they will not stick.

4. Put the nappy on, being very careful with nappy pins if used, and dress the baby.

5. Dispose of the soiled nappy – roll it up and put it into a nappy sack if disposable. If a terry nappy, dispose of the paper liner and put the nappy into a bucket of sterilising solution.

6. Wash your hands.

Terry nappies should be washed after soaking in solution, at a temperature of at least 60°C and in non-biological powder. They should be rinsed thoroughly.

Nappy rash

Nappy rash appears as a red, sore area over the buttocks. In severe cases it can look like chafing. Sometimes a baby can develop thrush on the buttocks; this can be seen as small outbreaks of spot-type lesions away from the main red area. Medical advice is needed to deal with a nappy rash caused by thrush.

A barrier cream applied to the napkin area is useful to prevent nappy rash, and petroleum jelly is a good standby. There are many different creams on the market, all claiming efficiency, but few babies will reach the age of two without ever having a nappy rash. The first defence to prevent nappy rash is not to allow a baby to spend too long in a wet nappy, and certainly never leaving a baby in a wet and dirty nappy. Applying a barrier cream is a second defence. All babies will benefit from spending some time each day without a nappy on. A warm room and a covered mat on the floor are a suitable place to let the child have time without a nappy.

Babies are prone to other types of minor health problems that can cause concern to parents. They are described in Figure 15.1.

Do IT

Demonstrate napkin changing and identify common skin problems that may occur.

You have been asked for advice from a new mother about the best way to care for her baby's skin, including his nappy area. Produce a short report for her, outlining how she can keep her baby's skin healthy.

Bathing a baby

Bathing a tiny baby can be a frightening experience – holding a wet, soapy, wriggling baby is rather like trying to hold a wriggling fish. It can also be most enjoyable, and provide a natural opportunity to play with a baby and introduce new toys as the baby gets older.

Good preparation is vital. Suddenly remembering that you have forgotten a towel is not very helpful when you have the baby in the bath. Expensive, special baby baths are not necessary – a tiny baby can be bathed in a washing-up bowl until he or she is big enough to go into a normal, family-sized bath.

- Make sure the room is warm and draught free, as babies rapidly lose heat. An ideal temperature is 20°C.
- Gather all the necessary equipment – towel, mild soap or baby bath liquid, cotton wool, clean clothes and nappy.
- Fill the bath with water at body temperature (37°C), always putting the cold

Figure 15.2 Some items you will need when bathing a baby

Problem	Description	Cause	Treatment
Sweat rash (milaria)	Rash of small red spots on face, chest	Overheating Immature sweat glands	Cool child down by removing clothes. Use cotton next to skin. Avoid overheating with cloths and room heating.
Cradle cap	Yellow/brown crusting on the scalp, particularly on anterior fontanelle	Build-up of sebum, failure to wash and rinse area properly	Soften with olive oil, shampoo and rinse well – special shampoos available.
Chafing	Soreness in body creases – neck, groin and armpits	Insufficient washing and drying of skin	Prevent by good skin care, especialy in the neck area due to baby dribbling. Apply mild cream – e.g. zinc and castor oil.
Eczema	Sore red rash, may affect face or any part of the body, particularly skin folds Can be very severe, with bleeding and weeping	Usually an allergic response – possibly to cows' milk	Requires medical treatment. Avoid soap and using detergents for washing clothes. Keep nails short to stop scratching. Use emulsifiers in the bath. Breast feeding helps to lessen severity and delay onset.
Constipation	Very hard, dry faeces, baby may cry on passing them	Insufficient liquids, especially water, and dehydration in warm weather	Try to ensure that the baby drinks enough water or diluted fruit juice.
Diarrhoea	Very smelly, loose faeces, at frequent intervals	Over-rich formula feeds Poor hygiene in making feeds Infection	Lots of water to drink. If it continues longer than 24 hours, seek medical help.
Urine infection	Smelly nappy, even when only wet Often produces a nappy rash	Infection	Seek medical advice.

Figure 15.1 Some possible health problems in babies

water in first. This will avoid potential accidents with older children putting their hands into hot water, or climbing into baths. This is a routine that should always be followed, to avoid any risk of scalding.

● Check the temperature with your elbow.

The best way, as with nappy changing, to learn how to bath a baby is to watch someone who is experienced. A guide to follow is shown below, and illustrated in Figure 15.3.

1. Undress the baby down to the nappy, and wrap in a warm towel. Do this on the floor or in another safe area.
2. Check the water temperature and adjust if necessary.
3. Wrap the baby in a towel and hold gently but securely. Using cotton wool, wash the face. Do not use soap on the face. Use a separate piece of cotton wool for each eye, moving from the inner corner to the outer.
4. Hold the baby over the bath and wash the head with water or gentle soap or shampoo, twice per week. Make sure that the fontanelle (the 'soft spot') is washed and rinsed properly, to prevent cradle cap.

5. On a firm, safe surface, unwrap the baby and remove the nappy. Clean the nappy area with wet cotton wool.
6. Holding the baby safely – with your arm under the shoulder supporting the head – gently lower into the water. Soap the baby all over the body if using soap, and then rinse thoroughly. Using baby bath liquid avoids the need for this. This is the ideal time for some gentle play and splashing, depending on the baby's level of enjoyment.
7. Lift the baby out of the bath and gently dry. Be particularly careful that creases are well dried.
8. Dress and put the baby into a cot, pram etc. before clearing the bath and clearing away equipment.

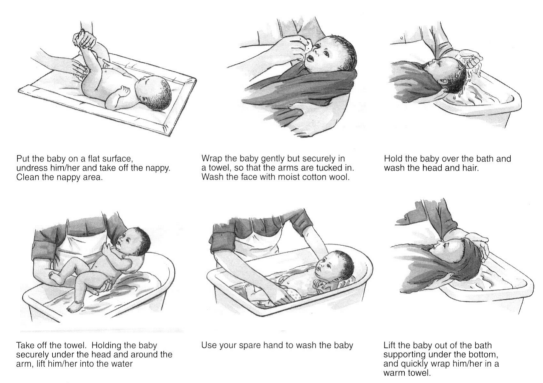

Put the baby on a flat surface, undress him/her and take off the nappy. Clean the nappy area.

Wrap the baby gently but securely in a towel, so that the arms are tucked in. Wash the face with moist cotton wool.

Hold the baby over the bath and wash the head and hair.

Take off the towel. Holding the baby securely under the head and around the arm, lift him/her into the water

Use your spare hand to wash the baby

Lift the baby out of the bath supporting under the bottom, and quickly wrap him/her in a warm towel.

Figure 15.3 The stages in bathing a baby

Two notes of caution: it is not necessary to poke around in any child's ears, especially babies', with cotton buds. Just clean around the outside with cotton wool if necessary. Secondly, baby boys' foreskins should be left alone, and they should not be pulled back at this age.

Topping and tailing

Very young babies may not be happy having a bath. This may be because of a sense of insecurity when they are undressed and exposed – tiny babies are happier wrapped up and feeling cosy. If a baby is not happy having a bath, then 'topping and tailing' can be done on several days a week. The face, head, hands and feet can be washed with cotton wool, and the baby's bottom can be washed with soapy water. Attention should also be paid to the skin creases, to check for signs of redness.

Older babies

Older babies usually thoroughly enjoy their baths, taking advantage of the chance to kick and splash. As soon as it is possible – and certainly by the time they are sitting with support at around five months – babies will enjoy going into a full-size bath, if possible with older siblings or a parent. A firm, non-slip mat should be placed in the bottom of the bath. Of course, you should never leave any child alone in the bath even for a second – they can slip and drown in a few centimetres of water.

If you are bathing an older baby in a baby bath, preparations should include protecting the surrounding floor areas from splashing. There is huge scope for play in the bath with an older baby – commercial toys are available that fit on or in the bath, or you can use plastic containers, ducks, sponges, plastic bricks and simply splash.

Care of teeth

As soon as a baby starts to get its teeth, you should start to clean them. Using a very soft baby toothbrush will be something of a game to the baby to start with. If the baby does not like the brush, you can use a soft piece of cloth with a tiny amount of toothpaste.

Prevention is better than cure with dental care. Avoid giving a baby fruit drinks through a teat, or dipping a dummy in juice or honey.

Do It

Prepare for and bath a baby.

Describe a bathtime routine for a baby three months old. How would you make it an enjoyable experience for you and the baby?

Respecting parents' wishes

Increased marketing by companies promoting new products to parents may mean that you are faced with new ideas about hygiene matters. As long as these ideas are not in opposition to basic safety and hygiene requirements, you should always respect parents' requirements. Examples of different ideas are to have bathtime in the morning rather than before bed, using terry nappies instead of disposables, and different methods of sterilising feeding equipment.

In some cases you may feel that the routines or techniques parents are using are not safe, putting you in a difficult position.

Do It

Describe how a carer would comply with parents' wishes relating to hygiene procedures.

Sam, aged three months, arrives at nursery with a new type of nappy – it looks like a shaped terry nappy with a sheet of plastic, and seems to need advanced skills in order to apply it.

Francis, aged two months, has not been sleeping very well. When you arrive to look after him for the evening his mother tells you to put a rusk in his bottle to help him sleep.

You are bathing a baby on a home placement and the telephone rings. The baby's mother is busy in the kitchen and calls you to answer the phone. She says the baby will be OK on the changing table for a minute.

A mother gives you some cotton buds and asks you to clean out her baby's ears inside, as they have been very waxy.

When you arrive to care for a new baby for the day, you are shown a bottle of milk that has been half consumed and then put on top of the gas fire to keep warm. It is suggested that you finish it off with the baby if she needs it before her next full feed is due.

Discuss these scenarios with a partner. Are the parents correct in their advice to you? What do you think you should do about these situations? Make notes on your ideas.

Bottle feeds and weaning foods

National dietary guidelines

National guidelines relating to the feeding of babies clearly state that breast feeding is the best for babies until they are at least three months old. From three months, solids may be gradually introduced, avoiding cows' milk, wheat, nuts, eggs, salt and sugar. Weaning is dealt with in greater detail later in this chapter.

The debate between breast and bottle feeding has raged on for many years. In the early 1900s babies who could not be breast fed had to be fed on variants of cows' milk, which is totally unsuitable for babies. Modern infant formula milks are scientifically modified to make them as near to human milk as possible.

Advantages of breast feeding

The main advantage of breast feeding are that:

- breast milk contains the right amounts of nutrients, at the right temperature, and is always available without risk of contamination
- breast milk contains antibodies to boost the immunity gained in the uterus
- it is less likely to result in an overweight baby
- it helps delay or avoid eczema
- it has little additional cost
- it helps in the bonding process
- it helps the uterus shrink more quickly
- it delays the return of the mother's periods.

Although breast feeding is the ideal way of infant feeding, not all mothers wish to use this method, or they may not be able to breast feed, for example if they are returning to work.

Bottle feeding does have some advantages in comparison to breast feeding.

- It is obvious how much milk the baby is taking.
- There is no risk of embarrassment with public feeding.

- Other people can feed the baby.
- It helps the mother who is returning to work.

Your role in the choice between breast and bottle feeding is only to give impartial information if asked, and then support the parents in their choice. The choice about feeding is a personal one for the parents of the baby, with support from midwives, health visitors and doctors.

Supporting mothers who wish to breast feed

Mothers who are breast feeding may need help to find some privacy when feeding their baby. Discreet public feeding is possible, as mothers can usually find a quiet corner away from the public gaze. Never suggest or support a suggestion that a mother could use a public toilet to feed – would you like to have your lunch in such a place?

Working mothers can use a breast pump to express milk, so that it can be kept in a bottle in the fridge until needed. You need to make sure that all the usual hygiene rules are followed to avoid the risk of infection.

Preparing formula feeds

Current formula infant feeds are almost a replica for breast milk, but the antibodies that breast milk passes to a baby cannot be replaced in formula milk. A well-prepared formula bottle given in a caring environment with close interaction between baby and feeder can, however, be a satisfying experience for both parties.

Equipment for feeding

Large chemists and baby shops have a wide range of bottles, sterilisers and associated equipment that if added together would be very expensive. Essentials for formula feeding are the following.

- Feeding bottles – up to 12 to allow rotation and advance preparation.
- Teats with holes of a suitable size to allow milk to flow without choking the baby.
- Covers for the teats – usually a top for the bottle that allows the teat to be put upside down in the bottle during storage in the fridge.
- Bottle brush and teat cleaner.
- Sterilising equipment.

There are several methods of sterilising:

1. Steam, using a special device.
2. Sterilising solution, made from tablets or concentrated solution. Bottles are soaked for a minimum time, usually 30 minutes.
3. Boiling for ten minutes – this tends to damage plastic bottles if used regularly.

Following the common sense rules of hygiene is the first step on the road to safe feeding. The chart in Figure 15.4 examines the principles of good practice.

Subject	Action required	Comments
Environment (kitchen)	Clean, dry worktops No other foodstuffs around Keep pets, etc. from surfaces	Contamination can easily occur due to carelessness
Operator (person preparing feed)	Always wash hands before starting work Do not touch any surface or equipment that will come into contact with milk Avoid touching the head, face, etc. during preparation Carefully read and follow the exact instructions on formula and sterilising solution packets Exact quantities of milk powder and water should be used	Risk of contamination, introduction of bacteria Very easy to make a feed that is too strong or too weak, as proportions are carefully calculated by the manufacturer
Equipment (bottles, teats, etc.)	All should be assembled before the start of preparation All bottles, teats, jugs, spoons must be thoroughly cleaned in hot soapy water, rinsed and left fully immersed in sterilising solution for minimum recommended time Formula should be checked as fresh and within date of use on packet Check that the water supply is a safe supply, and water is boiled before use	Milk and milk residue is an ideal medium for bacteria to breed Even a tiny amount of residue under the rim of a bottle can be enough to cause serious illness in a baby if bacteria multiply Any food stuff deteriorates with age and may cause harm if not within the use-by date Water supplies can carry bacteria that will cause gastroenteritis – this kills small babies due to the dehydration caused by vomiting and diarrhoea
Storage	Packets of formula should be kept in dry cupboard, tops safely and securely closed Bottles should be kept in refrigerator when made, teats covered Bottles should never be left out at room temperature Contents of part-used bottles should be disposed of	All vital practice to prevent contamination and potential gastroenteritis

Figure 15.4 Principles of hygiene for feeding babies

Another potential risk to babies is making up the feed with the wrong amounts of water or formula. Giving a baby stronger feed is dangerous because the feed will contain too much protein and too many salts – a baby's body cannot cope with this and convulsions and brain damage could occur. To avoid accidentally making the feed too strong:

- always check the number of scoops of powder that are needed
- only use the scoop provided in the packet
- do not be tempted to use heaped scoops – level off the powder with a plastic knife.

Too weak a feed will mean the baby is under-nourished, and will not thrive or develop to full potential.

Most people find it convenient to make up a supply of feeds for 24 hours and then store them in the fridge. Provided there are enough bottles, this is good practice. All the bottles that are going to be used for the next batch of feeds must have had enough time in the steriliser before they are re-used.

Giving the feed

A bottle feed can be given cold, but if it is heated to a suitable temperature it will be more enjoyable for the baby. Heating can be in a commercial bottle warmer or in a jug of water. Never use a microwave oven – there is a serious risk of hot spots in the formula that will scald the baby's mouth.

The feed is warm enough if a few drops sprinkled on the inside of your wrist feel comfortable.

When feeding, the bottle should be tilted to prevent air being swallowed with the milk, and pauses should be given to allow air into the bottle to prevent a vacuum forming.

Whenever possible, the baby should be fed by the main carer – ideally the mother – so that the same bonding will take place that breast-feeding promotes. Whoever feeds the baby, it should be done in a comfortable position that allows for eye contact and close bodily contact. Talking and smiling to the baby is an important part of the feeding experience.

Remember that a baby should never be left alone to feed from a bottle that has been propped up, because:

- there is a high risk of choking
- the baby being deprived of important contact with the carer
- too much air will be taken in.

Do it

Prepare a formula feed for a baby.

Give a demonstration of making up a bottle-feed. Design and produce an illustrated sheet showing the important safety points to consider when preparing feeds and feeding babies.

You should be able to do your demonstration in small groups using equipment at college. If this is a problem, write out a 'script' for a talk and note the equipment you would need to use.

Weaning

Weaning is the term used to describe the process of changing a child's feeding from being dependent on milk to eating family foods.

A newborn baby does not have the digestive system to cope with solid foods. A baby of one year has developed this system. The process of learning to enjoy a wide range of foods can be a simple, easy one, or it can be difficult for carers and the baby alike.

There are many fashions related to weaning. Ask your parents and grandparents when they weaned their children and what foods they used, and you will probably receive several different answers. Parents in Britain may say they started their child on baby rice, while parents in Israel may have used avocado pear as a first weaning food.

When should a baby start to be weaned?

There are national guidelines relating to the start of weaning, and it is a good idea to try to collect some government leaflets from baby clinics to check on the latest guidelines.

Ideally, a baby should have nothing but infant milk until at least three months of age, while the digestive system is maturing. A baby could thrive very well on milk alone until the age of 12 months. At this age, the iron stores from birth will be diminishing and the baby will be at risk of becoming anaemic. We could say therefore that weaning should start between three and 12 months. Leaving the start as late as 12 months could make it difficult for a baby to make the change from a breast or bottle to eating from a spoon.

At nine months a baby can pick up small items between finger and thumb, is sitting without support and is still exploring everything with his or her mouth. This is a time to introduce finger foods – that is, anything the baby can pick up and eat with the fingers – lumps of cheese, apple pieces, and small sandwiches. Weaning isn't just about eating different foods, it also develops independence in feeding, promotes fine motor skills, and develops the mouth muscles involved in speech.

There are several stages involved in weaning, as shown in the table in Figure 15.5.

Weaning stage	Suggested foods
First stage (3 months plus) Sloppy, slightly thicker than milk foods	**Bland tastes** Thickened milk – baby rice Pureed or stewed apple, banana, avocado
Second stage Thickness increasing, but no lumps	**Increase variety and strength of taste** First stage commercial foods Home-made pureed vegetables with gravy, e.g. carrots, yam, sweet potato Fruit and custard
Third stage Food less pureed – coping with thicker texture and some lumpiness Starting to finger feed	**Introducing slightly lumpier texture** Home-made food mashed with fork potatoes, vegetables, fish, fruits Rusks, bread crusts, peeled pieces of apple, banana or mango Cubes of cheese
Fourth stage (by 12 months) Eating most family foods	**Using family foods, avoiding tough or stringy textures** Very little that cannot be offered

Figure 15.5   The weaning process

There are a few safety rules that should be kept in mind during the weaning process.

- Never give a baby nuts of any description – there is a strong risk of allergy and also of choking.
- Avoid egg whites in the first year, as babies cannot cope with the protein albumin.
- Do not introduce cows' milk until six months of age, and then always use full-cream, pasteurised milk – to ensure full calcium and vitamin levels without the risk of infection.
- Never add salt to a baby's food – there is a danger of kidney damage.
- Avoid adding sugar or sweeteners – there is no need to develop a sweet tooth.
- Products containing wheat are best avoided until at least six months of age. Some babies are allergic to the gluten in wheat, resulting in coeliac disease.
- Avoid fatty foods at all ages, to help reduce unnecessary fat intake.

Think it through

Investigate all the different commercial weaning foods available in supermarkets, chemist's shops, etc. How easy do you think it would be to provide similar foods at home?

Do it

Explain national dietary guidelines relating to the feeding of babies.

Collect up-to-date information about the national dietary guidelines issued by the government. Prepare a checklist of the main points relating to the feeding of babies up to 12 months of age.

How to start weaning

A baby is ready to start weaning when he or she does not appear to be satisfied by milk feeds, despite increasing the amounts. Sucking the fists is not a sign of being ready for weaning this is a normal part of development.

Try offering the first spoonfuls part way through a milk feed, or near the end, when the first pangs of hunger have been satisfied. It takes some time for a baby to recognise that nourishment can come from a hard plastic object that has strange tastes on it, rather than from a soft, warm breast or rubber teat.

I know it goes in somewhere around here!

Gradually the amounts of solids taken will increase, and you should correspondingly decrease the amount of milk offered. By the time a baby is eating three substantial meals of solids a day, milk feeds should be reduced to night-time, with water or fresh juice at and between meals.

At six months old, a typical day's menu could be like the one shown below.

As soon as the baby starts trying, let him or her join in feeding – even though everything will fall off the spoon, and it will go anywhere but in the mouth! Offer finger foods as much as possible, as it all helps to aid independence. A vital piece of equipment at this stage is a sheet of plastic to protect the floor, if it is not washable!

Breakfast	Breast or bottle when woken Cereal, fruit, toast fingers Water or diluted juice in a cup
Lunch	Mashed fish or lentils with mashed vegetables Stewed fruit or milk pudding Water or diluted juice in a cup
Tea	Toast with a savoury spread, mashed banana or mango Water or well-diluted juice in a cup
Bedtime	Breast or bottle feed

Feeding difficulties

Refusing food is totally acceptable, because a baby will eat as much as he or she needs if opportunities are offered. This continues throughout childhood – eating and not eating only become a problem if the child's carers see them as a problem. A baby has every right not to eat if not feeling hungry – in the same way as you have.

New tastes should be introduced gradually. Babies are fairly conservative about new tastes, and trying too many ones in a short space of time will usually result in rejection. Offer only one new taste a day in the first months of weaning, and if a new food is rejected one day, try it again later.

Occasionally a baby may have an allergy to a particular food, and react with sickness, skin rashes or breathing problems. Usually the baby will have already shown this tendency with milk feeds if there is an allergy to cows' milk, or through the mother eating certain foods when breast-feeding. Babies can be allergic to eggs, seafood and nuts (which should not be given, as already discussed). Great care needs to be taken before deciding a baby is allergic to a certain food, as it is easy to deprive a baby or child of vital nutrients. If an allergy is suspected avoid that food, and seek advice from the child's doctor or health visitor.

Do IT

Describe what is meant by weaning.

You have been caring for a baby aged three and a half months at nursery. Plan the advice you would give to her mother on the best way to help her child reach the stage of eating normal family foods, from her present diet of milk. Present the information in a chart, or an easy-to-follow booklet, or any other suitable method including a video.

Supporting parents' wishes

Feeding a baby can be a difficult and emotional topic for parents. Many people see a thriving child as the sign of 'good' parenting. A child who does not eat well could be regarded as not being cared for properly. We develop our attitudes to food from a very early age, from our parents and our own experiences. Parents can become upset about what their child is or isn't eating, and many parents come under pressure from grandparents. Despite being aware of the latest healthy diet issues, they may find it hard not to follow their own parents' suggestions. As a childcare worker, you can offer support to parents in encouraging healthy eating in their babies.

When a child is at nursery this is fairly easy, but if you are working in a child's home it may be less so. It is important to remember that the final decision is that of the parents. Disagreements with them in front of the child will only make the situation worse. You may be able to have an informal chat with the parents about eating and diets, or show them an article you have read, but you cannot force your opinion on them.

As a worker in a care setting, you would be within your rights to contravene parents' wishes only if they were asking you to feed a baby with unsuitable foods – e.g. lightly boiled whole eggs to a baby under 12 months, gluten to a young baby, or unpasteurised milk to a toddler. Other than this you should as far as possible follow the wishes of parents. Cultural variations should be respected when you are designing menus for young children – at the very least, avoid offering 'forbidden' foods such as pork to Muslims, or meat to vegetarians.

DO IT

Describe the role of childcare workers in supporting parents' wishes relating to feeding their babies.

Survey the menus of all the babies at your placement. Do they all eat the standard menu of the nursery? If they do, find out what provision there is for following parents' wishes where they have different requirements for their child's diet. How would the nursery support those parents?

Creating a safe and stimulating environment

The role of the carer

Babies are unable to protect themselves from risks of injury or illness. Everyone who has any dealings with a baby is responsible for his or her safety. Thought needs to be given to all of the following points.

- Adequate clothing must be provided, suitable to the climate and room temperature, and it must be kept clean and maintained.
- The baby's surroundings should have appropriate levels of heating, light and cleanliness. An ideal temperature for a baby is one that you also feel comfortable in.
- Older children are naturally jealous of a new baby in the family – they feel that they will not be receiving as much attention. Even without intending any harm, toddlers can give cuddles that are over-zealous and could cause harm, or may 'offer' toys to the baby by throwing them into the pram.
- Animals can carry diseases that may be transmitted to humans. Never allow a dog to lick a baby or the equipment the baby will use. Never leave a dog alone with a baby – they can be as jealous as children.
- Protect from illness. Avoid contact with people who are ill. People are often infectious before symptoms show, so this is not always possible. Do not go to work if you are ill yourself, to avoid distributing an infection.

Hygiene

Careful attention to your own personal health and hygiene is the first step – remember the rules of hand washing, clean clothing, and the use of aprons for dirty jobs.

There should be a regular routine at nursery or the baby's home to ensure that the environment is clean and hygienic. Equipment and toys need regular washing and inspection for safety on a rota basis and also at any time you feel is necessary. Have a look around your placement – how do you find out about the routines that are related to providing a safe environment?

Safety

All equipment used with any child, including babies, should be checked daily for safety. The table in Figure 15.6 provides a safety checklist.

Item	Checks
Prams	Brakes working, catches to keep the pram opened working Harness safe and in use Shopping and other bags carried only in special carriers, not on the handles
Cots	Safety catches working, bars no more than 3 inches apart, mattress fits snugly Cot feels stable when gently shaken
Transport in cars, mini buses, etc.	Suitable safety seat provided, firmly fixed to body of vehicle – has BSI logo No wear on straps Straps adjusted to fit baby snugly
High chairs	Stable on the floor, cannot be easily tipped Have anchor points for harness – always used Tray firmly fixed, no cracks or chips
Safety gates	Good fit to size of opening When fixed and locked cannot be moved No horizontal bars to climb over
Fire guards	Firmly fixed to the wall Nothing to poke through into the fire No clothes on the guard for drying
Bouncing chairs, baby seats for use indoors	Harness or safety straps in use Never left unattended on a high surface
Baby walkers, bouncing swings	Seat adjusted to allow feet to sit flat on the floor Wheels and fixings safe
Toys	Check for cracks, breaks or loose parts Ensure nothing can be torn or pulled off and that there are no tears in fabric allowing fillings to escape

Figure 15.6 A safety checklist of equipment

Good practice when looking at baby equipment is to check that it has a British Safety Institute kitemark symbol attached, showing that it has been tested and meets safety requirements. Make yourself familiar with safety marks, and never use a toy or piece of equipment that does not have the appropriate mark. These safety marks are shown in Figure 12.4 on page 347.

Buying second-hand items is a sensible step in terms of cost, and for items that do not receive a lot of use. Care needs to be taken, however, that the previous owners have not altered the item at all, making it unsafe. For example, a second-hand cot might have been repainted with a lead-based paint, or have transfers that will peel off.

Do it

Explain the role of the carer in providing a safe and stimulating environment for babies.

Carry out a safety audit of all the equipment at your placement. List each item and the points that you feel need checking for safety. Briefly explain the routines at your placement relating to hygiene and safety.

How the stage of development relates to safety

By now you should be aware of the huge steps in development that take place in the first year of a baby's life. It will not surprise you that it is essential to mirror those changes in considering a baby's safety and play needs.

Suitable equipment and activities

The table in Figure 15.7 shows toys and activities that may be suitable at each stage of development.

Safety considerations must be at least one, and preferably two or three, steps ahead of the baby. Provide a safety gate for the stairs before the baby starts to crawl, always look at toys for loose parts, look for strings that could wrap around necks, always use a safety harness from the start of using a high chair, etc.

Do it

Describe how the developmental stage of the baby will affect selection and use of safety and play equipment.

Thinking about physical, intellectual, emotional and social development, plan at least one activity covering each aspect for a child at two months, six months, and ten months. What safety issues will you have to consider in your plans?

Age and stages	Toys and activities
Birth to 3 months Reacts to light, noise and touch Field of vision 20–25 cm	Cuddles, singing and talking Mobiles hung over cot, chair, changing mat Brightly coloured pictures and objects
3 to 6 months Able to hold objects Visual field expanding Mouthing Voluntary movements replacing reflex actions Kicking becoming vigorous Communication developing	Objects to hold and look at – range of textures, ideally sound-making toys such as rattles Over the cot, rods with range of objects on strings, cords Watching trees in the wind Time to enjoy freedom for kicking in the bath, on a changing mat without a nappy Noisy paper to kick against Finger games – e.g. 'This little piggy' Songs and movement
6 to 12 months Sitting with support, moving alone Increasing mobility – may be crawling to walking Anxious when carer is missing Enjoys exploring Start of imitative play Developing sense of self Interested in outside world	Great enjoyment of water play – in the bath with toys, in small washing up bowl Household opportunities – pots and pans, boxes, cans. Building stacks and knocking them down – toy bricks, boxes Games cleaning teeth, brushing hair Mirrors Outdoor trips to the park, shops, to see the cows … will enjoy repetition of these outings A treasure box made from a strong cardboard box, with changing items aimed at different senses Big, easy-to-hold crayons with big sheets of card to scribble on Push and pull toys, toys that make sounds or pop up when a button is pressed, etc.

Figure 15.7 Suiting activities to the age and stage of development of the child

Bonding, attachment and communication

All babies need to develop close links with at least one important adult. This is the start of a person's emotional security. Usually, we have close emotional links with several people.

The first link is usually the baby's mother. Before birth, the baby has been listening to the mother's voice, hearing her heart beat, and generally becoming familiar with the rhythms of the mother. In a normal delivery, the mother often holds the baby while the placenta is being delivered, and a breast-feeding mother may start to feed at this point. If there are complications in the birth every effort is made to ensure that the mother can hold or touch the baby as much as possible, even if the baby has to be in an incubator.

All this helps with the process of 'bonding', which is strengthened by:

- skin-to-skin contact
- familiar sounds of voices
- eye-to-eye contact
- familiar smells.

Ideally, a baby needs one or more constant caring figures – usually mother and father or grandparents. A good bonding relationship can and does develop with non-family members – you will see this yourself as you progress in your work with babies.

If a baby is cared for outside the home, then the carer should not be constantly changing. Many settings now use a key worker system, where one person has the prime responsibility for a child.

Think it through

Louie, aged nine months, attends a day nursery every day from 8 am to 6 pm. The baby room is staffed by whoever is available from the main nursery. Louie's mother is concerned because she never seems to see the same person when she drops Louie off or picks him up. Louie seems to be losing interest in nursery and cries or is miserable most of the time.

Leila is also aged nine months and also attends nursery from 8 am to 6 pm. The baby room has its own team of staff, with two key workers responsible for each baby. They are never on duty together, but have a good communication system to inform each other of how the babies are progressing. There is also a meeting once a week for the key workers to discuss 'their' babies. Leila's mother feels confident that she is leaving Leila with the same people all the time, and Leila greets her carers with a big smile every morning.

Why do you think Leila and Louie react so differently to their day care?

Apart from the security that consistent care gives to a baby, continuity of care is important in developing a baby's communication skills. From birth, you can see a baby trying to communicate with his or her main carers. Watch and listen to a new baby and mother. The mother will usually be talking in a language that to you may sound like nonsense, but this 'motherese' way of talking is an important part of initial communication for a baby. In response to talking, cooing, etc. from the carer, a baby will make noises back and then wait for a response – this is the start of 'turn taking'.

Separation anxiety

Forming close attachments to a person means that when a baby leaves that person he or she will probably be distressed. This will start to be obvious at around five or six months of age. If you are the new carer in a baby's life, there are ways of making this change easier for the baby.

- Approach slowly.
- Talk gently to the baby before you try to pick him or her up.
- Make sure that the baby can look at the parents as you take him or her from them.

From a very early age babies will show that they prefer the company of some people rather than others – usually by crying if they do not like a person. If you find that a baby does not respond well to you, speak to a supervisor about it and arrange for someone else to care for that baby.

More usually, the problem you encounter will be how to deal with the ending of your care for a baby. It may be at the end of a short placement, or once you are qualified, or as a baby moves to another nursery, or you change jobs. Always remember that you will have played an important role in the life of that baby. If possible, try to keep in touch with the family – continuing to visit a family where you were a nanny is perfectly acceptable, and will help the new person who is taking over. In a nursery, encourage the mother to bring the baby back for visits if possible, or if the baby has moved on to the next stage in nursery, there should be a transition stage during which you take the baby into the next room and stay for a time. All good child care settings accept the principle of bonding.

Do it

Explain the importance of bonding and attachment and the need to communicate at all stages.

In a small group, share your experiences of consistent care for babies under 12 months. This might be from a nursery, from discussions with parents who have changed the care for their baby on several occasions, or from observation. Chart your findings with a list of good practice and poor practice, giving examples and reasons.

FAST FACTS

Abuse   A term which covers a wide range of negative and damaging behaviour including: hitting, humiliation, exploiting, stealing from or neglecting others.

Access to Health Records Act 1990   An Act of Parliament which extended the law within the Data Protection Act to cover paper-based records kept by health services.

Access to Personal Files Act 1987   An Act of Parliament which extended the law within the Data Protection Act to cover paper-based records kept by local authorities and services that work for local authorities.

Activity planning sheet   Written plan for activities to be used with children, in nursery, school, etc. All activities should have a plan, with space for evaluating the activity.

APGAR score   The formal scoring system that identifies the condition of a new baby. Scores a baby on muscle tone, breathing, heart rate, reflexes, and colour.

Arthritis   A physical condition involving pain and difficulty in using or moving joints in the body.

Assessment   The process of finding out about the needs of a client and deciding how they can best be met.

Asthma   A long-term illness which affects breathing. Asthma affects over two million people in the United Kingdom.

Attachment   Close relationship that a baby has to his or her carers.

Attention deficit disorder   A term used to describe children who are extremely active, have a very short attention span and have behavioural difficulties.

Autonomy   The freedom and independence to choose what to do – within limits and boundaries. Most people are not free to do anything they like, but most adults are autonomous – they make their own choices within limits.

Bacteria   Micro-organisms that can cause disease in humans, e.g. streptococci. Many bacteria have a useful function in helping to keep the body healthy.

Behaviour modification   A method of helping children to alter aspects of their behaviour, usually by praising good behaviour and playing down unwanted behaviour.

Benefits   A range of rights which are aimed at supporting people in financial need.

Bereavement   A process of coming to terms with the loss of a loved person.

Body language   The language we use to send messages with the body. Body language is part of our 'non-verbal' communication.

Bonding   Forming an emotional attachment to a person. Babies usually make an attachment to carers during the first year of life.

Bottle feeding   Artificial feeding of babies, using modified infant formula. Used when a mother cannot or does not wish to breast feed.

Boundaries A line that you may go up to, but must not cross. Boundaries explain the limits of a carer's role.

Breast feeding The best method of feeding a baby. Clean, safe, convenient and protects a baby from gastro-enteritis. Also passes on natural immunity to the baby.

BSI logo The 'kitemark' of quality, showing that equipment has passed stringent safety tests.

Budgets The amount of money which is planned to be spent. Managers have to control spending budgets within services.

Cancer A disease where some body cells do not reproduce normally. Approximately one in four people in Britain die of cancer.

Carbohydrate A nutrient in food which provides energy for the body.

Cardiac arrest A health emergency when the heart stops beating.

Care plan A written document which outlines how the needs of an individual are to be met.

Care planning A process of working out how a person's needs can be met, which involves the client and the carers.

Care values Defined in NVQ. Current standards emphasise valuing diversity, rights and responsibilities and confidentiality.

Caste Rigid social divisions between groups – similar to social class, but people are born into a caste and cannot change caste, whereas people can change their class.

Casting The practice in children of about 12 months who seem to enjoy throwing toys from their chair and watching them fall to the ground. They are learning about cause and effect.

Census The questionnaire sent by the government of the United Kingdom every 10 years to every household. The information is analysed to help the government make planning and policy decisions.

Cerebral palsy The effect of a break in the message pathway from the brain to the muscles, which prevents limbs being moved at will, or speech occurring.

Children Act 1989 An Act of Parliament providing children with the right to be protected from 'significant harm'. Parents have responsibilities rather than rights with regard to their children. The Act also requires nurseries and residential schools to achieve standards and be inspected.

Chromosome All human cells have 23 pairs of chromosomes, containing the genetic material for the whole body.

Cleaning Activities taken to prevent the spread of harmful micro-organisms and to meet the social and emotional needs of individuals.

Clients' rights Rights to be different, free from discrimination, have confidentiality, choice, dignity, safety and security, and the development of personal potential.

Colostrum The fluid produced by the breasts in the first few days of breast feeding, containing a high level of antibodies and fat.

Comforter An item that a baby or child turns to when tired, upset or just resting, such as a piece of cloth, toy or dummy.

Communication cycle The process of hearing, watching non-verbal messages, feeling, developing understanding and finally sending a message back to another person.

Community Care Act 1990 An Act of Parliament intended to uphold the principle that people are best cared for in their own homes, or in other familiar surroundings, rather than being admitted into residential care as a matter of policy.

Confidentiality An important value which guides all care work. Information about clients must only be passed on to people with a need and a right to know it.

Conflict A situation that can develop when strong emotional feelings result in anger and a desire to fight.

Conservation The concept that an item retains the same mass or volume even if its shape changes, e.g. 100 ml of water is the same if it is in a long thin glass or a shallow bowl.

Constipation The passing of hard dry faeces, perhaps causing pain or bleeding. Caused by lack of fluids and roughage (vegetables, bran, and fruit) in the diet.

Control of Substances Hazardous to Health Regulations (COSHH) (1988) Regulations which specify how hazardous chemicals and materials must be kept and used, and the safety and emergency procedures which surround them.

Conversation sandwich The idea that all conversations should have a beginning or introduction, a middle and an end or finishing stage to create the right atmosphere.

Cradle cap A crust of dry skin cells on a baby's scalp, which may be brown and flaky. Often over the fontanels (soft spot) as carers may be wary of rubbing hard.

Culture The values and roles shared by social groups. Different cultures (values and roles) create different social groups.

Curriculum A scheme of work for the education of children. Outlines the aims of the child's education, what should be taught or covered and how.

Cystic fibrosis An inherited condition that affects a child's lungs and digestive tract, due to a lack of enzymes. People with this condition need drug and diet supplements.

Data Protection Act 1984 An Act of Parliament which requires computer records to be confidential, accurate and securely stored.

Desirable learning outcomes The list of outcomes a child should be capable of achieving when entering compulsory education at 5 years.

Direct discrimination Open and clear discrimination, where it is obvious that certain groups are being treated unfairly.

Disability The consequences of an impairment or other individual difference in a given social setting.

Disability Discrimination Act 1995 An Act of Parliament intended to create new rights for people with disability.

Discrimination In social care, treating some groups or types of people better than others, or giving a worse quality of service to some people because of the group they belong to.

Diversity The understanding that each individual is special and not exactly the same as anyone else. People are different or diverse in many different ways – these include age, gender, ethnicity, class, religion, sexuality, ability, health, relationships and beliefs. Diversity should be something that makes life interesting rather than a basis for discrimination.

Dyslexia A range of disabilities which can include difficulties with learning to read and to spell, although these disabilities are not related to any intellectual disability.

Eczema A skin condition with dry, itchy, flaky skin, which may weep. Ranges from isolated patches to extensive coverage of the body. May be caused by allergies.

Egocentric The stage of recognition of self by a young child, which shows as a child appearing to be selfish and self-centred. A normal stage of development at around 18 months.

Embryo The developing baby during the first eight weeks of life in the womb.

Environment Surroundings that a person lives in. Everything around people which affects them.

Equal Opportunities Commission The watchdog body protecting the equal opportunities of all people.

Equal Pay Act 1970 An Act of Parliament which made it unlawful for employers to discriminate between men and women in relation to their pay and conditions of work.

Ethnicity The social and cultural categories which people use to explain what race they are, for example white European, black British, or Asian.

Family A social group made up of people who are related to each other.

Fat A nutrient in food which provides concentrated energy.

Foetus The developing baby within the womb from eight weeks to birth.

Food safety A range of measures aimed at preventing the spread of harmful micro-organisms within food and drink.

Formula feed Cows' milk that has been modified to closely match human breast milk, to give to young babies whose mothers cannot breast feed.

Gastro-enteritis A serious illness for babies, caused by infection. Symptoms are vomiting and diarrhoea, with rapid dehydration. Can result in death of not promptly treated.

Gender The social role associated with being male of female.

Genes The biological set of instructions which influence the development of people. Genes interact with the environment to create individuals. Differences in people are always due to this interaction of genes and environment.

Harness Essential item of equipment fixed around a child's body and secured to a chair or pram to stop a child climbing out or falling.

Health and Safety at Work Act (HASAWA) 1974 An Act of Parliament placing responsibilities on employers and employees to create a safe workplace. The original Act has been updated and supplemented by many later sets of regulations and guidelines.

Immunisation The means of protecting people against certain illnesses by introducing a very mild or dead form of the virus into the body. The body's immune (defence) system develops antibodies to fight future exposure to the disease.

Impairment Physical damage or restriction to the functioning of the mind or body.

Incubator A plastic, heated cot, used to care for very ill or tiny babies.

Infection The spread of harmful micro-organisms such as viruses and bacteria.

Kinship The network of family and relatives of a person.

Labelling Fixed opinions about individuals or groups which are summed up in a word or phrase. People become labelled with a simple term in the same way that files or doors have a label stuck on them.

Letdown reflex The reaction of the breasts in breast feeding that releases the milk from the milk ducts. May be stimulated by the baby crying, or sucking on the nipple.

Life events Common events that happen to people within a society. Examples include going to school, starting work, retirement and bereavement.

Life stages Socially defined periods which are used to identify developmental stages such as infancy, childhood, adolescence and adulthood.

Listening Being able to understand fully what another person tells you – more than just hearing the words another person says.

Manual Handling Operations Regulations (1993) Regulations designed to minimise the risks of injury through carrying and handling at work.

Maslow's hierarchy The psychologist Abraham Maslow's description of human needs as belonging to the categories physical, safety, love and belonging, self-esteem and self-actualisation. Quality care does not address only physical and safety needs. Higher level needs are also important if people are to have quality of life.

ME Myalgic encephalomyelitis – an illness which can start with symptoms like a cold or flu, but which causes a person to feel tired and possibly depressed for a long period afterwards.

Medical model A view of society's reaction to disability, in which the person with the disability is seen as the problem.

Menopause The end of menstruation in women – usually some time between the ages of 45 and 55.

Mental Health Act 1983 An Act of Parliament providing for compulsory restriction of people to hospital if they are mentally ill. The Act restricts the freedom of individuals who are considered ill.

Merit chart A chart used to display a child's good behaviour, achievement, etc.

Milestones of development The age at which 95% of children have reached a certain point in development, e.g. the milestone for sitting alone is 9 months.

Minerals Nutrients in food which are needed in very tiny amounts to help the body to function correctly, for example iron needed for red blood cell production.

Mobility The ability to move and get to places independently. There are a wide range of aids to mobility including aids to walking and wheelchairs.

Motherese The interaction between a carer and baby, with 'baby talk' language from the carer.

Nappy rash A red, sore rash on a baby's nappy area, caused by the breakdown of ammonia in urine. The condition is made worse by leaving a baby in wet, soiled nappies for long periods.

National Curriculum The statement of subjects and levels of attainment that should be reached by all children at various stages and ages in their school career. Divides school years into four key stages.

National Health Service (NHS) The government-run service which provides doctors (GPs), hospitals and community health services.

Neonate A new baby from birth to 28 days of age.

NHS and Community Care Act 1990 See *Community Care Act.*

Nutrient A substance that nourishes or feeds the body.

Object permanence An object or person still exists even if it cannot be seen. Young children do not understand this concept until about the age of 12 to 18 months.

Parallel play The stage of play when a young child will play alongside another child, but not interact with him or her. The same game or activity may often be going on.

Piaget Jean Piaget (born 1896, died 1980) was famous for his early research on child development. He believed children's intellectual development could be described in four stages.

PIES Physical, Intellectual, Emotional and Social needs. PIES is one way of looking at human development and human needs.

Pincer grasp Grasping an object between the thumb and first finger. Starts as an immature pincer grasp using the pads of the finger and thumb, developing into a fine grasp with the tips of finger and thumb.

Placenta The life-support centre of a developing foetus in the uterus. Connected to the baby via the umbilical cord and attached to the wall of the uterus to nourish and supply oxygen to the baby, and remove waste products.

Policies Formal written statements explaining what to do within an organisation or work-setting.

Poverty Not having the economic resources (money) to meet your physical and social needs. Poverty usually causes stress because needs are unmet for a long period of time.

Prejudice Pre-judgement, where people have made fixed negative judgements about other people or groups.

Premature birth Delivery of a baby before the full 40 weeks of pregnancy is complete. Babies can survive from as little as 23 or 24 weeks but have an increased chance of survival from 28 weeks.

Pressure sores Sores that develop because the blood supply has been restricted to an area of tissue for too long. Pressure sores can develop if a person cannot move and sits or lies in the same position for too long.

Primary socialisation Primary means first. 'First' socialisation means learning to fit in with and develop the values of the first group you belong to. Usually this is a family group.

Primitive reflexes The automatic involuntary reactions to stimuli that a newborn baby displays, e.g. grasp and a sucking reflex. These reactions have to be lost before voluntary reactions can replace them.

Procedure The method by which a policy is put into practice.

Prone position The term used to describe a baby lying on his or her front, face down.

Prop feeding A practice of sitting a baby up, supported by cushions, and leaving the bottle in the baby's mouth, supported on the pillow. A lazy, very risky way of feeding, not recommended in any circumstances, as a baby may choke.

Prosthesis An artificial part which makes up for something that has been lost – such as an artificial leg.

Proteins Nutrients which help body cells to grow and repair. The body can also use protein to produce energy.

Race In the past, some people believed that there were biological differences between different 'races' of people. Nowadays, race usually means the socially defined groups that people understand themselves as belonging to.

Race Relations Act 1976 An Act of Parliament which makes discrimination on the basis of race illegal.

Reflection Within communication, reflection means checking your understanding of what another person has said by saying the words (or explaining your understanding of them) back to the person.

Registered persons Anyone deemed fit to be in charge of a nursery, nursing home, etc., under local authority legalisation.

Religion The term used to refer to traditions or to personal spiritual beliefs, or both. People grow up with different religious traditions.

Reporting of Injuries, Diseases and Dangerous Occurrences Regulations (RIDDOR) 1985 Regulations that aim to ensure all notifiable diseases, injuries and dangerous occurrences are reported and recorded.

Responsibilities Society's values create rights for people – but rights are rarely without boundaries. People have responsibilities as well as rights. Rights are balanced with responsibilities.

Rights Some rights exist because of laws or international conventions. Other rights exist within the values that guide care practice or society. Clients' rights relate to social and care value systems (see *Clients' rights*).

Rights of the Child Declaration of the United Nations, stating the basic rights of all children to be respected, cared for, and allowed to develop their potential.

Risk assessment Part of all health and safety procedures. Both employers and employees need to check situations for risks to health and safety.

Role The actions and attitudes that people take on in particular social situations. People act differently when they are with friends than when they are at work, because there is a professional role involved with being a carer, and a social role involved in being a friend.

Role play A type of play where children imitate others, e.g. in the home corner imitating their home circumstances.

Secondary socialisation Learning to fit in with groups, after first socialisation within a family or care group. Usually this means becoming part of friendship groups with other adolescents.

Security Feeling physically and emotionally safe. Security policies and procedures are necessary to ensure the safety of staff, clients and their possessions.

Self-actualisation The highest level of development in Maslow's hierarchy. It means fulfilling your potential and achieving everything you need to achieve.

Self-concept The way we understand who we are. It may be difficult to cope with life as an adult if you do not have an understanding of this.

Self-esteem How well or how badly a person feels about himself or herself. High self-esteem may help a person to feel happy and confident. Low self-esteem may lead to depression and unhappiness.

Sex Discrimination Act 1975 An Act of Parliament designed to prevent discrimination on the basis of gender.

Sexuality Sexual behaviour and orientation, i.e. attraction to same sex or opposite sex partners.

Social class The status given to different types of occupation or work. Comparisons of social class are used to help understand social differences.

Social model The idea of disability that sees society as the cause of difficulties for those with a disability. Society has been organised for the able bodied, and needs to be changed to allow easy access to buildings, transport, etc.

Socialisation Learning the values and normal behaviour of a group. Learning to become part of a group or culture.

Solitary play Play carried out alone, allowing children to have personal space.

Stereotype A fixed opinion or view of people that categorises groups of people as 'all the same'.

Stress An in-built reaction makes us want to fight or run when we feel threatened. It is possible to be threatened but not be able to fight or run, and symptoms of stress set in when this happens.

Supine position Used to describe the position of a child laid on his or her back.

Team A group of people working together for a shared purpose. Effective teams usually need a shared system of values and clear communication between team members.

Therapeutic Acting as a cure or offering improvement. Play can be therapeutic after a child has experienced some type of trauma, and expresses emotions, fears, etc., through play.

Thrush (candidiasis) A fungal infection of the digestive and genital tract. Shows as a white deposit, that will not rub off, in a baby's mouth, or as a distinctive nappy rash.

Time management A way of organising your time in order to prioritise important activities and ensure that your time is used effectively.

Topping and tailing The act of washing a baby's hands, face and bottom. Particularly useful for very young babies who do not enjoy bathing in the first few weeks.

Values Beliefs about what is valuable. Values guide professional care work. Shared values are necessary if people are to feel they belong together as a group, or if people are to work together as a team.

Virus The smallest of harmful pathogens (germs). They cause many different infections, e.g. the common cold, chickenpox and measles. Some viruses have vaccines available, but antibiotics cannot treat all viruses.

Vulnerability Being at risk of some kind of harm – not being protected from risk and harm.

Weaning The process of a baby changing from a milk diet, to eating a full range of family foods. Starts with sloppy, bland, soft foods, ideally from about 3 months to 6 months, with most children able to eat most foods by the age of 12 months.

Whistle-blowing Informing your manager of bad practice you have observed at work. It is important that everyone in the care field should feel they can do this if necessary.

INDEX